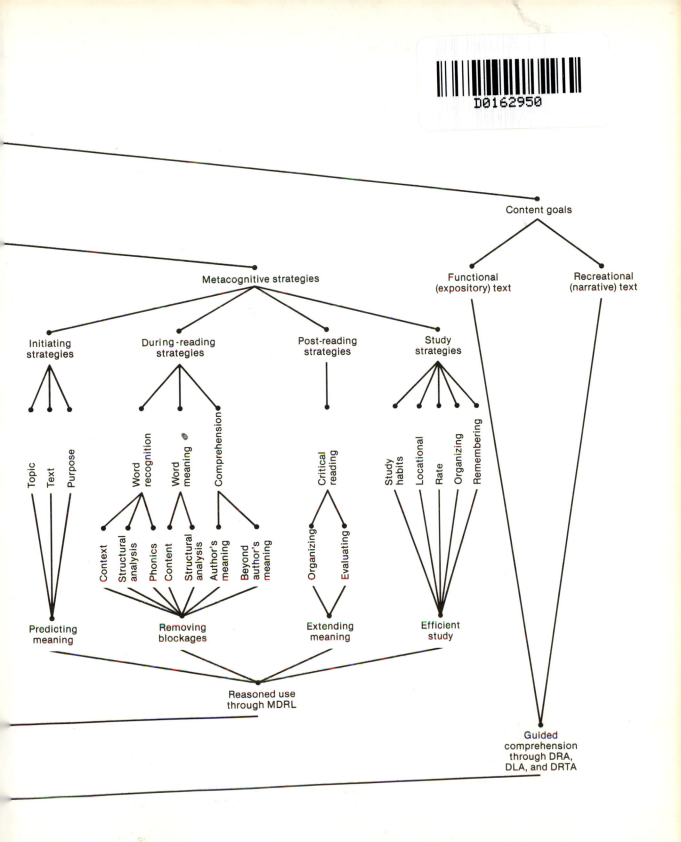

Content goals

Functional
(expository) text

Recreational
(narrative) text

Metacognitive strategies

Initiating
strategies

During-reading
strategies

Post-reading
strategies

Study
strategies

Topic

Text

Purpose

Word
recognition

Word
meaning

Comprehension

Critical
reading

Study
habits

Locational

Rate

Organizing

Remembering

Context

Structural
analysis

Phonics

Content

Structural
analysis

Author's
meaning

Beyond
author's
meaning

Organizing

Evaluating

Predicting
meaning

Removing
blockages

Extending
meaning

Efficient
study

Reasoned use
through MDRL

Guided
comprehension
through DRA,
DLA, and DRTA

IMPROVING CLASSROOM READING INSTRUCTION

IMPROVING CLASSROOM READING INSTRUCTION

A Decision-Making Approach

SECOND EDITION

Gerald G. Duffy
Michigan State University

Laura R. Roehler
Michigan State University

RANDOM HOUSE · NEW YORK

This book was developed for Random House by Lane Akers, Inc.

DEDICATION

To

Danise and Bob
Michael
Susinn and Matthew
Christopher
Kathy
Anne
Byrch

Second Edition
98765432
Copyright © 1989 by Random House, Inc.

Library of Congress Cataloging-in-Publication Data

Duffy, Gerald G.
    Improving classroom reading instruction.

    Biography; p.
    Includes index.
    1. Reading. I. Roehler, Laura R.
II. Title.
LB1050.D755 1989   428.4'07   88-26496
ISBN 0-394-38150-5

Manufactured in the United States of America

Cover Photo   Ken Lax/The Stock Shop

Part opener photos Part 1 Susan Lapides/Design Conceptions *Part 2* Sybil Shelton/Peter Arnold   *Part 3* Robert Bawden   *Part 4* Susan Lapides/Design Conceptions   *Part 5* Courtesy of Michigan State Univerity

Preface for Students

This book is written to help you become a professional teacher of reading. Professional teachers are in control of classroom instruction; they make the decisions. Control comes from knowledge and from a willingness to use knowledge. This book provides the knowledge and sets the expectation that you will use this knowledge to make instructional decisions.

Because the information load is heavy, the book has been carefully organized to assist your learning. Part 1 provides basic information about reading and explains what it's like to be a teacher. Part 2 describes how to teach reading to achieve various goals. Part 3 tells how to get organized for instruction; Part 4 provides specifics for teaching reading at various grade levels; and Part 5 presents some special issues as the basis for future professional growth.

The chapters are not separate and isolated. In a cumulative manner, each succeeding chapter uses information from previous chapters as a starting point. Similarly, concepts are continually developed throughout the book. For instance, *instruction* is discussed in virtually every chapter; as the book progresses, the meaning of the term becomes more and more refined as it is used in a variety of contexts and with a variety of examples.

To help you comprehend the content of the book, the following learning aids have been included:

1. *Advance organizers* Each of the 22 chapters begins with an overview, or Getting Ready, section. These overviews are followed by Focus Questions that direct you to specific information to be learned. Together these sections will help you activate the appropriate background experience needed to understand the chapter content.

2. *Chapter headings and subheadings* Headings and subheadings have been designed to guide your reading. They not only signal where important points are discussed, but, wherever possible, they are cued to the focus questions at the beginning of each chapter.

3. *Figures, tables, and examples* Numerous summarizing figures, tables, and examples have been provided to aid you in acquiring and reviewing key material. In addition, chapter photographs help you construct mental pictures of classroom reading instruction.

4. *Vocabulary aids* All professional terms are printed in boldface in the text and are also defined in the glossary.

5. *Chapter summaries* The essential chapter content is summarized at the end of every chapter to help you review major points and answer the Focus Questions.

One additional aid could not be built into the book. This is the opportunity for you to use what you learn with real students in real classrooms. Perhaps a supervised field practicum is part of your course work. If it is, use that situation as an opportunity to test and to apply what you learn in this book. If no such practicum is available, try to arrange classroom visits on your own so you can observe the teaching of reading and can try out the content of this book. The more you use the content, the better you will understand it.

You are embarking on a difficult task. Although teaching reading is complex, the rewards are satisfying and fulfilling. We hope this book—together with your real-world experience with students—will help you become a professional decision maker who reaps the rewards of being a classroom teacher of reading and literacy.

ACKNOWLEDGMENTS   We wish to acknowledge the contributions of the following people who helped make this book possible:

For helpful reviews of earlier versions of the text, Dr. Martha Combs, Oklahoma State University; Dr. Beth Ann Herrmann, University of South Carolina; Dr. Jerome Niles, Virginia Tech; Dr. Dixie Lee Spiegel, University of North Carolina at Chapel Hill; and Dr. Linda Vavrus, Stanford University. For providing excellent chapters for Part 5, Dr. Michael Kamil, University of Illinois at Chicago; Dr. Sandra Michelsen, Valparaiso University; and Dr. Maria Torres, Teachers College, Columbia University. For care, concern, and cheerfulness in preparing the manuscript, Karl Bellingar and Christine Harvey. Finally, for her unusually perceptive and thorough copyediting, which resulted in significant improvements of the manuscript, we express special thanks to Cynthia Garver.

Contents

IMPROVING CLASSROOM READING INSTRUCTION

Part 1

Perspectives on Reading Instruction

This section introduces you to the themes and terminology of reading instruction. Chapter 1 identifies the major theme—how to be in control of reading instruction when teaching in real classrooms where it is often difficult to be an independent decision maker. With classroom reality as a base, Chapters 2, 3, and 4 develop fundamental concepts of language learning, reading curricula, and instruction. The themes and terms introduced here will be returned to again and again as the specifics of classroom reading instruction are developed in subsequent sections of the book.

1 Reality and Reform in Reading Instruction

GETTING READY

Teachers make a difference. This is not a wishful statement or hopeful rhetoric. It is a fact established by more than 20 years of painstaking research, which shows that when teachers do certain things they produce higher achievement; when they do not do these things, they produce less achievement. Being an instructionally effective teacher, however, is not easy. Teaching is extremely demanding, and the constraints and realities of classroom life often cause teachers to favor mechanical instruction, which, although less effective in producing reading achievement, is easier and makes classroom life more manageable.

To help you get ready for real classroom teaching of reading, we start this book by discussing these realities, describing current instructional practices in reading, and explaining how classroom life encourages these practices. We then describe characteristics that you need to acquire to overcome the constraints of classroom life and to become a professional decision maker who is in control of your own instruction.

FOCUS QUESTIONS

- What characterizes the goals we try to develop through reading instruction?
- How is reading taught in today's schools?
- Why is it taught this way?
- What do teachers need to do to avoid teaching like technicians?
- What are the characteristics associated with teacher decision making in reading?

FOCUSING ON STUDENT OUTCOMES

In one second grade classroom a boy was observed working his way through a pile of six or seven worksheets that he had been assigned as **seatwork.** After much struggle and persistence he finally finished the last one, arranged them into a neat pile, heaved a huge sigh, and said out loud, "I don't know what they mean, but I did 'em."

This anecdote contains a serious message. The goal of reading instruction should be to develop students' understanding of and control over the reading process. If it is not—if instruction causes students to view reading as a series of tasks rather than as a sense-making process—students will probably never experience the full potential of reading.

To determine whether students understand and control the reading process, we interview students following their reading lessons. Consider, for instance, the following second grade student who was interviewed after a lesson on how to decode words with *ou* in them:

T: What were you learning today?

S: Sounds.

T: Okay. Why do you suppose you were learning that?

S: What do you mean?

T: Well, why do you think your teacher thought it was important for you to learn this?

S: I dunno. Maybe it'll help me when I grow up.

T: Okay. How do you do what you learned today?

Students learn what teachers emphasize. (Frank Siteman/Taurus Photos)

S: Like you could circle and underline.

T: Can you tell me more about how you do it?

S: No.

This student obviously does not understand what the teacher was teaching about how to use the *ou* sound. Consequently, he cannot be in control of this aspect of reading as he attempts to make sense of text.

In contrast, another second grader who was taught the same lesson by a different teacher said the following:

T: What were you learning today?

S: To pronounce words that have *ou* in them.

T: Why do you suppose you were learning this skill?

S: So it could help you decode words with *ou* in them.

T: How do you use *ou* to decode words?

S: First, you figure out the *ou* and what it sounds like. *OW*, like in loud. I'd go l-*ou*-d, loud.

Awareness such as this is an example of a student who understands how reading works, which in turn stimulates increased achievement and success in reading real books. Such results depend on what teachers say and do during instruction.

THE IMPACT OF THE TEACHER

Effective instruction depends on teachers because students learn what teachers emphasize. If we provide students with reading tasks that emphasize circling and underlining, as in the first example, students learn how to circle and underline. If we provide tasks that emphasize how to make sense out of text, students learn how to comprehend.

To illustrate, note the instructional emphasis in the following two lesson excerpts. Both teachers emphasize getting answers rather than making sense. The teacher's emphasis in the first excerpt, taken from a second grade oral reading session, is on accurate pronunciation of words with no attempt to discuss understanding or how the incorrectly pronounced words change the sense of the message:

T: Okay, Jack, go ahead and read.

S: Now Bobo also—

T: Not *also, al-ways.*

S: Always tried to do as he was told. So he picked up the light and put it outside. After time—

T: Another time.

S: Another time, Bobo's mother called him from the yard.

Answer getting rather than sense making is also emphasized in the following excerpt from another teacher's second grade reading lesson on the main idea of a text:

T: All right, now here are some possibilities for titles for that paragraph. "A Trip Downtown," "The New Shirt," "The Shirt That Didn't Fit." Let me read them again. "A Trip Downtown," "The New Shirt," "The Shirt That Didn't Fit." Now of those three possibilities, which one would go best? Annie?

S: "A Trip Downtown."

T: Okay. Tim, what do you think?

S: "The New Shirt."

T: I think the girls decided on "A Trip Downtown," and the boys like "The New Shirt." Mainly, what was the story about?

S: A trip downtown.

S: Getting a new shirt.

T: Getting a new shirt, wasn't it?

There is little evidence here of sense making or of how to go about determining the main idea. This teacher, like the first one, calls for answers from students, but offers no strategy for developing those answers. Once again there is no evidence of teacher concern for putting the reader in control.

What could you do to turn these instructional activities into sense-making episodes? You could establish as a base line the conceptual understanding that all reading is message getting and define the task as making sense of the message the author is sending. With such a foundation, in the first example you could respond to errors such as *also* for *always* and *after time* for *another time* by having the student explain how that "makes sense." In the second example, you could provide a piece of real text for students to read instead of an isolated practice paragraph about new shirts, establish why knowing what is the main idea is important to understanding the author's message, provide a suitable strategy, and model the use of that strategy with the real text.

When teachers emphasize mechanical procedures and recitation during instruction, students focus on mechanical procedures; when teachers emphasize conscious understanding, students learn to understand. Similarly, when the task emphasizes getting done and getting the right answers rather than knowing how to get the right answer, students may finish a task but they won't know what it all means. As a teacher, you can make a difference.

CURRENT INSTRUCTIONAL PRACTICE IN READING

Because reading instruction should put students in control of the reading process so they can become enthusiastic readers, one would expect to find sense-making instruction in most elementary classrooms. However, it is relatively rare. Instead, many teachers fill instructional time with activities that merely keep students busy. Positive attitudes, understanding, and conscious awareness of how to comprehend text receive relatively little emphasis.

This phenomenon appears to be prevalent at all grade levels. For instance, primary grade teachers spend much of their time monitoring students through workbook pages and work sheets without providing information about how to do a task or why it is being pursued. The work sheet directions to students in the following example are typical. Not only is there an absence of assistance to students, but the teacher defines the task as one of accurate answer getting. There is little concern about why the work sheet should be completed or how it contributes to the students' understanding of reading:

T: Okay. In the little paragraph that begins there, I would like to have you read the first one to yourselves and put a line under every word you can see that has the word *play* in it. Even if it has an *s* added to it. We're looking for the word *play*. Okay. Mary?

S: Look.

T: Okay. There's the word *look,* looked. But we're looking for *play.* John?

S: Playing.

T: Yes, *Playing* has *play* in it. How about the next one? Sue?

To illustrate an alternative, the teacher could have initiated the lesson by providing substantive information about what is to be learned, when it will be used, and how to do it:

T: Okay, today we are going to read a story that has lots of hard words in it. These words are alike because they end with either *s, ed,* or *ing.* I'm going to show you a strategy for figuring out these words. Where are we going to use this strategy, John?

S: In the story we read today?

T: Yes. Words like these will be in the story we read today. Now, let me show you a strategy for figuring out these words. Let's say we come to this word. [Writes *plays* on the board.] Okay, what I do is look at the word to see if it has one of my endings on it. Does it, Sarah?

S: Yes. It ends in *s*.

T: Okay. So then I cover the *s* and see if I know the root word. Do you know this word, Sam?

S: Play.

T: Yes. The root word is *play.* Now I uncover the *s*, say *play* and add the *s*. Plays. Does that word make sense in the sentence?

S: Yes.

T: Okay, then it is probably the right word. Now let's say we are reading along and we run into this word. [Writes *looked* on the board.] Can you use my strategy to figure out that word, Mary?

A similar pattern is seen in the other elementary grades. In these class-rooms, there is heavy emphasis on asking questions to assess whether students understand what the selection is about. The following excerpt from a third grade classroom is an example of how teachers "interrogate" during reading without providing instruction in how to answer the questions. This emphasis on time-filling activities such as oral reading followed by a period of questioning or monitoring students through work sheets is reflected in virtually all studies of classroom instructional practice.

S [reading orally]: It was morning. The sun was in the—

T: You can stop there. It was a good morning for doing something. What is it a good morning to do?

S: Jump.

T: Ed, will you read for me?

S: Hop, hop, hop—

T: He is going to talk to a rabbit, isn't he? Is it a small rabbit?

S: No, kind of big. Kind of big and kind of small.

T: It's Bill's turn to read.

S: The rabbit did not look happy. The rabbit had lost two little rabbits on the hill.

T: Why is the rabbit unhappy, Bill?

S [long pause]: I don't know.

T: Let's see if someone else knows.

s: I don't know.

t: Because he lost his two rabbits. You have to pay better attention.

Despite the fact that such tasks probably cause students to conclude that reading is answering questions rather than knowing how to answer questions, teachers persist in asking questions without telling students how to answer the questions. The driving force seems to be not what students will conclude about reading but, rather, occupying students' time. However, the teacher in the previous example could have inserted explanations that would have provided the information the students needed to answer the question about why the rabbit was unhappy:

t: Why is the rabbit unhappy, Bill?

s [long pause]: I don't know.

t: Let me show you a strategy you can use to figure out the answer to questions like that. First, go back and look at what the text says. For instance, it says, "The rabbit did not look happy. The rabbit had lost two little rabbits on the hill." When the question is asked, you have to ask yourself, "What do I know about things like that? What if I were the rabbit and I had lost two little rabbits, how would I feel?

s: You'd probably feel sad.

t: Yes. Now what would have made me sad? It was the fact that I lost the two little rabbits. Right? And that's why the rabbit was unhappy. You can figure out the answer to these kinds of questions by putting yourself into the story and thinking about how you would feel if you were in his place.

INSTRUCTIONAL CONSTRAINTS

Why don't teachers provide more explanations like this? Why do they emphasize the mechanical, routinized aspects of reading instruction rather than the cognitive and attitudinal aspects? It is not because they lack dedication and diligence. It is because of the **constraints** under which they work. We discuss these constraints in two categories: the complexity of classroom life and the dominance of the basal reading textbook.

The Complexity of Classroom Life

One of the unfortunate myths of our culture is that "anybody can be a teacher." The truth is that being a teacher is very difficult, especially if by "teacher" we mean a person who develops understandings and positive attitudes about reading. A major difficulty is the complexity of effectively managing daily classroom life. The energy expended on classroom manage-

A classroom is a complex place. (Robert Bawden)

ment too often leaves little energy for the kind of instructional decision making advocated in this book.

What is so difficult about managing classroom life? First, teachers must organize and smoothly manage the activities of 25 or 30 youngsters for five or six hours every day. It is difficult enough to keep one seven-year-old child occupied for five or six hours; it is incredibly more difficult to deal with 25 or 30 because of the social interactions that occur. Consequently, one of the first jobs a teacher faces is to create a socially acceptable environment where 25 or 30 distinct and captive personalities can exist in close proximity to each other for extended periods of time.

The problem is further compounded by the fact that in our society going to school is a serious business in which schools and teachers are held accountable for student achievement. To ensure this achievement, state and local boards of education require various kinds of achievement tests, and if the test scores are low the teacher is held accountable by parents and school officials. This **accountability** for good achievement test scores can be handicapping to teachers since achievement growth is affected by many factors outside the teacher's control, and since what is measured by tests often differs from what teachers know to be important.

Accountability pressures on students also add to the complexity of classrooms. For instance, students exchange performance in classrooms for grades, a fact that influences their classroom behavior. Students often avoid responding in class so they will not expose themselves to errors, and they negotiate for easier tasks to get better grades. This makes the teacher's job that much more difficult.

Classroom life is further complicated by the fact that teachers must constantly deal with dilemmas as well as with problems. Although problems can be resolved by rational problem solving, dilemmas have no "right" answers and create an ongoing climate of uncertainty. For instance, if you are teaching a reading group of ten students and you notice that two are whispering together while you are explaining something to another, you are faced with a dilemma. If you turn your attention to the two whispering students, the one you are interacting with suffers; if you ignore the whispering and attend to the student you are instructing, the whispering tends to spread. It is a dilemma.

Similarly, if you are teaching the same group of ten students and it becomes clear that five of them understand the task and five do not, you are faced with a dilemma. If you hold all ten until they have all learned satisfactorily, the five who can already do the task correctly will lose interest; if you dismiss them, you may embarrass the five remaining students because of their inability to perform as well. Such dilemmas are endless in the daily life of teachers and dealing with them makes teaching complex.

The problem of dilemma management is further complicated by the fact that teachers are often led to expect simple answers as, for example, when they are required to use certain instructional materials or certain procedures. These directives imply that problems of teaching can be solved if you use the right set of materials or procedures. Nothing could be further from the truth. Teaching is simply too complex; no one set of procedures or materials can possibly anticipate all the situations you will confront.

Classroom teaching is also difficult because of the constant need to adjust and adapt to changes. For instance, as our world changes we find that we are faced with more language and learning problems than ever before, and that there are more and more innovations to which teachers must adapt. (Chapter 19 describes how computers are changing instruction in reading and writing and Chapters 20 and 21 illustrate how special language and mainstreaming problems place unique demands on teachers.) To cope with such continuous change, teachers need to be flexible and adaptable.

Of all the difficulties of classroom life, perhaps none is harder to deal with than the isolation of teaching. The classroom is a crowded social environment, but it is an environment of children; as a classroom teacher, you are virtually isolated from other adults during the hours you are teaching. Consequently, you endure a professional loneliness as you try to cope with the dilemmas and difficulties of classroom life.

These are not the only difficulties classroom teachers face; they merely illustrate the complexity of the job. Contrary to public opinion, not everybody can be a teacher. Not everybody can deal with the complexities of classroom life and have the energy left to be effective decision makers when providing reading instruction.

The Basal Reading Textbook

The normal constraints of classroom life are more than enough for some teachers. After wrestling with them, they have little energy left to organize an instructional program in reading, so they look for something that will organize it for them. For 85 to 95 percent of American elementary school teachers, the answer lies with the basal reading textbook.

Whether or not you have recently been in elementary schools, you are probably familiar with **basal reading textbooks,** those carefully structured reading books that virtually every American identifies as the focus of reading instruction. These texts normally contain a series of fiction, nonfiction, and poetry reading selections, with fiction given the most emphasis. Each child in a reading group has the same book; children in different reading groups usually have different levels in the same series of books. During reading group time, students read the selections in the basal (either orally or silently), discuss the stories with the teacher, and complete the skill exercises in the workbook that accompanies the basal text. Most teacher questioning during elementary reading instruction focuses on what happens in the basal text selection being read, and most teacher monitoring focuses on the work sheets provided in the accompanying workbook.

Basal textbooks become a constraint because of the way so many teachers use them. Because of the complexities of classroom life, teachers often feel overloaded—there just seems to be too much to attend to and do. When this happens, many teachers turn to the basal textbook as a way to simplify their lives. They say, in effect, "I'll deal with all this complexity by simply follow-ing the 'expert' directions provided for me in this textbook." In saying this, they relinquish control of instruction, abdicating instructional decision mak-ing to the authors of the basal textbook. They stop thinking about their instruction and making their own decisions and start following: The teachers' guide becomes their leader. Merely having students "cover" the material—that is, correctly answer the questions in the basal textbook—becomes their goal.

The basal text thrives for two reasons. First, for teachers who have difficulty dealing with the complexity of classrooms and who consequently have little energy left to plan their own instruction, the basal text provides an organizational structure. It tells them what to do and say, puts materials in students' hands to keep them busy, and provides tests to determine whether progress is being made. In the fast-paced environment of classroom life, it seems to be a lifesaver because, by providing routines, procedures, and activities, it structures the program and promotes the smooth flow of classroom life.

Second, the basal text provides what appears to be a systematic and coordinated reading sequence from kindergarten to eighth grade. With its progression of levels, its skills sequence, and its massive assistance to teachers, it seems to be tailor-made for conducting instruction. In fact, the basal text is so ingrained in our educational system that even good teachers begin to doubt themselves if they are not religiously following the basal "system." For instance, despite tangible evidence that her students are not only in control of the reading process but are excited about it, the teacher in the following example feels guilty because she is not faithfully and mindlessly following the dictates of the basal system. Such is the pervasiveness of the basal text's influence!

> I sometimes feel I am struggling against odds to give my kids a worthwhile reading program. I have tried a different approach this year by balancing basal skills with children's literature. We read anything from Arnold Lobel and Shel Silverstein to Beverly Cleary and Judy Blume. Although I'm aware there is more to reading than the recreational end, I feel a small miracle has taken place with my kids. They sit on the edge of their seats, they laugh out loud, they hold their breath, they get angry but they can't wait to get to the next page! It never happened that way with the basal stories. Yet, I go through doubtful periods as I leaf through basal manuals wondering what horrible gaps I may be creating in these children's reading development.

Despite its systematic characteristics and its apparent usefulness in making classroom life more manageable, the basal text is not a panacea. There are problems associated with its use. As previously mentioned, too many hard-pressed teachers are willing to transfer responsibility for instruction from themselves to the basal. They expect the basal to provide the instruction, and if students do not learn, it is the basal's fault, not the teacher's. In other words, they operate on the principle that the basal program makes the difference, not that the teacher makes the difference.

Also, when teachers assign instructional responsibility to a basal text program, they stop teaching for understanding. They cover basal material mechanically, doing what the teachers' edition says to do and making sure that students "complete" the material. They focus on whether students get the right answer, assuming correct responses mean students are learning what the basal says they are supposed to learn. Such teachers seldom try to think of alternative strategies or activities because all the prescriptions are presumably in the teachers' edition. Hence, these teachers become technicians who follow someone else's plans rather than professionals who make their own instructional decisions.

The faith teachers place in basals is unwarranted. Recent studies indicate that basal materials often present information in confusing ways, that they emphasize practice and assessment exercises associated with answer-oriented instruction, and that the accompanying workbook exercises are often misleading or inaccurate.

It is unlikely that the content of basal texts will change dramatically in the near future. The reason is simple: They sell the way they are. Because teachers feel they need help in ordering classroom life, they favor basals; because publishers are in business to sell books, they include the routinized, answer-oriented materials some teachers favor. In short, since basals are going to be around for awhile, you must learn to teach reading effectively while using them.

The constraints of classroom life that drive teachers in the direction of basal text programs are summarized in Figure 1.1.

FIGURE 1.1   Why Teachers Teach Like Technicians

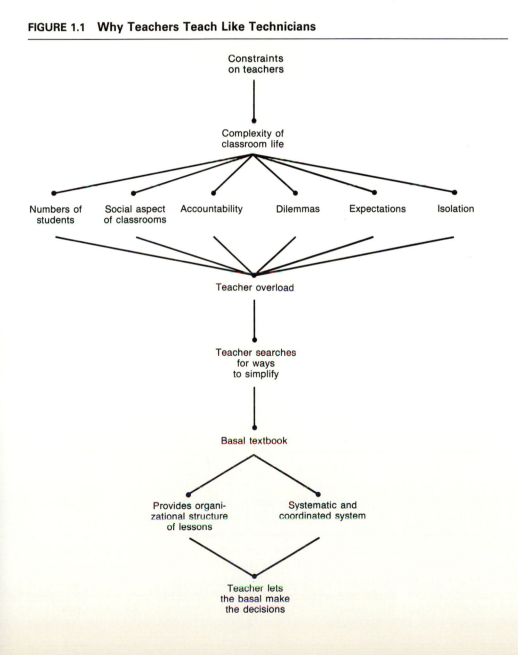

BECOMING AN INSTRUCTIONAL DECISION MAKER

The point here is not that teachers lack dedication and diligence. On the contrary, nearly all the teachers we encounter want to help students, want to be better teachers, and want to improve. Neither do we believe that teachers are unable to become professional decision makers who are in cognitive control of their instruction; we believe that teachers can and should.

This textbook emphasizes two important functions of being a decision maker when teaching reading. It puts a premium on (1) helping you become a good organizer and manager of reading curricula and instruction so you can reduce the complexities of classroom life and (2) teaching you how to make your own decisions about reading instruction even though you may be using basal textbooks. In the process, we hope you will develop the following seven characteristics emphasized in this book because they are associated with instructional decision makers.

First, teachers who are instructional decision makers view reading broadly. They see it not as a skill or series of skills, nor as an isolated subject, but as part of a language system whose purpose is communication and comprehension. Therefore, their reading instruction reflects language and the communication function of language.

Second, these teachers think in terms of what students should learn, not in terms of assignments for students to complete. In reading, the ultimate goal is for students to be in control of "real" reading as pursued by literate people. Therefore, instruction is designed to produce real readers, not students who can complete skill exercises accurately. Similarly, instruction is not effective when practice sheets are answered accurately; it is effective when students apply to real reading what was taught.

Third, these teachers understand that positive attitudes are as crucial as skills in learning to read. Teachers do many important things, but teaching children to like to read is especially important.

Fourth, teachers who are decision makers understand that comprehension is the result of cognition, awareness, and strategic thinking, not memory, rote, and accuracy. Therefore, a central question to students is not "Are you correct?" but rather "How do you know you are correct?"

Fifth, these teachers understand that basal textbooks cannot dominate reading instruction. They use them as tools, not as infallible guides and organize their reading program around an assigned basal but modify, adjust, and innovate according to chosen goals and the needs of their students.

Sixth, these teachers know that teachers' guides mainly provide tasks, activities, and directions. If students are to understand *how* to do tasks successfully, teachers must explain them and work hard to analyze them, using these analyses to create explicit "how-to" explanations.

Seventh, these teachers are not looking for "the" answer to reading instruction. They know that reading instruction is complex, classrooms are complex, and students and teachers are complex. There can be no panacea when so many complexities interact.

Eighth, these teachers know they must be life-long students of reading instruction. They will get more proficient from year to year, but they will never do things exactly the same. They are constantly thinking, changing, modifying, innovating, and looking for ways to improve instruction. The following list summarizes the ways in which decision makers think about reading instruction.

1. Think of reading broadly, not as a narrow skill.

2. Think in terms of what students learn, not activities.

3. Think that learning to like reading is as important as knowing how to read.

4. Think about the reasoning process involved in comprehending, not just the ability to get the answer.

5. Think that their job is to modify basal materials, not to follow them blindly.

6. Think that teachers should explain, not just assign tasks.

7. Think that there are many ways to teach reading, not just one way.

8. Think they should change and grow each year, not do the same thing each year.

Teachers who are decision makers are in control of their own instruction. One way to dramatize the difference between teachers who are in control from those who are not is to note how each one reacts to the same instructional task. In each of the following two examples, the teacher has presented a lesson and students' answers indicate a lack of understanding. The difference in what the two teachers do illustrates the difference between technicians and professional decision makers. The first teacher is a technician. She follows the teachers' guide and its prescriptions. When the need to explain arises, she does not know what to do, so she continues asking for the correct answer.

T: When you add an apostrophe *s* to boy, it shows that the boy has something. Can you make up a sentence for kitten? Something belongs to the kitten.

S: There's a basket full of kittens.

T: You added just an *s*. That's more than one kitten. This time make it ownership. Something belongs to this right here. Troy?

S: The kitten always owns the basket.

T: All right, but can you change your sentence around? You're saying the kitten owns the basket. Let's use kitten and basket.

S: Kitten basket.

T: But with the apostrophe *s*.

S: The kitten's basket.

T: The kitten's, that's the kitten's basket. All right. What belongs to the kitten? Troy?

S: The basket.

In contrast, the second teacher is not under the control of the basal. She possesses professional knowledge about reading and about how to instruct, and she uses this knowledge to generate a spontaneous explanation. As a result, the students' misconceptions are corrected, they become aware of how to do the task, and they achieve.

T: Connector words are what, David?

S: Two words put together.

T: What are connector words, Josh?

S: Two words hooked together.

T: They are not two words. Maybe I explained that incorrectly. A connector word is a word that connects one or more ideas. Okay, in this sentence, "They always walk to school together and they always walk home together," there are two ideas. They always walk to school and they always come home. Of the two connector words I put on the board [*and, but*], which word is connecting the two ideas, David?

S: And.

T: And. Do you see that? And. I have it underlined here. See how it is connecting the ideas of walking to school together and coming home together? It is sort of like a bridge that connects these two. Bridges connect different places, words connect ideas. Connector words connect ideas.

It is clear that reading instruction requires more than drilling children, asking them for right answers, and demanding that directions be followed accurately. Sense making must be emphasized. Students must understand what reading is, what they are trying to do when they read, how to get right answers, how reading works, and how to be in conscious control of their own cognitive processing as they read. The emphasis is on thought, not memory; on understanding, not mechanics; on application, not practice; on conscious awareness, not rote response; and on reading in the real world, not reading for school assignments only. What this requires is a teacher who adapts instructional materials by making appropriate decisions—a teacher who is in control of instruction and can modify it in ways that put students in control of their reading.

Sense making is promoted when the teacher asks students questions about the meaning of their reading. (RH Photo by Peter Vadnai)

SUMMARY

Reading instruction in elementary schools ought to be characterized by sense making, awareness, and positive attitudes. Unfortunately, many teachers emphasize fragmented, meaningless and mechanical elements of reading. This kind of reading instruction often occurs because of the constrained conditions of teaching, some of which are associated with the pervasiveness of basal textbooks and school policies about how these materials are to be used. In turn, these constraints cause teachers to follow the material technically rather than to make decisions about how to adapt it. To avoid teaching like a technician, you must assume regulatory control of your instruction by making your own decisions; doing so is the essence of being a professional.

SUGGESTED ADDITIONAL READING

ALVERMANN, D. E., & BOOTHBY, P. R. (1982). Text differences: Children's perceptions at the transition stage in reading. *Reading Teacher, 36*(3), 298–302.

BLANCHOWICZ, C. L. (1983). Showing teachers how to develop students' predictive reading. *Reading Teacher, 36*(7), 680–684.

DURKIN, D. (1984). Is there a match between what elementary teachers do and what basal reader manuals recommend? *Reading Teacher, 37*(8), 734–744.

HARRIS, L., & LALIK, R. (1987). Teachers' use of Informal Reading Inventories: An example of school constraints. *Reading Teacher, 40,* 624–631.

LEHR, F. (1982). Teacher effectiveness research and reading instruction. *Language Arts, 59*(8), 883–887.

SHANNON, P. (1982). A retrospective look at teachers' reliance on commercial reading materials. *Language Arts, 59*(8), 844–853.

SHANNON, P. (1982). Some subjective reasons for teachers' reliance on commercial reading materials. *Reading Teacher, 35*(8), 884–889.

SINGER, H. (1978). Active comprehension: From answering to asking questions. *Reading Teacher, 31*(8), 901–908.

STERN, P., & SHAVELSON, R. J. (1983). Reading teachers' judgments, plans, and decision making. *Reading Teacher, 37*(3), 280–286.

THE RESEARCH BASE

ANDERSON, L., BRUBAKER, N., ALLEMAN-BROOKS, J., & DUFFY, G. (1984). *Making seatwork work* (Research Series No. 142). East Lansing: Michigan State University, Institute for Research on Teaching.

DUFFY, G. (1983). From turn-taking to sense-making: Toward a broader definition of teacher effectiveness. *Journal of Educational Research, 76*(3), 134–139.

DUFFY, G. G., & ROEHLER, L. R. (1982). The illusion of instruction. *Reading Research Quarterly, 17,* 438–445.

DURKIN, D. (1978–1979). What classroom observation reveals about reading comprehension instruction. *Reading Research Quarterly, 14,* 481–533.

DURKIN, D. (1981). Reading comprehension instruction in five basal reader series. *Reading Research Quarterly, 16*(4), 515–544.

Language Learning and Reading Instruction | 2

GETTING READY

This chapter introduces you to four major themes: (1) the wholistic nature of language, (2) the nature of meaningful learning, (3) the goals of wholistic reading instruction, and (4) the characteristics of instructional decision making. It gives special attention to the big picture in reading instruction, which is based on two principles. The first is that reading, as one of the language arts, should emphasize the communication of meaningful messages. The second is that learning must be meaningful in order to be retained and applied.

FOCUS QUESTIONS

- What is the function of language?

- Why should reading be integrated with the other language arts?

- How are reading and writing similar?

- What is the main purpose of reading instruction?

- How do we know when reading instruction has been successful?

- What is the difference between short-term learning and meaningful learning?

- How do motivation and metacognition influence learning?

- What is the difference between metacognition and cognition?

- What are the three major goals of reading instruction?

- What are the characteristics of an instructional decision maker?

WHOLISTIC NATURE OF LANGUAGE

The function of language is communication. For communication to occur, there must be someone to send a message and someone to receive it. If a message is not worth sending or is of little interest to the receiver, there is little communication. Hence, instruction in the **language arts**—whether it is reading, listening, speaking, or writing—ought to include messages worth communicating.

Comprehension is the goal of all communication. In the **expressive language modes** of speaking and writing, comprehension means understanding the message well enough to compose it clearly. In the **receptive language modes** of listening and reading, comprehension means interpreting the message accurately enough to understand its meaning. Consequently, reading instruction focuses on getting meaning from text; writing instruction focuses on creating meaning in text. Because the various language modes are so inextricably bound up with one another, it is almost impossible to teach one in isolation from the others.

Comprehension makes the world of literacy available. **Literacy** is the sharing of recreational and functional messages through language. When creative writers compose messages that cause us to see the world differently, as with good literature, literacy is a recreational (and often aesthetic) experience. When writers share functional knowledge, as with written directions or textbooks, literacy is a practical experience. Therefore, the main purpose of reading instruction is to teach students to eagerly engage in literate activ-

The major goal of reading instruction is to develop students who eagerly seek literate activities. (Elizabeth Crews)

ities for both recreational and functional reasons. This is reading instruction's big picture. You will be keeping the big picture in mind if your reading instruction reflects the following characteristics of language:

- Reading instruction should be integrated in natural ways with the other language arts of listening, speaking, and writing.

- Students' reading and writing should always involve a message that is meaningful to them.

- The aim of all reading instruction is to help students control and enjoy the process of getting meaning from text.

- Reading instruction is successful when students eagerly read all kinds of written text.

Figure 2.1 summarizes the relationships among the major language concepts that are central to a **whole language approach** to reading.

FIGURE 2.1   Relationships among Major Language Concepts

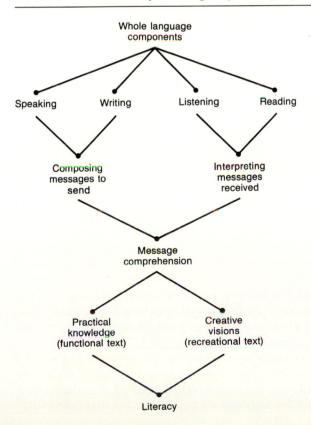

NATURE OF MEANINGFUL LEARNING

Traditionally learning was thought to be synonymous with simple remembering, and memorization skills were highly valued. For instance, do you remember the Friday spelling tests you took in elementary school? If you are like many people, you probably studied very hard on Thursday night, memorized all the target words, kept reciting them to yourself on the way to school on Friday, spelled them correctly on the test, and then promptly forgot how they were spelled because you did not use them. Psychologists call that kind of learning **short-term memory.** That is, you memorize something, and for a short time, you "know" it. However, most memorized information is forgotten because it is isolated from other actively used information and is relatively meaningless. Once forgotten, it is of no further use.

To be remembered in future situations, most learning must be conceptually meaningful—that is, you must understand individual concepts and the relationships among them. The human mind expedites meaningful learning by organizing experiences (such as reading about reading instruction) into networks of interlocking and related concepts called **schemata.** For example, your experiences with restaurants provide you with a restaurant **schema** that includes all your "restaurant" experiences, ranging from how the drive-through window at McDonald's works to the role of the maître d' in a four-star restaurant. All that restaurant knowledge is effortlessly remembered because it is meaningfully organized in your **long-term memory.** What students learn during reading instruction should be meaningfully organized so that it too can be easily retrieved.

Meaningful learning occurs when you create a new schema or modify an old one. For the learning to be meaningful, the concepts stored in the schema must be linked together in sensible ways, like they are in the figures in this chapter, for instance. To illustrate, if someone encounters a Japanese restaurant for the first time, that person will integrate procedures such as sitting on tatami mats instead of at a table into his or her existing restaurant schema, probably under a category "Oriental restaurants, Japanese." Long-term learning occurs when this new knowledge about restaurants is integrated meaningfully into a person's existing restaurant schema; that is, when it is linked in sensible ways with prior restaurant knowledge so that it can be remembered and used when needed. What students learn about reading in school should be integrated in similar ways into their prior schemata for reading.

Unfamiliarity with a Japanese restaurant's way of doing things may at first result in disorientation and frustration. If the disorientation and frustration are great enough, the person's motivation to eat there may disappear, and he or she may leave. In such a case, the restaurant schema remains unmodified, and no learning occurs. On the other hand, if the person stays and looks for analogous relationships from existing restaurant and Oriental culture schemata or receives instruction from someone—a waiter, for example—the existing restaurant schema is successfully modified. Similarly, during reading instruction students learn things on any given day that are modifications of the reading schemata they all brought to class. Effective instruction either corrects a previously held misconception about reading or embellishes an existing reading schema by adding new concepts.

Motivation, or the enthusiasm and perseverance a learner brings to a task, is obviously important in learning. We all want our students to be motivated. Motivation occurs if two factors are present—if there is a reasonable chance of success and if the end result is valued. In the case of the Japanese restaurant, the newcomer will enthusiastically persist in learning the etiquette of Japanese restaurants as long as it does not become too difficult to learn and as long as he or she continues to want to eat there. The same thing happens during reading instruction. Students are motivated if the work is not too hard and if the goal of being a reader is important.

Learning depends on more than motivation, however. The way a learner **mediates,** or thinks about, an experience is also important. For instance, one customer new to Japanese restaurants may think about the experience as a matter of making a few perfunctory adjustments, whereas another may think about the experience as the beginning of new cultural understandings and appreciations that go well beyond simple restaurant behavior. Because each person's schema for a particular topic is unique, each person uniquely mediates experiences and **restructures** them to create unique understandings. That is why no two people possess precisely the same conceptual understanding about any given topic. In the classroom situation, individual students mediate the reading instruction provided and restructure the understandings

---

Each student uniquely restructures the same reading instruction. (RH Photo by Peter Vadnai)

so they are unique to each of them. Consequently, every student comes up with slightly different understandings from identical learning experiences.

Learners mediate experiences better when they have been provided with information that helps them understand how to think about them. For instance, the learner who has been taught how to apply existing schemata to new experiences is more likely to create broader cultural understanding from the Japanese restaurant experience, whereas the learner who has not been taught how to activate existing schemata will probably be satisfied with "getting by" behavior. This awareness of how one thinks is called **metacognition.** Reading instruction focuses on providing students with information about how they think as they read. The result is readers who are metacognitive about how they read—who are aware of how to think when making sense out of text so they can control the comprehension process.

To summarize, learning can be short term or long term. Short-term learning is a relatively meaningless process of remembering isolated bits of information for short periods of time. Long-term learning is the active combining of new and old knowledge in meaningful ways so that a modified understanding results. Long-term learning is what teachers strive for, because students can recall and use it when needed. It is influenced by (1) metacognition, or how conscious the learner is in making linkages in the mind; (2) motivation, or how much or how little frustration and value is attached to the task; and (3) the information teachers provide to help the learner know how to mediate experiences in intended ways.

You will help students become enthusiastic readers if your reading instruction reflects the following characteristics of learning:

- Because learning occurs gradually, understanding about reading develops over time, not in a single lesson or a single experience.

- Because learning is an active process, students must be active participants, not passive recipients of knowledge.

- Because learning occurs by integrating old and new knowledge, students must have opportunities to integrate new content with existing schemata and thereby generate restructured understanding.

- Because metacognitive awareness of how one learns influences learning, students should be taught to be aware of how they read so they can control their own comprehension.

- Because humans are motivated when they are successful and when they value a task, reading instruction should emphasize activities that are low in frustration and high in value.

Figure 2.2 summarizes the major concepts about the learning process. Details of how to teach reading are provided in Chapter 4.

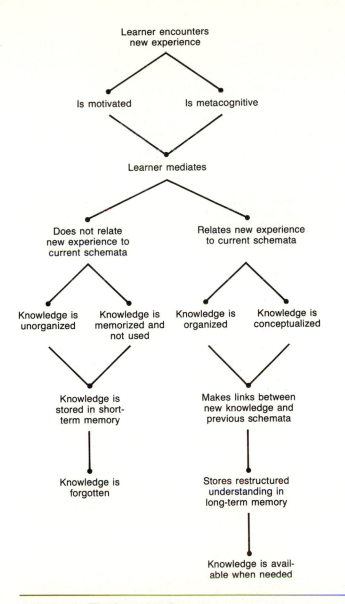

FIGURE 2.2 The Learning Process

GOALS OF WHOLISTIC READING INSTRUCTION

There are three major goals for reading instruction. Since the function of language is to communicate, the first goal is to have students comprehend what they read. They should understand the **content** of the selections they read. The second goal is students with positive **attitudes** about reading: They

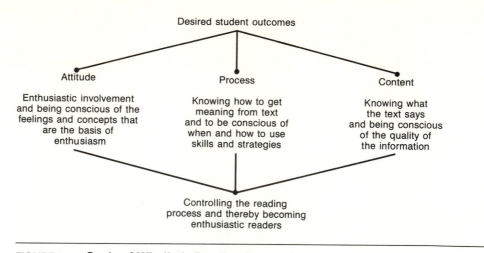

FIGURE 2.3   Goals of Wholistic Reading Instruction

should be enthusiastically involved in literacy events, they should love to read, and they should understand what reading can do for them. Finally, because the best learners are in conscious control of their reading, the third goal is students who comprehend and are also aware of *how* they comprehend. They should be metacognitive about the **process** of reading. When students are consciously aware of how reading works, they are able to figure out the meaning of difficult text when no teacher is available to guide them.

All three goals involve both cognition and metacognition. **Cognition** refers to the various mental processes you go through to comprehend the meaning of a text. Metacognition, as noted, is awareness of the mental processing you go through. Therefore, when you read a text, you are metacognitive if you not only comprehend the meaning but are aware of the mental processes that produced comprehension and use this awareness to regulate your comprehension.

To summarize, the three goals of reading instruction have two dimensions: the cognitive acts associated with reading and being metacognitive about these acts. Acquiring an awareness of these two dimensions puts students in conscious control of the process of constructing meaning from text, which is the key to being enthusiastic readers. Enabling students to develop such control is what reading instruction is all about. Figure 2.3 summarizes the goals of reading instruction.

The details of what you teach when you teach the three goals of reading are described in Chapter 3.

CHARACTERISTICS OF INSTRUCTIONAL DECISION MAKING

To help your students achieve these goals, you must be able to make your own decisions about instruction as you teach. As we mentioned in Chapter

Teacher decision making begins with careful planning. (Robert Bawden)

1, this is not easy. You must possess professional knowledge about language, learning, and instruction. This book starts you on the road to obtaining that knowledge. For this knowledge to be stored in your long-term memory, however, you must build a meaningful schema for "teaching reading" in which many concepts are linked together into a meaningful whole. This means creating an integrated mental structure for teaching reading in which you link, in sensible ways, the content from one chapter of this book with the content from other chapters.

You must be in metacognitive control of your knowledge so you can control your instruction just as you want your students to be metacognitive of how reading works so they can control the reading process. You must be conscious of how you organize your knowledge about the teaching of reading, and you must reflect on how the different categories of knowledge in your knowledge structure relate to one another.

You must also be flexible. Teaching reading is a highly complex endeavor; there are no pat answers. What works in one situation with one group of students may not work in another situation with another group of students. Therefore, change is a constant. The knowledge structure you create today will be adjusted or embellished tomorrow, not only while you are learning how to teach but throughout your entire career.

Decision making demands constant assessment. You must assess the students you are teaching, the situation you are in, and yourself. Assessment, provides the basis for the decisions you make. Without assessment data, you cannot know whether things are going well or poorly or whether any decisions need to be made.

Finally, decision making requires hard work and courage. It is easy to follow the directions someone else provides, and it is easy to justify doing so if you assume that the people who wrote the teachers' guide know more about teaching than you do. It is much harder to acknowledge that in the reality of the classroom you are in a far better position to judge how well students understand instructional content than the author of the teachers' guide. And it takes courage to steadfastly refuse to abdicate your responsibility for instructional decisions even when you make mistakes, as we all do.

Despite the difficulties, however, being a decision maker is worth the effort. The payoff comes in two ways. First, you will be more effective. You will help more students achieve literacy. Second, and equally as important, you will not "burn out" as a teacher. Instead, you will discover the joy and pride of creative work, of rarely doing anything the same way twice, and of striving to improve. Figure 2.4 summarizes the main points about decision making.

FIGURE 2.4   Teacher Decision Making

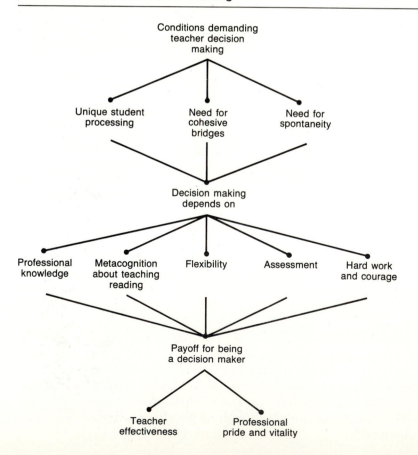

SUMMARY

Successful reading instruction is based on an understanding of how language and learning work. The function of language is communication, and since language includes listening, speaking, and writing as well as reading, reading instruction should be wholistic. That is, it should be integrated with the other language arts, particularly writing, since reading and writing both involve written text, and it should emphasize meaning getting. The goals of reading instruction are to have students comprehend what they read, be in control of the process of getting meaning from text, and be enthusiastic readers of various kinds of text. To accomplish these goals, instruction must promote the meaningful organization of knowledge associated with long-term memory, as opposed to memorization of relatively meaningless rules and facts associated with short-term memory. Meaningful organization is promoted when two conditions are present. First, students learn better when they not only know but also know how they know. Second, students who are motivated— who have a good chance to succeed at a task and who value the end product— learn better. The most successful teachers, therefore, are those who never lose sight of the goal of reading instruction and who are themselves in metacognitive control of their instruction as evidenced by the decisions they make as they teach.

SUGGESTED ADDITIONAL READINGS

AUTEN, A. (1983). The ultimate connection: Reading, listening, writing, speaking— thinking. *Reading Teacher*, 36(6), 584–587.

CLAY, M. (1986). Constructive processes: Talking, reading, writing, art and craft. *Reading Teacher*, 764–770.

GUTHRIE, J. T. (1983). Students' perceptions of teaching. *Reading Teacher*, 37(1), 94–95.

KOPFSTEIN, R. M. (1978). Fluent reading, language, and the reading teacher. *Reading Teacher*, 32(2), 195–197.

LIPSON, M. Y. (1984). Some unexpected issues in prior knowledge and comprehension. *Reading Teacher*, 37(8), 760–764.

OTTO, J. (1982). The new debate in reading. *Reading Teacher*, 36(1), 14–18.

PEARSON, P. D. (1976, March). A psycholinguistic model of reading. *Language Arts*, 53(3), 309–314.

SANACORE, J. (1984). Metacognition and the improvement of reading: Some important links. *Journal of Reading*, 27(8), 706–712.

SHUY, R. W. (1982). What should the language strand in a reading program contain? *Reading Teacher*, 35(7), 806–812.

STRANGE, M. (1980). Instructional implications of a conceptual theory of reading comprehension. *Reading Teacher*, 33(4), 391–397.

WEISS, M. J. (1986). Writers and readers: The literary connection. *Reading Teacher*, 39, 758–763.

WILDE, S. J. (1979). The experience and consequences of literacy: A case study. *Language Arts*, 56(2), 141–145.

THE RESEARCH BASE

DUFFY, G. G., ROEHLER, L. R., & MASON, J. (Eds.) (1984). *Comprehension instruction: Perspectives and suggestions.* New York: Longman.

HOFFMAN, J. V. (Ed.) (1986). *Effective teaching of reading: Research and practice.* Newark, DE: International Reading Association.

PEARSON, P. D. (Ed.) (1984). *The handbook of reading research.* New York: Longman.

ROEHLER, L. R., & DUFFY, G. G. (in press). Teachers' instructional actions. In R. Barr, M. L. Kamil, P. Mosenthal, & P. D. Pearson (Eds.), *Handbook of reading research* (2nd Ed). New York: Longman.

WITTROCK, M. (Ed.) (1986). *Handbook of research on teaching.* New York: Macmillan.

The Reading and Writing Curricula   3

GETTING READY

To be in control of reading instruction, you must know what reading is, what to teach, and why it is taught. This chapter defines reading, describes the reading curriculum and its relationship to writing, and provides a rationale for the reading curriculum goals emphasized at various developmental stages of reading growth. At the end of this chapter, you should have a global picture of the reading and writing curricula.

FOCUS QUESTIONS

- What is reading?

- How does it work?

- What is the role of concepts? prior knowledge? text? inferencing? strategies? context?

- How are reading and writing related?

- Given the nature of reading, what are the goals of reading instruction?

- How is the reading curriculum organized?

- How are the reading curriculum and the writing curriculum related?

- What do you teach when you teach reading?

- Why do you teach what you teach in reading?

DESCRIBING READING

Traditionally reading was described as a series of competencies or skills to be mastered. These competencies were identified by breaking the reading act into its component parts. It was logically assumed that the smallest unit in reading was the alphabet letter and its associated sound, and descriptions of reading often began with letters and letter sounds, then progressed to syllables, then to words, then to phrases, then to sentences, and so on. The idea was that the best way to understand reading was to isolate its individual aspects. Reading instruction consisted of teaching each of these separate parts, and students were considered good readers if they mastered each one. It was assumed that reading would result when all the separate parts had been learned. Given this point of view it is understandable why many teachers emphasize isolated skill instruction during reading.

However, reading is not performing a series of independent skills, but rather is the simultaneous interaction of various kinds of information. Neither does reading begin with the alphabet and proceed in an orderly progression to meaning; it starts by seeking meaning and uses a variety of sources, including the letters of the alphabet, to create meaning. Additionally, reading is not a matter of determining a single correct meaning in text; it is a matter of interpreting the text based on what the reader already knows.

Humans organize what they know about a topic (from **direct** or **vicarious experiences**) into categories or mental structures, which in Chapter 2 we labeled schemata. Whenever you begin talking or writing about a particular topic, you compose your message by drawing on the information you have in that schema. Whenever you read or listen to someone else talk about a topic, you interpret the message in terms of what you already know about the topic. The amount of information you have organized into a given schema depends on your experience with or prior knowledge about that topic. The more you know about a topic, the richer your schema is and the better you will understand messages about that topic; the less you know, the more barren your schema is and the less you will understand about that topic. For instance, the authors of this book have spent years studying effective reading instruction and, consequently, have a richer schema for reading instruction than you do. Hence, when we read a text on reading instruction, we comprehend more and detect more fine-grained levels of meaning than you do.

Concepts about Reading

Supporting any understanding of reading are your concepts about its essential functions. For instance, you conceptualize reading as a message-sending, message-getting activity. You know that at one end is a person (an author) who has a message to send, and at the other end is another person (a reader) who wants to understand the message. You want your students to demonstrate a similar understanding of this author-reader relationship. If they do not—if, for instance, they think reading is saying each word on a page correctly or that it is sounding out words—then they will have difficulty becoming truly literate.

Similarly, you want your students to articulate that reading is communication and that writing and reading are related. You want to know that they understand what reading can do for them and how important it is. And you

Teachers want students to understand what reading can do for them. (Freda Leinwand/ Monkmeyer)

want them to conceptualize reading as something that is controllable: to know that reading ability is not a matter of being smarter than someone else but of knowing how the comprehension system works and that they can use this knowledge to get meaning from text.

These concepts are essential because they provide motivation for learning to read. If students develop the understanding that reading is something done only in school and that it is an arbitrary and mysterious process over which they have little control, they probably will not want to learn to read. On the other hand, if you ensure that your students receive messages they really want to understand and that they feel empowered to make sense of these messages, they will develop accurate concepts for reading and will want to learn to read. These early concepts about reading form the basis of students' attitudes and responses toward it.

Making Sense Out of Reading

Language is the communication and clarification of thought from one person to another. In the case of this book, we (the authors) want to communicate to you (the reader) our thoughts about reading instruction so your schema will be more like ours. We want you to understand reading instruction as we do. Your ability to comprehend our text depends upon a variety of factors, which we now examine.

The Role of Prior Knowledge Various kinds of **prior knowledge** influence readers' ability to comprehend what they read about a topic. For instance, you have much prior knowledge about the topic of reading instruction simply by virtue of having gone to school. However, your prior knowledge about reading instruction differs somewhat from that of your classmates who went to different schools. When the information each of you gets from this book interacts with your prior knowledge about reading instruction, each of you actively interprets what you read in terms of what you have previously learned. Consequently, you and your friends construct slightly different meanings from this text.

In addition to prior knowledge about a topic, readers also use prior knowledge about language and how it works. For instance, you know from experience that certain language conventions are followed when you read (starting at the left side of the page and moving right); that certain combinations of letters (c-o-m-b) represent specific words; that certain words (because, next) signal particular relationships, such as cause-effect and sequence; that certain kinds of text (newspaper articles) are structured differently from other kinds of text (sonnets); that the meaning in one sentence can often provide clues to specific word meanings in another sentence; and that common meanings can be synthesized across large segments of text.

Some of this prior knowledge about language is automatic. That is, because some aspects of language are stable and used in the same form all the time, you memorize them. Examples include left-to-right directionality across the page, letter sounds, and instant recognition of common words. Other aspects of prior knowledge about language are strategic. That is, because comprehension of text demands flexibility, you must reason, must be aware metacognitively of how to figure out what makes the most sense. Good examples include predicting what is to come, using context clues to establish the meaning of an unknown word, inferencing, and synthesizing.

Readers also use their prior knowledge about the social situation within which comprehension takes place. For instance, when prior knowledge of a certain school situation tells you that the purpose of a reading assignment is to pass a factual test, you read differently than if the purpose is to draw generalized conclusions.

Similarly, prior experience with an author, such as Ernest Hemingway, or with a particular type of text, such as directions for completing tax returns, will influence how readers comprehend. Because of prior knowledge about Hemingway and tax forms, you use different comprehension strategies for each.

In a sense, even readers' prior feelings influence comprehension. If your previous experiences with reading have been generally positive, you tend to have a better attitude toward reading, are more motivated about it, and expect it to be a good experience. If, on the other hand, your previous experiences with reading have been negative, you either try to avoid it altogether or to develop strategies that allow you to minimize the amount you do.

The Role of Text The purpose of reading is to make sense out of text. The **text** is the printed matter an author creates to convey his or her ideas. The meaning is the author's, and the text carries that meaning. In composing text, authors use conventions of the language system to signal meaning to the reader. You use your understanding of those conventions as well as prior knowledge about the topic, purpose, and reading to reconstruct the author's message. Because your background knowledge is different from the writer's, you always construct a slightly different message than the author intended. Again, the meaning is not in the printed text; it is constructed by each reader, who uses prior knowledge about the topic, purpose, and language conventions to interpret the author's message.

The Role of Inferencing Because comprehension depends on interpreting new knowledge in terms of what readers already know about a topic, virtually all comprehension is inferential. Whenever you receive a spoken or written message, you make **inferences** or predictions about the intended meaning— that is, you infer or predict what the author is trying to communicate to you. These inferences are based on prior knowledge about language, the topic, the purposes for reading the text, and the strategic reasoning required to comprehend language.

It works like this. First, you look at the print (letters and words) for cues about the topic. You establish what the topic is and then use what you already know about that topic (your schema for the topic) to infer what the author intends to convey. You make inferences based on what you know about the author's purpose in writing the selection and your own purpose for reading it. Finally, you strategically adjust meaning as you are reading on the basis of your understanding of language. For instance, knowing that the text you will read is a political speech and knowing that the meaning of political speeches is different from that of a comedian's dialogue, you expect a certain type of meaning from the text.

The Role of Metacognitive Strategies Rather than constructing meaning randomly, readers use metacognitive strategies to reason about the author's meaning. **Metacognitive strategies,** in contrast to routine skills, require awareness, conscious thought, and reasoning. When *beginning to read,* you use initiating strategies to **activate background knowledge** and make initial predictions. When something does not make sense *while reading,* you stop, analyze the situation in terms of what is known about the reading system, and try to repair the blockage by using fix-it strategies. *After reading,* you use post-reading strategies to determine larger meanings. For instance, a reader who has a strong background in unions will initially predict that a passage titled "The Strike" is going to be about unions and will activate that schema and make appropriate predictions. However, when the first line of text starts out, "When Anne rolled her last ball and got her twelfth strike in a row . . . ," the reader will stop, confirm that the message is about a game instead of a union, and "fix" the situation by substituting a "bowling" schema for the "union" schema. After finishing the passage, the reader will reflect on it, perhaps drawing conclusions about the concentration demanded to roll 12 strikes in a row.

The Role of Situation   Inferencing and **strategic behavior** result from interactions between reader and text; also important is the situation or context in which reading occurs. If the situation is a casual look at a magazine while waiting to be picked up by a friend, the meaning you get will be different from reading the directions for your tax forms. Similarly, the school context influences meaning. For example, the meaning you get from reading a social studies text for a multiple choice test will be different from reading to prepare for an essay test on the same material. Hence, the context of the reading situation plays an important part in comprehension.

See Example 3.1 for an illustration of text comprehension.

Defining Reading

The focus of reading is meaning getting, or comprehending the content of a text for practical or aesthetic purposes. Meaning results from the simultaneous interaction of a variety of information that is available from the reader, from the text, and from the situation that directs the reading act. When reading is initiated these knowledge sources interact simultaneously. The reader predicts the meaning of the text, revises predictions on the basis of additional knowledge, and gradually constructs an interpretation of the message, employing fix-it strategies when the sense breaks down and reflective strategies following the completion of reading. We define reading as *purposeful reconstruction of an author's printed message for recreational or functional purposes.*

RELATING READING AND WRITING

Since reading is part of a whole language process, it should be taught in close association with oral language (listening and speaking) and writing. The relationship between reading and writing is particularly important because both are based on print; consequently, reading instruction should be closely tied to writing instruction.

Writing is important to reading growth for three reasons. First, readers and writers use the same set of written language signals. Writers must understand and manipulate these signals when composing a message that readers can reconstruct by interpreting the same signals. Thus, students' understanding of the system of language signals is enhanced when they use them in writing as well as in reading.

EXAMPLE 3.1   Comprehending Text

The Rotation

The rotation in a Piper Cherokee occurs at 60 miles an hour. When achieving that IAS, apply back pressure on the yoke and step on the right rudder. Soon you will achieve your best angle of climb.

When reading this text you use prior knowledge from a variety of sources simultaneously. You use what you know about print to identify the words "the rotation" in the title and probably predict a meaning associated in some way with turn taking or revolving. However, by the time you read the first line, you encounter other words, such as "Piper Cherokee" and "60 miles an hour," which cause you to revise that prediction. If you have enough prior knowledge about airplanes to include Piper Cherokee in your airplane schema, you probably predict an airplane topic at this point, although unless you have a very rich airplane schema you may not yet be able to construct a meaning for *rotation*. However, if you knew that this passage appeared in a chapter entitled "How to Take Off and Land a Small Plane," your choice of predictions for rotation narrows to airplanes landing and taking off. On the other hand, if this passage appeared in a book on Favorite After Dinner Jokes of Famous Toastmasters, you would start forming hypotheses about where the punch line is in relation to the word *rotation*—you abandon the schema "how to fly an airplane" and get your mind in gear for a joke. You use all these various knowledge sources almost simultaneously, monitoring your sense making as you proceed and being strategic about building meaning.

Every time you encounter unknown terminology, such as "IAS," or identify a word having a meaning you associate with a totally different topic, such as "yoke," you generate new hypotheses.

By testing hypotheses that are triggered by combinations of your knowledge of language and the topic, you gradually build a meaning for "The Rotation." You probably construct a message about the steps involved in getting a small airplane to take off. Depending on the richness of your small plane schema, you may correctly infer that rotation is that point when the plane first leaves the ground, or you may remain unclear about the precise meaning of rotation while still comprehending the essential message about taking off.

Differences in schemata are crucial. For instance, those who build a meaning for "The Rotation" based on a sparse schema for airplanes may get the essential sense of what is happening but will not have a clear understanding of where the yoke is, what a rudder looks like, what the best angle of climb is, and so on. Most licensed pilots, however, will not only construct those additional meanings but will be critical of the use of the term "best angle of climb" because they will feel it is not precise enough to describe that situation. In short, they go beyond the text passage and make a judgment.

Second, there is a close relationship between what readers do and think as they reconstruct meaning from text and what writers do and think as they compose text. For instance, both good readers and good writers understand that the purpose of written language is to communicate a message to someone who is not physically present to receive it. Consequently, both the act of composing and the act of comprehending require an empathy for the person at the other end of the communication channel, a monitoring of the sense-making process as it proceeds, and the use of strategies to clarify (in the case of writing) and to reconstruct (in the case of reading) meaning.

Third, writing is important to the development of reading because a good writing program increases the amount of time spent on text. No matter how much time is spent in the reading program, student learning is enhanced if additional time is devoted to composing text, a task that requires much the same kind of thinking. Consequently, good reading teachers work hard to integrate writing instruction into their reading programs.

BUILDING A READING CURRICULUM

The major goal of reading instruction is to put students in **metacognitive control** of the reading process: They should be conscious of how they make sense of text so they can independently comprehend the messages authors convey. Therefore, the major criterion for judging the success of your reading instruction is whether or not your students independently use reading for a variety of purposes.

Because reading is complex, this major goal is broken down into the following three subgoals: (1) **attitude goals,** or developing the positive responses and conceptual understandings that motivate reading growth; (2) **process goals,** or developing an understanding of how the reading system works; and (3) **content goals,** or using knowledge about the reading process to reconstruct messages in a text. If you develop all three subgoals you will produce readers who are in metacognitive control.

Although these three subgoals are separated for instructional purposes (both in this book and when planning reading instruction), they are not separated in reality. On the contrary, they are interactive—that is, each of the three subgoals influences and is influenced by each of the others. During classroom instruction, you will seldom focus on one subgoal to the total exclusion of all others. A particular lesson may have a process goal as a primary focus (the observable layer of the lesson) and still develop attitude and content goals (the hidden layers of the lesson). This is particularly true when instruction is examined in units or clusters of related lessons.

Figure 3.1 illustrates the nonlinear, interactive nature of reading. Note that the figure begins with attitude goals. This is not because attitude goals are necessarily taught first, but because students' attitudes about reading interact in a fundamental way with all the other goals. The process goals are listed next, not because they necessarily precede the reading of real text, but to illustrate the means-ends relationship that exists between process and content goals. Process goals have value only when they are applied to the content of real text. Finally, content goals are connected to attitude goals to illustrate that what students learn about comprehending text influences their understanding of reading and their attitudes toward it. The arrows are double-headed to emphasize the interrelationships among these outcomes.

We teach reading to develop the attitude, process, and content subgoals that together help students achieve the ultimate goal of being in control of reading. These subgoals are imbedded in the reading **curriculum**—the

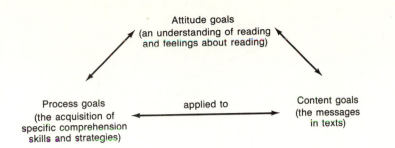

FIGURE 3.1   **The Interactive Nature of Reading**

planned learning experiences you design to produce motivated, independent readers.

Decisions about the reading curriculum, about what to teach in reading, are determined by the goals of reading instruction. Because students need to understand and enjoy reading, part of your curriculum focuses on building accurate concepts and positive responses to reading (attitude goals). Because students need to be conscious of how they get meaning from text, part of your curriculum focuses on how reading works (process goals). Because students need to understand the messages in texts, part of your curriculum focuses on helping them get content from text (content goals). Figure 3.2, an elaboration of Figure 3.1, shows how the three subgoals interact and contribute to the development of the major goal. A more extended discussion of the three subgoals follows.

Attitude Goals

For students to control the reading process, they must have a positive attitude about reading. That means they will not have incomplete or erroneous concepts about reading or perceive reading negatively. You will need to help them develop their concepts of reading and to instill positive responses.

Concepts   **A concept** is the combination of all the characteristics you associate with something. Every concept has an identifying word or label. For example, a familiar word like dog probably brings to mind many characteristics. For the word platypus, however, you may generate only a few characteristics and, as a result, your concept of platypus is not as rich as your concept of dog. Because everyone has had different experiences, everyone generates slightly different characteristics for identical concepts. Even a common word like dog results in slightly different mental images because of varying background experiences.

Similarly, different students have different concepts of reading. For instance, if school reading experiences primarily emphasize work sheets, drill, and correct answers, students will think reading is work sheets, drill, and

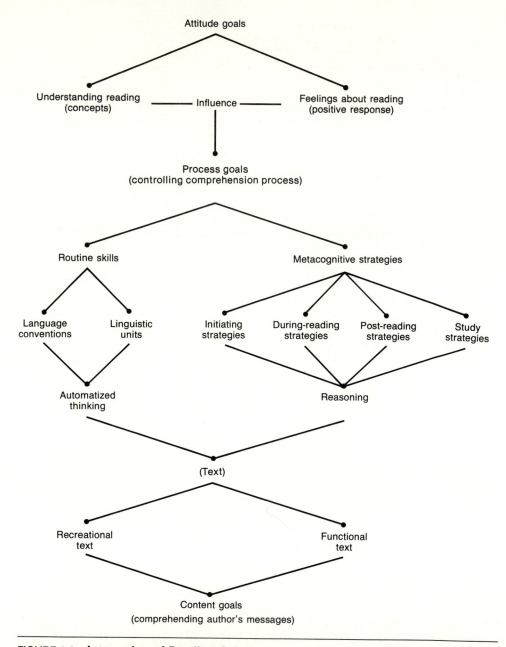

FIGURE 3.2   Interaction of Reading Subgoals

correct answers. If, in contrast, school reading experiences emphasize making sense out of written messages to meet needs and solve problems, students will think reading is meaning getting, sense making, and problem solving.

One of the fundamental goals in reading instruction is to help students understand that reading is a meaning-getting activity with the function of communication. Such a concept of reading contributes to a positive attitude about reading by setting for students accurate expectations about what real readers actually do. To build this concept, teachers provide positive experiences with reading that highlight the fact that text is produced by a writer who has a message to convey and that all reading involves interpreting the writer's message. Students' encounters with reading should emphasize the relationship among all four language modes: listening, speaking, reading, and writing. They will then learn that both speaking and writing involve a message sender who composes a message; that listening and reading involve a message receiver who interprets the message; and that reading and writing are not different subjects but opposite ends of the communication process.

Positive Responses Positive responses are closely tied to an understanding of reading since it is difficult for people to feel good about something when they have misconceptions about it. The chances of creating positive attitudes become better when students' reading experiences deal with messages of interest to them and are easy enough to be performed successfully. Hence, to create positive responses to reading you should provide reading experiences that have interesting content and that can be completed successfully.

Wholistic reading encounters emphasize listening, speaking, reading, and writing. (Robert Bawden)

When these conditions are present, your students will develop positive responses to reading. Details for teaching attitude goals are provided in Chapter 5, and suggestions for developing attitudes at various grade levels are provided in Chapters 15 through 18.

Process Goals

The second subgoal of reading instruction focuses on how reading works—that is, on the development of routine skills and metacognitive strategies.

Routine Skills Good readers do some things automatically and they think carefully (or reason) about other things. Those things done automatically are **routine skills** and include both language conventions and various linguistic units.

Language conventions are arbitrary rules that govern text. In English, examples include reading from the front of a book to the back, from the top of a page to the bottom, from the left side of the page to the right, and from the left side of a word to the right. Expert readers take such conventions for granted, but beginning readers who have no previous experience with English text may start reading at the back of a book, at the bottom of a page, or at the right-hand side of a page or word. Indeed, text in languages other than English may begin not at the front but at the back of the book, not at the top but at the bottom of the page, and not at the left but at the right sides of the page and word. To be in control of the reading process, students need to automatically apply these conventions when reading.

Linguistic units are letter combinations that students should learn to recognize without conscious effort, such as sight words, letter-name and letter-sound associations, and the meanings of common prefixes and suffixes. **Sight words** appear so frequently in English text that students should identify them instantly. It would be inefficient to expect readers to figure out common words such as "have" or "the" every time they encounter them. Instead, reading is more fluent when readers recognize most of these words at sight. That is, they memorize them through frequent use. Similarly, students should not have to consciously figure out the sound associated with every alphabet letter or letter-sound combination (such as *tr* or *th*). That would also be inefficient, if not impossible. Consequently, you should teach letter sounds as routine skills to be memorized so they can be recalled automatically when needed. The same is true of common prefixes and suffixes, as well as other linguistic units.

Metacognitive Strategies Although routine skills are important, an even more important part of being in control of reading involves metacognitive strategies. As noted earlier, three kinds of metacognitive strategies are particularly important.

Initiating strategies are used as you begin to read; they activate background knowledge especially of the topic, the type of text, and purpose in reading it.

During-reading strategies are used while comprehending and consist of two substrategies. The first is **monitoring,** in which you check the accuracy of your predictions and prepare to stop and generate new predictions if the text cues do not conform to your expectations. Monitoring refers to the constant test readers apply to what they read: "Is this the meaning I expected and does it make sense in terms of what I know about the world?" This strategy is the heart of comprehension; readers who do not monitor their meaning getting are not aware when their reading fails to make sense. Once monitoring reveals a problem with getting the meaning, readers must use **fix-it strategies** to generate new predictions or to remove the blockage to meaning. Ideally students would always be able to construct accurate meaning using initiating strategies. Such is not always the case, however. Frequently students will encounter words they cannot identify in print; will be unable to interpret the relationships being communicated by the author; will lose track of the gist of the message; or will be unable to make the inferences or draw the conclusions essential to the author's message. In such cases they need strategies they can apply to fix their comprehension—to remove the blockage, restore the meaning, and allow for the continuation of fluent reading.

Post-reading strategies are used after reading to organize, restructure, and make judgments about the author's message.

These three metacognitive strategies interact, with a reader making initial predictions about meaning; using during-reading strategies to monitor meaning getting to confirm or reject these predictions and to fix or construct new interpretations whenever needed; and using post-reading strategies to reflect on the author's message. This interactive process happens almost instantaneously. Following is an illustration of how these three metacognitive strategies might work in a comprehending book about the rules of baseball.

On the basis of previous experience with the topic (the rules of baseball), the kind of text it is (an information book on "How to Play the Game of Baseball"), and the purpose (to convey the basic procedures in playing the game), the reader initiates meaning getting by activating appropriate schemata and making predictions regarding what will be learned about baseball. In a sense, it is a getting ready step in which the reader activates appropriate background knowledge to prepare for making sense out of an author's message. Second, while reading, the reader monitors meaning getting. As each word or group of words on the page is identified, the reader attaches meaning based on his or her schemata for that topic, type of text, and purpose. The reader then confirms or rejects these predicted meanings by testing them against the **syntactic** or **semantic** cues imbedded in the text. If the prediction is confirmed, the reader goes on; if it is rejected in view of subsequent syntactic and semantic cues, the reader uses fix-it strategies to repair the blockage so that meaning getting can continue. Finally, after completing the reading, the information about baseball is organized and evaluated, particularly in view of the reader's purpose.

Study strategies, a fourth set of metacognitive strategies, are specialized strategies readers use to locate, organize, and remember text information, particularly the information found in textbooks, encyclopedias, and other functional text. For instance, expert readers locate information by using tables of contents, indexes, and card catalogs; they organize information by taking notes and outlining; and they remember information by using systematic study techniques. Because study strategies are usually used in association with content areas such as social studies and science, they are usually taught at the upper elementary grades.

Some people think of all the metacognitive strategies as "skills." However, skills are procedures to be memorized in isolation, and as a result, students use them automatically rather than thoughtfully and strategically. Although skills are useful and important for language conventions and linguistic units, comprehension of text requires flexible and adaptive reasoning—as opposed to routine and unvarying procedures—to reconstruct an author's meaning. So metacognitive strategies are not skills; rather, they are flexible and adaptable plans to be learned consciously. Once learned, the strategies may be applied automatically in highly familiar text situations that are easy for the reader to comprehend, but they will become conscious again when the reader encounters difficult text.

Details for teaching process goals associated with words are provided in Chapter 7, and Chapter 8 describes how to teach process goals associated with the strategies for comprehension. Suggestions for developing process goals at various grade levels are provided in Chapters 15 through 18.

Content Goals

Since the ultimate goal of reading is to interpret the author's message, readers have achieved the content subgoal when they can state what the author's message is. Process and content goals represent a means-ends relationship: Getting meaning from content is the end, and understanding how reading works is a means to that end.

Functional texts are those texts in which the content is utilitarian information. Normally, they are written as **expository text.** Textbooks are a good example; others are newspapers, catalogs, recipes, application forms, encyclopedias, various kinds of written directions, and so on.

When presenting such functional texts to your students, you should orient them to specific terminology or unknown words being employed, help them activate the appropriate **topic** schemata, provide information about the author's purpose in writing the text and their **purpose** in reading it, and help them anticipate and interpret the **text structure.**

Recreational texts are those texts in which the content is entertaining or enriching. Normally, recreational writing takes the form of **narrative texts.** These include nearly all forms of fiction, such as short stories, novels, and fictionalized biographies; other forms include fables, mythology, fairy tales, other folk literature, and poetry.

A major strategy used to involve students in recreational text is **uninterrupted sustained silent reading** (USSR) in which students and teachers quietly read books of their choice. Many teachers also plan daily sessions in which they orally read good literature to students, and teachers frequently have students share their favorite recreational reading with each other. The basal reading textbook typically contains numerous selections of recreational reading, many of which are excerpts from excellent examples of children's literature. When presenting such text to your students, you should provide guidance similar to that noted for functional text: Prepare students for the selection by helping them activate relevant background knowledge. In addition, you should often use recreational reading activities to teach such literary devices as metaphors, symbolism, and others.

It is important to note that the instructional focus of content goals is not so students can identify particular examples of text as "functional" or "recreational," but so they can get meaning from both kinds of text. Getting meaning in recreational text, which is primarily narrative, is a different task from getting meaning from functional text, which is primarily expository. Details for teaching content goals appear in Chapter 6. Suggestions for developing content goals at various grade levels are provided in Chapters 15 through 18.

Summary of Reading Curriculum Subgoals

A good reader is one who chooses to read independently, possesses the routine skills and metacognitive strategies to control the process of getting meaning, and applies what is known about how reading works to get the messages in functional and recreational text. No one of these three subgoals is more important than another, nor do you teach one as a prerequisite to another. Rather, all three are developed together and interact in supporting and encouraging reading growth.

The reading curriculum, then, is a direct reflection of the three subgoals that should be fostered in reading instruction. To build attitude goals, you create instructional encounters designed to build desired concepts and positive responses to reading; to develop process goals, you directly teach the routine skills and metacognitive strategies your students need to fluently generate predictions about the author's meaning and to restore meaning when the predictions are rejected; and to develop content goals, you guide your students' attempts to get the messages in functional and recreational text.

INTEGRATING THE WRITING CURRICULUM

Although this is a book about reading instruction, the close relationship between reading and writing means that reading teachers often integrate writing instruction with reading instruction. To help you accomplish such integration, we provide a brief description of the writing curriculum here and mention writing in subsequent chapters where appropriate.

There are many similarities between the reading and writing curricula. Just as the ultimate outcome of reading instruction is student control of the comprehension process, the ultimate outcome of writing instruction is student control of the composing process. Your students should know how to compose the functional and recreational messages they wish to write. To develop such conscious control, you must help students develop positive attitudes toward writing, knowledge of the content to be communicated, and an understanding of how the writing process works.

Attitude Goals

Like reading, writing growth depends upon good attitudes about writing. These attitudes are based in students' concepts about writing, which grow from their encounters with writing.

These concepts are virtually the same as those in reading. Students should understand the reader-writer relationship. That is, they should understand that writers are the first to read their own composed text; writing is

When students enjoy reading their own writing, the experience will be positive. (Susan Lapides/Design Conceptions)

message sending and always involves an audience; the audience can be oneself as well as others; writing is similar to speaking except that the audience is not physically present; and writing fulfills both functional and recreational needs.

Similarly, you should make sure students have positive encounters with writing. They should associate writing with enjoyment, fulfillment, and meaningful activity rather than with fear, work, and defeat. To develop accurate concepts and positive experiences you must provide students with writing experiences that are useful, pleasant, and reasonably natural. If this does not happen—if their writing encounters are useless, unpleasant, and contrived—students will develop inaccurate concepts and negative feelings about writing.

Content Goals

The content of writing is whatever message the writer wants to send. For instance, students should be able to compose such functional messages as business letters, friendly letters, simple expository text, reports, newspaper articles, and formal term papers. For recreation messages students should be able to compose diaries, journals, stories, poems, riddles, and jingles among others. Before composing various kinds of text, however, they must decide upon the purpose and content of the message. When students have clear and meaningful reasons for writing, they seldom have difficulty knowing what to say.

You should also help students distinguish between writing for oneself and writing for others. The content of personal writing (diaries, journals, reflections, recipes) is different from the content of writing produced for an outside audience. Text written for personal use is not so concerned with clarity or adherence to the mechanics of language, since there is little chance that writers will fail to understand their own messages to themselves, even when inaccuracies are present. When writing for others, however, both clarity and language mechanics must be emphasized to assist readers in reconstructing the message. In short, the content goals in a writing curriculum should help students identify the message they want to send, distinguish between writing for oneself and writing for others, and distinguish the text structures associated with various kinds of functional and recreational text.

Process Goals

Process goals in writing are divided into two categories: knowledge of the stages in the composing process and strategies for implementing each stage.

Knowledge of the Stages of Writing To be in control of the writing process, students must first know what stages writers go through in composing text. All writers must plan, draft, and edit.

The **planning stage** emphasizes reflection. A writer decides upon the purpose of a message, the central meaning to be conveyed, and the supportive information to be included. An important part of the planning stage is to think about who will read the message and how to adapt it to that audience. For instance, when writing about a complex topic for a knowledgeable audience, elaborate background information is not needed. On the other hand, when the intended audience is relatively unsophisticated about the topic, it is necessary to build a background before launching into the central message. Consequently, the planning stage must take into account the intended reader's values and schemata.

The planning stage also includes organizing the message into an appropriate text structure. For instance, in composing a story, the text structure usually follows a progression from the setting to the main character, to the character's problem, to a series of events that occur, to a resolution of the problem. In contrast, in composing a news article, the usual text structure is to have all the relevant information in the first paragraph and to assign the details to subsequent paragraphs. Planning is especially crucial when the audience is someone other than oneself, since the text structure helps the reader reconstruct the message.

In the **drafting stage** the writer composes a message in rough form, concentrating on producing a coherent and cohesive text. Coherence (the ideas fit together) and cohesiveness (the central message is maintained throughout the text) are important whether the writer is producing functional or recreational text.

In the **editing stage** the writer critically reads his or her text, trying to anticipate where readers might have difficulty. All stages of the composing process are important, but editing is particularly important because it is here that the message is honed and polished to ensure that the reader makes an interpretation close to what the writer intends. Editing encompasses all aspects of the writing process: The writer edits in terms of the planning stage (content and audience), the drafting stage (text structure, coherence, and cohesiveness), and the finer points of the editing stage (word and phrase choice, punctuation, grammatical accuracy, and spelling).

These stages are not necessarily linear. Writers often move from planning to drafting and back again before all the planning is complete. Similarly, editing often occurs before the drafting stage is complete. This is particularly true when writing for an audience other than oneself. Nevertheless, the typical progression is as follows. A writer plans for the content, the audience, and the basic text structure; this plan is then used to produce a coherent and cohesive first draft; the draft is then edited for content, clarity, and the mechanics of written language, a process which often proceeds through several additional drafts.

Strategies to Be Used at Each Stage The strategies used in writing are similar to those in reading. Whereas readers consciously monitor their understanding of an author's message and stop when there is a blockage and activate a fix-it strategy, writers consciously monitor what they are composing for potential blockages to readers' comprehension. When a potential blockage is detected, the writer calls on a planning, drafting, or editing strategy to remove it.

Three strategies are helpful at the planning stage. The first planning strategy involves getting the necessary information, either by brainstorming, reading, interviewing, or observing. An important distinction must be made here: When students complain that they do not know what to write about, it is often because the writing task is not meaningful to them—it is busy work. Since the problem is not a lack of information but a meaningless assignment, the solution is to give students a good reason for writing rather than strategies for getting more information. If students do lack information about a real message that will be sent to someone, then ways to gather information must be taught. The second planning strategy involves focusing on what is to be said, which often involves clarifying the purpose of the writing. Students can accomplish this by grouping or categorizing gathered information. The third planning strategy focuses on organizing: it calls for procedures such as outlining, in which related concepts are grouped together in a chosen text structure.

Drafting-stage strategies focus on creating coherence and cohesion in the message. To ensure coherence, the age-old method of adding introductory and summary statements and wrapping them around the central message is a reliable remedy. This solution can be adapted to both functional and recreational writing. It is most often associated with expository text, in which it is used to provide coherence to paragraphs, sections, and entire texts. Another way to make expository text coherent is to carefully use headings and subheadings to guide the reader. For narrative text students can follow a story map, which sequences the events. To ensure cohesion students may insert transition statements between paragraphs and sections and insert signal words that key one section of text to another. Particularly useful is the strategy of including periodic summaries. In functional text summaries remind readers of key points, concepts, or the main idea; in recreational text summaries can remind readers of the problem, the sequence of events relating to the problem, or the theme.

Editing-stage strategies focus on helping the reader reconstruct the intended meaning. Editing requires the writer to play two roles simultaneously: During this process the writer is also a reader. Although multiparagraph organizational characteristics are sometimes modified at the editing stage, most editing focuses on the sentence and word levels. For instance, writers use synonyms and a thesaurus to make more precise word choices; syntactic changes to improve meaning through word order; punctuation to help the reader understand what the author intended, and spelling to help the reader identify the words. These strategies are often referred to as the mechanics of writing and are sometimes incorrectly taught as skills to be memorized through synonym and antonym drills, sentence diagramming, punctuation drills, and weekly spelling tests. When students are taught writing mechanics in this way, they seldom apply them to the actual task of composing. When taught as strategies to be used when editing a real message, however, mechanics suddenly become more meaningful and useful.

To summarize the writing curriculum involves giving students information about how the writing process works, just as the reading curriculum involves giving information about how the reading process works. In both cases the intent is to have students who are in cognitive control of the communication process and who can apply appropriate strategies to repair actual or potential blockages to meaning getting. Suggestions for integrating writing into various reading goals are provided in Chapters 5 through 9, and suggestions for using writing when teaching various grade levels are provided in Chapters 15 through 18.

STAGES OF DEVELOPMENTAL READING GROWTH

A reading curriculum is organized as a **developmental progression.** That is, some attitude, process, and content goals are emphasized in the early elementary grades and others are emphasized later. The different points along this developmental continuum are called **stages of developmental reading growth.** This book refers to five stages, each of which slightly overlaps the preceding one.

The first level, the **readiness stage,** includes preschool, kindergarten, and first grade students. At this level most students are not actually reading but are preparing to do so. Oral language activities are generally used to help them learn the attitude, process, and content goals needed to begin actual reading. In writing, there is an emphasis on **preliterate writing** in which students begin to use their individual, nonstandard language systems to create and share written messages.

The second level, the **initial mastery stage,** ordinarily begins in first grade and continues into second grade. At this stage most students actually begin to read and write print. During the initial mastery stage students learn to read preprimers, primers, and other materials associated with beginning reading. Attitude, process, and content goals are taught with a particular emphasis on word identification.

The third stage, the **expanded fundamentals stage,** ordinarily begins in second grade and continues into fourth grade. At this stage students' reading levels expand into second, third, and fourth grade materials due to increased mastery of the fundamentals of reading. The curriculum continues to include attitude, process, and content outcomes, but the emphasis on word identification diminishes and emphasis on comprehension increases.

The fourth stage, the **application stage,** ordinarily begins at about fourth grade and continues into eighth grade. Along with basal reading textbooks students increasingly use textbooks for other curricular areas such as social studies, science, and mathematics. They apply what they have learned about reading to these other content areas. At this stage emphasis is on attitude, process, and content goals that support such application.

The fifth stage, the **power stage,** typically begins in eighth grade and can continue long after formal schooling ends. Readers at this level can handle almost any kind of reading. Because it typically occurs at the post-elementary school level, the power stage is not emphasized in this book.

As Table 3.1 illustrates, the relative emphasis given the three curricular goals varies according to the stages of developmental growth even though all three goals are taught at every developmental stage. For instance, a kinder-garten teacher expects to emphasize attitudes almost 50 percent of the time and content less than 25 percent of the time, whereas a twelfth grade teacher reverses this emphasis. Similarly, the emphasis within any particular goal

TABLE 3.1   Relative Curricular Emphasis across Developmental Stages*

	READINESS	INITIAL MASTERY	EXPANDED FUNDAMENTALS	APPLICATION
Attitude goals				
Concepts and positive responses	Stressed in listening comprehension	Stressed	Continued development	Maintained
Process goals				
Routine skills	Stressed in print awareness			
• vocabulary		Stressed	Maintained	Maintained
• word recognition		Stressed	Continued development	Maintained
Metacognitive strategies	Stressed in listening comprehension			
• initiating strategies		Stressed	Continued development	Continued development
• during-reading strategies		Stressed	Continued development	Continued development
• post-reading strategies		Introduced	Introduced	Continued development
• study strategies	Not dealt with	Introduced	Introduced	Stressed
Content goals				
Recreational text	Stressed	Stressed	Continued development	Continued development
Functional text	Introduced	Introduced	Stressed	Stressed

* The power stage is not discussed in this book.

varies from one developmental level to another. Content goals heavily emphasize recreational reading at the readiness and initial mastery levels, where narrative text is frequently used, and heavily emphasize functional reading at the application and power levels, where expository text is emphasized. Process goals are heavily emphasized at the initial mastery and the expanded fundamentals levels, where many fix-it strategies are taught, and are emphasized less at higher levels.

THE IMPORTANCE OF WHY

Professional teachers understand why they teach what they teach. Technicians who have no such rationale blindly follow directions contained in teachers' manuals and workbook pages. They do not know why they are doing what they do, so they have no basis for making their own decisions. Knowing why things are done in a certain way provides the cohesiveness that glues the instructional reading program together. The technician's emphasis on isolated tasks, mechanics, and surface answers, in contrast, tends to create a disjointed and mechanical instructional program.

Knowing why you are doing things is the first step in becoming a professional decision maker. You must know why reading and writing are related and why particular reading and writing lessons contribute to the ultimate content, attitude, and process goals.

This book emphasizes justifying instructional decisions by referring to desired reading goals. While many classroom constraints limit what teachers can do and the materials they can use, professionals rise above these constraints. They shape instructional encounters to create desired attitude, process, and content goals. Thus, professional teachers are in cognitive control and are prepared for continuous modification, refinement, and improvement of instruction.

SUMMARY

Writers purposefully construct text to have messages read and readers purposefully reconstruct text to receive messages. To get messages from text, readers simultaneously combine cues the author embeds in the text and cues from their own prior knowledge about the topic and about reading itself, strategically inferring the meaning the author intended. Consequently, the reader must have a positive attitude based on a conceptual understanding of reading and its function; an understanding of the mental processing good readers engage in to construct meaning; and ultimately an understanding of the content of the message. These three components—positive attitudes about reading, awareness of the processes involved, and understanding the content of text—are the goals of reading instruction: What you teach when you teach a reading curriculum is attitudes about reading, mental processes employed by good readers, and comprehension of text content. Because reading and writing are so closely related, analogous attitude, process, and content goals are developed during writing instruction. Both reading and writing curricular goals are developed gradually over the course of years.

SUGGESTED ADDITIONAL READINGS

ARTLEY, A. S. (1980). Reading: Skills or competencies? *Language Arts*, 57(5), 546–549.

AUTEN, A. (1985). Focus on thinking instruction. *Reading Teacher*, 38(4), 454–456.

BABBS, P. J., & MOE, A. J. (1983). Metacognition: A key for independent learning from text. *Reading Teacher*, 36(4), 422–426.

CANADY, R. J. (1980). Psycholinguistics in a real-life classroom. *Reading Teacher*, 34(2), 156–159.

CHOMSKY, C. (1971). Write now, read later. *Childhood Education*, 47, 296–299.

CHOMSKY, C. (1976). After decoding, what? *Language Arts*, 53, 288–296.

DIONISIO, M. (1983). Write? Isn't this reading class? *Reading Teacher*, 36(8), 746–750.

DOWNING, J. (1982). Reading—skill or skills? *Reading Teacher*, 35(5), 534–537.

FITZGERALD, J. (1983). Helping readers gain self-control over reading comprehension. *Reading Teacher*, 37(3), 249–253.

GAMBRELL, L. B. (1985). Dialogue journals: Reading-writing interaction. *Reading Teacher*, 38(6), 512–515.

GARNER, W. I. (1984). Reading is a problem-solving process. *Reading Teacher*, 38(1), 36–47.

GEMAKE, J. (1984). Interactive reading: How to make children active readers. *Reading Teacher*, 37(6), 462–466.

GOLDEN, J. M. (1984). Children's concept of story in reading and writing. *Reading Teacher*, 37(7), 578–584.

GUTHRIE, J. T. (1984). Comprehension instruction. *Reading Teacher*, 38(2), 236–238.

GUTHRIE, J. T. (1984). Writing connections. *Reading Teacher*, 37(6), 540–542.

JONES, L. L. (1982). An interactive view of reading: Implications for the classroom. *Reading Teacher*, 35(7), 772–777.

PARIS, S., OKA, E., & DEBRITTO, A. (1983). Beyond decoding: Synthesis of research on reading comprehension. *Educational Leadership*, 41, 78–83.

RAND, M. K. (1984). Story schema: Theory, research and practice. *Reading Teacher*, 37(4), 377–383.

RONEY, R. C. (1984). Background experience is the foundation of success in learning to read. *Reading Teacher*, 38(2), 196–199.

TATHAM, S. M. (1978). Comprehension taxonomies: Their uses and abuses. *Reading Teacher*, 32(2), 190–194.

TIERNEY, R., & PEARSON, P. D. (1983). Toward a composing model of reading. *Reading Teacher*, 37, 568–580.

WILSON, C. R. (1983). Teaching reading comprehension by connecting the known to the new. *Reading Teacher*, 36(4), 382–390.

THE RESEARCH BASE

ANDERSON, R. C., & PEARSON, P. D. (1984). A schema-theoretic view of basic processes in reading comprehension. In P. D. Pearson (Ed.), *Handbook of reading research*. New York: Longman.

KING, M., & REUTEL, V. (1981). *How children learn to write: A longitudinal study.* Final report. Columbus, OH: Ohio State University.

PEARSON, P. D., & TIERNEY, R. (1984). On becoming a thoughtful reader: Learning to read like a writer. In A. Purves & O. Niles (Eds.), *Becoming readers in a complex society.* Eighty-third Yearbook of the National Society for the Study of Education. Chicago: University of Chicago Press.

PEARSON, P. D., DOLE, J., DUFFY, G. G., & ROEHLER, L. R. (in press). Developing expertise in reading comprehension: What should be taught and how should it be taught? In J. Farstrup & J. Samuels (Eds.), *What research says to the teacher of reading* (2nd ed). Newark, DE: International Reading Association.

Instruction, Motivation, and Methodology

4

GETTING READY

To control instruction you must first understand the components of instruction and methodology. This chapter describes these components, providing you with an introduction to how to conduct reading instruction in elementary school. Three major topics are discussed: the nature of instruction, motivating through integrated instruction, and approaches to organizing reading instruction.

FOCUS QUESTIONS

- What is the distinction between teaching and instruction?

- What are the three main characteristics of instruction?

- How do academic tasks influence what students learn?

- What is the distinction between direct instruction and indirect instruction?

- What are the two ways to motivate students?

- How does integrating within lessons and integrating across lessons enhance motivation?

- What is the distinction between the basal textbook approach to reading instruction and the language experience approach, the personalized reading approach, and a combined approach?

NATURE OF INSTRUCTION

Teachers expedite the learning of students. That is, teachers instruct. According to Lee Shulman:

A teacher is someone who knows something not understood by others, presumably his students. He is capable of transforming his own comprehension of the subject matter, his own skills of performance or desired attitude values, into pedagogical representations and actions. There are ways of talking, showing, enacting or otherwise representing the ideas so that the unknowing can come to know, those without understanding can comprehend and discern, the unskilled can become adept.[1]

The Distinction between Teaching and Instruction

The first step in understanding instruction is to distinguish it from other elements of teaching. Although learning, teaching, and instruction tend to occur together, they are not synonymous. Learning can occur without teachers or any formal instruction. **Teaching** encompasses all that you do in the course of the school day, including instruction. What you do to keep your class moving smoothly, to keep up morale, and to make children feel good about themselves are not instructional activities. They are part of the important general activities associated with teaching school but are not specifically tied to intentional efforts to develop specific curricular outcomes. This does not mean that these more general classroom activities are unimportant. Collecting milk money, taking lunch count, supervising recess, consoling an injured child, and countless other activities that make up the daily classroom routine are essential for effective operation of a classroom. However, they are noninstructional because they do not involve intentionally using professional knowledge to achieve curricular goals.

Instruction is intentional and goal directed. As a teacher, you plan an encounter between your student's schema and a specified experience with the intention that your student will modify that schema. **Instruction,** therefore, is a conscious attempt to modify another's understanding (or schema) in a specified way, with the intention of producing specific curricular outcomes. It may or may not cause your students to modify their schemata, which is to say it may or may not result in learning.

Characteristics of Instruction

Instruction is characterized by three properties: caring, information giving, and mediation of student construction of meaning. Teachers must do more than simply tell students what they need to know or give them an activity to do, because students are not passive participants in learning. They have feelings, and they already possess conceptions (and, sometimes, misconceptions) about what is being taught. While you certainly need to provide students with knowledge, you must also account for students' feelings as human beings and for their active role in redefining, on the basis of their conceptions and misconceptions, what it is that you are teaching them. The first characteristic of instruction is sensitivity to learners' thoughts and feelings in accomplishing the desired goal.

1. Shulman, L. (1986). *Knowledge and teaching. Foundations of the new reform.* Unpublished paper, Stanford University.

A second characteristic of instruction is information giving. Learning occurs when students modify an existing schema or create a new schema from information they receive. Students can receive information directly, as when you **model,** that is, show them exactly how to do a task; or less directly from the classroom environment as they participate in activities intended to encourage them to infer the information. In either case students must receive information in order to build schemata about curricular goals.

The third characteristic of instruction is mediation of student restructuring of the information provided. Students mediate what happens during instruction. That is, they filter information through their minds and, in the process, restructure the message so that it fits their respective schemata.

This is not the way instruction has always been viewed. People used to think of instruction as a single cycle in which the teacher "poured" information into students' minds. Research has shown, however, that students are not passive recipients of instructional information but active mediators of experiences that they encounter. They pass instructional information through their existing schemata and, in the process, negotiate a meaning consistent with those schemata. This modern view of learning and instruction requires teachers to do more than care and more than simply "pour in" information. They must also allow time for students to express their restructured understandings and then decide what instructional elaborations, if any, to provide to help students reach the intended curricular goal.

Teachers must allow students time to express their understanding of instruction. (Will McIntyre/Photo Researchers)

How students mediate instruction is crucial to what they learn because they learn the interpreted or reconstructed goal, not necessarily the intended one. For instance, if you want students to learn letter sounds, you might assign a ditto sheet and tell students to draw lines from each letter to a picture of an animal whose name begins with that letter sound, expecting this exercise to cause students to use letter sounds when reading. Students, however, may think about this task in terms of how to finish it quickly and, acting upon this interpretation, will learn how to get done quickly. They complete the dittos but do not learn what you intended—about how to use letter sounds in reading.

You combat such situations by carefully structuring the **academic task,** the work teachers give students to do. Students decide what they must learn by noting what the teacher accepts as a satisfactory performance of the task. For instance, a ditto sheet on letters means one thing if the completed ditto sheet is what the teacher grades, and it means another if students' use of letters when reading a simple story is what the teacher grades. In the first case, students interpret the task as one of drawing lines from letters to pictures, and that is what they learn; in the second case, students interpret the task as one of using letters when reading text, and that is what they learn.

Good instruction, then, can be summed up with the following three points:

1. Instruction is the intentional provision of academic tasks designed to help students modify their schemata in ways specified in the curriculum.

2. Academic tasks can be embedded in the classroom environment or directed by the teacher.

3. Student feelings must be considered in relation to every academic task as well as the fact that students will restructure the task on the basis of what they already know.

DISTINCTION BETWEEN DIRECT AND INDIRECT INSTRUCTION

Instruction can be direct, indirect, or a combination of both. **Direct instruction** occurs when teachers present an academic task to students. For example, a mother teaching a baby to say the new word *Daddy* and a teacher teaching a student to read the printed word *Daddy* are examples of direct instruction. **Indirect instruction** occurs when academic tasks are embedded in activities in the classroom environment to lead students to some desired goal. Leaving computer catalogs in the classroom so students will examine them and, hopefully, understand that reading includes catalogs as well as the more traditional books typically found in school is an example of indirect instruction. Most instruction contains elements of both direct and indirect instruction, since you verbally direct some student experiences. The following discussion gives details on using these types of instruction.

Direct Instruction

Teachers who instruct directly play a structured and active role. They rely on what they say to ensure that students interpret academic tasks in the intended way. That is, they provide information to students directly and expect students to respond. Each response provides an opportunity for students to express their understanding of the information the teacher provides, and each of these expressions offers the teacher a window into students' minds. By looking through this window you then interpret to see how students have restructured the task; you use what you learn through each interaction as a basis for providing elaboration. Consequently, successful direct instruction depends as much on your spontaneous elaborations as on your initial presentation of information. Hence, direct instruction is an ongoing process of reciprocal mediation. Caring teachers plan encounters to provide students with information about the curricular goal that is mediated and restructured by students, fed back to the teacher, and, when necessary, followed by elaborated information keyed to this feedback. This interactive cycle continues until students reach the desired goal, whether during a single lesson or, in the case of more complex understandings, after a series of lessons. (See Figure 4.1.) Four characteristics are associated with direct instruction: assessment, explanation, practice, and application.

Assessment involves collection of the data used to make decisions. It is crucial to all instruction, especially direct instruction because teachers cannot make good decisions unless they assess student performance.

Data can be collected either formally (using standardized tests) or informally (using teacher-made measures). Clinicians and reading specialists make much use of **formal tests,** but most classroom teachers rely on **informal tests.** That is, they observe their students, question and talk with them, examine their written work, and make instructional decisions from these data. One example of informal assessment is the teacher's observation of students' restructuring in the description of instructional mediation. Chapter 11 provides details about how to assess.

Explanation is verbal assistance. It is extremely important in direct instruction because it is during explanation that teachers initially provide the information students need to construct an understanding of what is being taught. Explanation provides the "how-to" bridge between not knowing and knowing. It plays a major role in determining how students will interpret a task, because they tend to think about tasks in the ways teachers talk about them. In short, students learn what teachers emphasize.

Explanation consists of two parts. First is the initial instructional presentation—a series of brief teacher statements about what is to be learned, why it is to be learned, and how to do it. This information giving usually includes explicit teacher modeling of how to do a task and, as such, relies greatly on teacher talk. Second is the interaction between teacher and students as students restructure the teacher's presentation. This is where teachers gradually shift the responsibility for doing and understanding a task to their students

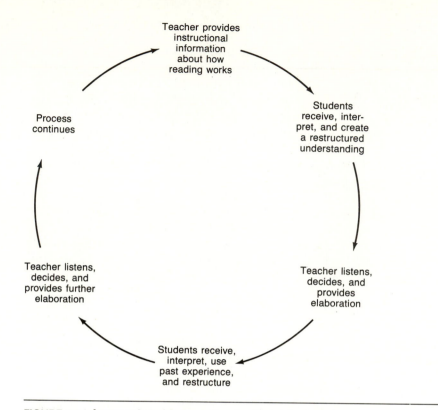

FIGURE 4.1   Instructional Interaction in Direct Instruction

by providing a series of opportunities for students to express their understanding. Students complete succeeding items in the series of opportunities with less and less assistance from the teacher (with less and less teacher talk and more and more student talk). The goal is for students to comprehend without teacher assistance. This interactive part of instruction calls for much flexibility from teachers, since students constantly restructure explanations in terms of their prior knowledge. Chapter 13 provides details about how to explain.

Practice is repetition, and its function is to make habitual, or solidify, initial understanding developed during explanation. For instance, explanation helps students understand how to figure out the theme of a story, but practice makes the strategy a habit. Practice is generally characterized by repetition and drill, whereas explanation is characterized by information giving and sense making.

Practice usually consists of activities rather than teacher talk. To give students practice, teachers involve them in activities with either controlled or natural text. **Controlled text** is intentionally structured to include many repetitions of whatever knowledge or strategy is being taught; **natural text** is an unaltered example of text, such as a library book, that includes sufficient examples of what is to be practiced. In most reading classrooms practice activities employ controlled text such as workbook pages or ditto sheets in which students respond several times to a similar kind of task because it is efficient and easy to use. However, controlled-text practice activities do not encourage application of the learning to natural text. Since the ultimate goal is "real" reading, natural text is often a more useful practice, despite the relative scarceness of examples.

Whereas explanations must be teacher led, practice can be either teacher guided or independent. Practice is guided when teachers directly supervise it: for instance, monitoring each student's response to practice items or listening to each student read aloud during the reading group. Practice is unguided when teachers have students work independently: for instance, giving students unsupervised seatwork or assigning practice sheets for homework.

Along with assessment and explanation, practice is part of the bridge teachers provide during direct instruction to help students achieve the desired goal. It is intentional (you decide what the practice is to be) and **strategic** (you design the practice to solidify a specific curricular goal). However, practice is distinct from explanation. Explanation comes first, and then practice solidifies what has been explained and understood. Because it would be foolish to practice something one does not understand, explanation is a prerequisite to practice. More information on practice is provided in Chapter 13, and examples of practice appropriate for various goals are provided in the chapters devoted to specific grade levels (Chapters 15 through 18).

Application is designed to help students **transfer** what has been learned from an instructional setting to a real world setting. Whereas teachers' explanations develop students' understanding of a goal and practice provides repetition in using that understanding in a somewhat artificial situation (the text is controlled rather than natural), application helps students apply to natural settings what was understood and practiced. For instance, explanation helps students understand how to figure out the meaning of an unknown word from context, and practice helps them use what has been learned when reading self-selected material. When students use what they learn when reading a newspaper or reading a library book, they are applying what they learned. To accomplish this, teachers must provide opportunities for such application.

Assessment, explanation, practice, and application in direct instruction are distinguished from each other by their functions. If you intend to develop initial understanding, explanation is needed; if you intend to solidify understanding, practice is needed; if you intend to test understanding, assessment is needed; and if you intend to help students transfer understanding to real reading, application is needed.

Example 4.1 is an illustration of a typical direct instruction lesson, including examples of assessment, explanation, practice, and application. Detailed directions for planning and teaching direct instruction lessons are provided in Chapter 13.

EXAMPLE 4.1   Direct Instruction

This example of direct instruction is designed to develop students' understanding about how to make predictions while reading. The instruction is based on the teacher's assessment that the students do not actively predict what meanings will come next.

The teacher's instructional plan calls for a task that requires predicting and a two-part explanation. First, the teacher presents initial information by explicitly stating what is to be learned (how to make predictions), why it is important (because good readers think along with the author), and when it will be used (in a story to be read that day, which the teacher shows to the students). Then the teacher models what good readers think about as they make predictions while reading. In the second part of the explanation the teacher listens to students' interpretations of how to make predictions, de-

cides if additional elaboration is needed to guide students to the desired goal, and provides such elaboration as needed.

The teacher then provides practice in making predictions, using excerpts from real text, which have been put together on a single practice sheet. The teacher has the students complete the practice under guidance and provides corrective feedback as appropriate.

Once the students understand how to make predictions, the teacher introduces them to the targeted text and cites the importance of applying what has been learned when reading that text. Students are then directed to read the text and to make predictions as they read. The subsequent discussion focuses not only on what the selection was about but also on the students' application of their newly acquired prediction strategy.

Indirect Instruction

In contrast to direct instruction, indirect instruction depends more on classroom activities than on teacher talk. That is, the activities themselves provide the information, shaping students' interpretations of the task and leading them to discover the intended instructional goal. Since the activities in the environment contain information that is self-evident, teachers assume a relatively covert role. A strength of this approach is that student interest and motivation increase with independent (or semi-independent) pursuit of activities. A weakness is that because students are not working as closely with teachers there are fewer teacher-student interactions and, as a result, fewer opportunities to monitor and respond to students' restructuring.

When using indirect instruction, teachers build a literate environment that features activities—academic tasks—that contain information students can use to build schemata about instructional goals. For instance, teachers might encourage students to send handwritten notes to each other at any time during the school day. This is an academic task. The task has embedded in it the information that writing and reading are message-sending, message-getting activities. By engaging students in the task of passing notes, the teacher hopes that students will infer the information about these characteristics of language and will use it to revise their schemata for reading and writing.

Teachers orchestrate activities in three aspects of the environment: the physical, the social-emotional, and the intellectual.

The **physical environment** refers to what is seen in the classroom. It includes such things as seating arrangements, types of furniture, decorations on the wall, work that is displayed, and bulletin boards. Teachers can structure a physical environment to highlight certain activities that stimulate specific reading goals. For instance, a positive response to reading could be developed by including in the physical environment lots of attractive books and inviting places to read them, such as bean bag chairs; this physical environment invites the activity of pausing and relaxing with books. Because such an arrangement is intended to stimulate activities that contain self-evident information about appreciation of reading as a recreational activity, it is a form of indirect instruction.

The **social-emotional environment** refers to activities that involve social interactions among classroom participants. For instance, teachers may wish to develop the concept that reading is a form of communication between reader and writer similar to the speaker-listener relationship. Although the teacher does not directly explain it, the social activity of pairing students to exchange first oral and then written messages demonstrates that all language is a process of sending and receiving messages. Such teacher orchestration of a classroom's social-emotional activities is an example of indirect instruction.

The **intellectual environment** refers to activities in which teachers model, set expectations, challenge, and stimulate interests. For instance, to develop the concept that reading is an enjoyable leisure-time pursuit, teachers may provide pleasure-reading activities and personally model their own enjoyment of reading, or they may read a story to their students. The instruction is not overt; there is little or no direct teacher talk about how to enjoy books. Instead, these teachers arrange for activities to carry the message that reading is an enjoyable leisure-time activity. This is indirect instruction.

Instruction is indirect when you intentionally orchestrate classroom activities to lead students to specific goals. It may not appear that you are providing information students can use to build schemata about reading when you are sitting and reading a library book or quietly observing students interacting in pairs, but you are. It is, therefore, an example of indirect instruction, because you assume a relatively passive and covert role and permit the activities to do the instructing. Example 4.2 provides an example of indirect instruction. Detailed suggestions for building a literate environment in your classroom are provided in Chapter 10, and suggestions for planning and teaching lessons that are indirect are provided in Chapter 13.

Summary of Direct and Indirect Instruction

Both direct and indirect instruction are intentional efforts by teachers to achieve specified curricular goals; both employ academic tasks, presentations, and interactions with students, and both are teacher led. The difference is

EXAMPLE 4.2   Indirect Instruction

This example of indirect instruction is designed to develop students' appreciation for how books can produce a sense of wonder.

The teacher first engages the students in a task of book sharing. Children's books that typically stimulate a sense of wonder are collected—examples include McCloskey's *Time of Wonder,* Sperry's *Call It Courage,* L'Engle's *Wrinkle in Time,* and Lewis's *Moment of Wonder.* The teacher displays these books prominently in the classroom as part of the physical environment, reads certain excerpts aloud, and features the theme of wonder on a bulletin board.

Then the teacher discusses the books with the students. This activity combines the intellectual and social-emotional environments. To an observer, the academic task looks casual, informal, and unplanned. In reality, however, the teacher has deliberately selected the books, carefully selected which segments to read, and planned what to say to students to draw unusual experiences described in the books to their attention.

Then the teacher involves the students in choosing and reading books, guiding them as they talk about passages that stimulate interest and reinforcing them as they respond positively to the chosen passages. This task again reflects both the intellectual and social-emotional environment.

one of degree. In direct instruction a teacher presents the academic task in a more direct and straightforward manner (usually through teacher talk) to achieve desired goals; in indirect instruction a teacher's intervention is through involving students in activities. Good teachers use both direct and indirect instruction.

The decision to employ direct or indirect instruction depends on two things. The first is the desired curricular goal. If you want to develop a conceptual understanding about reading or good feelings about reading (that is, attitude goals), indirect instruction is usually best. If you want to develop knowledge about how reading works or the ability to get meaning from a text (that is, process and content goals), direct instruction usually works best. The second condition is the aptitude of the student. If a student learns to read easily, indirect instruction is often effective; if a student has difficulty learning to read, better results are usually obtained with direct instruction.

Whether instruction is direct or indirect, however, it always reflects your intention and involves information-giving through an academic task. In direct instruction, you take more responsibility for providing information about what is to be learned; in indirect instruction, the information is implicit in the activity students engage in.

Combining Direct and Indirect Instruction

Direct and indirect instruction are not mutually exclusive. Rather, instruction is a continuum, ranging from extreme examples of direct instruction in which teacher talk is dominant, through gradually diminishing amounts of teacher intervention, to a point where student involvement in activities is dominant.

Instruction can be direct, indirect, or a combination of both. (Susan Lapides/Design Conceptions)

Hence, you may choose to teach in more or less direct or indirect ways depending on what the curricular goal is and on how difficult you expect it to be for a particular group of students.

Because effective teachers combine direct and indirect instruction, the classroom reflects both a literate environment and direct teacher guidance. The **literate environment** emphasizes activities that literate people pursue, rather than the typical classroom "work." For instance, the physical environment includes many reading and writing opportunities, and students use them for genuine communication: students read books of their choice, write real messages to real people, and use reading and writing to achieve both aesthetic and pragmatic goals. In short, classroom activities indirectly instruct students in both the joys and practicalities of literacy. The teacher actively guides students' evolving understanding about how reading works. While exhibiting humaneness and sensitivity in responding to students, the teacher provides explicit information students can use to construct accurate concepts about reading and teaches them how to gain metacognitive control of meaning getting. Figure 4.2 summarizes the important components of instruction.

MOTIVATING THROUGH INTEGRATED INSTRUCTION

One of the major instructional concerns of teachers is motivation, and a frequently asked question is, "How do you get kids to *want* to learn to read?" There are two keys to motivation. The first is success. As human beings, we all enjoy doing things successfully, and we all dislike doing things we cannot

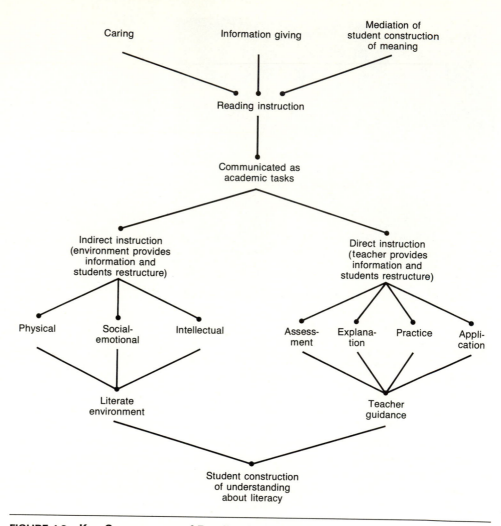

FIGURE 4.2   Key Components of Reading Instruction

do well. To motivate students you must make sure their encounters with reading are reasonably successful ones by assigning tasks at which students can succeed. Chapter 11 discusses this in detail.

This chapter focuses on the second key to motivation, the usefulness of reading. Human beings all enjoy learning things they can use in some important way, and they dislike doing things that seem to be busy work. You must make sure your students' encounters with reading lead to some useful end as opposed to isolated tasks with little perceived value. Creating useful reading tasks means you must **integrate** or combine reading with something else your students value. The two following examples of integration are illustrative.

Integration within a Single Lesson

The simplest way to illustrate the usefulness of reading is to integrate within a single lesson. When you present a skill or strategy in isolation from real reading, students are not able to understand why it is useful and, consequently, are not motivated to learn it. For instance, a lesson about prefixes that is limited to finding and circling prefixes in lists of words has little perceived usefulness. Students conclude that the task is busy work, and they are not motivated by it. However, if you present the prefix task in combination with reading an interesting story containing unknown prefixed words, your students will conclude that the task is worthwhile and they will be inclined to learn the prefixes. By integrating the skill or strategy with real reading you create usefulness, and motivation results.

Integration across Lessons

Another more elaborate kind of usefulness involves integrating tasks across lessons. Teachers often teach several related aspects of reading and writing in a series of connected lessons that are planned as cohesive and wholistic units of instruction. For instance, if your students participate in a series of lessons about how to read directions in order to build and fly kites and they are interested in flying kites, the task of learning to follow directions possesses usefulness. Since the task helps them build kites they conclude that the series of lessons are useful, and they are motivated. By integrating the series of lessons with a project the students value, you show them the usefulness of the lessons, and motivation results.

Examples of integration are virtually endless. You can integrate reading with writing, listening, speaking, previously learned reading content, or a variety of different subject areas. In all cases, your intent is to hook reading content to another activity where it will be immediately used. This is a much more powerful motivator than telling students that what they learn in reading will help them at some vague time and place in the distant future.

APPROACHES TO ORGANIZING READING INSTRUCTION

Instruction, whether it is direct or indirect, has to be organized. Teachers call their year-long series of organized reading activities the **reading program.** Every classroom has such a program; that is, every teacher organizes the teaching of reading into a set of year-long activities. The different ways to organize programs are usually discussed in terms of approaches to the teaching of reading. Although there are many such approaches, the three major ones are: the basal text approach, the language experience approach, and the personalized reading approach. In practice, the basal text approach is used by most classroom teachers.

Basal Text Approach

As noted in Chapter 1, basal reading textbooks are used in the **basal text approach** in almost all elementary classrooms in the United States. For many teachers a basal textbook *is* the reading program, and their year-long set of activities comes primarily from the teacher's guide that accompanies the text.

Publishers invest millions of dollars in developing, packaging, and marketing these instructional materials. Despite publisher competition, however, the differences among the major basal reading programs are marginal. All follow essentially the same format including a multilevel series of 15 to 20 books beginning with **readiness** books for kindergarteners and proceeding through **preprimers** and **primers** to texts designed for use in the eighth grade. Usually a publisher provides two separate books, one slightly more difficult than the other, for use at each grade level. In actuality, however, several levels may be in use in any given classroom at any time because of the wide differences in students' reading abilities. This explains why U.S. schoolchildren identify each other's relative reading status by asking the question, "What book are you in?"

Each level of a basal reading series includes a student text containing the selections to be read, a workbook with exercises to be completed, and a teachers' edition with extensive teaching suggestions and directions. The teachers' edition for any given level is a massive book that contains:

1. Copies of both the selections and the workbook pages that appear in the student's edition.

2. Extensive descriptive material regarding the philosophy of the basal program.

3. Organizational procedures teachers should follow in implementing the program.

4. Specific directions to follow in presenting prescribed skills.

5. Suggested questions to ask when discussing selections with students.

6. Enrichment activities for use as follow-up or culminating activities.

7. End-of-unit tests that can be used to evaluate student achievement.

In addition, most basal reading series provide supplementary charts, work sheets, games, and other instructional devices useful to a teacher, as well as

EXAMPLE 4.3   Basal Text Lesson

Typically, teachers use basal texts in the following way. They call the reading groups together, often referring to the group by the title of the basal text being used (e.g., "Would the Windchimes come to the reading table now?"). The lesson typically begins with the teacher introducing the reading selection using the suggestions provided in the teachers' edition. The teacher then introduces and teaches the vocabulary words, gives students a purpose for reading the selection, and has them read the story (often orally in the very early grades and silently once students are in second grade or beyond).

After the selection has been read, the teacher discusses the content with students by asking questions suggested in the teachers' edition and often has students do oral or silent rereading of certain parts to elaborate on some point. Then the teacher refers to the teachers' edition for suggestions regarding what skills to teach, uses these in introducing the skills, and assigns students to the associated workbook pages to give them practice in the skill. Finally, the teacher closes the lesson using one or more of the teachers' edition suggestions for enrichment activities and pupil evaluation. Ordinarily, this series of activities requires three or four days for each selection. Once the cycle is completed with one selection, it is repeated with the next. In this way each basal reading textbook is completed, and reading instruction gets accomplished.

an elaborate **scope-and-sequence chart,** which details the development of every skill and strategy across all levels of the program. Example 4.3 outlines the procedure of a typical lesson using the basal text approach.

There are advantages to the basal text system. From the teachers' standpoint, a basal simplifies the complexity of teaching reading. All the techniques, activities, and materials are provided and have been organized into manageable three- to four-day units. Consequently, the demands on teachers are lessened. When one considers the complexity of the classroom, as noted in Chapter 1, this advantage is compelling.

However, the basal also has disadvantages. First, because the basal is organized into a set of routine activities, teachers tend to conduct instruction in a technical manner; they assign the instructional responsibility to the basal and become technicians who follow directions rather than professionals who maintain control of their own instruction. Second, because of the emphasis placed on the stories in the basal, teachers tend to believe that all children learn how to read simply by reading. While high-aptitude students sometimes learn to read by reading, low-aptitude students seldom do. Third, despite the emphasis on stories, basal programs provide little opportunity for sustained reading of text. Instead, reading is often disrupted by the need to respond to teacher questions or by requests to read orally in turn. Finally, basals emphasize isolated workbook-type activities more than real comprehension outcomes and, as a result, tend to convey the impression that reading is a mechanical process of getting answers rather than a cognitive process of making sense out of an author's message.

Language Experience Approach

The **language experience approach** (LEA) is organized around personal experiences that students translate into written text and then read. Consequently, what students read describes personal experiences using familiar words. Students are in control of comprehension because the words, prior knowledge, author purpose, and text structure are all familiar.

The language experience approach is most frequently associated with beginning reading. However, because of the dominance of the basal text approach, it is seldom used exclusively.

More than any other approach, the language experience approach emphasizes the interrelationships among the language modes. It starts with an experience (such as a field trip), continues with oral language (students talk about the field trip and listen to others express their thoughts), results in a written product (the talk about the field trip is written down), and culminates in students reading what they have written (their own stories). Students learn the role of reading within the overall language system: that thoughts can be communicated in spoken messages, that what can be spoken can be written down, and that what is written can be read.

In the early grades the language experience approach usually involves taking dictation from children, since young students cannot yet write. However, young students can write their own stories using **invented spelling** to make up for what they have not yet formally learned about spelling. In later grades, students do their own writing. Language experience stories for primary grades are frequently composed in the following sequence.

1. Start with an experience—a holiday, the weather, a story they read, or any other common experience.

2. Discuss the experience with students.

3. Suggest that the students' ideas be written by the teacher on a large piece of chart paper displayed at the front of the room.

4. Direct students to suggest a title and a first line, and write these on the chart paper.

5. Solicit subsequent contributions from others in the group and write these on the chart paper.

6. When complete, read the product orally to the group.

7. Direct students to read the story or parts of the story on the chart to you.

8. Have students copy the story for themselves and illustrate it.

9. Make the resulting book part of the growing library of material students can read.

Language experience stories for upper-elementary grades are somewhat different in that students can write and do not need to copy a group story. The pattern for upper grades usually follows the following sequence.

1. Discuss an experience with students—a field trip, a sporting activity, a visitor to the classroom, an adventure they have had.

2. Brainstorm with students about ideas regarding the topic—sequences of action, descriptive words, conclusions.

3. Write ideas so they can be seen visually, such as on a chalkboard.

4. Guide students in developing an opening and possible plots or sequence of events.

5. Have students complete their own stories.

6. Edit completed stories—editors can be students or teachers.

7. Prepare final copies as books for the room or school library, or for home.

The language experience approach has many advantages. It emphasizes the language concepts that undergird reading (the relationship between read-

The language experience approach emphasizes the interrelationships among speaking, writing, and reading. (Robert Bawden)

ing and writing, for instance). It also puts students in control of the reading process (they know the words because they were used in the oral discussion, they have prior knowledge because the text is based on a shared experience, and they understand both the author's purpose and the text structure, because it was self-written). In addition, it is always fresh and motivating, since the experiences that are the basis for the stories are real, not contrived. As such, it is probably the best single approach to early reading instruction.

However, there are disadvantages to language experience. The most serious one is that it does not have the built-in organization of materials and activities found in the basal text. Instead, teachers and children generate all the reading materials, and teachers are totally responsible for creating both the curricular structure and the necessary materials. A teacher's organizational task is therefore very difficult and the energy demands on teachers are high.

Another disadvantage of the language experience approach is its heavy reliance on indirect instruction. Although effective for developing positive attitudes and an understanding of language, it is less effective in developing an understanding of specific skills and strategies, especially for low-aptitude students. Instruction that is more direct is most effective in developing these outcomes, and there is little emphasis on direct instruction in the language experience approach.

A final disadvantage of the language experience approach is that very few schools allow teachers the latitude to use it as the primary means for organizing the reading program. Instead, they either mandate a specific basal text or provide several different basals, thereby setting the expectation that a reading program should be organized around basal materials and activities.

Personalized Reading Approach

The **personalized reading approach,** sometimes called **individualized reading,** is based on self-selection in which children choose the library books they wish to read and the words they wish to learn. Students read these selections independently, and the teacher instructs each student through individual conferences. During these conferences the teacher discusses the book currently being read by the student, assesses the student's needs and achievements, and provides individual instruction. Because students must be independent readers to employ this approach, it tends to be associated with the middle and upper grades but is seldom used exclusively. The following list shows the key points involved in organizing a personalized reading program.

1. Start collecting a variety of books. For the average classroom, try to collect 100 books, or at least three different books per pupil. If there are not enough available in your school, borrow, trade, and ask for donations.

2. Set up an interesting library area with a rug, pillows, and some furniture. Try to arrange the books with the covers facing the students.

3. Teach your students the "rule of thumb." If they are primary age, tell them to select a page in the middle of the book and begin reading it silently. Each time they miss a word, they should put up a finger. If all their fingers are up before the page is finished, the book is too hard. Older students can just count up to five words missed.

4. Teach them to get books quietly.

5. Teach them how to get help with a word. They could go to the dictionary, an aide, experience charts, other books that they know, a friend, the teacher, or they could try to figure it out.

6. Teach them to prepare for a conference with the teacher by:
   a. Selecting a book.
   b. Reading silently to themselves or reading aloud to a friend.
   c. Signing up for the conference.

7. During the conference, which should last five to ten minutes, discuss with the student interesting information, the author's purpose, and how the story can be applied to other situations. Finally, to check performance, have the student read a portion of the story aloud.

8. Meanwhile, the rest of the class are reading their books or doing an original activity to follow up something they have read. Examples of creative activities are writing for a class newspaper, keeping track of books, choral reading, dramatization, writing letters, and creative writing.

9. Occasionally you may form temporary groups to work on a particular reading goal.

The personalized reading approach has many advantages. It is highly motivating, since the students are personally involved in selecting their reading materials. Vocabulary control is not imposed by an outside source; instead, students expand their vocabulary as they read a variety of books. This approach, through the use of teacher-student conferences, promotes personal interaction between students and teacher. Most important, however, the personalized reading approach encourages the reading habit, promoting reading as reading and not as some boring school task that has no relation to the real world.

Personalized reading also has disadvantages, however. There is a lack of emphasis on systematic instruction. Strategies, for instance, are not taught systematically, but are taught as they happen to appear in self-selected materials. It takes a highly skilled teacher to determine needs as quickly and as accurately as demanded by this approach, and it takes a highly organized teacher to find the time to conduct conferences and also to teach the strategies once the need is recognized. Most teachers feel they cannot do this adequately because other demands of the classroom are just too great.

While the personalized reading approach is seldom used as the only reading program in a classroom, elements of it are often incorporated into existing programs. For example, many classrooms have regular free reading periods in which students select what they read and occasionally have conferences with the teacher about them.

Combined Approach

As you can see, each approach to reading instruction has advantages and disadvantages. None is totally satisfactory in itself. Consequently, we recommend a **combined approach** for organizing your reading program. Because basals are often mandated (explicitly or implicitly) and because most teachers appreciate their organizational comfort, they are the foundation for this combined approach.

By making a basal the foundation of a combined reading program, certain activities and routines get established—reading groups, directed reading lessons, and instruction that tends to be direct. If this is the total program of reading instruction, however, it will be out of balance. Consequently, features of the language experience approach and the personalized reading approach are combined with the basal approach to create a balanced instructional program. For instance, a portion of each school day can be scheduled for free reading of self-selected books. You can also plan frequent language experience activities in which each student or group of students creates text based on a real experience and then reads it. You can use such activities to develop your students' understanding of reading's relationship to language, the relationship between reader and writer, language as communication, and other aspects of whole language. An example of a combined approach is shown in Example 4.4.

At the core of this combined model is a basal textbook and instruction that tends to be direct. Added to this core are daily personalized reading activities and frequent language experience activities. Instruction occurs both directly (with the basal text activities) and indirectly (with the language experience and personalized reading activities).

A WORD ABOUT SPECIAL STUDENTS

One of the difficult aspects of teaching reading is that we must teach so many different kinds of students. For instance, as Chapters 20 and 21 describe, elementary school reading teachers are routinely expected to teach students with special learning problems or unique language differences. Sometimes teachers have the expectation that such different students require different instruction. This is not so. You must adapt your instruction to the level at

EXAMPLE 4.4   Combined Approach

A third grade teacher using a combined approach to reading instruction might organize a reading period as follows.

The first 15 minutes are a free reading period in which students silently read books of their own choice (personalized approach). During the bulk of the reading period, the teacher meets separately with three different reading groups, each using a different level of the basal textbook (basal text approach). While the teacher is working with each basal text group, those students not in a group are individually writing news articles about classroom events for publication in a classroom newspaper; the newspaper was stimulated by a trip to the local city newspaper (language experience approach). Thus, all three approaches are combined into a single reading period.

which such students are working, but your basic instructional techniques remain the same.

For instance, you build a literate environment for all students, regardless of language or learning problems; you care about all students regardless of language or learning problems; you provide all students with explicit information about what is to be learned, when it will be used, and how to do it regardless of language or learning problems; you guide students' construction of instructional understandings regardless of language or learning problems; and you use a combination of approaches regardless of language or learning problems.

Consequently, the instructional question when faced with students who have special language and learning problems is not, "What new approach should I use here?" but rather, "How can I adjust what I know about effective instruction to best help these students?"

SUMMARY

Teaching is used in this book to encompass all the classroom roles and responsibilities a teacher assumes in the normal course of a day; *instruction,* in contrast, refers to those roles and responsibilities specifically associated with developing curricular goals. There are three main characteristics of instruction: a humane caring about children and their well-being; a provision of information that students can use to build a schema for a curricular goal; and mediation of students' restructuring as they build understanding about a curricular goal. These characteristics can be developed directly by having a teacher provide information for student use in creating schemata or less directly by including activities in the classroom environment that contain implicit information students can use to build curricular schemata. In any case, students must be motivated and instruction must be organized. Teachers motivate by giving students tasks they can succeed at and by integrating what is to be learned with activities that are meaningful. Teachers organize reading instruction by employing a basal text approach, a language experience approach, a personalized reading approach, or a combination of these.

SUGGESTED ADDITIONAL READINGS

ALLEN, E. G., & LAMINACK, L. L. (1982). Language experience reading—It's a natural! *Reading Teacher, 35*(6), 708–714.

ALLEN, R. V. (1968). How a language experience program works. In E. C. Vilscek (Ed.), *A decade of innovations: Approaches to beginning reading.* Newark: International Reading Association.

ASHTON-WARNER, S. (1963). *Teacher.* New York: Bantam Books.

BLAIR, T. R. (1984). Teacher effectiveness: The know-how to improve student learning. *Reading Teacher, 38*(2), 138–142.

CRISCUOLO, N. P. (1979). Effective approaches for motivating children to read. *Reading Teacher, 32*(5), 543–546.

DUFFY, G., & ROEHLER, L. (1982). The illusion of instruction. *Reading Research Quarterly, 17*(3), 543–546.

FARRAR, M. T. (1984). Asking better questions. *Reading Teacher, 38*(1), 10–20.

HALL, M. (1979). Language-centered reading: Premises and recommendations. *Language Arts, 56*(6), 664–670.

HARE, V. C. (1982). Beginning reading theory and comprehension questions in teachers' manuals. *Reading Teacher, 35*(8), 918–923.

HILL, S. E. (1985). Children's individual responses and literature conferences in the elementary school. *Reading Teacher, 38*(4), 382–386.

HUNT, L. C. (1971). Six steps to the individualized reading program (IRP). *Elementary English, 48*(1), 27–32.

KING, R. T. (1982). Learning from a PAL. *Reading Teacher, 35*(6), 682–685.

LAMBIE, R. A., & BRITTAIN, M. M. (1983). Adaptive reading instruction: A three-pronged approach. *Reading Journal, 37*(3), 243–248.

MALLON, B., & BERGLUND, R. (1984). The language experience approach to reading: Recurring questions and their answers. *Reading Teacher, 37*(9), 867–871.

PEARSON, P. D., & DOLE, J. (1987). Explicit comprehension instruction: A review of research and a new conceptualization of instruction. *Elementary School Journal, 88*, 151–166.

ROEHLER, L., & DUFFY, G. (1981). Classroom teaching is more than an opportunity to learn. *Journal of Teacher Education, 32*(6), 7–13.

ROEHLER, L., & DUFFY, G. (1982). Matching direct instruction to reading outcomes. *Language Arts, 59*(5), 476–481.

ROSENSHINE, B. (1983). Teaching functions in instructional programs. *Elementary School Journal, 83*, 335–352.

VENEZKY, R. (1987). A history of the American reading textbook. *Elementary School Journal, 87*, 247–266.

THE RESEARCH BASE

BARR, R. (1984). Beginning reading instruction: From debate to reformation. In P. D. Pearson (Ed.), *Handbook of reading research.* New York: Longman.

BROPHY, J. E., & GOOD, T. L. (1986). Teacher behavior and student achievement. In M. Wittrock (Ed.), *Handbook of research on teaching*. New York: Macmillan.

DUFFY, G. G., ROEHLER, L. R., MELOTH, M. S., & VAVRUS, L. G. (1986). Conceptualizing instructional explanation. *Teaching and Teacher Education, 2*, 197–214.

ROEHLER, L. R., & DUFFY, G. G. (in press). Teachers' instructional actions. In R. Barr, M. L. Kamil, P. Mosenthal, & P. D. Pearson (Eds.), *Handbook of reading research* (2nd ed.). New York: Longman.

Part 2

Structuring and Teaching the Reading Curriculum

A teacher must possess a vast amount of professional knowledge. Of fundamental importance is knowledge about what to teach and how to teach it. The chapters in this section will help you build this understanding. The chapters are organized around the major subgoals of reading: Chapter 5 develops attitude goals, Chapter 6 develops content goals, and Chapters 7, 8, and 9 develop various kinds of process goals.

5 | Helping Students Feel Good about Reading: Attitude Goals

GETTING READY

This chapter describes in greater details the attitude goals for each stage of developmental reading growth in elementary school. Both what attitude goals to teach and how to develop them are discussed. More detailed suggestions for developing positive attitudes are described in the appropriate chapters in Part 4.

In this chapter you will meet four teachers who will illustrate how attitude goals can be developed at various grade levels. Ms. Chang is a kindergarten teacher, Ms. Walters teaches first grade, Mr. Gutierrez teaches third grade, and Ms. O'Malley teaches fifth grade. These teachers will help illustrate points in Chapters 6 through 9 also.

FOCUS QUESTIONS

- What are the components of attitude?

- Why are attitude goals important?

- Why should students be metacognitively aware of their concepts and feelings about reading?

- What role does the literate environment play in developing attitude goals?

- What role does direct teacher guidance play in developing attitude goals?

- What are the major attitude goals developed at the readiness stage? at the initial mastery stage? at the expanded fundamentals stage? at the application stage?

WHAT ARE ATTITUDES AND WHY ARE THEY IMPORTANT?

"Attitude" is a frequently misunderstood word in education. Often, it is used to describe unmotivated students, as in "Sam has a poor attitude." In this book, however, attitude refers to students' conceptual understandings and feelings about reading; the goals are accurate concepts and positive feelings. A "bad attitude" can be changed by determining whether the difficulty lies with misconceptions about reading or bad feelings about it, or both, and then developing the needed concepts or positive feelings.

Students' attitudes often determine whether they develop reading ability, for misconceptions and negative feelings about reading rarely lead to reading competence. Consequently, attitude goals are the curricular foundation to a good elementary school reading program.

At the readiness and initial mastery stages, the foundation for reading should be that reading is a joyful and useful activity. For this reason, pre-school, kindergarten, and first and second grade teachers spend much of their instructional time and effort developing attitude goals. Although this emphasis lessens in later years, it nevertheless remains a permanent part of the elementary reading curriculum. Kindergarten teachers may spend as much as 50 percent of their instructional time developing attitude goals, whereas seventh and eighth grade teachers may spend only 20 percent.

DEVELOPING METACOGNITIVE CONTROL

To reach attitude goals, you want students to become metacognitive about what reading is and about the value of reading. Such metacognitive awareness is often revealed in student interviews. For instance, when asked what reading is, students who answer, "Reading is getting an author's message" possess a more accurate concept of reading than those who say, "Reading is sounding out words." Similarly, when asked what reading is used for, students who answer, "It's used for sending messages" possess a more accurate concept than students who say, "It's used in school." Interview responses also reveal students' metacognitive awareness of their own feelings about reading. We know that when students are aware of what reading is and of their own positive feelings toward reading, they understand why they are learning to read. This provides a motivational basis for learning.

Metacognitive awareness is an intermittent rather than a permanent state of mind, of course. For instance, students with positive attitudes may routinely enjoy reading without being consciously aware of it; when questioned about their concepts and feelings, however, they should be able to access and articulate them. This ability to be metacognitive results only if early instructional experiences develop awareness.

INSTRUCTIONAL EMPHASIS IN ATTITUDE GOALS

Attitudes are sometimes discussed as if they are inherent in students and beyond the teacher's control, but this is not the case. Poor student attitudes in reading are usually tied to misconceptions and negative feelings about it. If you can change these, your students' attitudes about reading will change.

It is crucial that you be as systematic and as dedicated to developing attitude goals as you are to teaching other aspects of reading. At any stage of developmental reading growth, you must include attitude development as an integral part of your reading curriculum.

Instruction in attitude goals, like all reading instruction, involves two kinds of academic tasks. One centers around the literate environment (or indirect instruction), and the other around teacher-directed activities (or direct instruction).

The Literate Environment

The literate environment plays a major role in developing attitude goals by emphasizing activities that provide natural opportunities for students to communicate personally meaningful messages. In this way students come to view reading and writing as useful, not artificial. For instance, classrooms with a literate environment typically display different kinds of reading materials and include opportunities for students to use them to solve real problems. Similarly, opportunities for composing, sending, and receiving meaningful written messages are provided.

The intention is that the activities of the classroom itself, by virtue of

When students communicate personally meaningful messages, they learn that reading and writing are satisfying activities. (RH Photo by Peter Vadnai)

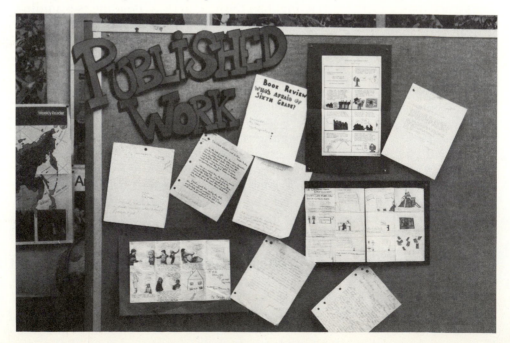

emphasizing literate encounters, will cause students to conclude that reading and writing are valued pursuits that fulfill genuine functions. Even though this is an indirect form of instruction, it is nevertheless a powerful way to help students develop their reading schemata.

Direct Teacher Guidance

Direct instruction plays a relatively minor role in developing attitude goals, basically because actions speak louder than words where attitudes are concerned. Direct teacher guidance does play a role in developing attitude goals, however, since students are influenced by what teachers say. It is crucial that teachers look for every opportunity to make statements that reflect accurate concepts of reading and provide tangible evidence of their own enthusiasm for literate activities. In doing so, teachers help students construct accurate understandings and enthusiastic responses to reading.

TEACHING ATTITUDE GOALS AT VARIOUS DEVELOPMENTAL LEVELS

The following sections provide initial suggestions for teaching attitude goals. More specific suggestions for teaching attitude goals are provided in Chapter 15 for preschool and kindergarten, in Chapter 16 for primary grades, in Chapter 17 for middle grades, and in Chapter 18 for upper grades.

Readiness Stage

At the preschool and kindergarten levels, teachers want students to develop fundamental conceptual understandings, such as that reading is talk written down by someone and that it communicates entertaining and useful messages. It is also crucial that students begin to associate reading with good feelings. Consequently, teachers of young children plan and conduct a variety of activities designed to cause students to conclude that reading can be a satisfying, exciting, and useful activity.

Because students at the readiness stage are not yet reading print independently, attitude goals are primarily developed through oral language activities. Teachers read stories to students, have them listen to recordings of stories, create stories with them on the basis of shared experiences (language experience activities), or help them tell stories they have composed using their own preliterate form of writing. Just because students are not yet reading independently does not mean they cannot engage in communication using written language. Moreover, because of the close relationship between reading and writing, teachers develop children's positive attitudes about writing as they develop attitudes about reading. Example 5.1 illustrates how to develop positive reading and writing attitude goals at the readiness stage.

EXAMPLE 5.1   Developing Attitude Goals at the Readiness Stage

I. Attitude goals

   A. *Concepts—reading is*
      1. Talk written down
      2. Someone saying something
      3. For enjoyment

   B. *Positive responses—readers feel*
      1. Excitement
      2. Satisfaction

Linda Chang began the afternoon session of her kindergarten class with a lesson using Leo Leonni's *Swimmy.* This delightful story describes the adventures of a little black fish who thwarts the eating habits of bigger fish by arranging little red fish in the shape of one big fish with Swimmy becoming the eye.

Ms. Chang used the oral reading of Leonni's *Swimmy* to develop the attitude goal that reading is someone saying something. To stress that books are written by someone who wants to send a message to others, Ms. Chang described Leo Leonni as a real person who liked friends and wanted to tell others about his feelings. Therefore, he took his message and put it into a book to be shared with them.

The following afternoon, Ms. Chang illustrated to her students that they, too, could share a message with others. After recalling how Leo Leonni had shared with them his message about liking friends, the children decided they wanted to share similar messages, and Ms. Chang recorded it. Afterward, Ms. Chang read their messages about liking friends to them and gave each student a copy to take home for the parents to read aloud. In this way, Ms. Chang developed attitude goals about what reading is, especially the close relationship between reading and writing.

Initial Mastery Stage

As students begin to read print in first and second grade, teachers continue to devote about half their time to developing conceptual understandings and positive feelings about reading. The major difference between teaching attitude goals at the initial mastery stage and teaching them at the readiness stage is that students can now read simple text. Even though stories, as opposed to functional text, are widely used at the initial mastery stage, teachers can begin developing the concept that reading is also used to satisfy curiosity and provide information. They continue simultaneous development of positive attitudes about writing by having students act out the role of author as well as reader.

Language experience activities continue to play a major role in building the reading-writing connection. Students and teachers spend much time talking about shared experiences, writing down these experiences, and reading what they have written down. These language experience activities help develop accurate concepts about what reading and writing are all about and demonstrate that communication through written language can be useful and fun. Example 5.2 illustrates how to develop positive attitude goals at the initial mastery stage.

EXAMPLE 5.2   Developing Attitude Goals at the Initial Mastery Stage

I. Attitude goals

A. *Concepts—reading is*

  1. A message written by an author for a reader

  2. For enjoyment

  3. For information

B. *Positive responses—readers feel*

  1. Excitement

  2. Satisfaction

  3. Knowledgeable

  4. Their curiosity satisfied

In Kelly Walters' first grade room, the morning reading period began with the sharing of Judith Viorst's *Alexander and the Terrible, Horrible, No Good, Very Bad Day.* Alexander had a day where everything went wrong. He counted wrong, lost his best friend, and the dentist discovered he had a cavity. Ms. Walters chose this book to develop the attitude goal that reading brings satisfaction. Ms. Walters read the book to the class, and they discussed their own horrible days and how reading about Alexander's horrible day made them feel that they were not the only ones who have bad days.

Ms. Walters used a follow-up activity to help her students realize the connection between reading and writing as well as the satisfaction and pleasure that comes with sending a written message. When she told them that their principal, Mr. Jennings, had had a day like Alexander, the students decided to send him a letter about their horrible days to help make him feel better. After dictating a letter that Ms. Walters printed on the board, the children copied the sentences and added at least one more of their own. Then all the letters were sent to Mr. Jennings. After reading his letters, Mr. Jennings strengthened the students' understanding and positive responses by coming to the classroom and telling them how much better he felt because of their letters.

Expanded Fundamentals Stage

At the expanded fundamentals stage, third and fourth grade students begin developing the flexibility and independence associated with expert reading. Although attitude goals no longer dominate instruction, they continue to be important despite three noticeable changes.

The first change involves the time devoted to attitudinal instruction. Teachers in these grades devote about a third of their energies and resources to these goals, rather than the earlier 50 percent. This does not mean that attitudes diminish in importance once students begin reading at the third and fourth grade levels. But because solid attitudinal foundations have already been developed at the readiness and initial mastery stages, teachers at the expanded fundamentals stage can maintain that foundation while devoting proportionately more time and energy to their instructional goals.

The second difference focuses on how reading works. At this stage, conceptual understandings are expanded to include the concepts that reading is part of a language system, the system is based on making sense of written messages by making predictions based on prior knowledge of both topic and language, and reading can be controlled by using the language system strategically. This conceptual awareness, and its related feelings of self-control, is the heart of developing metacognitive readers.

The third difference involves the transition from narrative to functional text. Whereas students' initial understanding of reading is based primarily on stories, there is a movement at the expanded fundamentals stage to develop the concept that reading provides information and know-how. That is, the concept about reading being a message-sending and message-getting activity is expanded from narrative story telling to include a variety of expository text forms, such as textbooks, newspapers, and printed directions. While this conceptual understanding is being built, the teacher simultaneously attempts to develop positive feelings about reading as a functional tool. Example 5.3 illustrates how to develop positive attitude goals at the expanded fundamentals stage.

Application Stage

If attitude goals have been properly developed at earlier stages, attitude development at the application stage is often a matter of maintenance. That is, teachers of students reading at the fifth through eighth grade levels ensure that the accurate concepts and positive feelings developed at earlier levels are reinforced and strengthened. Within that general framework, however,

---

EXAMPLE 5.3   Developing Attitude Goals at the Expanded Fundamentals Stage

I. Attitude goals

A. *Concepts—reading is*

1. Communication between a writer and a reader
2. For enjoyment
3. Predicting meaning
4. Making sense
5. A tool for gathering information

B. *Positive responses—readers feel*

1. Excitement and joy
2. Satisfaction in solving problems
3. Knowledgeable
4. Curious
5. A sense of power

John Gutierrez's third graders were busily preparing for a visit from an opthamologist. Before the visit, they read Ellen Raskin's *Spectacles,* a story about Iris, who sees strange things because she is nearsighted. However, visits to the opthamologist and the optician enable Iris to see like everyone else.

As his attitude goal, Mr. Gutierrez wanted to teach the concept that reading is a tool for gathering information. In addition, he chose to illustrate the connections between oral language and written language by having each student write a question and send it to the opthamologist prior to her talk. As the opthamologist presented her information, the students listened for the answers to their questions and, if the answers were not provided, asked them in person. After the opthamologist's talk, the students wrote informational booklets about a first visit to the optometrist. These books were then read to students in another third grade classroom.

EXAMPLE 5.4   Developing Attitude Goals at the Application Stage

I. Attitude goals

A. *Concepts—reading is*

1. Authors have purposes for writing text; readers have purposes for reading text
2. Reading can clarify knowledge, feelings, and attitudes
3. Reading can expand knowledge, feelings, and attitudes
4. Reading is a valuable tool that meets needs

B. *Positive response—readers feel*

1. Excitement
2. Satisfaction
3. Knowledgeable
4. Curious
5. A sense of power

As part of a fifth grade unit on animal behavior, Donna O'Malley had a small group of students read Jean George's *Julie of the Wolves.* Julie survived alone in an area of the Artic Circle known as the Northern Slope because she developed an understanding of wolves' social behavior and, as a result, was allowed by the wolves to share their food and become a member of the wolf pack.

After a lengthy discussion of the wolves' social behavior as it affected Julie, the group prepared a written report for the entire class to read and use. For her attitude goal, Ms. O'Malley developed the concept that reading is a tool for information gathering that enables one to become knowledgeable from reading. In discussions with the group, she illustrated how they had used reading to gather information about wolves' social behavior. In addition, the students saw the natural relationship between reading and writing.

there is a transition from reading stories to reading informational material such as that found in social studies and science. Example 5.4 illustrates how to develop positive attitude goals at the application stage.

SUMMARY

Students are not likely to develop control of their reading if they feel negative about it. Positive attitudes for reading depend on students being metacognitively aware of concepts about what reading is and about their feelings for participating in reading activities. The major instructional technique for developing attitude goals is the literate environment, in which students develop accurate concepts and good feelings by engaging in meaningful reading and writing activities. While you may occasionally develop attitude goals through direct teacher guidance, this form of instruction generally plays a relatively minor role. As students move through the grades, instructional emphasis on attitudes moves gradually from simple concepts of reading and enjoyment of stories to more complex concepts about the function of reading and the variety of responses one can have to reading.

SUGGESTED ADDITIONAL READINGS

FREDERICKS, A. D. (1982). Developing positive reading attitudes. *Reading Teacher, 36*(1), 38–40.

GENTILE, L. M., & HOOT, J. L. (1983). Kindergarten play: The foundation of reading. *Reading Teacher, 36*(4), 436–439.

HEATHINGTON, B. S., & ALEXANDER, J. E. (1984). Do classroom teachers emphasize attitudes toward reading? *Reading Teacher, 37*(6), 484–488.

MAGER, R. (1960). *Developing attitudes toward learning.* Palo Alto, CA: Fearon.

MASS, L. N. (1982). Developing concepts of literacy in young children. *Reading Teacher, 35*(6), 670–675.

ROETTGER, D. (1980). Elementary students' attitudes toward reading. *Reading Teacher, 33*(4), 451–453.

TEMPLETON, S. (1980). Young children invent words: Developing concepts of "wordness." *Reading Teacher, 33*(4), 454–459.

THE RESEARCH BASE

BROPHY, J. E. (1983). Research on the self-fulfilling prophecy and teacher expectations. *Journal of Educational Psychology, 75,* 631–661.

BROPHY, J. E. (1986). *Socializing student motivation to learn* (Research Series No. 169). East Lansing: Michigan State University, Institute for Research on Teaching.

WEINSTEIN, R. (1983). Student perceptions of schooling. *Elementary School Journal, 83,* 287–312.

WIGFIELD, A., & ASHER, S. R. (1984). Social motivational influences on reading. In P. D. Pearson (Ed.), *Handbook of reading research* (pp. 423–452). New York: Longman.

Helping Students Comprehend Text: Content Goals 6

GETTING READY

This chapter describes the content goals that are taught at each stage of developmental reading growth in elementary school. Again, both what content goals to teach and how to teach them are discussed. More detailed suggestions for teaching content goals are described in the appropriate chapters in Part 4. Ms. Chang, Ms. Walters, Mr. Gutierrez, and Ms. O'Malley again provide illustrations for various grade levels.

FOCUS QUESTIONS

- What should students be able to do as a result of being taught content goals?

- What three factors influence student comprehension of text content?

- What should students be metacognitive about when pursuing content goals?

- How does a literate environment contribute to the development of content goals?

- What direct teacher actions contribute to the development of content goals?

THE COMPONENTS OF CONTENT GOALS

Understanding the content of written messages depends on three components: prior knowledge of topic, text structure, and purpose. How these components influence understanding of content is the focus of this chapter.

Role of Prior Knowledge of Topic

Students' ability to comprehend the content of written messages depends heavily on how much they already know about the topic. If students know a lot about the topic, they also know the meaning of most words associated with that topic and will therefore understand the content of the message; if students have limited experience with the topic, they will not know many words, and chances are good that they will not understand the content.

When teaching to develop content goals, you should try to make sure students know the meaning of all the words used and, if some words are not known, provide them with experiences designed to develop those word meanings.

Role of Text Structure

The print that contains a written message is called the text and takes various forms. Narrative text (referred to as recreational text in this book) entertains and includes stories, plays, and poems. Expository text (referred to as functional text in this book) informs or persuades and includes textbooks, newspapers, encyclopedias, recipes, etc.

Text is a major concern when you teach content goals because each kind places different demands on the reader. One of the demands relates to text structure, that is, to the overall pattern followed when writing a particular kind of text. For instance, when writing stories, writers use narrative structures such as the following.

1. Establish the setting.

2. Introduce the main character.

3. Describe the problem or conflict.

4. Describe the events related to resolution of the problem.

5. Resolve the problem.

When writing textbooks, they use expository structures such as the following.

1. Introduction (tell them what you're going to tell them)

2. Body (tell them)

3. Conclusion (tell them what you told them)

Similarly, when writing Haiku poetry, writers follow a structure in which five syllables appear in the first line, seven syllables in the second line, and five syllables in the third line; when writing a business letter, managers use a business letter structure; and when writing a news story, reporters state the main points about what, who, where, when, and why in the first paragraph, with subsequent paragraphs offering supporting facts in descending order of importance.

To help students comprehend various kinds of text, you should provide opportunities for them to read them and then guide their reading by informing them about the text structure employed.

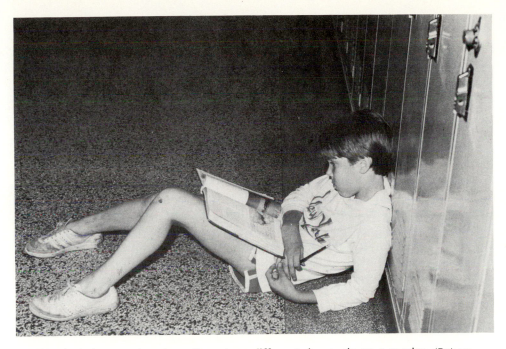

Textbook and recreational reading place different demands on a reader. (Robert Bawden)

Role of Purpose

A newspaper account of a baseball game can be read to find out who won, or how the teams ranked as a result of the game, or what the hero of the game said in the post-game interview, or all of these things. What students actually understand depends largely on their purposes for reading. When teaching, you should help students understand the content of the text by providing them with purposes or by helping them select their own purposes.

WHO IS IN METACOGNITIVE CONTROL?

When developing content goals, your role is to organize students' encounters with text to focus on understanding the content, not on improving their strategies for understanding. Therefore, you should have students focus on the author's message and on being metacognitively aware of whether their purposes for reading are being met. When planning instruction to meet content goals, the teacher examines the text, decides what type of text it is and what words are unknown (and, sometimes, what the purpose for reading should be), and then presents the lesson in ways that emphasize understanding the content. As a result, students are focused on the content and they learn the content, which was your intention.

INSTRUCTIONAL EMPHASIS IN CONTENT GOALS

Content-oriented instruction centers around both indirect instruction, which employs the literate environment, and direct instruction, in which the teacher actively guides.

The Literate Environment

To develop content goals, a literate environment physically demonstrates to students the role played by reading and various kinds of recreational and functional text. The classroom and the library include many examples of recreational and functional text appropriate for the grade level being taught, and teachers encourage students to use these texts both for pleasurable reading and for solving problems.

In a literate environment, the importance and function of various kinds of text become self-evident. Because students are surrounded by a variety of functional and recreational text matched to their reading levels, interests, and assignments, they are encouraged to pursue independent reading. This kind of indirect instruction is crucial to developing content goals.

Direct Teacher Guidance

In content-oriented reading teachers guide students' understanding of text. This means they assume metacognitive control of the task, figuring out ahead of time the word meanings to be developed, the structure of the material to be read, and (sometimes) the purposes for reading the text. Then they decide what assistance students will need to understand the content of the selection.

This assistance is usually provided in three phases: things to do before, during, and after the reading assignment. Before the reading, teachers help students activate prior knowledge about the topic, develop necessary word meanings, and establish purposes for reading that particular text. During the reading, they help students monitor their meaning getting, especially in terms of established purposes. After the reading, they help students demonstrate their understanding by summarizing and clarifying the message. The most common tool for conducting this kind of instruction is the **directed reading lesson** (DRL), which is summarized as follows.

1. **Introduce the selection to be read:** Activate students' background knowledge about the topic, direct student attention to necessary words, and establish appropriate purposes.

2. **Have students read the selection:** Ask questions to monitor students' meaning getting.

3. **Discuss the selection:** Ask clarifying and summarizing questions, check to see that the purposes of the reading have been met, and extend students' understanding of the meaning of the text.

There are several variations on the directed reading lesson, all of which begin with teachers analyzing the demands of the text and then providing their students with guidance to help them focus on the text's content.

Role of Teacher Questioning

The questions teachers ask play a crucial role in developing students' understanding of text content. It is often the teacher's questions that get students to focus on a particular meaning.

You can ask **literal questions** when you want students to comprehend an author's explicit meaning. You can ask **inferential questions** when you want students to understand implied meanings found between the lines of a text and to construct meanings the author only hints at. You can ask **critical questions** when you want students to understand meanings that go beyond what the author said—such as to analyze the author's message critically or to pass judgment on the validity of what the author was saying. In the Aesop fable "The Tortise and the Hare," a literal question would ask who the participants in the race were; an inferential question would ask why we expect the hare to win the race; and a critical question would ask whether such a race is likely to occur in reality. These three types of teacher questions are crucial to content goals since they focus students' attention on the kind of meaning you want them to get from the text.

However, while teacher questioning helps students focus on the level of meaning, questions do not necessarily result in student metacognitive control of comprehension. In a directed reading lesson *you* are in metacognitive control, deciding what prior knowledge needs to be activated and then asking questions designed to access it. Likewise, during the reading it is *you* who decides what meaning must be monitored and asks questions that focus students on that meaning. Finally, it is *you* who decides what meaning needs to be clarified and summarized after the reading. In all three instances, students merely follow your lead. You are in metacognitive control of comprehension, not they. In short, the reasoning involved in knowing what prior knowledge to activate as reading begins, what inferences to make during reading, and what critical judgments to make following reading is directed by you, not your students. Questioning is a crucial teacher action to focus students' attention on particular levels of text meaning. But such questions will not help students learn how to do the reasoning associated with answering the questions. Chapters 7 and 8 provide details on using questions to teach the reasoning associated with process goals.

CONTENT GOALS AND WRITING

Although writers are concerned with composing rather than interpreting the content of a message, the components remain the same. Just as background experience, text structure, and purpose are the keys to interpreting a message,

EXAMPLE 6.1   Developing Content Goals at the Readiness Stage Using a DLA

I. Introduce the selection

   A. Activate background knowledge

   B. Direct attention to necessary words

   C. Establish purpose

II. Read the selection

   A. Ask questions to check comprehension

III. Discuss the selection

   A. Ask clarifying and summarizing questions

   B. Check that purposes for listening have been met

   C. Expand on students' understanding of text

Linda Chang had prereading, during-reading, and after-reading purposes when she read *Swimmy* to her kindergarten children. She first activated her students' background knowledge about oceans or large bodies of water by conducting a short discussion on fish and where they live, the different sizes of fish, and what it feels like to be small and alone. Then Ms. Chang developed an understanding of new words (such as *mussel, shell, marvel,* and *school of fish*) by talking about what they are and what they are for and by providing some examples and nonexamples of each. Finally Ms. Chang directed students' attention to the purpose for listening to the book by alerting them to any information that would help them understand what Swimmy did when he found himself alone with big fish around him.

During the reading, Ms. Chang stopped at several places to help students monitor their own meaning getting. She asked literal questions about what was happening and inferential questions about how Swimmy was feeling.

After the story was read, Ms. Chang asked questions to clarify and summarize the story.

She wanted to be certain students understood why Swimmy arranged the little fish in the shape of a big fish and why he acted like the big fish's eye. Activities were complete when the students answered critical questions about how working together can help get a task done and how belonging to a group can help combat the fears associated with being alone and small.

The following day, Ms. Chang used *Swimmy* as the basis for creating a class-written story entitled "When I Feel Alone and Small." She helped students during prewriting activities by reminding them of what Swimmy did when he felt alone and small, and by emphasizing words that the children contributed as description words. Ms. Chang helped the children create their story by providing a text structure as follows: "When I feel alone and small, I _____. Then I feel _____." After the story was written, Ms. Chang read the story to the children, asking them to listen carefully to see if it made sense and if it told how they feel and what they did when they were feeling alone and small.

so they are the keys to composing a message. Writers must match the words they use with their audience, must arrange those words into familiar patterns or structures, and must maintain a consistent focus or purpose for their message. Since much of a written message's content is determined at the planning stage, content goals in writing are developed mainly during the planning of the written text.

Integrating content goals into writing helps students understand the reciprocal author-reader relationship while also reinforcing the roles of prior knowledge of topic, text structure, and purpose in written literacy.

TEACHING CONTENT GOALS AT VARIOUS DEVELOPMENTAL LEVELS

Readiness Stage

Even though most preschool and kindergarten children cannot read yet, they can understand the meaning of text read to them. Content goals in preschool and kindergarten focus on helping students get meaning from the simple narratives they listen to.

The major instructional tool at this stage is the directed listening activity (DLA). Basically the **directed listening activity** is the same as the directed reading lesson except that students listen while the text is read to them. Before listening, the teacher activates appropriate background experience, develops word meanings, and sets the purpose. During the lesson, the teacher asks questions to help students monitor their meaning getting. After the lesson, the teacher helps students answer questions related to the purposes for the reading. The goal, of course, is student understanding of the content

---

EXAMPLE 6.2   Developing Content Goals at the Initial Mastery Stage Using a DRL

I. Introduce the selection
   A. *Activate background knowledge*
   B. *Direct attention to necessary words*
   C. *Establish purpose*

II. Have students read the selection
   A. *Ask questions to check comprehension*

III. Discuss the selection
   A. *Ask clarifying and summarizing questions*
   B. *Check that purposes for reading have been met*
   C. *Expand on students' understanding of text*

The first graders in Kelly Walters' room were settling down for a reading lesson using Judith Viorst's *Alexander and the Terrible, Horrible, No Good, Very Bad Day*. During the prereading activities to activate their background knowledge, Ms. Walters led her students through a discussion of bad days in which everything seems to go wrong. Students quickly contributed to the discussion so Ms. Walters began introducing words with which she felt they would have difficulty. Finally, the purposes were set when Ms. Walters asked her students to answer literal and inferential questions about how Alexander helped himself feel better when it seemed like everything was going wrong. As the group read the book aloud together, Ms. Walters periodically asked questions to see if students under-stood the story. After the story ended, she asked students other questions—such as, "What do you think this story is about?"—to see if students understood how Alexander made himself feel better about his bad day.

On the next day, the students decided to help Mr. Jennings feel better about his bad day by sending him letters (see Example 5.2). The students began their prewriting activities by remembering Alexander's horrible day, and then they generated a list of the horrible things that had happened to Mr. Jennings. Then they created their letters. Using the text structure of a friendly letter, each student wrote about at least two bad incidents. For the post-writing activities, the students edited each other's letters for content and mechanics.

of the text that was read to them. Example 6.1 illustrates how to develop content goals at the readiness stage.

Initial Mastery Stage

It is at the initial mastery stage, usually during the first grade, that most students first learn to read independently. This transition from readiness to initial mastery is a gradual one in which the focus shifts from understanding content of text read orally to understanding content of text students read themselves. Of course, first and second graders often have many listening activities as they begin to read simple books on their own. Although teachers continue to emphasize recreational text (especially narrative text) at the initial mastery stage, students also read simple expository text and other forms of functional text.

Teachers of first and second grade rely heavily on two techniques for guiding student comprehension of the texts they read. The first technique is the directed reading lesson. Example 6.2 illustrates how to use DRL to guide student understanding of content at the initial mastery stage.

The second technique is the language experience approach, in which

---

EXAMPLE 6.3   Developing Content Goals at the Initial Mastery Stage Using the LEA

I. Introduce common experience—initiate a direct experience

  A. Field trip

  B. Classroom visitor

  C. Vicarious experience, such as a story

II. Discuss the experience

  A. Solicit student ideas about topic

  B. Write down key ideas and words

III. Help students write a story

  A. Help students devise title and opening

  B. Solicit more ideas

IV. Read the story with students and help them produce copies to take home

The first graders eagerly gathered around Ms. Walters to hear Judith Viorst's story of *Alexander and the Terrible, Horrible, No Good, Very Bad Day.* After quickly introducing the book and its characters, Ms. Walters read the story using an opaque projector so the children could join in during the repetition parts. Afterward the children discussed the story with Ms. Walters, highlighting visually and auditorily the repetitive pattern found in the story. The discussion then moved into bad days experienced by the stu- dents. Incidents were recorded on the board and words that described the incident were added. Ms. Walters then had the students select certain incidents and the class created their own story, *Ms. Walters' Class and Their Terrible, Horrible, No Good, Very Bad Day.* Ms. Walters typed the story and made each student a copy. Students illustrated their own books, and then took the books home to read to their families, showing and explaining their illustrations.

students and teacher collaboratively write a story based on a common experience. Because the story involves a shared experience (and thus shared word meanings) and because all the students shared in constructing the text, understanding the content is virtually assured. Example 6.3 illustrates how to use the language experience approach to teach content goals.

Expanded Fundamentals Stage

At the expanded fundamentals stage, which usually occurs in third and fourth grade, students significantly expand the kinds of text they read. The earlier focus on narrative stories broadens to include various literary genres. Stu-

---

EXAMPLE 6.4   **Developing Content Goals at the Expanded Fundamentals Stage Using a DRTA**

I. Introduce the selection
   A. *Activate background knowledge about topic, purpose, and type of text*
   B. *Teach new vocabulary words*

II. Make predictions
   A. *Have students survey the selection's illustrations, headings, and other clues*
   B. *List their predictions on the board*

III. Have students read the selection and check their predictions

IV. Discuss the selection
   A. *Have students discuss the accuracy of their predictions*
   B. *Provide follow-up activity that involves story content or predicting skills*

The All Stars reading group joined Mr. Gutierrez at the third grade reading circle. He handed every student a copy of Ellen Raskin's *Spectacles* and asked them to examine the front of the book only. He activated background knowledge by a discussion of eyeglasses—who wears them, what they are for, what types there are, and so on. He then carefully related the unknown word spectacles to eyeglasses. On the basis of their discussion, Mr. Gutierrez asked every student to make a prediction about the content of the book. [This book is particularly good for making predictions because the strange creatures that Iris thinks she sees are exposed on the following pages when an adult corrects her.]

After the predictions were recorded, Mr. Gutierrez established the purpose of the lesson by telling students they were going to see if their predictions about the story were accurate. After the first two pages were read, he had each

student note the accuracy of their prediction, and, if necessary, make a new prediction. As the story was read students predicted, verified, and made new predictions. When the story was finished, the students discussed how Iris' nearsightedness created problems, and they all checked to see how accurate they had become in making predictions.

Because an ophthalmologist was coming to provide information on eye examinations, all students in the group used their predicting ability while reading informational books about opthamology. The students took notes on what they read and contributed their notes to the group. From the notes, the group created an outline for a book on eye examinations, and each student wrote a section. The group compiled their book, edited it, and shared it with the rest of the class in preparation for the ophthalmologist's visit.

dents now encounter text structures associated with poetry, with various kinds of folk tales, and with simple drama, as well as traditional narrative stories. Similarly, functional reading expands beyond the simplest form of expository text to include textbooks, newspapers, magazines, and other common forms of informational text. Consequently, content goals at the expanded fundamentals stage focus on helping students understand the content of various types of text.

Teachers at the expanded fundamentals stage continue to rely heavily on the directed reading lesson to develop understanding of content, often with modifications. One example is the **directed reading-thinking activity** (DRTA), which actively involves students in setting purposes by having them predict what the content of the text will be. Example 6.4 illustrates how to use a DRTA to teach content goals at the expanded fundamentals stage.

FIGURE 6.1   Content Goals across Developmental Stages

Readiness stage

Recreational text
    Getting meaning from narrative text read to students
Functional text
    Getting meaning from simple expository text read to students

Initial mastery stage

Recreational text
    Getting meaning from narrative text
Functional text
    Getting meaning from simple expository text

Expanded fundamentals stage

Recreational text
    Getting meaning from various forms of narrative text
    Getting meaning from various genre of literature
Functional text
    Getting meaning from expository text (e.g., textbooks)
    Using question-answer relationships to get meaning from content

Application stage

Recreational text
    Getting meaning from various forms of narrative text
    Getting meaning from various genre of literature
Functional text
    Getting meaning from expository and content-area text
    Using question-answer relationships to get meaning from content
    Getting meaning from text with heavy conceptual content

EXAMPLE 6.5   Developing Content Goals at the Application Stage Using QAR

I. Introduce the lesson

   A. *Activate background knowledge*

   B. *Direct attention to necessary words*

   C. *Discuss how to use QARs to find answers to questions*

II. Demonstrate (model) **how you identify what type of question is used**

   A. *Right there—answer is found on page*

   B. *Think and search—answer requires information from more than one sentence or paragraph*

   C. *On my own—answer is not in the selection but is found in the reader's own knowledge*

   D. *Explain how you thought about the question, the information in the text, and where to find the answer*

III. Interaction with students

   A. *Give students samples of text and related questions*

   B. *Have students explain how they looked through the text information to decide how to answer the question*

   C. *Gradually increase text complexity as students become more proficient at answering questions*

IV. Closure—have students apply their understanding of QARs to another assignment

The Max Headroom reading group in Ms. O'Malley's fifth grade class was preparing to read Jean George's *Julie of the Wolves,* a story of how an Eskimo girl survives in the wilderness with the help of a wolf pack. Because Ms. O'Malley wanted her students to gain information from the text about the social behavior of wolves, she developed lessons using question-answer relationships (QARs). The lesson began as Ms. O'Malley led the students through the lesson introduction where motivation, background, purpose, directions, and word meanings were developed. Motivation was high because the task focused on wolf behaviors that were like human behaviors, so the students knew the story would be helpful in developing their reports on animal social behavior.

With the background in place, Ms. O'Malley directed students to questions about how human parents feed their young, how they reprimand others for inappropriate behavior, how they show affection, and so on. The students examined questions and predicted whether they would find the answer explicitly stated in the text ("right there"), whether the answer would be implied by the author ("think and search"), or whether the answer required them to make an independent judgment ("on-your-own"). Then students read the selection and answered the questions. When the students were ready to write their reports on the social behavior of animals, they were able to refer to their questions and answers about wolves. Ms. O'Malley's strategy succeeded in teaching both reading and writing content goals.

Application Stage

Content goals are particularly important at the application stage (grades 5 through 8) because it is here that the instructional emphasis shifts from learning how to read to using reading as a tool to get meaning from a variety of text. Now, students learn about various forms and genres of literature and begin in-depth study of content areas such as social studies and science. Not only are students expected to understand various story, poetry, and drama forms, but also they are expected to understand expository text containing heavy conceptual loads (such as encyclopedia articles, information books, specialized directions, and technically oriented texts). Figure 6.1 illustrates the progression of content goals from the readiness to the application stages.

Because of the increased conceptual load and the variety of texts encountered at the application stage, teachers work hard at providing guidance in these texts. The DRL and DRTA continue to be used heavily. In addition, other specialized techniques are used, some of which focus on word meanings (such as **structured overviews** and **semantic maps**), some on how to locate answers to the questions posed (such as **question-answer relationships**, or **QARs**[1]), and some on the structure of the text itself (**story maps**). Example 6.5 illustrates how to use a QAR, which is a variation of the DRL, to help students understand a reading selection at the application stage.

SUMMARY

Content goals focus on helping students understand the message in written texts. Understanding the content of written text depends on the reader's background experience for the topic, the type of text, and the purpose for reading the selection. When teaching content goals, you want students to be conscious of the content of the text, and you are less concerned about whether your students understand the process by which they came to understand the text. Consequently, you develop content goals by establishing a literate environment, which calls for the reading of meaningful text, and asking students questions and employing directed reading techniques that make you responsible for the comprehension process while freeing your students to focus on content. The curricular emphasis on content goals gradually increases from one grade level to the next as students encounter more and more difficult types of text.

SUGGESTED ADDITIONAL READINGS

CHOATE, J., & RAKES, T. (1987). The structured listening activity: A model for improving listening comprehension. *Reading Teacher, 41,* 194–200.

NESSEL, D. (1987). The new face of comprehension instruction: A closer look at questions. *Reading Teacher, 40,* 604–607.

[1] Raphael, T. Question-answering strategies for children. *Reading Teacher, 36*(2), 186–191.

OGLE, D. (1986). K-W-L: A teaching technique that develops active reading of expository text. *Reading Teacher, 39,* 564–571.

PALINCSAR, A. M. (1986). Interactive teaching to promote independent learning from text. *Reading Teacher,* 771–777.

POOSTAY, E. J. (1984). Show me your underlines: A strategy to teach comprehension. *Reading Teacher, 37*(9), 828–830.

RAPHAEL, T. E. (1984). Teaching learners about sources of information for answering comprehension questions. *Journal of Reading, 27*(4), 303–311.

RICHGELS, D. J., & HANSEN, R. (1984). Gloss: Helping students apply both skills and strategies in reading content texts. *Journal of Reading, 27*(4), 312–317.

ROEHLER, L., DUFFY, G., & MELOTH, M. (1986). What to be direct about in direct instruction in reading: Content-only versus process-into-content. In T. Raphael (Ed.), *Contexts of school-based literacy.* New York: Random House.

SMITH, M., & BEAN, T. W. (1983). Four strategies that develop children's story comprehension and writing. *Reading Teacher, 37*(3), 295–301.

STAUFFER, R. G., & HARREL, M. M. (1975). Individualized reading-thinking activities. *Reading Teacher, 28*(8), 765–769.

WIXSON, K. K. (1983). Questions about a text: What you ask about is what children learn. *Reading Teacher, 37*(3), 287–294.

WONG, J. A., & HU-PEI AU, K. (1985). The concept-text-application approach: Helping elementary students comprehend expository text. *Reading Teacher, 38*(7), 612–618.

WOOD, K. D., & ROBINSON, N. (1983). Vocabulary, language and prediction: A prereading strategy. *Reading Teacher, 36*(4), 392–395.

RESEARCH BASE

AU, K. H. (1979). Using the experience-text-relationship method with minority children. *Reading Teacher, 32,* 677–679.

BECK, I., & MCKEOWN, M. (1981). Developing questions that promote comprehension: The story map. *Language Arts, 58,* 913–918.

BLOOM, B. (1956). *Taxonomy of educational objectives: Cognitive domain.* New York: McKay.

GUZAK, F. J. (1967). Teacher questioning and reading. *Reading Teacher, 21,* 227–234.

PEARSON, P. D. (1981). *Asking questions about stories.* Occasional Paper Series. Lexington, MA: Ginn.

RAPHAEL, T. (1987). Research on reading: But what can I teach on Monday? In V. Koehler (Ed.), *Educator's handbook: A research perspective* (pp. 26–49). New York: Longman.

7 | Helping Students Use Words: Process Goals

GETTING READY

A major part of reading involves words—decoding what they say and attaching meaning to them. These are process goals and are commonly labeled word recognition and vocabulary. This chapter describes the process goals for teaching word recognition and vocabulary at each stage of developmental reading growth in elementary school. Related writing goals are also described. Again, both what word recognition and vocabulary goals to teach and how to teach them are discussed. More detailed suggestions for teaching are described in the appropriate chapters in Part 4. Ms. Chang, Ms. Walters, Mr. Gutierrez, and Ms. O'Malley again provide illustrations for various grade levels.

FOCUS QUESTIONS

- What is the difference between word recognition and vocabulary?

- What are some examples of routine word recognition skills and metacognitive strategies for word recognition?

- What is an example of a routine vocabulary skill and a metacognitive strategy for vocabulary?

- What is fluency?

- In word recognition and vocabulary, when should students be in metacognitive control and when should these functions be automatic?

- How do instructional actions differ in teaching routine skills and metacognitive strategies for word recognition? in teaching routine skills and metacognitive strategies for vocabulary?

- What role does teacher questioning play in developing word recognition and vocabulary goals?

- What word recognition and vocabulary goals are emphasized at the readiness stage? at the initial mastery stage? at the expanded fundamentals stage? at the application stage?

THE WRITTEN CODE

One way to describe reading is to say that it is "talk written down." Writing down talk creates the need for written symbols and a system of conventions to ensure that the symbols are employed in uniform ways. The symbols and the governing conventions are like a code. A message is encoded in print and the resulting text is sent to the reader in various forms (letters, newspapers, books, etc.). Both the writer and the reader must be in agreement about the code, or the messages cannot be communicated.

Understanding the written code is an important part of the reading curriculum. If your students are unfamiliar with the written symbols (letters and words) and with the conventions governing their use (how to examine the letters, how letters form words, what sounds go with what letters, how words are separated in print, and so on), they cannot reconstruct messages authors embed in text.

This chapter focuses on what parts of the code to teach at various grade levels. Because the smallest meaningful product of the code is a word, word recognition and word meaning (vocabulary) are the focus.

DISTINGUISHING BETWEEN WORD RECOGNITION AND VOCABULARY

Readers can have two different kinds of problems with words. First, they may encounter a word they have never seen in print before and are thus unable to identify, even though they may know what it means when someone says it to them. This is a **word recognition** problem. A good example is the word *know*. A reader who understands this word in conversation may not recognize it in print because it sounds like it should be spelled *no*. This is a word recognition problem—the word is not recognized in print.

Readers can also encounter words for which they have no meaning. This is a **vocabulary** problem. For instance, you can pronounce the word *aglet*, but you probably do not know the meaning of the word. This is a vocabulary problem—you do not know the meaning for a word.

In order to focus instruction, it is important to know whether you want students to recognize words unknown in print but known in oral language or whether you are trying to teach them the meaning of words.

COMPONENTS OF WORD RECOGNITION

The ability to recognize words in print consists of both routine skills and metacognitive strategies. Routine skills are associated with recognizing words

Integrating word recognition and vocabulary ensures that students will be able to both pronounce and understand unfamiliar words. (Susan Lapides/Design Conceptions)

instantly; metacognitive strategies are associated with figuring out unknown words.

Routine Skills

Routine skills are those skills that expert readers perform automatically with little thought or reasoning. In word recognition, they consist of both language conventions and linguistic units that contribute to recognizing words instantly.

Language Conventions Language conventions associated with word recognition govern how printed language works. For instance, to recognize words instantly, readers must know how to examine print—that to start at the top left-hand side of the page and move across the lines in a left-to-right direction from the top of the page to the bottom. Further, readers must know that the beginning and end of words are marked by a space on either side of the word and that words start at the left and go to the right. These conventions are part of the written language code, and readers must use them routinely in order to recognize many words instantly.

Linguistic Units Linguistic units associated with word recognition consist of both words and letters. To read text easily, the reader must instantly recognize most of the words on the page. Such instantly recognized words are called sight words. Teaching readers to recognize words at sight—or instantly—is an important part of word recognition. A list of 325 basic sight words, organized into four lists starting with the easiest and moving to the hardest, is provided in Figure 7.1.

Letters are also important linguistic units. For instance, to figure out unknown words young readers can sound out each letter or letter combination in turn and then blend the sounds together. In order to use such a strategy, however, they must first recognize, without conscious effort, the individual letters and their associated sounds. This associating of letter and sound is commonly called phonics. (See pp. 112–114 for a list of phonic elements.)

Metacognitive Strategies

Metacognitive word recognition strategies are used to figure out what a word says while in the midst of reading a text.

Monitoring Monitoring is the key to word recognition strategy use. That is, the reader is always alert for situations in the text that do not make sense and is always ready to say something like, "Oh, oh, something's wrong here." In the case of word recognition, the problem is an unrecognized word. In monitoring for unrecognized words, readers consciously acknowledge that they do not recognize a word and pause momentarily to decide what to do about it. This is a conscious reasoning process and is therefore a metacognitive strategy.

Fix-It Strategies Once they are conscious of an unrecognized word, readers must **decode,** or figure out, the word. Decoding is also sometimes called **word analysis** or **word attack.** To decode, readers apply fix-it strategies, of which there are three.

The first way of decoding is using **context clues:** That is, the reader quickly uses the words around the unknown word to figure out its meaning. Context is usually the most efficient method to decode unrecognized words because it is usually the fastest. Examples of the most common context clues are provided in Figure 7.2.

If using the context clues does not work (and if the unrecognized word contains an **affix**), the expert reader will often try structural analysis since it is the next fastest means of decoding. **Structural analysis** is the breaking apart of an unrecognized word by its structural units (prefixes, suffixes, inflectional endings, and root words) and then identifying the word by pronouncing each separate structural unit in turn. For instance, if *unhappy* is an unrecognized word, it could be pronounced un-happy. A list of common structural units and their meanings is provided in Figure 7.3.

Finally, the reader might use **phonics,** which is the blending together of

FIGURE 7.1   325 Basic Sight Words

List 1: Easiest

I	green	mother	on	but	what
and	blue	girl	some	an	all
the	yellow	look	you	be	been
a	one	on	jump	they	her
to	two	after	little	for	much
was	three	get	then	were	them
in	four	is	we	out	about
it	five	not	did	him	too
of	six	she	father	us	baby
my	seven	who	make	or	
he	eight	boy	cat	have	
white	nine	go	get	new	
black	ten	good	sit	sad	
red	saw	like	hot	this	

List 2: More difficult

something	other	old	day	when	full
from	laugh	there	our	talk	horse
house	ball	again	with	today	orange
want	some	his	bigger	as	keep
went	pretty	chair	do	off	table
where	surprise	push	know	child	which
door	water	any	put	take	guess
dog	woman	by	will	tell	give
shall	word	how	are	children	right
pull	write	song	busy	walk	find
if	before	very	just	wash	would
long	please	am	apple	first	

List 3: Still more difficult

draw	does	ready	bird	miss	ear
feet	family	store	break	nice	lion
many	funny	end	drink	air	point

individual letter sounds as a means of figuring out an unrecognized word. That is, the individual letter sounds learned routinely (see Figure 7.4) are consciously combined and blended. Phonics is the slowest of the three decoding methods because it requires that each separate letter-sound unit be retrieved from memory and then blended together. *Unhappy,* for instance, would be pronounced u-n-h-a-p-p-y. Further, phonics is not always reliable because letter sounds are not always consistent and predictable.

FIGURE 7.3   Some Common Structural Units

Some common prefixes

Prefix	Meaning
dis-	not; the opposite of
in-, im-, il-, ir-	not
pre-	before
re-	again, back
un-	not; the opposite of
anti-	against; opposed to; stopping
inter-	together; between
under-	below; beneath

Other prefixes

mal-	pro-
mid-	super-
mis-	

Some common suffixes

Suffix	Meaning
-age	act or result of; cost of
-dom	position or rank of being; condition of being
-hood	state or condition of being
-ist	person who does or makes or works

Other suffixes

-able	-ful
-an; -ian	-ic
-ant	-ly
-ern	-meter

Some Latin roots

Root	Meaning	Example
cred	believe	credence, credo, incredible
cur	run, flow	current, curriculum
fac, fec	do, make	factory, defect
gen	kind, type	generation, generic
mit, miss	send	admit, dismiss, transmission
scrib, script	write	describe, inscribe, prescription
stat	stand, put in place	stature, station
struc	build, prepare	construction, instruct
voc	call	vocal, vocation
volv	roll, turn	evolve, revolve

FIGURE 7.4   Common Phonic Elements in English

Consonants: *b, c, d, f, g, h, j, k, l, m, n, p, q, r, s, t, v, w, x, y, z.* The letters *b, d, f, h, j, k, l, m, n, p, r, s, t, v, w, y,* and *z* have corresponding sounds that are quite consistent in English. The letters *c* and *g* have two associated sounds. One is referred to as hard and the other as soft:

Hard *c* cane, cat, cow		Soft *c* cent, certain, city
Hard *g* go, good, gone		Soft *g* gene, gent, gem

Consonant blends: A consonant blend or cluster is a combination of two or three consecutive consonants in one syllable. When the blend is pronounced, each letter in the blend has its own distinct sound. The following blends occur frequently in English:

bl	*cr*	*fl*	*gr*	*sc*	*sn*	*str*	*tw*
br	*dr*	*fr*	*pl*	*sk*	*sp*	*sw*	
cl	*dw*	*gl*	*pr*	*sm*	*st*	*tr*	

Consonant digraphs: Two consecutive consonants that represent only one sound are called consonant digraphs. The following are examples of consonant digraphs:

ch	*sh*	*wh*	*gh*
ph	*th*	*ck*	*ng*

The *th* may occur voiced or voiceless (if your vocal cords vibrate, it is voiced; if they do not, it is voiceless):

voiced *th*   *th*ere, *th*is
voiceless *th*   *th*in, *th*ing

Silent consonants: Certain consonants sometimes have no sound value in spoken English.

gh	*gh*ost	*kh*	*kh*aki	*pn*	*pn*eumonia	*rh*	*rh*ubarb
gn	*gn*at	*kn*	*kn*ot	*ps*	*ps*alm	*wr*	*wr*ong
h	*h*onor						

Vowels: There are two categories of vowel sounds that most frequently occur in English:

Long vowels		Short vowels	
ate	*ro*de	*am*	*o*dd
eel	*u*se	*e*nd	*u*s
ice		*i*ll	

---

meanings are known instantly through routine development of vocabulary; others must be figured out through the use of metacognitive strategies.

Routine Vocabulary Skills

Many new word meanings are learned routinely when new experiences are encountered. For instance, when teaching content goals (see Chapter 6) such

FIGURE 7.4   continued

Vowel digraphs: Two consecutive vowels that represent only one sound are called vowel digraphs. The following are examples of the most common vowel digraphs:

ai	rain	*ee*	meet	*au*	August	*oa*	boat
ay	play	*ei*	ceiling	*aw*	awful	*oe*	toe
ea	easy	*ie*	pie	*ow*	grow	*ue*	true

Diphthongs: Two consecutive vowels with one sound but in which the tongue starts in one position and moves rapidly to another are called diphthongs. The following are examples of diphthongs:

oil   boy   owl   out

Schwa: The *schwa* sound can best be described as an unstressed short *u* sound and is symbolized phonetically by /ə/. The *schwa* sound is the most frequently occurring vowel sound in the English language and occurs with all vowels. The vowels in the following *unstressed* syllables stand for the *schwa* sound:

a	e	i	o	u
coma	beaten	imitate	button	column
bedlam	taken	nostril	summon	

Syllable: A syllable is the smallest pronouncable unit of a word. In defining a syllable, direct the emphasis at the idea of vowel sounds. Children will be able to recognize that *all* of the following words have only one syllable because there is only one vowel sound:

so   two   seed   charge   stretch   straight

All of the following words have two syllables because they have two distinct vowel sounds:

hotel   picnic   country   preacher

Phonetic and syllabic generalizations: Syllabication rules and phonetic generalizations have been the subject of some controversy at various times throughout the course of educational history. Whereas many of the rules or generalizations are quite useful, the utility of others is open to question. What is of utmost importance is that a teacher of reading be familiar with the commonly taught generalizations and realize the limitations that the various rules have.

---

as a unit on community helpers, a first grade teacher includes direct and vicarious experiences to help students routinely build concepts for key words such as *community, mayor,* and *utilities.* Similarly, a sixth grade social studies teacher who wants students to read and understand a textbook chapter on ancient Egypt helps students routinely build concepts for key words such as *pharaoh, pyramid,* and *sphinx.* The goal in such cases is for students to know instantly the meaning of necessary words. They may not be conscious of how they know the meanings, but they do know them.

FIGURE 7.4   continued

Phonetic generalizations for vowels

1. When a syllable has one vowel and that vowel is not in final position, the vowel *generally* sounds short (unglided):

cat, cut, cot, in-dex

2. When a syllable has one vowel and that vowel is in final position, the vowel *generally* sounds long (glided):

me, my, hel-lo

3. When a syllable has two digraph vowels, the long sound of the first is generally pronounced:

meat, plain

4. The vowel digraph *oo* stands for both a long and a short sound:

room, wood

Syllabication generalizations

1. Most affixes and inflections are syllables:

un-like, tell-ing

2. When two consonants in a root are preceded and followed by vowels a syllabic division *generally* occurs between them:

bul-let, af-ter

Certain basic reading series have adjusted this rule to state that the syllable division occurs *after* the *second* consonant:

happ-en.

3. When vowels precede and follow a single consonant, a syllabic division *usually* occurs between the preceding vowel and the consonant:

ho-tel, po-lice.

4. When a root ends in a consonant followed by *le,* the consonant plus *le* generally make up its final syllable:

tum-*ble.*

5. For purposes of syllabication, consonant digraphs *generally* function as if they were one consonant:

o-ther

6. For purposes of syllabication, vowel digraphs *generally* function as if they were one vowel:

de-tail, aw-ful

Metacognitive Vocabulary Strategies

Knowing a word meaning from experience with a topic such as ancient Egypt is one thing; figuring out word meanings on your own is another. Consequently, teachers help students develop metacognitive strategies that can be applied to figure out word meaning. For instance, they teach students to monitor in order to spot words for which they have no meaning. And once such unknown words have been spotted, students can begin thinking of ways to figure them out. Just as in decoding, the two most commonly used strategies are context clues and structural analysis. As context clues can be used to decode a word's pronunciation, they also can be used to figure out a word's meaning (refer to Figure 7.2). And as students can use root words, prefixes, suffixes, and inflectional endings to identify a printed word, they can use these same structural elements to figure out what an unknown word means. For instance, *un*-happy, is *not* happy.

As with word recognition strategies, you teach metacognitive vocabulary strategies to help students reason about words that are unknown in meaning. Again, it is a problem-solving situation in which readers monitor to locate unknown words, choose an appropriate strategy (context, structural analysis, or a combination of these) to solve the problem, implement the strategy, and then check to see if the problem (the unknown word meaning) has been solved.

Developing Student Metacognitive Control

Metacognitive control is a primary emphasis in word recognition and vocabulary. However, its role varies. It is of central concern when teaching metacognitive strategies, but it has little to do with teaching routine skills. In word recognition, for instance, students need not be metacognitive (i.e., conscious) of their use of linguistic units and language conventions. They should be automatic about such things as reading pages from left to right and also in their recognition of letter names and sight words. However, students should be metacognitive about monitoring and decoding unknown words. Consequently, instruction in monitoring and fix-it strategies emphasize conscious reasoning.

Similarly, in vocabulary instruction there are some things that receive a metacognitive emphasis and some things that do not. The routine development of new vocabulary when reading for content goals, for instance, is not done with a metacognitive emphasis. Students develop new word meanings as they engage in such reading, but they are not particularly conscious of how they are learning these words. In contrast, strategies for how to figure out unknown word meanings found in print *are* taught with a heavy metacognitive emphasis. Students should be consciously aware of what they do when they encounter an unknown word so that, in future situations, they will be able to think through the problem themselves and resolve it independently.

Teaching with a metacognitive emphasis requires that you recast as reasoning processes those skills that are traditionally taught as memorized routines. In word recognition, for instance, context clues, structural analysis, and phonics are commonly presented to students as skills—that is, as certain rules to memorize and follow exactly the same way each time. Unfortunately, this does not work very well because readers must construct meaning flexibly. To teach context clues, structured analysis, and phonics as metacognitive word recognition strategies, you must present them as something other than routine and fixed rules. Specifically, you must present them as reasoning processes that are modified and adapted to fit a problem to be solved. Structural analysis, for instance, is not presented as a routine matter of dividing root words from prefixes and suffixes but rather as an adaptive process of consciously thinking about how the meaning of a prefix and suffix are combined with a root word meaning and about the reasoning that must be done to arrive at the new meaning.

It is important to understand that expert readers are not forever metacognitive when faced with word recognition and vocabulary problems. In fact, as students become more and more expert, there is less need for conscious word recognition and vocabulary strategies because experience with reading makes virtually all situations routine. However, metacognitive control is essential at the earlier stages of reading when problems are encountered frequently. At the later developmental stages when faced with occasional unrecognized or unknown words, if your students' original instruction emphasized conscious awareness they will be able to access the knowledge and assume control over the situation. However, in order for this to happen, word recognition and vocabulary must be initially taught as metacognitive strategies, not as routine skills.

INSTRUCTIONAL EMPHASIS IN WORD RECOGNITION AND VOCABULARY

As with other goals, instruction for word recognition and vocabulary instruction is discussed in terms of (1) the indirect instruction associated with a literate environment and (2) the direct instruction associated with the teacher's role as a mediator.

The Literate Environment

The major function of the literate environment is to promote conceptual understanding of reading and positive feelings about literacy. Because word recognition and vocabulary focus on words (sometimes in isolation), it is particularly crucial that a literate environment be much in evidence to counter indications that reading is just a matter of knowing words. In the absence of a literate environment, your students are likely to develop the misconception that the most important thing about reading is knowing isolated words. Consequently, your classroom should provide tangible evidence that word recognition and vocabulary are used as part of the message-sending, message-getting function of reading.

To enhance word recognition and vocabulary, the literate environment should provide a word-rich environment. Written words, and messages composed of written words, should be much in evidence, whether through labeling various objects in the room, bulletin boards with written messages, a classroom postal system in which the teacher and students exchange written messages, or other ways. Similarly, oral vocabulary games and the sharing of special words, funny words, strange words, and so forth can help students develop positive attitudes about words generally and about word recognition and vocabulary in particular.

Direct Teacher Guidance

There are two kinds of direct instruction in word recognition and vocabulary, depending on whether the goal is to develop routine skills or metacognitive strategies. Because routine skills should be automatic, there is a **drill and practice model,** which emphasizes repetition to teach these skills. However, the repetition is sandwiched between other crucial elements. First, provide an explanation in which you activate students' background knowledge, make explicit statements about what is to be learned and when it will be used, and model what is to be learned so students have a tangible example to follow. Second, provide an opportunity for students to practice under your guidance. Finally, provide an opportunity for students to apply the routine skills. To illustrate, consider instruction in a routine skill such as learning the sight word *the*. You would drill and practice as follows. To provide an explanation, make sure students' background knowledge of the word *the* is activated— they recognize it when it is spoken; then tell them that they are going to learn to recognize the printed version of the word so they can say it instantly when they encounter it in the story you are going to read together. To model, show students the word in context (such as in the sentence, "*The* doll is mine"), say the sentence, point to *the* and say it. Then have your students do the same. Practice the procedure repeatedly with other sentences until students display accuracy in recognizing the target word. Finally present the story to be read and direct your students to use their newly acquired sight word knowledge of *the* when they encounter it in the story. You employ a similar procedure when teaching other linguistic units and language conventions. A three-step drill and practice lesson model is shown in Figure 7.5.

A modification of this three-step lesson can be adapted to the direct teaching of vocabulary (see Figure 7.6). To illustrate this procedure, consider a situation in which you want to teach the meaning of *platypus* to fifth graders. First, give students experiences with a platypus, perhaps by showing them a picture of one, and use the experience (the picture, in this case) to identify characteristics of a platypus. It is often helpful to organize these characteristics according to the class it belongs to, its identifying properties, some examples of it, and some nonexamples of it (a duck, for instance, which shares some properties of a platypus but is not a platypus). As you do so, say the word to associate it with the experience. You might say, "This is called a platypus. An animal with these webbed feet and a broad bill is called a platypus." Finally, have your students use the new word in oral or written expression.

The routine drill and practice model is not appropriate for metacognitive strategies. Instead, you should use a **modified directed reading lesson (MDRL)** (see Figure 7.7). You will remember from Chapter 6 that the directed reading lesson (DRL) is used for developing content goals, and is structured to get students thinking about the content of the text. In contrast, when

FIGURE 7.5   Drill and Practice Model

Step 1   Explanation

Teacher activates students' background knowledge, specifies what is to be learned and when it will be used in the immediate future.

Model-repetition cycle

Teacher demonstrates what is to be learned, and students repeat demonstration.

Step 2   Guided practice cycle

Student practices under teacher's guidance.

Student has repeated opportunities to do the task.

Teacher provides corrective feedback and re-models as needed.

Step 3   Application

The learning is immediately applied to a real reading situation.

---

developing metacognitive strategies, students should think not so much about the content but, instead, about the reasoning they do in order to understand the content. Consequently, you modify the DRL so that your students will think about *how* they get meaning rather than the meaning itself.

For instance, when teaching context clues, you would introduce a selection to be read, state (or show) that it will contain unknown words, and set as a main purpose of the lesson learning how to figure out those words when they are encountered in the selection. Next, you would model the reasoning expert readers employ when using context clues to figure out unrecognized words and would provide opportunities for your students to practice that reasoning. Then you would introduce the selection to be read, set the dual goals of understanding the selection's content and using context to figure out any unrecognized words, have your students read the selection, and then discuss both the content of the selection and how context was used to figure out the unrecognized words. Hence, the DRL with its emphasis on understanding the content of a selection is modified to focus mainly on the process used to overcome problems related to understanding that content.

FIGURE 7.6   Teaching Vocabulary Using a Modified Drill and Practice Lesson

Step 1   Provide an experience.

Step 2   Identify the properties or characteristics associated with the concept.

Step 3   Say the name of the concept.

Step 4   Give students opportunities to express themselves using the new word.

FIGURE 7.7   Teaching a Process Goal Using MDRL

Step 1   Introduce the selection to be read (activate prior knowledge about topic) and introduce the reading problem to be encountered.

Step 2   Model the use of the strategy to be used, guide students' practice solving similar problems and set the purpose that the strategy will be used in the selection to be read.

Step 3   Reintroduce the selection to be read, set the dual goals of understanding the content (content goal) and applying the newly learned strategy (process goal) and have students read the selection.

Step 4   Discuss the selection in terms of the content and application of the strategy to solve the problem.

Step 5   Close the lesson by summarizing both the content of the selection and the strategy used to solve the problem.

Direct instruction in word recognition and vocabulary, then, depends on whether the goal to be developed is an automatic, memorized response (a routine skill) or conscious reasoning to solve a problem of getting meaning (a metacognitive strategy). When the goal is routine skill, a drill and practice model is used; when the goal is strategic reasoning, a modified directed reading lesson is used.

Integration of Word Recognition and Vocabulary

There is obviously some overlap between word recognition and vocabulary. Both focus on words, both demand monitoring, both make use of context clues and structural analysis as strategies and neither is "reading" in the true sense of constructing meaning from text because the focus is individual words, not connected text. Both, therefore, are prerequisites to the process of creating meaning.

Because word recognition and vocabulary focus on different functions (what the printed form of a word says and what it means), we present each separately here. However, because they are so closely associated, when we present them to children it is best to teach them together. Integrating word recognition and vocabulary is not only efficient in terms of time but also helps ensure that students will not become **word callers** who pronounce words they read but do not understand what they mean.

Role of Fluency

A term frequently associated with word recognition and vocabulary is **fluency,** which usually refers to how smoothly and expressively a student orally reads a text. If students can read text with no hesitations or mistakes and use intonation patterns consistent with the text's meaning, they are said to be fluent readers. If, on the other hand, they read in a slow, choppy manner characterized by many errors and poor intonation patterns, they are not fluent. The typical instructional activity associated with fluency is **oral round robin reading,** in which each student in the reading group takes a turn reading orally.

Fluency is an important but complex goal of reading instruction. It involves much more than oral round robin reading. In fact, oral round robin reading is probably a destructive instructional activity since it often causes students to conclude that the goal is for them to never hesitate, and to know every word instantly. In actuality, you want your students to conclude that reading involves thoughtful reconstruction of meaning from text.

A student's poor fluency may be rooted in routine skills (not knowing enough words and word meanings) or in metacognitive strategies (not knowing how to figure them out). The skill most commonly associated with poor fluency is sight word recognition, because when students instantly recognize all the words in a selection, they tend to read smoothly. Similarly, prior knowledge of topic affects fluency since students with rich conceptual networks about a topic know more word meanings and are better able to create meaning fluently. Finally, students' ability to apply metacognitive strategies to text blockages also affects fluency because the better they are with strategies, the faster and smoother they are in removing blockages to meaning.

Fluency, then, results when students possess both routine skills and metacognitive strategies associated with all aspects of reading, not just word recognition and vocabulary, and it really means smoothness of meaning getting, not smoothness of oral reading. Consequently, fluency is better defined as smoothness in constructing meaning from text using all aspects of the reading process, not just those relating to words.

Role of the Dictionary

Dictionary usage is frequently associated with word recognition and vocabulary instruction. This is because students are often told to look up unknown words in the dictionary. However, dictionaries are virtually useless for figuring out unrecognized words until the application stage (which usually occurs in grades 5 through 8). Using a dictionary for word recognition purposes requires so many skills (use of alphabetizing, guide words, entry words, pronunciation keys, and so forth) that it is virtually impossible to teach its use for pronunciation purposes before the fifth grade. By this time relatively few words need to be decoded because so many are known as sight words.

Dictionaries are more easily used to determine word meanings. However, even when used for this purpose, the disruption they produce poses a serious disadvantage. When a reader stops reading to look up the meaning of a word in a dictionary, so much time is consumed that the train of thought is interrupted, and sometimes the reader loses the text's message.

Dictionaries are most useful in study strategies, particularly at the application and power stages of developmental reading growth. Consequently, dictionary usage is emphasized in Chapter 9.

Role of Teacher Questioning

As noted in Chapter 6, teacher questions serve to focus students' attention on particular aspects of an instructional task. For content goals, your questions focus students on the desired level of meaning (literal, inferential, or critical). For word recognition and vocabulary goals, your questions focus students on the specific goal. Your questions help students determine, for example, whether the lesson is on how to say a word (word recognition) or on what a word means (vocabulary). Similarly, your questions help focus a lesson on automatized responses (as with routine skills) or on reasoning (as with metacognitive strategies).

However, these kinds of questions do not cause students to develop the desired reasoning associated with metacognitive control of word recognition and vocabulary. For instance, asking your students the meaning of an unknown word will not develop their reasoning associated with how to use context to figure it out. Even asking what metacognitive strategy was used to figure out a word meaning will not by itself cause your students to develop the desired reasoning. For reasoning to develop, two conditions must be present. First, you must ask questions about the reasoning students used, not about the word's meaning. Therefore, the relevant question to ask is not, "What does the word mean?" but, rather, "How did you figure out what the word meant?" Second, your question about the reasoning must follow an explanation and demonstration of how to figure out word meanings. It is assumed that your students do not have adequate schemata for figuring out word meanings, so you must explain and demonstrate the metacognitive strategy before asking questions about it.

Integration with Writing

Word recognition and vocabulary are equally important in writing, but the perspective shifts from interpreting to composing text. The more vocabulary words a writer knows, the more clearly the message can be composed, just as the more vocabulary words a reader knows, the more clearly the message can be interpreted.

Similarly, metacognitive strategies can be used when composing text. For instance, context strategies, usually associated with reader comprehension, can be inserted by the writer into written messages as clues designed to help the reader construct the writer's intended meaning.

Word recognition skills and strategies such as sight words and phonics also have analogous uses in writing. In spelling, for instance, it is important to be able to remember visually (at sight) some words that do not use phonetic principles (such as *come* and *pneumonia*) while also using phonetic and structural analysis principles strategically when spelling words that do conform to these principles (*rabbit* and *hat*).

TEACHING WORD RECOGNITION AND VOCABULARY AT VARIOUS DEVELOPMENTAL LEVELS

Readiness Stage

In preschool and kindergarten, both vocabulary and word recognition are developed through listening and language experience stories, since few students at this stage can read text independently. Many of the skills and strategies taught at this level are labeled readiness, since they get students ready to read independently.

The preschool and kindergarten emphasis on vocabulary development is twofold. First, teachers provide students with direct and vicarious experiences that both broaden their backgrounds and, in the process, increase their meaning vocabulary. Preschool and kindergarten teachers often take their students on field trips or engage in other activities to bring students into contact with new experiences; as a follow-up, they then use these activities to create language experience stories using newly acquired vocabulary. Simultaneously, and often as part of the same language experience activity, teachers show students how context can be used to predict meaning. For instance, a teacher might show students how to predict the next word in a sentence.

Word recognition instruction at the readiness level emphasizes routine skills. Students are taught about the basic conventions of language such as left-to-right movement, linguistic units such as letters and letter sounds, and general **print awareness.** Emphasis is placed on visually distinguishing between letters (called **visual discrimination**) and auditorily distinguishing between letter sounds (called **auditory discrimination**). In addition, students at this stage learn high utility sight words, such as their own name. Example 7.1 illustrates how to teach vocabulary and word recognition at the readiness stage.

Initial Mastery Stage

Word recognition and vocabulary are heavily emphasized at the initial mastery stage. This is the time when most students independently read text for the first time, and, consequently, knowing words is a major concern. In vocabulary development, there continues to be a heavy emphasis on providing both vicarious and direct experiences that result in development of new vocabulary. Additionally, however, there is an increase in the emphasis on fix-it strategies, such as context clues and structural analysis, to figure out the meaning of unknown words. The goal is to increase the number of word meanings the students know.

EXAMPLE 7.1   Developing Word Recognition and Vocabulary at the Readiness Stage

I. Word recognition

A. *Routine skills*

1. Print awareness regarding conventions of letter and word usage
2. Visually discriminate among letters and words
3. Auditorily discriminate among letter sounds
4. Associate letters and sounds
5. Identify the highest utility words at sight

B. *Metacognitive strategies*

1. Monitor language experience text for words that are recognized and unrecognized
2. Access fix-it strategies for unknown words
   a. Using context to identify words in a language experience activity

b. Blend sounds together in combination with context to identify simple words

II. Vocabulary

A. *Routine skills*

1. Build vocabulary by discussing experiences that employ new words
2. Build meaning of concrete words

B. *Metacognitive strategies*

1. Monitor oral language and language experience stories for words that are unknown in meaning
2. Access fix-it strategies for meaning getting
   a. Use context in oral language to predict unknown word meanings
   b. Use context in language experience stories to predict unknown word meanings

Linda Chang, who planned to read *Swimmy* to her kindergarten class, decided to introduce the vocabulary associated with oceans before reading the story to them. As she introduced concrete words such as *jelly fish, seaweeds, sea anemones, school of fish,* and *eel,* she used illustrations in *Swimmy* to help explain what each word meant: "Seaweeds are plants that grow in the ocean." Next, she introduced some of the identifying characteristics of these new concepts: "Seaweeds are like the weeds around us except they grow under the water, are soft, and float in water." Next, she showed how seaweeds are different from the local weeds: "Local weeds have hard stems, have firm leaves, and stand upright by themselves, whereas seaweed stems are not hard, the leaves are not firm, and the plants can't stand by themselves, they float in the water." Finally, Ms. Chang showed how all the new words were connected to living things found in the ocean.

As Ms. Chang began the story about Swimmy, she told the children that books are read from left to right, and as the story progressed, she periodically showed them how she was doing this. Then she questioned them about left-to-right progression, and finally she supported their responses when they showed her where to start and which way to go. As she read the story, Ms. Chang also showed the children pictures to illustrate new vocabulary words.

In subsequent days, after the children had created their language experience story about feelings of friendship (described in Chapter 5), Ms. Chang read their story back to them, deliberately leaving out words that could be predicted from context. Following a short lesson on predicting, the children predicted words that would fit in the empty spots in their story. All the children then took their story home to read to their families. Ms. Chang had achieved the word recognition and vocabulary objectives of developing language conventions (left to right), building vocabulary through discussions of vicarious experiences found in *Swimmy,* and developing an understanding about the role of prediction in reading.

In word recognition, the emphasis shifts from readiness skills associated with visually discriminating print conventions and auditorily discriminating letter sounds to increasing the number of words the student can recognize in print. This is done in three ways. First, a heavy emphasis is placed on sight word recognition, in which more and more of the high-utility words in English are instantly recognized. As part of this effort, students are taught to discriminate visually among easily confused words such as *was-saw, them-then,* and *there-where.* Second, students are taught during-reading strategies, specifically to monitor their reading so that they are conscious of encountering unrecognized words and, if they become aware of a word they do not recognize, to stop and apply an appropriate fix-it strategy to identify the word. At the initial mastery stage, there is a heavy emphasis on all three decoding strategies for word recognition: context clues, structural analysis, and phonics.

Fluency of word recognition receives some emphasis at the initial mastery stage. However, the focus is less on fluency in saying every word accurately than on effective monitoring and the efficient application of fix-it strategies when unrecognized words are encountered. In short, stopping to fix blockages is encouraged. It is during these pauses in reading that the student accesses the repertoire of available strategies and selects an appropriate one for application in the particular situation. Example 7.2 illustrates how to teach vocabulary and word recognition at the initial mastery stage.

Expanded Fundamentals Stage

Word recognition and vocabulary instruction continue at the expanded fundamentals stage (grades 3 and 4), but the emphasis shifts from the most basic skills and strategies to more sophisticated ones.

Vocabulary development shifts from learning new word meanings through direct experiences to learning new word meanings from more formal word study efforts. That is, as students begin to encounter difficult terminology associated with content areas such as social studies and science, the teacher directly teaches the meanings of these words (refer to Figure 7.6). Simultaneously, efforts to teach monitoring and fix-it strategies for figuring out unknown word meanings continues.

In word recognition, the emphasis shifts from basic to more sophisticated metacognitive strategies. Consequently, teachers of students reading at third and fourth grade levels continue to teach word recognition, but the more difficult elements are emphasized.

Example 7.3 illustrates how to teach word recognition and vocabulary at the expanded fundamentals stage.

Application Stage

By the time students move into the application stage (fifth through eighth grade), they should have most of the skills and strategies associated with

EXAMPLE 7.2   Developing Word Recognition and Vocabulary at the Initial Mastery Stage

I. Word recognition

A. *Routine skills*

1. Identify words at sight
2. Recognize easily confused words
3. Fluently recognize sight words in connected text

B. *Metacognitive strategies*

1. Monitor for unrecognized words and fluently access appropriate fix-it strategies
2. Access fix-it strategies for unknown words
   a. Identify words by using the context of a sentence
   b. Identify words by using common structural units such as compound words, contractions, prefixes, and suffixes
   c. Identify words by using initial and final consonant sounds and common phonogram units
   d. Use context clues, structural analysis, and phonics in combination

II. Vocabulary

A. *Routine skills*

1. Build vocabulary through discussion of vicarious and direct experiences
2. Continue emphasis on concrete words

B. *Metacognitive strategies*

1. Monitor for words unknown in meaning and fluently access appropriate fix-it strategies
2. Access fix-it strategies for meaning getting
   a. Using context to predict the meaning of unknown words in print
   b. Using structural analysis to predict the meaning of unknown words in print

Kelly Walters decided to teach her first grade students how to use phonics as a decoding strategy to identify unknown printed words. She also decided to build their vocabularies by discussing both vicarious and direct experiences. *Alexander and the Terrible, Horrible, No Good, Very Bad Day* had many examples of closed, short vowel words (*bad, get,* etc.) and multiple opportunities to build vocabulary.

While reviewing the book, Ms. Walters picked out words that fit a simple phonic pattern (*gum, get, bed, bad, box, kit, let, got,* etc.). She grouped the words (*bed* and *bad, got* and *get, kit* and *sit,* etc.), and taught a phonics lesson of letter substitution in closed, short-vowel words. She taught students that you can pronounce an unknown word by recognizing the pattern it belongs to, substitute a new letter in it, and say it. Immediately after the phonics lesson, the students, each with their own paperback version of Viorst's book, went through the story looking for words that fit. When a word was found, they pronounced it, and then discussed the part of the story in which the word was used. As they discussed the parts of the story, each event was listed. Using all the events listed, they brainstormed descriptive words that fit each event. For instance, for the event where one student was blamed for getting the library books out of order when she was only trying to help a friend who didn't know how to check a book out of the library, the students developed the descriptive words of *quiet, orderly,* and *librarian.* These events and descriptor words were then used when the entire class wrote their letter to the principal about their bad days (as described in Chapter 5).

EXAMPLE 7.3   Developing Word Recognition and Vocabulary at the Expanded Fundamentals Stage

I. Word recognition

A. Routine skills

1. Recognize a wide variety of words instantly
2. Fluently recognize sight words in connected text

B. Metacognitive strategies

1. Monitor for unrecognized words and fluently access appropriate fix-it strategies
2. Access fix-it strategies for unknown words
   a. Identify words by using the context of surrounding sentences and paragraphs
   b. Identify words by using less common prefixes and suffixes
   c. Identify words by using vowel generalizations and common syllabication principles
   d. Use context clues, structural analysis, and phonics in combination

II. Vocabulary

A. Routine skills

1. Build vocabulary through direct study of words associated with content being studied
2. Shift emphasis from concrete words to multiple meaning words, homonyms, synonyms, antonyms, and other special categories of words

B. Metacognitive strategies

1. Monitor for words unknown in meaning and fluently accessing appropriate fix-it strategies
2. Access fix-it strategies for meaning getting
   a. Use large chunks of context around the unknown word to figure out meaning
   b. Use less common prefixes and suffixes to figure out meaning
   c. Introduce the dictionary for determining word meaning

John Gutierrez's third grade students were completing lessons that helped to develop understanding about vocabulary and word recognition skills. For the word recognition parts of his lessons, he decided to teach students how to recognize unknown words that had the relatively uncommon suffix of *-er* since the book *Spectacles* had many examples of such words. After presenting information about *-er* words, modeling how to say unknown words that end in *-er,* and helping students learn to use the *-er* endings with unknown words on their own, he had them read *Spectacles* for content goals as well as to note *-er* words. Since some of the students included words like *Chester* and *mother,* Mr. Gutierrez took that opportunity to clarify that all *-er* words do not fit the pattern and broadened their understanding of the uses of both phonics and structural analysis.

Because an ophthalmologist was coming to visit the classroom, Mr. Gutierrez taught a vocabulary lesson with words taken from the story that were directly associated with eye exami-

nations. Using the words *prescribed, contact lens, glasses, frames,* and *spectacles,* he took the students through a four-step lesson. First, Mr. Gutierrez provided experiences with these words by bringing in some contact lenses for the students to examine. Second, he used the experiences to generate characteristics associated with the words: For contact lens they generated words like *small, not flat, clear,* and *bendable sometimes.* These characteristics fit into four categories: They decided contact lenses were a way to see, they were small, they were not flat, and they were clear. They also decided that some contact lenses were rigid while others were flexible or soft. Third, the students visually connected the printed words *contact lens* with its characteristics, and finally they discussed possible questions they might ask the ophthalmologist about contact lenses. After meanings for all the words were developed, the students generated and wrote questions to ask the ophthalmologist about eye examinations.

EXAMPLE 7.4   Developing Word Recognition and Vocabulary at the Application Stage

I. Word recognition
  A. *Routine skills*
    1. Not emphasized
  B. *Metacognitive strategies*
    1. Maintain monitoring for unrecognized words and fluent accessing of appropriate fix-it strategies
    2. Maintain fix-it strategies for recognizing words unknown in print

II. Vocabulary
  A. *Routine skills*
    1. Build vocabulary through direct study of words encountered in content area subjects
    2. Emphasize abstract words
  B. *Metacognitive Strategies*
    1. Maintain monitoring for words unknown in meaning and fluently accessing appropriate fix-it strategies
    2. Maintain fix-it strategies for figuring out the meaning of unknown words

Donna O'Malley's fifth grade students in the Max Headroom reading group were completing lessons that combined understandings about vocabulary and word recognition with the attitude and content goals. Ms. O'Malley decided to teach her students how to identify unknown words using a variety of fix-it strategies, since the book *Julie of the Wolves* has several unknown words, such as *predicament, kayak, Nunivak, gussaks, ilaya,* and *ulo.* After a brief discussion that activated the students' knowledge about phonics, structural analysis, and context clues, Ms. O'Malley taught them to use a combination of all three strategies when encountering unknown words. She presented information to the students, modeled how to use a combination of the strategies, and provided opportunities for student practice. Students were asked to jot down any words they figured out using their new skill as they continued to read *Julie of the Wolves.*

For the vocabulary portion of the lesson, Ms. O'Malley taught them how to use context clues to figure out the meaning of an unknown word. *Julie of the Wolves* contains many passages where context can be used to figure out unknown words, such as *warily, quickened,* and *vaulted.* After the lesson, the students applied the strategy as they read *Julie of the Wolves,* and finally they used their new vocabulary as they wrote reports on the social behavior of animals.

word recognition and vocabulary. Word recognition and vocabulary tasks at this level are primarily a matter of maintaining and extending the skills and strategies developed earlier.

In vocabulary, the emphasis is on learning specialized vocabulary associated with content area subjects such as social studies, science, and literature. In word recognition, the emphasis is on maintaining students' fluency in reading, monitoring, and applying fix-it strategies. Example 7.4 illustrates how to teach word recognition and vocabulary at the application stage.

SUMMARY

Readers need to decode and understand the meaning of words in order to read. Word recognition focuses on decoding; vocabulary focuses on word meaning. Some of what students must learn consists of routine skills. For instance, students must routinely and automatically know letter sounds to decode and must routinely and automatically know the meaning of words associated with their background experience. Similarly, some of what students must learn about words consists of metacognitive strategies. For instance, students must be conscious of how they use context to decode a word unknown in print and they must be conscious of how they use prefixes to determine the meaning of unknown prefixed words. Your instructional role differs depending on whether you are teaching routine skills, in which case you will use a drill and practice model, or metacognitive strategies, in which case you will use a modified directed reading lesson. In any case, instruction on words requires that you do more than simply develop fluency in reading orally or ask students questions about content. Instead, you must teach the routine skills and metacognitive strategies, question students about how they used those skills and strategies, and check to see that students are applying them when reading. While word recognition and vocabulary are most heavily emphasized in the early developmental stages, words continue to receive some emphasis even at the application stage.

SUGGESTED ADDITIONAL READINGS

BECK, I. L., & MCKEOWN, M. G. (1983). Learning words well—A program to enhance vocabulary and comprehension. *Reading Teacher, 36*(7), 622–625.

BLACHOWICZ, C. L. (1978). Metalinguistic awareness and the beginning reader. *Reading Teacher, 31*(8), 875–882.

BLACHOWICZ, C. (1985). Vocabulary development and reading: From research to instruction. *Reading Teacher, 39*, 876–881.

BLACHOWICZ, C. (1987). Vocabulary instruction: What goes on in the classroom? *Reading Teacher, 41*, 132–137.

BURKE, E. M. (1978). Using trade books to intrigue children with words. *Reading Teacher, 32*(2), 144–148.

CLYMER, T. (1963). The utility of phonics generalization in the primary grades. *Reading Teacher, 41*, 252–258.

CULYER, III, R. C. (1979). Guidelines for skill development: Word attack. *Reading Teacher, 32*(4), 425–433.

CUNNINGHAM, J. W. (1979). An automatic pilot for decoding. *Reading Teacher, 32*(4), 420–424.

CUNNINGHAM, P. M. (1980). Teaching were, with, what, and other "four-letter" words. *Reading Teacher, 34*(2), 160–163.

DICKERSON, D. P. (1982). A study for use of games to reinforce sight vocabulary. *Reading Teacher, 36*(1), 46–49.

GROFF, P. (1986). The maturing of phonics instruction. *Reading Teacher, 39*, 919–923.

GROFF, P. J. (1984). Resolving the letter name controversy. *Reading Teacher, 37*(4), 384–388.

JIGANTI, M., & TINDALL, M. (1986). An interactive approach to teaching vocabulary. *Reading Teacher, 39*, 444–451.

JOHNSON, D., PITTELMAN, S., & HEIMLICH, J. (1986). Semantic mapping. *Reading Teacher, 40*, 778–783.

MARZANO, R. J. (1984). A cluster approach to vocabulary instruction: A new direction from the research literature. *Reading Teacher, 38*(2), 168–173.

MORRIS, D. (1982). "Word sort": A categorization strategy for improving word recognition ability. *Reading Psychology, 3*(3), 247–259.

RIBOVICH, J. K. (1979). A methodology for teaching concepts. *Reading Teacher, 33*(3), 285–289.

SCHWARTZ, R., & RAPHAEL, T. (1985). Concept of definition: A key to improving students' vocabulary. *Reading Teacher, 39,* 198–205.

TAYLOR, B. M., & NOSBUSH, L. (1983). Oral reading for meaning: A technique for improving word identification skills. *Reading Teacher, 37*(3), 234–237.

RESEARCH BASE

BECK, I., MCKEOWN, M., & MCCASLIN, E. (1983). Vocabulary development: All contexts are not created equal. *Elementary School Journal, 83,* 177–181.

GOODMAN, K. (1972). Reading: The key is in the children's language. *Reading Teacher,* 1254–1261.

JOHNSON, D., & PEARSON, P. D. (1984). *Teaching reading vocabulary* (2nd edition). New York: Holt, Rinehart & Winston.

LABERGE, D., & SAMUELS, J. (1974). Toward a theory of automatic information processing in reading. *Cognitive Psychology, 6,* 293–323.

PARIS, S., LIPSON, M., & WIXSON, K. (1983). Becoming a strategic reader. *Contemporary Educational Psychology, 8,* 293–316.

8 Helping Students Use Comprehension Strategies: Process Goals

GETTING READY

Comprehension is what reading is all about. Consequently, comprehension is the most important process goal. This chapter describes the process goals for comprehension taught at each stage of developmental reading growth in elementary school. Related writing goals are also described. Again, both what comprehension goals to teach and how to teach them are discussed. More detailed suggestions for teaching are described in the appropriate chapters in Part 4. Our sample teachers again provide illustrations for various levels.

FOCUS QUESTIONS

- How are comprehension processes distinguished from what was learned in earlier chapters about attitude, content, and word recognition and vocabulary goals?

- What strategies help students become self-regulated comprehenders?

- What comprehension strategies are used as one begins to read? during reading? after reading?

- What can teachers do to develop student understanding of comprehension processes?

- How are reading comprehension processes related to writing?

- What are the curricular emphases when teaching comprehension processes at various levels of developmental reading growth?

IMPORTANT DISTINCTIONS ABOUT COMPREHENSION

Comprehension is the essence of reading. The writer creates a text to communicate a message; the reader's task is to comprehend that message. To teach comprehension effectively, however, you must make three important distinctions.

Distinguishing Comprehension from Word Recognition and Vocabulary

Word recognition and vocabulary (see Chapter 7) usually receive heavy instructional attention in the beginning stages of reading acquisition. This is because both recognizing and knowing the meanings of words are basic to comprehension. Because students must recognize and attach meaning to individual words when reconstructing printed messages, word recognition and vocabulary are actually part of the comprehension process.

Understanding this subtle interrelationship is important when teaching reading because it is the key to achieving balance between word knowledge and comprehension instruction. Although word recognition is a prerequisite to comprehension, it is only a small part of the overall process. Being able to pronounce the word *halberd*, for instance, does not necessarily mean that you comprehend its meaning.

Distinguishing Comprehension from Remembering

Some teachers equate comprehension and **remembering,** particularly remembering factual information. These teachers require students to answer questions about information contained in the reading selection, with recall being the primary focus.

However, comprehension and remembering are not synonymous. Comprehension is reconstruction of an author's message. As detailed in Chapter 4, it involves combining new information from text with old information from prior experiences and actively building new understandings. While recall of what was read is important, it is distinct from reconstructing a message. When you recall, you do not construct; you memorize. Good readers use comprehension processes to reconstruct an author's message. They then employ memory strategies to remember that message for a test or other purpose. Remembering strategies are separate from comprehension strategies and are taught as study strategies (see Chapter 9).

Distinguishing Comprehension Processes and Content Goals

Distinguishing between process and content is crucial in comprehension instruction. To comprehend the content of a text, the author's message (see Chapter 6), you must engage in mental processes, or reasoning. Although the two goals are interrelated, they are distinct, and you must always remember that knowing the content, repeating it on a test for instance, does not always mean students understand the process of reasoning. This book emphasizes throughout that you want your students to learn how they process rather than simply recall facts.

There is a means-ends relationship between process and content. Although the end product of comprehension is understanding specific content,

Word recognition receives much attention in the beginning stages of reading instruction. (Elizabeth Crews)

the means to that understanding is the reasoning used to reconstruct text. If you limit comprehension instruction to the content of the immediate text, then your students receive no explicit information about *how* to comprehend. Consequently, you will be unable to gradually shift control of the comprehension process to students.

Although teacher-posed comprehension questions are useful in guiding students to important content, they do relatively little to focus students on comprehension reasoning. To ensure that your students learn how expert readers comprehend, you must explicitly teach both the reasoning employed by experts when making sense of text and how to apply these mental processes while reading. Some students, particularly those with rich language backgrounds, incidentally discover these mental processes while reading. Other students, however, find it is too confusing to answer questions about a selection's content while simultaneously figuring out for themselves how comprehension works. They need explicit demonstrations of how good readers comprehend, and they need practice in using these reasoning processes.

This chapter focuses on the mental processes involved in comprehension. While these processes are discussed separately from content here, they are not taught in isolation from content. As you explain comprehension processes to your students, you should immediately help them apply these processes to the context of texts they are reading.

TYPES OF COMPREHENSION STRATEGIES

In contrast to word recognition and vocabulary, comprehension has no routine skills that, once mastered, are forever automatic. Instead, all **comprehension strategies** are metacognitive. That is, you teach your students to be conscious of when and how to use them so they can access them when reading text on their own.

This does not mean that comprehension strategies never become automatic. On the contrary, through repeated use, comprehension reasoning becomes increasingly automatic, especially when reading easy or familiar text. This is another form of fluency (see Chapter 7) in which students smoothly construct meaning from text without hesitations, false starts, and errors. This fluency develops after your students have had extensive experience in consciously adapting strategies to a variety of text situations. However, even the best readers occasionally encounter a difficult text and, consequently, must be able to consciously access these strategies.

Like all metacognitive activity in reading, comprehension strategies are based in monitoring. That is, readers expect the message in the text to make sense, and as they read, they listen to see if it does.

Within the framework of monitoring, comprehension strategies can be described in terms of strategies readers employ as they begin to read (initiating strategies), as they are in the midst of reading (during-reading strategies) and when reflecting on meaning after reading (post-reading strategies).

Initiating Strategies

When initially encountering text, readers immediately become strategic. They examine the text (and the situation in which the text is to be read) for clues about its meaning, and they predict what the content will be about. These are called initiating strategies.

There are three sources of clues for making predictions about the selection. One is topic clues, which are often found in a selection's title, in its pictures, or in the first or second paragraph. Using a story about rainfall, for instance, you could model by saying, "I see that the title is about rainfall, and the pictures all show people standing around looking sad in the rain, so I think the topic must be something about rain and how it affects people." Also teach students to recall what they already know about those clues— what their background experience tells them. You could model by saying, "I know from my own experience that too much rain can make things messy and even cause floods, which hurt people." Then teach students to use topic clues and prior experiences to make predictions about what the author's message will be. You could model by saying, "I think this story is about the bad things that can happen to you when you get too much rain."

A second source of clues for making predictions about a selection is text clues. A selection on rain will stir different expectations if it is found in a collection of humorous tales, a geography book, or a poetry book. You could model by saying, "This story about rain is in a section of our textbook that has the theme 'courage,' so I think this story, like the others in this section of the book, must be about courage." Then show your students how to predict on the basis of that information, saying, "Because the topic is rain and appears in a section of the book about courage, maybe this selection is going to be about the ways people are courageous when there is lots of rain." Another kind of text clue is the internal text structure. Teach your students to identify whether a selection to be read is a story, an expository article, a poem, or some other kind of text. Then, teach them to use what they know about each type of text structure to predict what will happen in the selection. You could model by saying, "Since this is a story, and stories usually start by describing the main character and the problem, I think the next page or so should tell me who the main character is and what problem the main character is going to have with the rain."

A third source of clues for making initial predictions is the purpose for reading the text. Your students may be reading a text for enjoyment, for a homework assignment, to solve a particular problem, or for other reasons. Purpose shapes perceptions, whether one is looking for a particular person in a crowd or looking for meaning in a text. For instance, when you read a newspaper article, you predict different meanings depending on what you are looking for. You could model how readers use purpose to make predictions about meaning by saying, "Because we are reading the stories in this section of our book to learn about different kinds of courage, I think I'm going to find that this is a story about a different type of courage."

To summarize, initiating strategies focus on what readers think about to make predictions as they begin to read. You should provide your students with explicit information about how to generate predictions using topic, text, and purpose clues. These are the first steps in reconstructing the author's message.

During-Reading Strategies

No matter how strategic a reader is when initiating reading, some predictions may prove to be inaccurate. During-reading strategies are used to check and, if necessary, to modify initial predictions when something unexpected is encountered. The essence of being metacognitive is the reader's regulation of these unexpected blockages to meaning. The reader stops and says, "Oh, oh, something's wrong here. This doesn't seem right in light of what I expected," and then consciously activates a fix-it strategy to correct the situation. This regulation of meaning getting is repeated frequently when reading a difficult selection.

During-reading strategies for comprehension are used to resolve two kinds of problems. The first focuses on the author's message—what the author wants readers to understand. This can include information the author explicitly states in the text or implies. In either case, the focus of the problem is on what the author intended. The second focuses on meaning that goes beyond the author's message. What meaning does the reader construct beyond that intended by the author?

Continuing the illustration from the preceding section on initiating strategies, assume that your students made initial predictions that the story was going to be about one boy's courage in the face of floods caused by excessive rainfall. However, while reading the opening paragraphs of the story, cooperative rather than individual action is favored. Readers must use strategies for determining the author's message to identify this subtle change. For instance they may use strategies they have been taught for making inferences to identify the author's implication that cooperative rather than individual effort is to be the focus. Similarly, when reading this passage readers can use what they have been taught about how to construct meaning beyond what the author intended. They might draw conclusions about whether cooperative effort would be more or less efficient than individual effort, regardless of whether the author intended that they create this meaning or not.

As was noted in Chapter 7 regarding word recognition and vocabulary, many traditional reading comprehension skills typically learned in isolation can be recast as during-reading strategies. For instance, skills such as noting details; determining pronoun referents, main idea, and author purpose; classifying; recognizing relationships (e.g., causal, sequencing, compare-contrast); identifying character traits; and constructing inferences based on author cues can be taught as strategies for determining an author's message. And constructing inferences based on reader background knowledge, drawing conclusions, and making critical judgments can be recast as strategies for going beyond the author's meaning.

To accomplish such recasting, you present what is to be learned not as a rule-driven procedure to be routinely employed in exactly the same way in all instances but, rather, as a process of thinking about solving a problem in which the reasoning employed must be modified to adapt to each new situation. Consequently, you would not present main idea as a set of rules to follow but, rather, as an adaptive thinking process in which the reader uses clues in the text to reason about what major point the author is making.

To summarize, expert readers routinely use during-reading strategies to regulate the ongoing process of getting meaning. They monitor emerging meaning to determine whether initial predictions were accurate, and if they were not, they use fix-it strategies to generate new predictions that fit the new information. The reasoning involved in accomplishing this regulatory function includes monitoring, accessing appropriate strategies, reasoning with the strategies, forming a new prediction, and testing the new prediction.

Post-Reading Strategies

Meaning getting is not complete when a reader finishes the last words in a text. Some of the most significant comprehension occurs after reading is completed. **Organizing strategies** include the processes of summarizing, determining the main point or theme, drawing conclusions; **evaluative strategies** include making judgments. These processes usually occur after reading is completed and so are called post-reading strategies.

Good readers use such strategies to reflect after they read. Like during-reading strategies, many of these post-reading strategies have traditionally been taught as skills, but they are actually flexible plans for constructing meaning, not proceduralized routines to be memorized. This book describes two types of post-reading strategies. The first focuses on organizing—or re-structuring—text meaning. After reading, a reader may wish to summarize, clarify, or draw conclusions about an author's main idea or literary theme. The second focuses on evaluating and judging—or doing **critical reading**—about an author's message. A reader may make judgments about the credentials of an author, an author's relative use of facts, bias, and propaganda, or the validity of an author's conclusions.

To illustrate, consider the previously described selection about group courage in the face of a flood caused by rainfall. You teach students to reflect on the thematic meaning of this selection as it relates to other selections in the section on courage. A reader may wish to summarize the author's message about group courage and compare it to other kinds of courage described in earlier selections. Or, a reader may wish to judge the validity of the author's argument for group efforts rather than individual efforts.

Such post-reading reflection requires strategic thinking. A reader must regulate, or be in control of, the reasoning involved in organizing an author's information or making judgments about it. This post-reading **self-regulation,** like initiating strategies and during-reading strategies, requires instruction to help students be conscious of what they are doing, why they are doing it, and how to do it.

To summarize, like all metacognitive strategies, comprehension strategies are taught to help students reason about solutions to comprehension difficulties. When students begin reading, you want them to approach it as a problem to be solved; to access and use appropriate topic, text, and purpose initiating strategies; and to make initial predictions. When students encounter comprehension difficulties during reading, you want them to access the appropriate strategies for determining author's meaning and for constructing meaning beyond what the author intended; and to use these strategies to solve any problems. When students finish reading you want them to access appropriate post-reading strategies to reflect about the text's meaning.

INSTRUCTIONAL EMPHASIS IN COMPREHENSION PROCESSES

As with other goals, instruction in comprehension processes can be discussed in terms of the literate environment (indirect instruction) and the teacher's role as a mediator (direct instruction).

The Literate Environment

Since comprehension is the heart of reading, the classroom environment should feature getting meaning from connected text. **Connected text** is any printed matter that represents a complete message being conveyed in a meaningful environment. For instance, a note the teacher writes to a student about progress in school is connected text. Similarly, written directions for how to run the classroom movie projector, invitations asking community leaders to speak to the class, poems written by students in the class, storybooks students choose from the library, classroom newspapers, comic strips, and various forms of language experience stories all are examples of connected text. The literate environment should abound with such materials.

When connected text pervades the classroom environment, students are constantly confronted with real-life reading experiences that demand com-

When students are constantly confronted with real reading experiences, they learn why it is important to understand comprehension strategies. (Robert Bawden)

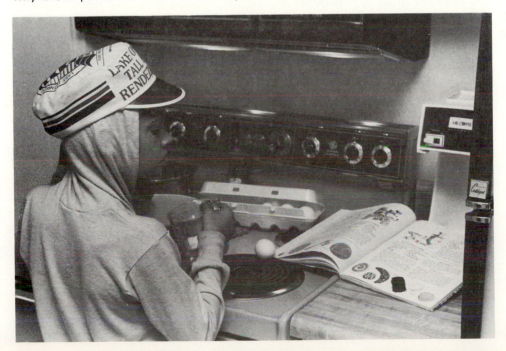

prehension, and consequently, they learn first-hand why it is important to learn comprehension strategies. This understanding is the basis for motivation: Because your students understand what real reading is all about, they are willing to expend the necessary energy to learn comprehension strategies. Without these experiences, students construct alternative schemata for reading. If a classroom environment emphasizes isolated reading tasks, such as those typically found in workbooks, students will conceptualize reading as busy work. If a classroom fails to build an understanding of what reading is, students see no compelling reason why they should try to learn comprehension strategies.

Direct Teacher Guidance

Direct instruction in comprehension processes focuses on helping your students become metacognitively aware, using techniques such as the modified directed reading lesson developed in Chapter 7. Like word level strategies, instruction in comprehension strategies focuses students on the reasoning that leads them to meaning. The idea is not to teach students to master individual strategies but to teach them to use strategies flexibly and in combination.

In teaching students to activate background knowledge before beginning to read, organize your instruction using an MDRL. First, introduce the selection to be read, so that the strategy is presented as part of a real reading task. Then, state the purpose of the lesson—that is, how to use clues to make predictions about meaning before reading even begins. Use the selection to be read as an example along with other examples of similar text. Then, model how to use text clues and background knowledge to make initial predictions about the meaning in the text; check students' understanding of the strategy by giving them other textual examples and guiding them as they try out the strategy. Once you are reasonably sure your students understand how to use the strategy, have them read the selection and apply the strategy. Thus, students immediately apply the strategy in a real reading situation.

Follow the same format when you teach during-reading and post-reading strategies. Always introduce the strategies within the context of a real reading task so your students have a place to apply it. Mediate students' understanding about how to use the strategy by providing explicit introductions, modeling the mental processing involved, assessing their responses during the course of guided practice and providing appropriate additional assistance as needed. Then have students apply the strategy immediately in the daily reading selection.

Role of Teacher Questioning

Comprehension questions are probably the most prevalent activity in comprehension lessons. That is, teachers have students read a selection and then ask comprehension questions about it. When your goal is to develop comprehension strategies, this practice is questionable for two reasons.

First, as noted earlier, such comprehension questions focus students on content, not on the mental processes used to acquire that content. Consequently, students do not attend to the reasoning involved in answering your questions. From your perspective, questions about content provide useful assessment data about who is comprehending and who is not, but the questions themselves do not teach students to comprehend.

Second, such comprehension questions are frequently asked before students have been given explicit instruction in how to comprehend. The point is not that you should ask no comprehension questions. That would be foolish. It is virtually impossible to conduct instruction without asking questions. Rather, you need to give students explicit instruction about how to comprehend before you ask questions to see if they can comprehend. After you model how to reason and provide graduated assistance in doing such reasoning, questions help keep students focused on the reasoning they are doing. Question asking alone, however, does not provide students with the raw materials needed to build schemata for how to comprehend.

Integration with Writing

Reading comprehension strategies can also be used in writing. If good readers initiate meaning getting by looking for clues with which to predict meaning, then good writers should provide such clues when composing messages. If good readers use text clues to fix blockages to meaning, good writers should include such clues in the text they compose. And if good readers find meaning through post-reading strategies such as organizing and evaluating, good writers should embed in the text information to assist readers in constructing such meaning.

TEACHING COMPREHENSION AT VARIOUS DEVELOPMENTAL LEVELS

Readiness Stage

Comprehension at the readiness stage emphasizes listening comprehension, since students in preschool and kindergarten cannot yet read. Consequently, at the readiness stage comprehension processes are taught through listening, and what is learned is later transferred when students begin reading at the initial mastery stage.

Listening comprehension is virtually the same as reading comprehension. It is enhanced when background knowledge is activated and predictions are made before beginning to listen, when sense making is monitored and breaks in meaning getting are repaired during listening, and when information is organized and judged after listening. Consequently, the thinking students do to comprehend text in listening situations serves as a useful foundation for the thinking required for reading comprehension.

At the readiness stage, you should also employ language experience stories to help students make the transition from strategic listening to strategic reading. You could use a common class experience to build a story with students and use that story to illustrate how readers use initiating strategies, monitor and repair meaning as the text is processed, and finally organize and judge information in the text after reading.

Example 8.1 illustrates how to teach comprehension at the readiness stage using both listening and language experiences.

EXAMPLE 8.1   Developing Comprehension Processes at the Readiness Stage

I. Initiating strategies

    A. *Activate background knowledge of topic*

        1. Predict content as signaled by picture and title

    B. *Activate background knowledge of text*

        1. Recognize story structure to predict content

    C. *Activate knowledge about author's purpose*

II. During-reading strategies

    A. *Use monitoring strategies to identify problem*

    B. *Access strategies*

        1. Determine author meaning—recognize details in a listening situation and make inferences about relationships when key words are stated

        2. Beyond the author's meaning—make inferences about relationships based on readers' background knowledge

    C. *Implement the strategy*

    D. *Verify that problem is solved*

III. Post-reading strategies

    A. *Use organizing strategies*

        1. Recall what is important through story structure: beginning, middle, end

    B. *Use evaluating strategies*

        1. Judge fantasy or reality

Linda Chang wanted to develop comprehension processes. She used the oral reading of *Swimmy* to develop three comprehension strategies: predicting content from pictures and title (initiating strategies); monitoring the accuracy of the predictions (during-reading strategies); and recalling what's important by using the story structure of beginning, middle, and end (post-reading strategies).

For the initiating strategy of predicting from the title and pictures, Ms. Chang showed the children the cover, which depicts an underwater scene, read aloud the title, *Swimmy,* and modeled for them how to predict what the story was about. She helped them by showing how she thought about things that swim under water. When Ms. Chang and the children had created their predictions, she read the book aloud showing them all the illustrations. Periodically she helped the children monitor their predictions by comparing their predictions to the actual text in order to see which ones were accurate. After the story was finished, Ms. Chang helped the children recall what was important in the story by using the story parts of beginning, middle, and end. They decided the following events were important: Swimmy finding himself alone; Swimmy swimming through the water; Swimmy finding a school of red fish; and Swimmy teaching them to swim in formation so they looked like one big fish. As the students recalled the important parts, Ms. Chang wrote them on the board. When their recall was completed, Ms. Chang and the students read this jointly constructed text.

Initial Mastery Stage

As students begin to accumulate a sight word vocabulary, you will help them make the transition from listening comprehension to reading comprehension. Show students how the thinking they do when listening to a story is essentially the same thinking they do when reading a preprimer or primer on their own. Show them how to initiate reading comprehension by activating appropriate background information and making initial predictions about the meaning of the text; show how to monitor and repair breaks during reading; and help students engage in post-reading thinking.

However, the task gradually becomes more complex at this stage. The initiating strategies expand to include simple expository text as well as narrative text; the during-reading strategies include typographic cues, such as question marks and exclamation points, which do not appear in listening situations, as well as more complex kinds of relationships, such as sequence and cause-effect; and the post-reading strategies include main idea thinking and using certain word clues to judge author bias. Example 8.2 illustrates how to teach beginning readers to apply strategic comprehension processes at the initial mastery stage.

Expanded Fundamentals Stage

As students progress to reading third and fourth grade text, the comprehension emphasis broadens. Now you will teach students to use initiating strategies with a greater variety of text and for a greater variety and complexity of purposes. During-reading strategies focus on how to monitor and repair increasingly complex kinds of comprehension problems, such as how to use key words to identify compare-contrast relationships, how to infer such relationships when key words are not provided, and how to use background experience to make inferences beyond what the author implies. Finally, post-reading strategies focus on determining what is particularly important in the text by summarizing and by making judgments based on the author's use of **denotative** (emotionally laden) and **connotative** (neutral) language. Example 8.3 illustrates how to teach comprehension at the expanded fundamentals stage.

Application Stage

As students move into the upper grades, they spend a great deal of time working in content areas such as social studies, literature, science, and mathematics. Consequently, reading content area materials becomes very important and is reflected in the comprehension instruction provided at the application stage.

Here, comprehension strategies emphasize initiating reading in a variety of text types, repairing problems encountered in content area materials, and following up the reading with sophisticated organizational and evaluation strategies, such as drawing conclusions and determining the validity of the

EXAMPLE 8.2   Developing Comprehension Processes at the Initial Mastery Stage

I. **Initiating strategies**

   A. Activate background knowledge of topic

      1. Predict content as signaled by picture and title

   B. Activate background knowledge of text

      1. Recognize story structure and expository structure to predict content

   C. Activate knowledge of author's purpose

II. **During-reading strategies**

   A. Use monitoring strategies to identify problem

   B. Access strategies

      1. Author's meaning

         a. Recognize details

         b. Use typographic cues

         c. Recognize key words

         d. Make inferences about relationships when key words are stated

         e. Make inferences based on author's purpose

         f. Make inferences based on cause and effect, comparisons, sequence, and series

      2. Beyond the author's meaning

         a. Make inferences based on reader's background knowledge

   C. Implement strategies

   D. Verify that the problem is solved

III. **Post-reading strategies**

   A. Use organizing strategies

      1. Recall what is important using text structure

      2. Classify words and phrases

      3. Determine main ideas of expository text

   B. Use evaluating strategies

      1. Judge message content by author's word usage

Kelly Walters had three comprehension strategies that she wanted her first graders to learn as they listened to and read *Alexander and the Terrible, Horrible, No Good, Very Bad Day.* She wanted them to learn how to predict content using story structure knowledge (initiating strategy), how to monitor and verify the accuracy of predictions as they read (during-reading strategy), and how to organize important information by using story structure knowledge (post-reading strategy).

Ms. Walters introduced the book by telling the students that the book described a day where everything went wrong for Alexander. She asked the students to remember things that had gone wrong for them. After they had generated several instances, Ms. Walters moved to her lesson on predicting and verifying predictions using the story structure of beginning, middle, and end as cues for the predictions. Since the students already knew story parts, she taught them how to activate what they knew about the topic and to use the pictures to predict what was going to happen at the beginning, middle, and end of the book.

When the predictions were completed and grouped, the students listened to the story. Ms. Walters periodically stopped to have them verify predictions at the beginning, middle, and end of the book. When predictions were accurate, she acknowledged this and when predictions were inaccurate, she helped them as they created new predictions for each section. When the story was finished, Ms. Walters moved to the post-reading strategy of organizing what was important using their knowledge of story structure. She had the students recall events at the beginning, middle, and end as she wrote their responses on the blackboard. When the responses were completed for each section, Ms. Walters helped the students decide if each response was important or not and had them explain why. They returned to the book as necessary. The final list of important events was read and then recorded so that other students could use their list as they read about Alexander.

EXAMPLE 8.3   Developing Comprehension Processes at the Expanded Fundamentals Stage

I. **Initiating strategies**

   A. *Activate background knowledge of topic*

      1. Predict content as signaled by title and subtitles of text

   B. *Activate background knowledge of text*

      1. Recognize different kinds of meaning are conveyed by different types of text to predict content

   C. *Activate knowledge of author's purpose; combine with reader's purpose to predict*

II. **During-reading strategies**

   A. *Use monitoring strategies to identify problem*

   B. *Access strategies*

      1. Author's meaning

         a. Use key words to note sentence relationships

         b. Recognize pronoun referents

         c. Make inferences about relationships when key words are not stated

         d. Make inferences based on author's cues

      2. Beyond the author's meaning

         a. Make inferences based on reader's background knowledge

   C. *Implement strategies*

   D. *Verify that the problem is solved*

III. **Post-reading strategies**

   A. *Organizing strategies*

      1. Recall what is important

         a. Recognize different types of text structure (stories, articles, poems, letters)

         b. Classify sentences according to common idea or theme

         c. Determine main ideas

   B. *Evaluating strategies*

      1. Judge content of message by author's word usage—denotative and connotative words

      2. Judge content of message by completeness of content development

For his third graders who were reading the book *Spectacles*, John Gutierrez had selected the comprehension strategy of recognizing the author's purpose and combining that with the reader's purpose to predict content (initiating strategy). Since Ellen Raskin wrote *Spectacles* to show that things can be seen in two different ways, Mr. Gutierrez used her purpose to begin a unit about point of view. He told the students that they were beginning a unit that dealt with seeing things from varying points of view.

After describing why varying points of view were important, Mr. Gutierrez introduced the book, *Spectacles,* telling the students why the author had written the book and that the book was about a girl who was nearsighted and had to get glasses. Taking the author's purpose and their own purpose, Mr. Gutierrez helped the students predict what the story was going to be about. After several predictions had been generated, the students read *Spectacles,* stopping periodically to verify predictions and to generate new ones (during-reading strategy).

After the story was read, the students discussed how the author uniquely showed readers that things can be seen in two different ways and how important that is for developing varying points of view. Mr. Gutierrez then used the students' new knowledge about seeing things in two ways as a basis for recognizing the point of view in *Billy Goats Gruff* and had them rewrite that story from the troll's point of view. The stories were shared and added to the class library.

EXAMPLE 8.4   Developing Comprehension Processes at the Application Stage

I. Initiating strategies

   A. *Activate background knowledge of topic*

      1. Predict content as signaled by opening and summarizing paragraphs

   B. *Activate background knowledge of text*

      1. Recognize different types of text have various text structures to predict content

   C. *Recognize reading makes most sense when author's purpose and reader's purpose coincide*

II. During-reading strategies

   A. *Use monitoring strategies to identify problem*

   B. *Access strategies*

      1. Author's meaning

         a. Use key words to note paragraph relationships

         b. Make inferences about relationships between paragraphs based on author's cues

      2. Beyond the author's meaning

         a. Make inferences based on reader's background knowledge

   C. *Implement strategies*

   D. *Verify that the problem is solved*

III. Post-reading strategies

   A. *Organizing strategies*

      1. Recall what is important

         a. Use knowledge of the different types of text structure

         b. Classify paragraphs

         c. Determine main ideas

      2. Draw conclusions

      3. Summarize content

   B. *Evaluating strategies*

      1. Judge content of text in reference to prior experience

      2. Judge author's structuring of text in reference to content

The fifth graders in Donna O'Malley's room were beginning a unit on courage in their reading group. Ms. O'Malley had selected *Julie of the Wolves* as the first selection because Julie showed great courage when she found herself alone and starving on the North Slope of Alaska.

author's position. In general, comprehension strategies taught at the application stage are more complex because the text being read is of greater variety and complexity. Also, signals provided by the author are more subtle, and the reader must be more active in inferring meaning. Example 8.4 illustrates how to teach comprehension at the application stage.

SUMMARY

Comprehension processes focus on the reasoning involved in comprehending, not on the attitudes required or the content of the message itself. The goal is to make students conscious of the reasoning employed by self-regulated readers. You want students to know how to activate background knowledge and make predictions as they begin to read; you want them to monitor their meaning getting and employ strategies if blockages to meaning occur

EXAMPLE 8.4   continued

Julie established social relationships with a pack of wolves in order to survive and eventually helped the wolf pack survive. Ms. O'Malley chose the initiating strategy of recognizing that reading makes most sense when author's purpose and reader's purpose coincide. This fit because she wanted her students to generate characteristics of courageous people, and Jean George had written extensively about Julie's courage.

As the unit began, Ms. O'Malley established with students that a purpose for reading *Julie of the Wolves* was to discover characteristics of courageous people. She followed that with a short lesson on the effectiveness of predicting when author and reader purposes coincide. She modeled how to use the book's cover flaps, where the publisher states that courage was a major component of the book, to establish the author's purpose. The students were alerted as they read to see if they could discover more information about how their purposes and the author's purposes coincided.

Ms. O'Malley's during-reading strategies involved teaching students to make inferences based on their background knowledge. For instance, when Julie made initial contact with the wolf pack leader, he showed anger, but, rather than retreating, she moved closer and triggered acceptance by patting him under the chin. Ms. O'Malley used this instance to model for her students how to make inferences about courage based on their background. She asked her students to recall when they had been confronted by a strange, large dog that had growled or seemed angry. When several did, she asked them what they had felt or done. All said they had been scared and had run away. Ms. O'Malley then related that Julie also was scared and wanted to run away but understood that the only way to get food from the wolf pack was to move forward to get acceptance. Julie showed courage.

For the post-reading strategy, Ms. O'Malley modeled how to draw conclusions by examining what Julie had done and deciding if Julie's behavior showed courage or not. Ms. O'Malley gradually moved from telling her students how to draw conclusions to asking them to draw their own conclusions as she supported them. This reading lesson closed when Ms. O'Malley had her students write stories about people showing courage. These stories became a book that was placed in the classroom library for other students to read as they completed units on courage.

while reading; and you want students to organize and evaluate what they read once they finish. Your role in teaching these strategies is to develop a classroom environment that emphasizes the reading of connected text and to explain to students the strategic reasoning to use when engaged in such reading. You can enhance students' learning of comprehension processes by showing them how many of the same strategies are used by good writers as they compose text. Instruction in comprehension processes begins with listening comprehension at the readiness stage and progresses gradually through more and more complex processes and types of text.

SUGGESTED ADDITIONAL READINGS

BAUMAN, J., & SCHMITT, M. (1986). The what, why, how and when of comprehension instruction. *Reading Teacher, 39,* 640–647.

FARRAR, M. T. (1984). Why do we ask comprehension questions? A new conception of comprehension instruction. *Reading Teacher, 37*(6), 452–456.

GARNER, R. (1982). Resolving comprehension failure through text lookbacks: Direct training and practice effects among good and poor comprehenders in grades six and seven. *Reading Psychology, 3*(3), 221–231.

GORDON, C. (1985). Modeling inference awareness across the curriculum. *Journal of Reading, 28,* 444–447.

GORDON, C. J., & BRAUN, C. (1983). Using story schema as an aid to reading and writing. *Reading Teacher, 37*(2), 116–121.

HOFFMAN, J. V. (1979). Developing flexibility through reflex action. *Reading Teacher, 33*(3), 323–329.

KIMMEL, S., & MACGINITIE, W. (1985). Helping students revise hypotheses while reading. *Reading Teacher, 38*(8), 768–771.

MCGEA, L., & RICHGELS, D. (1985). Teaching expository text structure to elementary students. *Reading Teacher, 38*(8), 739–749.

MCINTOSH, M. (1985). What do practitioners need to know about current inference research? *Reading Teacher, 38*(8), 755–761.

MCKEOWN, M. G. (1979). Developing language awareness, or why leg was once a dirty word. *Language Arts, 56*(2), 175–180.

MOLDOFSKY, P. B. (1983). Teaching students to determine the central story problem: A practical application of schema theory. *Reading Teacher, 36*(8), 740–745.

POINDEXTER, C., & PRESCOTT, S. (1986). A technique for teaching students to draw inferences from text. *Reading Teacher, 39,* 908–911.

READENCE, J., BALDWIN, R. S., & HEAD, M. (1987). Teaching young readers to interpret metaphors. *Reading Teacher, 40,* 439–443.

REUTZEL, D. R. (1985). Story maps improve comprehension. *Reading Teacher, 38*(4), 400–404.

TAYLOR, K. (1984). Teaching summarization skills. *Journal of Reading, 27,* 389–393.

RESEARCH BASE

BAKER, L., & BROWN, A. (1984). Metacognitive skills and reading. In P. D. Pearson (Ed.), *Handbook of reading research* (pp. 353–394). New York: Longman.

DUFFY, G., ROEHLER, L., & MASON, J. (1984). *Comprehension instruction: Perspectives and suggestions.* New York: Longman.

PARIS, S., OKA, E., & DEBRITTO, A. (1983). Beyond decoding: Synthesis of research in reading comprehension. *Educational Leadership, 41,* 78–83.

TIERNEY, R., & CUNNINGHAM, J. (1984). Research on teaching reading comprehension. In P. D. Pearson (Ed.), *Handbook of reading research* (pp. 609–656). New York: Longman.

TIERNEY, R., & PEARSON, P. D. (1983). Toward a composing model of reading. *Language Arts, 60,* 568–580.

Helping Students Study: Process Goals | 9

GETTING READY

Studying is an important part of learning to read. It involves special kinds of reading, traditionally called study skills. However, study skills are more properly described as strategies, since students must be in metacognitive control of the mental processes involved. This chapter describes the process goals for study strategies taught at each stage of developmental reading growth in elementary school. Related writing goals are also described. Again, both what study strategies to teach and how to teach them are discussed. More detailed suggestions for teaching are described in the appropriate chapters in Part 4. Our sample teachers again provide illustrations for various levels.

FOCUS QUESTIONS

- How do study strategies differ from comprehension strategies? from content goals?

- What kinds of study strategies help students become self-regulated?

- What specific strategies are taught to help students locate information? determine reading rate? remember information? organize information? develop study habits?

- How do teachers develop student understanding of study strategies?

- How are study strategies related to writing?

- What are the curricular emphases when teaching study strategy processes at various levels of developmental reading growth?

DEFINING STUDY STRATEGIES

Very early in their school experience students learn that reading is closely associated with study. They learn that books are not only a source of pleasure but also a source of homework. They also learn early that various kinds of text can be used to find needed information. Efficiently finding and using information from various kinds of text requires special abilities.

Study strategies, like word knowledge and comprehension strategies, are process goals because they are the means in a means-end relationship. The end goal is the effective use of textbooks and other study materials, but the means to that end are the strategies good readers use.

Distinguishing Study Strategies from Comprehension

Comprehension is constructing understanding of a given unit of text. The reader processes the text, combines the text information with prior knowledge, and reconstructs the author's message.

Study goes beyond comprehension. Although understanding is a prerequisite, students must do more than simply understand. They must efficiently locate, sort, and remember particular kinds of information, often from a variety of sources. In short, study strategies are more complex than comprehension. While students must comprehend whenever they read, study requires strategies for efficiently dealing with the demands of text. When reading a history text, students must not only comprehend but also must know which parts of the text to read slowly and which to skim, how to organize the material for recall at a later date, and how to restructure the content for use as specified by the context of the content area of history.

Distinguishing Study Strategies from Content Goals

Study strategies are closely associated with **content area reading,** that is, the textbook reading done in association with content areas such as science, mathematics, English, and social studies. To help students understand a textbook author's message, you structure the instructional situation, as described in Chapter 6, to guide students to the desired understanding.

Study also involves locating and using information from a variety of other textual sources in order to achieve some specific goal. Therefore, study strategies go beyond content goals because they focus on textbook use and on gathering and using information from other textual sources.

To summarize, study strategies are those used by expert readers to gather and to use information efficiently from a variety of text sources in order to meet the demands of study. They encompass the efficient use of all types of functional text including textbooks, dictionaries, encyclopedias, newspapers, magazines, and journals. These strategies are used in study situations in which students need to gather, organize, and remember specialized information for particular purposes.

COMPONENTS OF STUDY STRATEGIES

Study strategies are organized into five categories, all of which are used metacognitively. You should teach students to be conscious of how to access

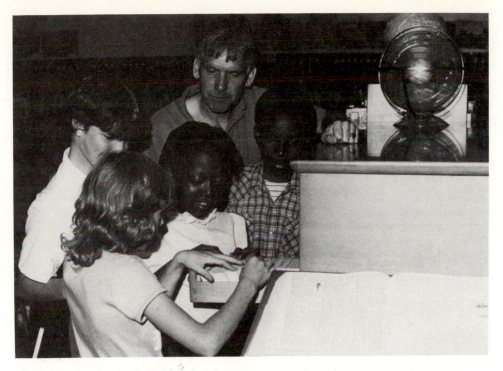

Library strategies include learning how to use card catalogs. (Robert Bawden)

these strategies so they can regulate their meaning getting in specific study situations.

Locational Strategies

Locational strategies, as the name implies, are strategies used to locate information. Your students may need to find specialized information in a particular type of book, periodical, or graphic reference source typically found in libraries or other public agencies. When this occurs, expert readers stop and think, "What do I know about finding such information?" You teach locational strategies to answer that question.

Locational strategies include book part strategies, library strategies, reference source strategies, and graphic strategies. **Book part strategies** include learning how to find specific information in books, through efficient use of the table of contents, index, and glossary. **Library strategies** include learning to use card catalogs and the Dewey Decimal System. **Reference source strategies** include learning how to use dictionaries, encyclopedias, atlases, and other major reference sources. **Graphic strategies** include learning how to use graphs, charts, tables, and other graphic means for displaying information. Table 9.1 pairs the source of information with the applicable strategies.

TABLE 9.1   Strategies for Locating Information

SOURCE	USING
Books	Table of contents, index, glossary, preface, footnotes
Library	Dewey Decimal System, card catalog, indexing
Reference sources	Dictionaries, encyclopedias, atlases
Graphic devices	Charts, maps, tables, figures, illustrations

Rate Strategies

Rate strategies follow logically from locational strategies because once information is located, it must be read. Good students do not read all study materials at the same rate. Instead, they read at varying rates of speed, depending upon the situation. The curricular goal here is to teach your students to ask themselves, "How fast should I read this material in order to get the information I need?" and then to show them how to vary reading rate according to the demands of the situation.

Using a variety of reading rates is not the same as speed reading. In fact, speed reading has no real place in the elementary reading curriculum because it is highly specialized and of limited use. Adjusting the rate of reading to one's purpose, however, is something all your students can learn to do, and it is applicable to many study situations. It involves teaching your students that good readers read at a very rapid **scanning** pace when previewing material or glancing through it to see if it contains the information being sought, at a rapid, **skimming** pace when looking for a key word or key idea that locates the information being sought in that particular section, and at a slow and careful pace when the reader has located the exact part of the text where specific information is located. In preparing a report on atomic energy, for instance, a student might scan a book on nuclear reactors to see if it contains relevant information, skim a particular chapter in the book to locate particular sections of interest, and then read those sections slowly.

Reading rate is one of the keys to efficient study. Instead of reading every word, expert readers scan to find potentially helpful information, skim that information to locate key words that signal discussion of the information they need, and read carefully only the text that is particularly helpful.

Remembering Strategies

Remembering strategies follow logically from rate strategies because once information has been read, students must remember it, particularly in study situations. When the need to remember information arises, your students should stop and think, "This is information that I am going to have to remember. What do I know about remembering difficult material that will help me here?"

The best-known technique for remembering what is read is SQ3R. **SQ3R** stands for the following steps: survey, question, read, recite, and review. With this system, you teach students to survey the text to be read to get the general idea of what is coming; use the headings, subheadings, and other graphic cues to predict what questions might be asked at the end of each chapter; read the text with those questions in mind; check to see if they know the answers to these questions after reading the text; and review the material for answers to any questions that they were unable to recite. This simple five-step pattern has repeatedly proven effective in improving students' retention of the material read in texts. It works well because it involves readers in establishing purposes for reading, allows them to get a feel for the text through an initial survey, encourages reading to confirm or disprove predictions embodied in the questions, and promotes the habit of checking to make sure that predictions have indeed been confirmed.

Summarizing is another good technique for remembering. Summarization requires that after reading a passage of difficult text the reader should extract the important points and then restate the passage in terms of just those points. In doing so, students are aided in separating less important information from crucial information. Similarly, main idea strategies, in which students distinguish passage details from the gist, are helpful for remembering. Other strategies for remembering, similar to SQ3R and summarizing, are detailed in Chapter 18.

Organizing Strategies

Reading for study purposes is characterized by two kinds of difficulties: The material is often complex, and it is often necessary to collect information from more than one source. You teach **organizing strategies** when your students are faced with such difficulties and say to themselves, "How am I going to put all this information into a sensible order?"

There are three major kinds of organizing strategies: note taking, outlining, and semantic maps. Note taking involves teaching students to identify both the purpose of note taking (what information is needed?) and the structure of the text (what headings, subheadings, and other devices does the author provide to help?); to use both the purpose and the text structure to identify particularly important information; and to condense relevant information into note form. It is helpful to teach your students how to use 3" by 5" note cards for note taking.

Outlining involves teaching students to organize their notes into a series of major headings and more detailed subheadings. You might show them how to physically group note cards in piles under each major heading and then to put the note cards in each category into the desired sequence.

Semantic mapping can be used both before and after reading to organize information. Before reading, you can put the topic for the day on the blackboard and have students tell what they know about it. As they provide concepts and ideas from their prior knowledge, organize them into categories.

For instance, if the topic is Alaska, students might suggest *cold, Eskimos,* and *igloos* as ideas they already possess about Alaska. Organize these into a semantic map with the categories *climate, people,* and *housing,* respectively. After reading, have your students contribute additional ideas and concepts that might alter the semantic map, noting for instance that parts of Alaska are relatively warm, that many different kinds of people live in Alaska, and that there are modern buildings and houses throughout Alaska. Through the use of semantic mapping, your students can organize large amounts of information.

Such organization strategies serve three purposes. First, they help students sort out complex material or combine material from several sources into a comprehensible form. Second, they help students remember important information. Finally, they help students transform what they have read into written form.

Study Habits

Study habits include a variety of abilities crucial to effective studying. One is organizing time to study. When students wonder why they are falling behind their classmates, the answer may be that their peers are making better use of their study time. Your students can learn to control this problem if you teach them to use free time efficiently, by estimating available study time, by prioritizing study assignments, and by making a "time budget" to distribute available time according to priorities.

Other important study habits include learning to follow directions and how to take tests. Students can be taught to follow directions and to be strategic when taking tests. Table 9.2 gives examples of some test-taking strategies.

To summarize, like metacognitive strategies for word recognition and vocabulary and for comprehension, study strategies are taught in a problem-solving mode. That is, readers are taught to monitor their study and to access and use strategies appropriate for solving specific problems. If the study problem is one of locating information, you want students to use locational strategies. If the problem is determining how carefully material must be read, you want students to use rate strategies. If the problem is one of recalling text information, you want students to use remembering strategies. If the problem is organizing information, you want students to use organizational strategies. If the problem is efficient study, you want students to use study habit strategies.

INSTRUCTIONAL EMPHASIS IN STUDY STRATEGIES

As with other curricular goals, instruction in study strategies can be discussed in terms of indirect instruction in a literate environment and the more direct instruction associated with teacher mediation.

TABLE 9.2   Strategies for Taking Tests

TEST SITUATION	STRATEGY
Students psychologically freeze and forget what they know	Complete practice tests for familiarization with materials, environments, and expectations
Students start answering questions too soon	Practice looking over the test to see what is required
Students do not plan time well and end up without time to finish	Allocate a specific amount of time to teach part of the test before beginning
Students do not read the directions carefully	Teach students to read directions and to follow directions as stated
Students get stuck on one hard question and do not answer other questions	Teach students to answer questions they know first and to save the hardest questions for the end
Students skip questions they are unsure of	Teach students to make educated guesses unless there is a penalty for wrong answers
Students spend extra time on questions that have little value	Teach students to answer first those questions that have the most value
Students leave no time to check over their tests	Teach students to save the last 2 or 3 minuts to check over their tests
Students do not read multiple choice tests carefully	Teach students to read questions carefully, to find answers that are clearly wrong first and to select the best answer from among those choices remaining
Students do not prepare themselves physically or mentally for the test	Teach students to get a good night's rest, to eat before the test, and to review before taking the test
Students do not look at corrected tests	Teach students to analyze to determine whether incorrect answers were due to misinterpreting directions, faulty time allocation, lack of information, etc. so that the same mistakes will not be repeated

The Literate Environment

The primary function of the literate environment is to help students develop accurate conceptual understandings and positive feelings. This is a particularly difficult task when teaching study strategies because most students have negative feelings about studying.

A properly developed literate environment helps transform studying from boring work on meaningless topics into a satisfying experience involving curiosity and empowerment. To accomplish this, you must structure a classroom environment in which required topics are presented in light of your students' interests, and you must ensure that your students interact with content in meaningful and interesting ways. If the class is studying Alaska, you and your students might decide to produce travel brochures designed to entice tourists to visit Alaska, rather than simply read a textbook chapter on Alaska and then answer a few end-of-chapter questions. To produce the brochures, you would have to teach your students to locate information, how to use reading rate strategies, how to remember pertinent information, and how to organize it in preparation for writing the brochure. Hence, study strategies become part of an environment that emphasizes pursuit of an interesting and meaningful project. As a result, your students develop better concepts about study, have more positive feelings about engaging in study activities, and are better motivated.

The trick in developing a literate environment for study strategies is to make every effort to transform study content into projects meaningful to students. **Teacher-pupil planning** is often useful here. This technique calls for you to introduce new subject matter content by talking with your students about their interests with that topic. Then use the expressed interests to develop meaningful study projects. Such planning demands extra effort from you, but the payoff in your students' motivation to study justifies it.

Direct Teacher Guidance

Whereas efforts to develop positive study environments are covert, developing study strategies is an overt process. In teaching study strategies, you focus on helping students become metacognitively aware of what the study strategies are, when it is appropriate to use each one, and the mental processes they should employ with each.

In providing such overt instruction, use the modified directed reading lesson presented in Chapter 7. Start by identifying the situation where the study strategy will be used in that day's work, and then provide explicit information about what the strategy is, when it will be used, and how to use it (including a model or demonstration). After modeling the strategy, provide students with opportunities to try out the strategy themselves, giving additional help as needed. Finally, when your students understand how to use the strategy, return to the task for the day, reminding students that they should apply the newly learned strategy in completing the task.

In the previous example about making brochures about Alaska, your students may have to read information books that contain difficult terminology. Therefore, you may decide to teach a lesson on dictionary usage so that while using the information books students will be able to locate the meaning of difficult words. Consequently, you would introduce the lesson by referring to the difficult words students are likely to encounter in the reading they are doing in preparation for making the brochures. State that you are going to provide them with a strategy for finding out the meaning of such words, and give them explicit instructions for using the dictionary. Part of this instruction

Students learn to use the dictionary as a study strategy for finding the meaning of unknown words. (RH Photo by Peter Vadnai)

involves expressing your thought processes as you use the dictionary. Then give students the opportunity to use the dictionary to find the meaning of unknown words, and provide assistance as needed. After students have demonstrated competence with the dictionary, have them return to their reading assignments about Alaska using the dictionary as needed.

Integration with Writing

Study strategies are not limited to reading. In fact, because most study involves written assignments of some kind (reports, essays, homework), study strategies are as applicable to writing as to reading. Consequently, students should be taught study strategies as part of the writing curriculum as well.

In the previous example, study strategies are used both in reading about Alaska and in preparing the brochures about Alaska. Hence, study strategies can be taught in an integrated reading-writing situation.

TEACHING STUDY STRATEGIES AT VARIOUS DEVELOPMENTAL LEVELS

There is relatively little instructional emphasis on study strategies at the readiness and initial mastery stages, but a progressively heavier emphasis as students move through the expanded fundamentals and application stages. This is because formal study of subject matter such as social studies and science begins to receive emphasis at about fourth grade.

Readiness Stage

There is very little emphasis on study strategies at the readiness stage. Students at this level do not read and write, and their listening comprehension activities call for little subject matter learning involving complex material or multiple information sources. The only study strategy that receives any emphasis at this stage is learning to follow oral directions involving two or three steps. This is the beginning of instruction in following directions that increases in complexity as students move to the more demanding situations at higher grade levels. Example 9.1 illustrates how to teach following directions at the readiness stage.

Initial Mastery Stage

As with the readiness stage, there is little emphasis on study strategies in first and second grade. This is because the academic efforts of students at this stage are devoted almost exclusively to learning how to read, and relatively little emphasis is placed on learning any subject matter or on associated study activities.

However, first and second grade teachers do provide initial instruction in study strategies, which forms the basis for more in-depth study at later stages. For instance, first and second grade teachers continue to provide instruction in following directions and introduce such study habits as getting

---

EXAMPLE 9.1   Developing Study Strategies at the Readiness Stage

I. Study strategies

  A. *Study habits*

    1. Following simple oral directions

For study strategies, Linda Chang taught her kindergarten class how to follow oral directions. Since they had already heard the story of *Swimmy*, she used that information as the content for a lesson on following directions. First, she modeled how she successfully follows directions. Then, in small groups, each student was given a picture of Swimmy the black fish, a big fish, some red fish, and a jellyfish. Ms. Chang began with two directions, telling the children to put Swimmy at the left corner of their page on the first line and then to put the big fish next to Swimmy on the same line. She continued giving directions for two items until every member of the group was successful. The students worked in pairs checking each other's work. Ms. Chang then increased the number of directions to three and continued having children work in pairs. Toward the end of the lesson, students were asked to give three directions to the other members of the group, using the *Swimmy* characters. The lesson ended when Ms. Chang had the students review what they had learned about following directions.

proper rest in order to pursue study tasks. Additionally, students at this level are introduced to locational skills through picture dictionaries; they are taught simplified versions of SQ3R to help them remember certain kinds of information; and they use simple semantic maps to organize information. These efforts are introductory in nature, however, because in the absence of heavy subject matter demands in first and second grade, there is relatively little call for study strategies. Example 9.2 illustrates how to study strategies at the initial mastery stage.

Expanded Fundamentals Stage

By grades 3 and 4, instruction in study strategies noticeably increases. Students encounter their first subject matter, such as social studies and science, and are first assigned to read textbooks that typically accompany the study of these subjects. As subject matter instruction increases, the need for study strategies becomes apparent, and more and more instructional time is devoted to it.

Students at the expanded fundamentals stage receive serious instruction in locational strategies, including use of the library, book parts, and dictionaries and encyclopedias, as well as interpretation of simple graphs and charts. Students are taught to make initial adjustments in reading rate, to use

---

EXAMPLE 9.2   Developing Study Strategies at the Initial Mastery Stage

I. Study strategies

   A. Study habits

      1. Follow directions
      2. Proper rest for academic work

   B. Locational strategies

      1. Picture dictionaries

   C. Remembering strategies

      1. Simple SQ3R

   D. Organizing strategies

      1. Simple semantic maps

A group of first graders eagerly gathered around Kelly Walters for their reading class. Earlier she had asked them to remember what happened to Alexander in *Alexander and the Terrible, Horrible, No Good, Very Bad Day* and had told them they would use what they remembered in their reading lesson. Ms. Walters planned to use what they remembered to teach them how to follow directions. Each student was given a set of cards with each card having one event from the story about Alexander printed on it (going to the dentist, getting shoes, seeing Dad, riding in the car, etc.). After modeling how to follow directions and reading the phrases aloud, Ms. Walters began with two directions that required students to put the "seeing Dad" card first and the "riding in the car" card second. When the students were easily handling two directions, she began giving them three directions. The students worked in pairs, checking to see if the cards were placed in the order given by the teacher. The lesson ended when the students reviewed what they had learned about following directions.

SQ3R and summarizing techniques to remember information, and to increase their use of both semantic maps and techniques for following directions. Example 9.3 illustrates how to teach study strategies at the expanded fundamentals stage.

Application Stage

The heaviest emphasis on study strategies occurs in the upper grades. This is because in grades 5 through 8 the instructional emphasis shifts from learning how to read to learning through reading. At the upper grades teachers expect students to already know the rudiments of how to read so they devote much of their instructional effort to the more specialized demands of study. Because most middle schools and junior high schools are departmentalized by subject matter, students are taught study strategies in the context of their social studies, science, English, and math classes.

The strategies also become more complex at this stage. Study habits no longer emphasize following directions, but focus on helping students organize study time and take tests; locational strategies move into indexing, the

---

EXAMPLE 9.3   Developing Study Strategies at the Expanded Fundamentals Stage

I. Study strategies

A. Locational strategies

1. Use the library card catalog to locate books by title or author
2. Use a book's table of contents and glossary to locate information
3. Use a dictionary to find word meanings
4. Use simple bar and line graphs to gain meaning

B. Rate strategies

1. Use a slow pace for careful reading
2. Use a fast pace for skimming

C. Remembering strategies

1. Summarize

D. Organizing strategies

1. Develop semantic maps

E. Study habits

1. Follow written directions involving three or more parts

In John Gutierrez's third grade class, the students read *Spectacles* as part of a unit on the care of eyes. Mr. Gutierrez decided to have the students organize the information on eye care by creating a semantic map. After reading the book, students listed all the things they remembered about eye care. Since *Spectacles* describes the sequence of getting glasses (recognizing a problem, visiting the eye doctor, visiting the optician, selecting frames, wearing glasses, correcting the problem), Mr. Gutierrez used sequence as the way to organize the semantic map. As a group, the students classified the events under what happened first, second, third, and so forth as Mr. Gutierrez completed a semantic map on the board. Multiple copies of the semantic map were made, and it became a source of information as students completed the unit on eye care.

EXAMPLE 9.4   Developing Study Strategies at the Application Stage

I. Study strategies

  A. *Locational strategies*

    1. Use a book's table of contents, glossary, and index to locate information
    2. Use library card catalogs and the Dewey Decimal System to locate information
    3. Use dictionaries, encyclopedias, atlases, thesauri, etc. to locate information
    4. Use graphs, charts, tables, etc. to locate information

  B. *Rate strategies*

    1. Scanning pace
    2. Skimming pace
    3. Careful slow pace

  C. *Remembering strategies*

    1. SQ3R—survey, question, read, recite, and review (and variations of this technique)
    2. Summarizing

  D. *Organizing strategies*

    1. Note taking
    2. Outlining
    3. Semantic maps

  E. *Study habits*

    1. Organizing time
    2. Test taking

The students in Donna O'Malley's fifth grade class were well into their unit on courage. Because they were very excited by the unit and wanted to find out more about courage, she taught them study strategies they could use to find more information on their own. For locational strategies, she taught them how to use the subject index of the card catalog in the library and gave them opportunities to use it during reading time and free time in order to find more information on courage. For rate strategies, Ms. O'Malley taught her students how to scan so they wouldn't have to read every word they found about courage. When the students knew how to scan, they could more easily decide if the information they found was suited to their purposes. For remembering strategies, the students learned how to summarize. First Ms. O'Malley modeled summarizing; then the students practiced summarizing as they collected information on courage. For organizing strategies, Ms. O'Malley taught her students how to take notes in which they primarily recorded summaries in phrase form. The students used their summarizing strategies and note-taking strategies as they collected information about courage.

When the students showed signs that they were ready to move to the next section of the unit, Ms. O'Malley helped them generate a lengthy list of the information they had collected about courage. Because the students knew how to group and classify, they created a semantic map from this list. Small groups of students then chose the part of the semantic map about which they had gathered information and decided how to present it to the rest of the class. Some students wrote stories like *Julie of the Wolves,* while others created plays and others wrote factual articles. The unit culminated with a "courage seminar" for the principal and parents during which the students shared their knowledge about courage.

thesaurus, atlases, and complex graphic material; reading rate breaks fast reading down into skimming and scanning; and organizing is broadened to include heavy emphasis on note taking and outlining. Example 9.4 illustrates how to teach study strategies at the application stage.

SUMMARY

Although study strategies are based in comprehension processes and are used in situations where the focus is text content, they are different from both comprehension processes and content goals. This is because study strategies go beyond the construction of meaning to focus on how to deal efficiently with the demands of study. The intent is to help students become metacognitive about study strategies so they can be in control of the studying they are faced with. Five kinds of study strategies help students become more efficient about study demands: strategies for locating information, for determining rate, for remembering information, for organizing information, and for using helpful study habits. Your role is to create an environment where study is meaningfully employed and to explain to students the reasoning involved when using study strategies in those situations, both in reading and in writing. Instruction in study strategies receives relatively little emphasis at the early developmental stages but gradually increases as students encounter more and more complex text in the upper grades.

SUGGESTED ADDITIONAL READINGS

BEAN, T., SINGER, H., & COWAN, S. (1985). Analogical study guides: Improving comprehension in science. *Journal of Reading, 29,* 246–250.

BROMLEY, K. D. (1985). Precise writing and outlining enhance content learning. *Reading Teacher, 38*(4), 406–411.

FINLEY, C., & SEATON, M. (1987). Using text patterns and question prediction to study for tests. *Journal of Reading, 31,* 124–132.

LANGER, J. (1986). Learning through writing: Study skills in the content areas. *Journal of Reading, 29,* 400–406.

MUIR, S. (1985). Understanding and improving students' map reading skills. *Elementary School Journal, 86,* 207–216.

REINKING, D. (1986). Integrating graphic aids into content area instruction: The graphic information lesson. *Journal of Reading, 30,* 146–151.

ROGERS, D. G. (1984). Assessing study skills. *Journal of Reading, 27*(4), 346–354.

SIMPSON, M. (1984). The status of study strategy instruction: Implications for classroom teachers. *Journal of Reading, 28,* 136–143.

STEWARD, O., & GREEN, D. S. (1983). Test-taking skills for standardized tests of reading. *Reading Teacher, 36*(7), 634–638.

WRIGHTS, J. P., & ANDREASEN, N. L. (1980). Practice in using location skills in a content area. *Reading Teacher, 34*(2), 184–186.

RESEARCH BASE

ANDERSON, T. H., & ARMBRUSTER, B. B. (1984). Studying. In P. D. Pearson (Ed.), *Handbook of reading research.* New York: Longman.

BEACH, R., & APPLEMAN, D. (1984). Reading strategies for expository and literary text types. In A. Purves & O. Niles (Eds.), *Becoming a reader in a complex society.* Eighty-third Yearbook of the National Society for the Study of Education (Part 1). Chicago: University of Chicago Press.

Part 3

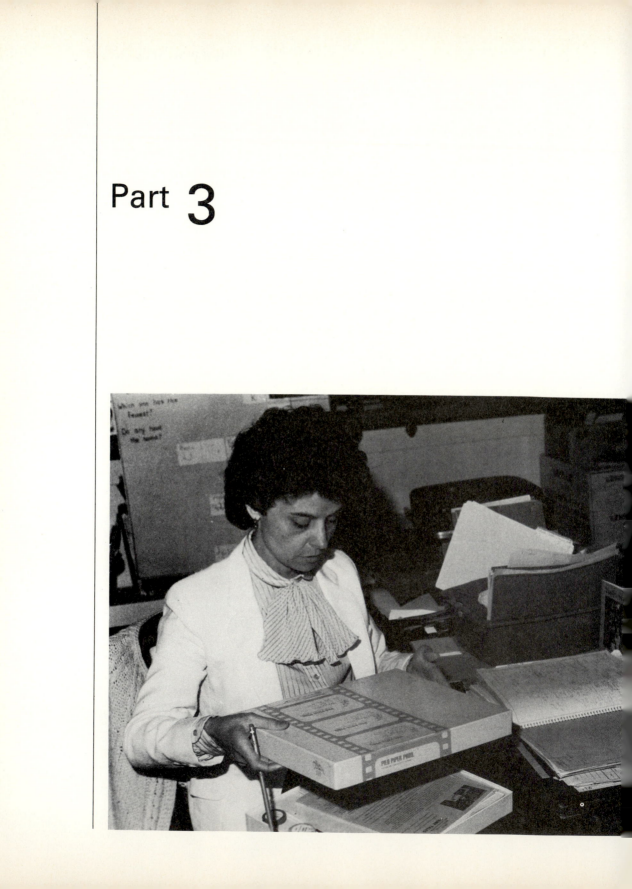

Getting Organized for Instruction

The knowledge about what to teach provided in previous chapters represents an important foundation for reading instruction. In addition to knowing what to teach, however, you must also know how to organize for instruction. The five chapters in this section provide suggestions that will help you to arrange your classroom environment to promote literacy, to group students, to adapt basal textbook prescriptions, to organize instruction into units and lessons, and to manage classroom reading instruction efficiently.

10

How to Establish a Literate Environment:
The Key to Whole Language Instruction

GETTING READY

What your students think and feel about reading depends on the environment in which they learn to read. Different concepts develop depending on whether the environment you create emphasizes nonliterate tasks or whole language activities involving books, libraries, and writing.

This chapter describes how to promote accurate concepts about reading by establishing a literate environment in the classroom. Creating such an environment, which emphasizes the pursuit of literate activities, is a fundamental part of organizing for instruction.

FOCUS QUESTIONS

- Why is a literate environment necessary?

- What does the physical environment consist of?

- What does the intellectual environment consist of?

- What does the social-emotional environment consist of?

- How do I get ready to use the literate environment for indirect instruction?

IMPORTANCE OF A CONCEPTUAL FOUNDATION

Reading cannot be taught in isolation. The instructional environment must provide a supportive conceptual foundation for what reading is and for what good readers do by emphasizing the pursuit of literate activities.

What happens if reading is taught in an environment that does not emphasize literate activities? Consider the experience of one teacher. A new student came to her fifth grade class from a large-city school district where heavy emphasis was placed on mastering long lists of skills and in which

164

instruction consisted of following the teacher's directions. The day the new boy arrived, the teacher was confronted with a negative attitude.

T: I'm going to explain how to use a strategy to solve a problem encountered when reading.

S: How many of these dumb things do I have to learn?

T: Only as many as you need to make sense out of what you read.

S: And you call yourself a teacher?

It is clear that students' understandings about reading are a product of the interpretation they make of their environment. The student in this example interpreted his previous school environment to mean that reading is learning a list of skills dictated by the teacher. He had no idea that reading is a meaning-getting process or that making sense of text depends on the reader's ability to impose meaning on it. He carried this concept from his former school into the new classroom. If the old understandings remain unchanged, no amount of explicit teacher explanations about strategy use will work, because the boy will continue to try to make the new teacher's explanations fit his old understandings of skills and following teacher directions.

Another teacher related that she was having trouble getting her fourth grade students to use fix-it strategies because they refused to admit they had problems with reading. When her students encountered an unknown word or an unfamiliar idea, they tried to maintain an illusion of fluency by bluffing their way through it. It is not hard to understand why they did this. Their first, second, and third grade instruction had emphasized fluency, accuracy, and oral round robin reading, and their former teachers had chastised them for not knowing all the words or not instantly answering all the comprehension questions. These teachers conveyed the message that reading is knowing words and answers instantly, not that reading involves reasoning. Consequently, when these students got to fourth grade, they operated on the concepts learned from earlier teachers. If these old concepts remain unchanged, these students will continue to try to make their fourth grade teacher's instruction fit their old concept that reading is error-free fluency.

In both cases, the new teacher's success depends on changing students' concepts about reading and about what good readers do. That is, the teacher must build an instructional foundation that causes students to think differently. A literate environment in the classroom is a major force in building desired conceptual understandings about reading.

PURPOSE OF A LITERATE ENVIRONMENT

In a literate environment, the most visible classroom activities illustrate, in an atmosphere of love and fun, how language is used for real purposes. For

165

instance, there is an emphasis on free-choice reading; on student authorship; on various kinds of writing for communicating real and important messages; on projects that involve reading directions and other kinds of functional materials; on a variety of different kinds of text, from newspapers and catalogs to student-written books; on the teacher's own engagement in reading and writing activities; and on the sharing of enjoyable and functional literacy events. Although the more traditional tasks associated with school are also evident, the emphasis is on real language, and the classroom reflects the flair and excitement that comes with real language use. The teacher's intent is to provide daily evidence that reading is a meaning-getting process and that what we are trying to learn during reading class is to send and receive real messages. When provided with such evidence, students become aware of why they are learning what they are learning about reading. In short, the reading instruction becomes meaningful, and students gradually build accurate concepts that provide a foundation for instruction. In contrast, if the classroom environment emphasizes nonliterate tasks, such as isolated work sheets, memorized rules, procedures, and endless skill tests, students tend to conclude that the name of the reading game is to "get done," and reading instruction is based on inaccurate concepts.

WHAT A LITERATE ENVIRONMENT LOOKS LIKE

In a literate environment, the classroom should emphasize whole language. There should be many examples of literacy and language in action—real language and real literacy. Instead of the traditional situation in which a teacher talks and everyone else is quiet, the literate environment encourages various kinds of oral and written student communication. Instead of limiting written material to textbooks, many other kinds of printed materials are used as well, including trade books, magazines, comic books, catalogs, recipes, and newspapers. Writing is not taught as a separate subject with an emphasis on neatness and accuracy of script, but is integrated into reading activities along with speaking and listening.

In a global sense, then, a literate environment provides numerous opportunities for students to encounter and participate in real language and literacy experiences, thereby increasing the chances they will develop accurate concepts about reading and positive feelings for it. Teachers deliberately create these opportunities.

Consider seatwork and how it can be changed to match the characteristics of a literate environment. In many classrooms it is not unusual to see students sitting at desks completing piles of ditto and practice sheets geared to habituate isolated skills and bits of knowledge. Communication is at a minimum, and the emphasis is on busy work. In contrast, in a literate environment seatwork might include independent reading for information or pleasure or journal writing for reflective or expressive purposes. Seatwork is often done in pairs rather than individually, and it includes shared oral reading, think

Teachers should provide daily evidence that reading class teaches about receiving and sending oral messages. (RH Photo by Peter Vadnai)

aloud activities to develop reasoning abilities, peer tutoring, interviews, and **author's chair** activities in which student authors are interviewed about their creativity and craftsmanship. Small-group activities include collaborative group assessment of stories and articles, creative drama development, teacher-made games for practicing strategies and skills, and cooperative group discussions of other content areas. All of these examples of seatwork reflect literate activity and would be part of a literate environment.

A classroom environment is what the teacher makes it. It *is* possible to create alternatives to traditional classroom environments so that students build accurate conceptual foundations about what reading is and what it is used for.

COMPONENTS OF A LITERATE ENVIRONMENT

You create a literate environment by orchestrating physical, intellectual, and social-emotional environments. The physical environment refers to things physically evident in the classroom; the intellectual environment consists of mental challenge; and the social-emotional environment encourages socialization with language. Use these environments to create an atmosphere in which meaningful language becomes an integral part of daily activities.

Physical Environment

To establish a physical environment conducive to literacy, print must be everywhere. In most areas where Americans live, print guides and challenges our everyday lives. A trip to the store is guided by stop signs, yield signs, walk and don't walk signs. Printed sales slips record our purchases, and we keep track of them in checkbooks. Billboards and written advertisements challenge and entice us to try certain products. Consumer magazines assist us as we attempt to select the best products. Editorials persuade us to consider a certain point of view, and books and magazine provide challenges, enticements, and entertainment.

You should create a similar environment in your classroom by displaying print prominently and using it in a variety of ways. Display classroom rules, directions, and procedures in print. Encourage your students to verify uncertainties by referring to a printed reference. Encourage recreational activities, such as free reading, choral reading, sharing of poetry, etc., and encourage sharing of reference work, as when students turn to a recipe book for a class cooking project or to directions for assembling something the class has ordered. Display printed language that issues challenges to the students; and display thought-provoking questions around the room on bulletin boards, chalkboards, and display tables with printed answers to the questions placed close by or with written directions for where to find the answers attached to the questions.

Draw your students' attention to the integrated nature of language use, to the way all the language modes are used for communication. Your students will learn what you emphasize; if you talk about the integrated nature of language, your students will become aware of it. Consequently, your physical environment should include not only the prominent display of print but also tangible evidence of the integrated nature of print and its relationship with other language modes.

Intellectual Environment

You cannot base a literate environment on physical environment alone; an intellectual environment must accompany it. You orchestrate the intellectual environment by creating challenges. This is done by setting expectations, by modeling, and by capitalizing on your students' interests and motivation.

Expectations Challenges always involve the possibility of failure; the trick is to choose the right challenge. Part of choosing the right challenge lies with the concept of **expectations.**

The expectations of those around us influence how we view ourselves. Consequently, the expectations you communicate to your students can lead

Teachers model recreational reading as part of the intellectual environment. (Robert Bawden)

them to believe that they can become literate. Do your words and actions convey negative feelings about risk taking, or do they convey trust and the feeling that it is okay to fail when trying something new because we learn from our mistakes? Do your words imply that only perfection is acceptable, or do you value ever closer approximations as students move toward a final goal? You should set the expectations that all your students can learn, that learning takes time, that failures and mistakes are inevitable and no reason to quit. By setting positive expectations, you make it easier for your students to accept challenges and to persevere in completing them.

We communicate expectations about language as well as about people. For instance, in talking with your students, you establish expectations about the integrated nature of language by ensuring that what is written will be read by someone; by emphasizing that language is a tool for conveying information, ideas, and experiences; and by making sure reading is seen as one of the four language modes, not as an isolated skill.

Modeling Modeling, a powerful tool for learning, influences us at all levels of development. At a very early age, we watch others and then do what we see them doing. Much of our early learning comes from emulating a model, and you can use this phenomenon to develop a strong intellectual environment. You can model the reading of books and how we use reading to understand others, and you can model the need to communicate in writing (with the principal's office, with other teachers, and with the parents). Make an effort to model all possible uses of the written word.

Interests Student interests are the areas of knowledge your students are curious about and want to explore. Topics such as dinosaurs, tornadoes, horses, and unexplained events fall into this category for many children. When you want your students to use language (especially reading), high-interest topics such as these can be used to create challenges they are willing to pursue.

One strategy is to have your students themselves become resident experts on topics of interest to them. Each student selects an interest area such as whales, doll making, or computers and becomes the class expert through extensive reading. You then direct all questions on the topic to that student. This is also an excellent way to illustrate the integrated nature of language, since all four language modes are typically used when the resident experts are consulted.

Internal Motivators Most students possess a set of **internal motivators** that, when activated by well-chosen activities, produce a positive attitude toward the activity and result in higher achievement.

The first internal motivator is choice. Whenever students are provided choice during activities, motivation is activated. You are employing choice when you include the selection of two or three activities or topics for your students to choose from, the selection of the language mode to use (listen or read, speak or write), and the selection of the time necessary to complete the activities.

A second internal motivator is the opportunity to act like an adult. Most students enjoy opportunities to pretend being the teacher, whether it is with pairs of students, a small group of students, or an entire class of students. You can add this internal motivator to many different types of activities.

A third internal motivator is the opportunity to alter language. Activities such as creating new definitions for words (*illegal* is a sick bird; *bulldozer* is a sleeping bovine) are helpful; students may also create new words for definitions (a very fast car is a *zoommobile;* an awesome football team is the *terror machine*).

Another internal motivator is the opportunity to create language. You can do this by having your students create poems, stories, or articles. A sixth grade student created the following story patterned after Remy Charlip's *Fortunately.*

> Fortunately I had a friend
> Unfortunately he died.
> Fortunately there was a funeral.
> Unfortunately it was sad.

Fortunately there were flowers.

Unfortunately I wish there were more.

Fortunately everyone was there.

Fortunately so was I.

Fortunately I want to be just like him.

A second grade student created the following paragraph as part of an activity that encouraged him to create language.

All about Computers

I will answer five questions about computers.

What are the five main parts of a computer? The five main parts of a computer are the control unit, the arithmetic unit, memory devices, input devices, and output devices.

Where did the word computer get its name? The computer got its name from compute.

Why do computers punch holes? The holes are for computers to read.

What does COBOL stand for? COBOL stands for common business oriented language.

Is there any such thing as a computer language? Yes, COBOL is a computer language.

The main idea is about computers, how come they punch holes, what the five main parts of a computer are, and what COBOL stands for.

Whenever you activate these internal motivators, you increase the possibility of student engagement and success.

One example of how the intellectual environment can be orchestrated using expectations, modeling, interests, and motivation is a technique called uninterrupted sustained silent reading (USSR). USSR is a good example of indirect instruction designed to develop accurate concepts and positive feelings about reading. The technique is deceptively simple: you and your students read books of their choice individually for sustained periods of time each day. The purpose is to get your students hooked on reading and to offer them sustained opportunities to practice real reading. It works because you set an expectation that all students will read, you model reading and students emulate you, you account for the interest of every student through individual choice of books, and you account for motivation by allowing your students choice of what to read, how much to read, and how to follow up on the reading. The steps in establishing USSR in the classroom are listed in Figure 10.1.

FIGURE 10.1   Establishing USSR in Classrooms

Step 1   Establish a spot in the room for a room library.

Step 2   Choose three to five books per student.

Step 3   Select books that range in topic and difficulty.

Step 4   Include magazines, newspapers, comics, and catalogs.

Step 5   Have each student choose something to read.

Step 6   Keep the first session only 5 minutes long (or less).

Step 7   Increase each succeeding session by 1 minute until the desired length of time is attained.

Step 8   Periodically change the books, usually every month or so.

Step 9   Have students keep some sort of record of what they are reading, but do not give grades or establish competitions for the most books read.

Step 10   Periodically have sessions with your students to share what they've read and to talk about the nature of reading. Keep these sessions very informal.

Social-Emotional Environment

Literacy and the social-emotional environment in which literacy occurs are closely related. Literacy is the communication of ideas and, as such, is a social event influenced by the emotions of the communication. Consequently, you should orchestrate social-emotional factors when building a literate environment. These factors include social interactions and collaborative sharing.

Social Interactions   The quality of the social interactions accompanying reading activities influences your students' feelings and concepts about reading. When your students discuss a book together (such as Sendak's *Where the Wild Things Are* or White's *Charlotte's Web*), they not only have the opportunity to express their own concepts and feelings but to hear others expressing theirs. As a result of this social interaction, they modify their own feelings and concepts about reading. Social interactions help promote the understanding that reading is communication and that communication brings satisfaction.

Collaborative Sharing   Collaborative sharing is a specialized type of communication that assists in developing positive attitudes about reading. In **collaborative sharing,** you assign each member of the group a responsibility. One student is the facilitator, another the recorder, another the researcher, and so on. Group size is determined by the number of responsibilities; the usual number is three or four. The facilitator keeps the group on task and makes certain everyone participates; the recorder keeps a written record of the interaction; and the researcher goes back to the original source of the information when needed. If any group member has difficulty, all group members help. Since everyone has a responsible role to play within the group, social interactions bring high status to everyone, not just to those who already enjoy it. When you arrange your environment to include such sharing, the high status felt by all students increases the feeling that reading is satisfying while also enriching the concept that reading, writing, talking, and listening are all elements of communication.

CREATING A LITERATE ENVIRONMENT

The planning of a literate environment starts with the three goals of reading instruction developed in Chapter 3. You first decide what curricular goals to work toward, then build a literate environment designed to support these goals. Use the following six-part guide to build a literate environment.

1. Decide on the goals you wish to develop. Attitude goals are best developed through activities associated with the literate environment. For these goals, the environment plays the dominant role, whereas for process and content goals, the teacher plays the dominant role. Select the curriculum goals you wish to achieve with your class (see Chapter 3). At the readiness and initial mastery stages, you might select feelings such as "reading satisfies the need to know" or concepts such as "reading is for information." At the expanded fundamentals and application stages, you might select feelings such as "reading helps you feel good about yourself and others" and concepts such as "reading is a tool that can clarify knowledge, feelings, and attitudes." The curriculum goals you select depend on the development stage and the needs of the students. However, you must select the curriculum goals before establishing activities to develop those goals.

2. Allocate sufficient time for instruction. We know that time is connected to learning; that is, the more time given to a goal, the more that is learned. Similarly, the less time allocated, the less that is learned. Activities in the literate environment must be allocated sufficient time if the goals are to be achieved.

3. Employ indirect instruction. Organize activities such as learning centers, classroom libraries, and visual displays to indirectly lead your students to achievement of the goals.

4. Orchestrate the physical, intellectual, and social-emotional environments to create desired conditions.

Physical environment: At the readiness and initial mastery stages, the following examples illustrate what could be done: Install a cooking center or a science center with written directions; prominently display books that provide either information or enjoyment in the classroom library; title a bulletin board "the wonders of the animal world" and post pictures of such

A rich literate environment encourages students to accomplish goals independently through indirect instruction. (Robert Bawden)

wonders as flying squirrels or the 16-foot white shark with questions to be
answered in print. At the expanded fundamentals and application stages,
activities could include the following: Install a science center or an anthropological center involving a dig; develop a time capsule; prominently display
books that provide additional information on digs or time capsules in the
classroom library; post a bulletin board with pictures of the products of a dig;
develop the progress of the dig in a time line or chart. The range and variety
of goal-directed activities is limitless.

Intellectual environment: At the readiness and initial mastery stages,
similarly develop elements of the intellectual environment (expectations,
modeling, interests, and motivation) in several ways. In the cooking and
science centers set the expectation that all students will use them; model the
desired outcome; use the interests of specific students (such as one student's
interest in octopuses or another's interest in kangaroos) as topics in the
science center; use pictures to stimulate motivation. At the expanded fundamentals and application stages, employ similar procedures. Set the expec-

tation that all students will be involved in the anthropological center, that the student experts are ready to be called on for help, that any developing interest in digs or other related activities will be included, that new experts might emerge, and that the teacher will model the desired outcomes.

Social-emotional environment: Social interactions and collaborative sharing support the goals selected. At the readiness and initial mastery stage, allocate time for informal social interactions about the work in the center. Establish collaborative endeavors for more formal interactions among students, in which you predetermine the tasks and outcomes but the groups implement them. At the expanded fundamentals and application stages, allocate time for informal social interactions about the anthropological center and keep formal social interactions in the collaborative groups.

5. Match groupings to specific activities and goals. During indirect instruction in the literate environment, students normally work in small groups or as individuals. At times, however, you may wish to explain certain procedures to the whole class. Some groupings may be formally established by you, as for collaborative groups, but many will be informal.

6. Monitor activities in terms of desired goals. Once the literate environment has been planned and is operating, you monitor its effectiveness. Activities that do not lead to the desired goal can be dropped, and more effective activities can be substituted.

SUMMARY

It is crucial that you create a literate environment in your classroom if you want your students to develop accurate concepts about reading and what it is for. Students can develop such concepts only if they participate in experiences that represent what literate people actually do with reading. Your role in creating a literate environment is primarily one of providing activities for students to pursue. One way to think about creating such an environment is in terms of what is physically present in the classroom to stimulate literate activities, whether intellectual challenges and expectations you set encourage pursuit of literate activities, and whether the social-emotional climate of the classroom promotes literate activity.

SUGGESTED ADDITIONAL READINGS

ALLINGTON, R. (1977). If they don't read much, how are they ever gonna get good? *Journal of Reading, 21,* 57–61.

BERGLUND, R. L., & JOHNS, J. L. (1983). A primer on uninterrupted sustained silent reading. *Reading Teacher, 36*(6), 534–539.

BOODT, G. M. (1982). Up! up! and away! writing poetry in the reading class. *Language Arts, 59*(3), 239–244.

COODY, B., & NELSON, D. (1982). *Successful activities for enriching the language arts.* Belmont, CA: Wadsworth.

DUFFY, G. G. (1967). Developing the reading habit. *Reading Teacher, 21,* 253–256.

EVANS, H. M., & TOWNER, J. C. (1975). Sustained silent reading: Does it increase skills? *Reading Teacher, 29,* 155–156.

GENTILE, L. M., & MCMILLAN, M. M. (1978). Humor and the reading program. *Journal of Reading, 21*(4), 343–349.

HAMILTON, M. C. (1974). Read aloud to children. *Instructor, 84,* 129–130.

HAMILTON, S. F. (1983). Socialization for learning: Insights from ecological research in classrooms. *Reading Teacher, 37*(2), 150–156.

HOLBROOK, H. T. (1982). Motivating reluctant readers: A gentle push. *Language Arts, 59*(4), 385–390.

HUBBARD, R. (1985). Second graders answer the question "Why publish?" *Reading Teacher, 38*(7), 658–662.

JANNEY, K. P. (1980). Introducing oral interpretation in elementary school. *Reading Teacher, 33,* 544–547.

JENNINGS, M. (1978). *Tape recorder fun.* NY: David McKay.

LANGER, J. A. (1982). Reading, thinking, writing and teaching. *Language Arts, 59*(4), 336–341.

LEVINE, S. (1984). USSR: A necessary component in teaching reading. *Journal of Reading, 28,* 394–400.

MANNA, A. L. (1984). Making language come alive through reading plays. *Reading Teacher, 37*(8), 712–717.

MARTIN, C. E., CRAMOND, B., & SAFTER, T. (1982). Developing creativity through the reading program. *Reading Teacher, 35*(5), 568–572.

MCCRACKEN, R. A. (1971). Initiating sustained silent reading. *Journal of Reading, 14,* 521–524; 582–583.

MCCRACKEN, R. A., & MCCRACKEN, J. J. (1978). Modeling is the key to sustained silent reading. *Reading Teacher, 31*(4), 406–408.

MENDOZA, A. (1985). Reading to children: Their preferences. *Reading Teacher, 38*(6), 522–527.

MIKKELSEN, N. (1982). Celebrating children's books throughout the year. *Reading Teacher, 35,* 790–795.

MILLER, G. M., & MASON, G. E. (1983). Dramatic improvisation: Risk-free role playing for improving reading performance. *Reading Teacher, 37*(2), 128–131.

MOORE, J. C., JONES, C. J., & MILLER, D. C. (1980). What we know after a decade of sustained silent reading. *Reading Teacher, 33*(4), 445–450.

NESSEL, D. D. (1985). Storytelling in the reading program. *Reading Teacher, 38*(4), 378–381.

ODLAND, N. (1979). Planning a literature program for the elementary school. *Language Arts, 56*(4), 363–367.

RADENCICH, M. C. (1985). Books that promote positive attitudes toward second language learning. *Reading Teacher, 38*(6), 528–530.

RASINSKI, T., & NATHENSON-MEJIA, S. (1987). Commentary: Learning to read, learning community: Considerations of the social contexts for literacy instruction. *Reading Teacher, 41,* 260–265.

SCHEU, J., TANNER, D., & HU-PEI AU, K. (1986). Designing seatwork to improve students' reading comprehension. *Reading Teacher, 40,* 84–87.

SEAVER J. T., & BOTEL, M. (1983). A first-grade teacher teaches reading, writing, and oral communication across the curriculum. *Reading Teacher, 36*(7), 656–664.

SIDES, N. K. (1982). Story time is not enough. *Reading Teacher, 36*(3), 280–283.

WAGNER, B. J. (1979). Using drama to create an environment for language development. *Language Arts, 56*(3), 268–274.

WETZEL, N. R., DAVIS, L., & JAMSA, E. (1983). Young authors conference. *Reading Teacher, 36*(6), 530–533.

WHITE, J., VAUGHN, J., & RORIE, I. (1986). Picture of a classroom where reading is for real. *The Reading Teacher, 40,* 84–87.

WINOGRAD, P., & SMITH, L. (1987). Improving the climate for reading comprehension instruction. *The Reader Teacher, 41,* 304–310.

RESEARCH BASE

DUFFY, G., & ROEHLER, L. (1987). Building a foundation for strategic reading. *California Reader, 20*(2), 6–10.

EVANS, H., & TOWNER, J. (1975). Sustained silent reading: Does it increase skills? *Reading Teacher, 29,* 155–156.

FADER, D., & MCNEIL, E. (1968). *Hooked on books: Program and proof.* New York: Berkeley.

HOLDAWAY, D. (1979). *The foundations of literacy.* Sydney, Australia: Ashton Scholastic.

JOHNS, J. (1977). Children's concepts of reading and their reading achievement. *Journal of Reading Behavior, 4,* 56–57.

THOMAS, J. (1975). *Learning centers: Opening up the classroom.* Boston: Holbrook.

11 | How to Form Reading Groups

GETTING READY

One of the things that makes reading difficult to teach is the fact that students in one class can represent several levels of developmental reading growth. To deal with individual differences, you form reading groups so that students with similar needs are taught together. In this chapter we recommend two types of groups, describe them, and explain the assessment decisions that you must make in forming such groups. You must begin making these assessment decisions as soon as your literate environment is created. Consequently, assessment is crucial to your efforts to organize instruction.

FOCUS QUESTIONS

- Why are reading groups desirable?
- What characteristics distinguish collaborative groups?
- What characteristics distinguish ability groups?
- How do you decide what students to assign to a collaborative group?
- How do you decide what students to assign to an ability group?
- How can you determine student needs for attitude goals? for process goals? for content goals?

PURPOSE OF READING GROUPS

Some reading instruction occurs in large group settings. However, small reading groups are found in virtually all elementary classrooms because students vary so much in their reading levels. In a third grade class with 24 students, for instance, reading levels will normally range from beginning reading (about first grade) to upper grade reading (about sixth grade). If you try to teach all 24 children in one large group, advanced readers will get bored and lose interest while low-aptitude readers will get frustrated and lose interest. When students are grouped by ability, however, each group receives instruction at an appropriate level.

To deal with individual differences, you must first understand why they occur. To some degree, individual differences can be attributed to varying quality of instruction. That is, a student may be behind because he or she received poor instruction. However, even when instruction is excellent, differences in student progress occur.

Aptitude for Verbal Learning One of the influences on student ability to understand and respond to instruction is aptitude for **verbal learning.** Some of your students have an aptitude for reading. Just as some people have an aptitude for mechanics or mathematics or poetry writing and others do not, some people have more aptitude for learning to read than others. There is nothing wrong with either the fast developers or the slow developers, it is just that some have more aptitude than others.

Background experience influences verbal learning and, ultimately, reading development. Some of your students come to school with rich experiences that enhance verbal learning. They have been to many different places, they have had a variety of vicarious experiences through the media, they have encountered many different ideas and concepts, their oral vocabulary is rich and varied, and their families value accepted school behavior. Conversely, other students have seldom been outside their immediate neighborhood, they have had limited vicarious experiences, they have been exposed to few ideas and concepts, their oral vocabulary is limited, and their families may not value accepted school behavior. Since reading involves constructing meaning using prior knowledge and text information, students with rich background experience can be expected to construct meaning easier and progress faster than students whose background experience is sparse.

Similarly, culture and cultural variations influence one's aptitude for learning to read. Our society includes children from various cultural backgrounds, including upper, middle, and lower class; white, yellow, and black; Mexican, Vietnamese, and other ethnic groups; small town and urban, to mention but a few, and they must all learn side by side. Even when language is no problem, each culture may have its own traditions and its own expectations for how to do things. The ways of one culture are not better than the ways of another, they are just different. Some cultural values, however, are more supportive of what is considered appropriate school behavior than others. The expectations associated with school materials, rules, and teacher attitudes may be new to students from certain cultures. Conversely, students whose cultural traditions match the expectations of schools have less trouble adapting to the materials, rules, and teachers because of background familiarity with the way things are done. For example, Oriental cultures revere teachers, and teacher-student interactions are very formal; consequently, Oriental students may have difficulty adjusting to the more informal teacher-student interactions typically found in American schools. These cultural dif-

Individual aptitude and perseverance influence rate of reading growth. (RH Photo by Peter Vadnai)

ferences may affect verbal learning and, ultimately, progress in learning to read.

Language variations of several kinds influence students' verbal learning. For instance, it is not unusual in many American schools to find students who do not speak English well or at all since they have another native language at home. These students generally move more slowly through the developmental stages. Similarly, some students have dialects that differ greatly from the dialect used for instruction, which occasionally impedes students' movement through the developmental stages. Special language problems such as these are discussed in greater detail in Chapter 21.

Keep in mind that differences in developmental reading growth are found in all classrooms and may stem from factors that influence students' verbal learning. You will see such differences in every class you teach. You must take them into account to understand why some students are learning more quickly than others.

Perseverance Verbal learning problems account for some differences in the rate of developmental reading growth, but they do not account for all. Perseverance also explains some differences in the rate of reading growth. Three conditions affect perseverance: expectations, self-concept, and motivation.

Expectation is the most influential condition. Children from homes where reading and learning are valued tend to have positive expectations about these activities. Because important people in their lives expect them to learn to read, they learn to read. This phenomenon is called a **self-fulfilling prophecy** because humans tend to fulfill the expectations set for them.

Teachers' expectations can be quite subtly communicated. For instance, by regularly calling on certain students more than others, by regularly praising some students more than others, and by setting slightly higher academic standards for some students than for others, teachers create an expectation that certain students are smarter and more capable of learning than others.

Communicating expectations can be insidious; you can communicate negative or positive expectations without knowing you are doing so. For instance, you may unconsciously work harder with students of one gender, thereby setting more positive expectations for the favored group and less positive expectations for the other group. Such positive and negative expectations influence your students' perseverance and, ultimately, their rate of developmental reading growth. Students for whom positive expectations are set tend to persevere and to learn to read faster than those for whom negative expectations are set.

Self-concept is closely related to expectations; it refers to the image that people hold of themselves. If a student has a positive self-image, the chances for normal developmental reading growth are good; if a student has a negative self-image, the chances for normal developmental reading growth are not as good. People's positive and negative self-images are closely related to expectation because we develop our self-images from our perceptions of what other people think of us. If you set high expectations for your students, they tend to develop positive self-images. If you set low expectations for your students, or expect them to be ineffective or unimportant, they tend to develop less positive self-images. The more positive a self-image, the more confidence there will be in attacking difficult tasks such as learning to read. Hence, positive self-images help students persevere in moving through the stages of developmental reading growth.

Motivation is another major influence on your students' ability to persevere. As noted in Chapter 2, motivation is influenced by both whether the student values what is being learned and whether it can be learned relatively easily. Your students will value what they learn when you present content meaningfully, usually through integration within and across lessons. Your students' success in learning, however, depends on whether you assign tasks matched to their ability level. That is, students who are assigned reading tasks they can succeed at are motivated and they persevere in the task; students who are assigned tasks that are very difficult for them become discouraged and unmotivated, and they do not persevere during instruction.

To summarize, a student's rate of progress throughout the stages of developmental reading growth is greatly influenced by both perseverance and aptitude for verbal learning. Both are necessary for learning to read. Since your students possess different amounts of aptitude for verbal learning and perseverance, you can expect them to move through the stages of developmental reading growth at different rates of speed, even if your instruction is excellent.

Assessing Individual Differences

If there are stages of developmental reading growth, and if students in any particular classroom move through these stages at different rates of speed, then each classroom will contain students from several stages. How can you determine at what stage each of your students is and, if appropriate, the reasons why a student is moving faster or slower than expected?

One reading specialist argues that a student's health as a reader can be determined by checking the vital signs of reading, just as the physical health of a person can be determined by checking the vital signs of the body.[1] The vital signs of reading health are the three curricular goals specified in Chapter 3. If students have an accurate concept of what reading is and respond positively to reading (attitude goals), understand how reading works (process goals), and can get content meaning from functional or recreational text (content goals), then they are "healthy" readers. If students are deficient in one or more of these categories, a problem exists.

To make decisions about a student's reading health, you use knowledge about the goals of reading (the vital signs) and knowledge about what constitutes normal progress for the student's age (stages of developmental reading growth). You can modify the check list shown in Figure 11.1 to fit each stage of developmental reading growth and use it as an initial tool in deciding about a student's vital signs. For each student check *yes* or *no* in the left-hand column for each of the vital signs at a particular stage of developmental reading growth, making the necessary decision on the basis of data collection techniques such as those listed in the right-hand column. If you check *yes* for each vital sign at the developmental level, a student can be said to be a healthy reader at that stage of reading growth.

Making this kind of assessment is a first step toward forming reading groups. Once you get a sense of each student's stage of developmental reading growth, you can begin thinking about how many groups you will need, what kind of groups you want in your classroom, and how to collect student data to help you decide what group each student should be in.

KINDS OF READING GROUPS

Many classrooms have only one kind of reading group—the traditional basal textbook ability group formed on the basis of reading level. There is a serious weakness in this practice. While basal textbooks are helpful in developing process and content goals, they are less helpful in developing attitude goals. Hence, when you have only ability groups, the instructional emphasis tends to be on the former, to the neglect of the latter.

---

[1] Sherman, G. (1985). A personal communication. Michigan State University.

This problem can be eased by having two kinds of reading groups. Just as a literate classroom environment must have a variety of activities reflecting the three goals of reading instruction, grouping patterns must match various goals. We suggest collaborative groups to promote attitude goals and ability groups to promote process and content goals. **Collaborative groups** are temporary groups. They are heterogeneous in that three to four children of varying abilities work together on a particular project. For purposes of reading instruction, collaborative group projects are directed toward attitude goals. For instance, you may form temporary collaborative groups to create language experience stories; to read and discuss certain kinds of books; to discuss themes and issues relating to outside reading; to organize and prepare presentations to the rest of the class or to other classes; to produce various kinds of text, such as poetry, drama, letters to the editor, and essays; to follow written directions, such as recipes; and to engage in a variety of other activities that result in positive responses and conceptual understanding of reading. The group members normally divide up the work according to their particular strengths. Seldom do all the group members perform the same functions or do the same reading. Such grouping is sometimes called **cooperative grouping** because all group members contribute to the completion of the activity.

Ability groups, in contrast, are homogenous groups in which, four to eight students are grouped together because they are all working at the same ability level. Consequently, you can give them all the same written material in the expectation that all will be able to read it and perform the required tasks. In contrast to collaborative groups in which each participant contributes to a group goal by performing a different task, ability groups require each member of the group to perform the same tasks to ensure that everyone achieves certain goals. For instance, you may teach how stories are structured to an ability group, so all your students in that group can use this as a strategy to predict meaning; or you may demonstrate a study guide to the same group, which will help them locate and comprehend salient information in a selection they will read together.

Both ability groups and collaborative groups are important. Collaborative groups provide opportunities for students to develop the attitude goals of reading, while ability groups permit teachers to show how reading works and how to understand the messages in texts. The greatest benefit of using both kinds of groups may lie with the potential for neutralizing negative expectations. One of the persistent problems in grouping only by ability is that negative expectations are communicated to students in the low group. Low-group students are publicly labeled dummies. No matter what you say to soften this label, the fact remains that the students are in the lowest reading group and everyone knows it. These negative expectations are neutralized somewhat if collaborative groups also exist. In collaborative groups each student is a worthwhile contributor to a heterogeneous group, and consequently, morale and perseverance are maintained.

FIGURE 11.1   Vital Signs of Reading Check List

Student's name _____

Student's age and grade _____

Student's expected stage of developmental reading growth _____

		The vital signs of healthy reading associated with the stage of reading growth normal for that age and grade	How to find data to answer questions
Yes	**No**	**I. Attitude Goals**	
		A. Accurate concept of reading	
_____	_____	Understands that reading is meaning getting?	Interview students about reading. Observe how student makes use of reading.
_____	_____	Has a rich concept of the function of reading?	Same as above.
		B. Positive response	
_____	_____	Has positive feelings toward reading?	Interview student. Observe student during free time, reading times, etc.
_____	_____	Likes to read?	Observe student's response to various kinds of reading situations.
		II. Process Goals	
		A. Routine skills	
		1. Language conventions	
_____	_____	Routinely uses language conventions such as left-to-right direction?	Observe how student moves eyes across a page of text.
		2. Linguistic units	
_____	_____	Knows most words instantly?	Listen to student read text at grade level. Are 95% of the words recognized instantly?
_____	_____	Has meaning for words met in reading?	Select words from text materials and ask student to use them orally in sentences.
		B. Metacognitive strategies	
		1. Initiating strategies	
_____	_____	Uses knowledge of topic to predict meaning?	Give student several reading tasks and ask student to tell how

FIGURE 11.1   continued

_____ _____   Uses knowledge of au-
                    thor's purpose to predict
                    meaning?

meaning is obtained and how
words, topic, purpose, and text
structure are used to predict.

Ask student to state predictions
and how decided on those predictions.

_____ _____   Uses knowledge of text
                    structure to predict mean-
                    ing?

Same as above.

2. During-reading strategies

_____ _____   Reads with fluency?

Listen to student read and note
number of hesitations, repetitions, etc.

Analyzes unknown words

_____ _____   ● using context clues?

Give student a sentence that can
be read but has a word missing. Is
the missing word correctly predicted?

_____ _____   ● using structural analysis?

Give student words with affixes.
Are the words correctly identified?

_____ _____   ● using phonics?

Give student nonsense words containing phonic elements that
should be known at that level. Are
the words correctly pronounced?

_____ _____   Generates new predictions?

Give student passages to read that
are somewhat difficult and have
student read them out loud. When
student encounters difficulty observe whether student looks back,
and starts over with a new prediction.

_____ _____   Constructs meaning using ty-
                    pographic cues

_____ _____   ● using roots and affixes?

Give student affixed words and
have student explain how the
meaning of the root word was
changed.

_____ _____   ● using key words?

Give student a grade level paragraph with relationships signaled
by key words and ask student
questions about the relationships.

_____ _____   ● using context?

Give student a grade level sentence with one unknown word and
ask student to predict what the unknown word means.

FIGURE 11.1   continued

——— ———	Analyzes text and text structure?	Give student samples of text and ask student to tell you what clues they offer for meaning.
——— ———	Matches author's purpose with reader's purpose?	Give student sample of text and ask student to identify author's purpose, student's own purpose, and how these relate to meaning getting.

3. Post-reading strategies

——— ———	Constructs meaning by classifying?	Give student a list of grade level words and have student classify them into categories and label them.
——— ———	Infers from gist?	Have student read a grade level paragraph and ask questions that require inference from gist.
——— ———	Draws conclusions?	Have student read a grade level paragraph and ask questions that require drawing conclusions.
——— ———	Makes judgments?	Have student read a grade level paragraph and ask questions that require making judgments.

III. Content Goals

A. Functional text

——— ———	Reads and understands expository text?	Give student samples of functional text and check understanding by having student summarize and/or answer questions about text content.
——— ———	Reads and understands specialized kinds of functional text (recipes, application forms, etc.)?	Same as above.

B. Recreational text

——— ———	Reads and understands narrative text?	Give student samples of narrative text and check understanding by having student summarize and/or answer questions about text content.
——— ———	Reads and understands poems?	Same as above but with poetry.
——— ———	Reads and understands specialized kinds of narratives (fantasy, folk literature, etc.)?	Same as above but with specialized narrative.

Collaborative groups help to develop attitude goals. (Robert Bawden)

DATA NEEDED TO FORM READING GROUPS

Having two kinds of reading groups means that you must decide how to assign students to each kind of group. The following section describes the data needed to make such decisions.

Collecting Data to Form Collaborative Groups

A collaborative group must work together to accomplish a goal despite student differences. This means that you must avoid assigning existing cliques of children to the same collaborative groups simply because they know how to get a job done. To form collaborative groups, you collect data about students' interests, about their ability to get along with others, and about the current social relationships in the classroom. There are several ways to do this.

The most useful is daily observation. Much can be learned about your students simply by watching what they do and say in a variety of situations. Whom do they talk to? Who talks to them? Who are the leaders and who are the followers? Who is being picked on? What interests, strengths, and weaknesses do various children display?

Another useful technique is to use a questionnaire to solicit your students' interests and attitudes. You can administer it in interview form in kindergarten and the primary grades and in its written form with more mature students. Such questionnaires should be simple and easy to complete. For instance, sentence completion tasks such as the following are useful:

My idea of a good time is _____ .

The smartest person in the class is _____ .

I like _____ because _____ .

Another simple technique is to give your students a list of statements and ask them whether these are true or false about themselves:

I think most of the kids in school like me.

I get nervous when I have to talk in front of the class.

Another useful technique is to talk casually to each student. You can engage a student in conversation while supervising recess or while waiting to go to lunch. Such conversations, because they are so informal and nonthreatening, can yield valuable information.

A sociogram is often a useful indicator of the social relationships in the classroom. A sociogram is administered by asking students to list the three children in the class that they would most and least want to be with in a group. As shown in Figure 11.2, the results can be plotted to graphically display who the popular children are, who the isolates are, and where the cliques exist. You can use such information when forming collaborative groups to help decide where to place the isolates, whether to split up a clique, and how to separate class leaders. Sociogram data are useful in making a variety of grouping decisions.

There is no totally systematic way to form collaborative groups. However, because group composition changes from activity to activity, it is a decision that you must make frequently. Your decisions will be better if you base them on data you have gathered about your students, their preferences, their own perceptions about themselves, and the way other students view them.

Collecting Data to Form Ability Groups

Since ability groups are composed of students with similar abilities, you collect data about student ability. The question is, "What kind of ability?"

Traditionally, teachers have assessed reading levels by asking students to read aloud progressively more difficult paragraphs and to respond to a series of questions about the content of those paragraphs. To determine if a student has a third grade reading level, for instance, the teacher would make an oral reading assignment from a third grade book and then ask questions about the paragraph's content. If the student is 99 percent fluent in identifying words in the text and 90 percent accurate in answering questions about the passage, that level of text is considered to be the student's **independent reading level**; that is, the child can read material from that level without

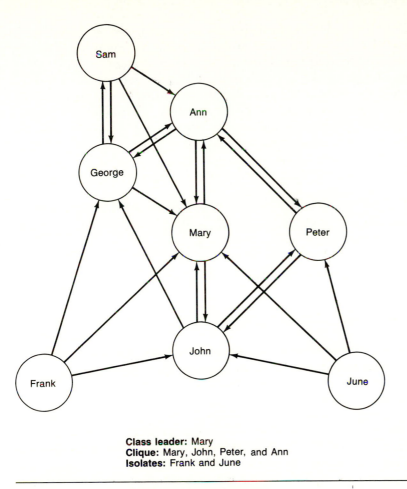

Class leader: Mary
Clique: Mary, John, Peter, and Ann
Isolates: Frank and June

FIGURE 11.2   Sample Results of a Sociogram

assistance from the teacher or another adult. If the student reads with 95 to 99 percent word recognition and 75 to 90 percent accuracy in comprehension, that level of text is considered the student's **instructional reading level;** that is, material from that level can be read by the student with some assistance from the teacher. If the student reads the material with less than 95 percent fluency in word recognition or less than 75 percent accuracy in comprehension, the material is considered to be the student's **frustration reading level;** that is, such material is too difficult for the child to read under any circumstances.

It is important to keep students' motivation in mind when placing them in reading groups. If you place students in groups in which the reading tasks are at their frustration reading level, they will be unmotivated and they will not persevere in the task of learning to read. Similarly, if you place them in groups in which the reading tasks are at their independent reading level, they will not learn new things because they know everything at that level. If, however, you place them at their instructional reading levels, they benefit from an appropriate blend of new information and challenge.

While it is comforting to have such quantitative guidelines for determining reading levels, current knowledge about how reading works suggests that using this technique alone may not be completely adequate. A student's reading level is not entirely revealed by number of words identified and the number of the questions answered in a sample of graded text. Whether students can read a passage or not depends first on their prior knowledge—on whether they have a schematic structure for the topic being discussed. In other words, an individual's reading level in a particular text depends on the topic being discussed. A selection on one topic from a typical third grade book may be easy for one student because of familiarity with that topic, while another student in the same reading group may find it quite difficult due to lack of background about the topic. In addition, factors such as syntax and special vocabulary can affect text difficulty. Consequently, if the practice of establishing independent, instructional, and frustration reading levels implies a single, static reading level for each child, it is misleading.

In view of the above, how do you assign students to the "proper" text in a basal series when each level consists of a variety of selections, some of which may reflect a student's background experience and some of which may not? This is a classic example of a teaching dilemma. As with all dilemmas, there is no single right answer; instead, you must use available data to make the best decisions possible and, when additional data become available, remain flexible enough to modify your decision.

A good practice when beginning the school year is to listen to each student read passages selected at random from various levels of a basal text series as previously described. If you are teaching third grade, for instance, ask your students to read samples of basal text from the first, second, third, and fourth level books. As students read, note any breaks in fluency: Note any places where the student's intonation pattern does not match the meaning of the text; where words are miscalled or omitted, where words are inserted or substituted; where words are repeated or identified incorrectly and then corrected; where noticeable hesitations are made before words; where the pattern does not match the meaning of the text; where punctuation is ignored; and where any other indications of nonfluent reading occur. You should note particularly breaks in fluency that alter the meaning of the text and remain uncorrected by the student, because such breaks suggest that the student is not self-monitoring the meaning-getting process. After oral reading is completed, assess comprehension by having the student first retell or summarize what the selection is about. If important meaning relationships are omitted, probe with questions designed to assess the student's comprehension of that particular relationship. After the student reads successively more difficult passages, examine the student's performance pattern across the various passages. Using the criteria for independent, instructional, and frustration levels as a guide (but not as an iron-clad rule), ask and answer questions such as the following.

- What passages did the student read with no apparent difficulty?

- In what passage did the student first begin to show some frustration?

- At what point did the reading become clearly frustrating for the student?

- On the basis of the student's reading performance across these paragraphs, what basal text seems to be comfortable—not too frustrating and not too easy?

It is sometimes difficult to decide on initial student placements in a basal text despite having listened to each student read. In such cases, check other data sources. The previous year's teacher can tell you what level text the student was in before, and you can look in the student's cumulative record folder for recommendations from other teachers and for the results of other tests.

If placement is still difficult, it is best to follow the rule, "When in doubt, go low." If you cannot decide between placement in a second or third level book, it is probably best to begin with the second level book. By doing so, you protect students' self-concepts. If you start high and later on move students to a lower group, they are bound to feel discouraged, and it can cast a pall on their motivation for the rest of the year. If you begin by making the lower of the two placements and later assign students to the higher level, they will be encouraged and motivated.

The assessment task is not over when you assign students to groups, however. As noted before, reading ability level is not static, and you must continue to collect and act upon fresh data. Because the level of difficulty in a basal text selection depends partly on a student's background experience regarding the topic, you must make adjustments for individual students despite the fact that all the students are supposedly at a particular reading level. A selection on sheepherding in the Rocky Mountains will be easier for students who have some prior knowledge about sheep, sheepherding, or the Rocky Mountains. In this sense, the students in a group are never reading at the same reading level. Consequently, you must continually monitor students' prior knowledge to ensure a match between student and text.

MONITORING STUDENT PROGRESS IN GROUPS

Although students are assigned to an ability group, they do not necessarily stay in it all year. Depending on their progress, individual students may be moved to a higher or a lower level. To make decisions about when to move a student to another group, you should regularly collect data about his or her progress in the three major goals of reading instruction.

Collecting Data about Attitude Goals

To monitor your students' conceptual understanding of reading, conduct interviews and ask questions such as, "What is reading? Why do people read?

What is the purpose of reading?" and "Where did the writing on the page come from?" Observe how your students use reading: Do they read to solve problems or for pleasure? Do they treat reading as a communication process? Do they understand the relationship between reading and the other language modes, particularly writing? Then compare the information you obtain from these observations and interviews to the typical curricula found at the various stages of developmental reading growth to determine which concepts must yet be developed (use the examples in Chapter 5 to help you).

Use similar techniques to monitor your students' responses to reading. In interviews ask your students what feelings they experience when reading, what they appreciate about reading, how often they read, what their favorite book is and why, and so on. Observe whether your students choose to read during leisure time, whether they respond emotionally to what is read, whether they seem to value what has been read, and so on. Again, compare the information you obtain to the attitude goals listed in Chapter 5 for the various stages of developmental reading growth. By comparing your data about your students' attitudes with the expectations for each stage of growth, you can determine which feelings and concepts must yet be developed.

Collecting Data about Process Goals

Process goals are divided into routine skills and metacognitive strategies.

Collecting Data on Routine Skills Routine skills focus on the language conventions and linguistic units that are used identically on every occasion. As such, routine skills are automatic responses requiring little conscious reasoning. Good examples are moving across the page in a left-to-right progression (a language convention) and word knowledge (a linguistic unit).

To assess language conventions such as left-to-right progression, observe your students' eye movements as they read. While no reader, no matter how expert, moves his or her eye steadily across a page without any regression at all, good readers do process text in a left-to-right progression. You can assess student use of this convention by watching eye movements or, in the case of very young readers, the movement of the finger being used to keep their place in the text. If the movement is in a generally consistent left-to-right order, students can be said to be employing this language convention.

The task of assessing linguistic units is more complex because there are more things to consider. For instance, in the case of words, you need to determine two things. First, you need to know what printed words can be identified, since individual words must be recognized in order to predict meaning. This can be determined by having students read a sample of text at the appropriate reading level and noting all the words that are not recognized, are miscalled, or cause the student to break the fluency of reading. Another technique is to use a graded list of words. Put each word on a card and flash these to the student one at a time. Those the student identifies instantly are sight words; those that cause hesitation or cannot be identified must be learned. For a student who is at the readiness level, the same

To make decisions about when to change a student's reading group, teachers routinely collect data about the student's progress. (RH Photo by Peter Vadnai)

technique can be used to determine how many alphabet letters are known (since, at the readiness level, the students have not yet learned many words).

The second thing you need to find out about students' word knowledge is their understanding of the meaning of words encountered in text. To gather this information, first pronounce the word and then ask the student to use the word aloud in a sentence. If the word is correctly used, the student knows the meaning of the word in that context. By identifying what words the student does not know (that is, words that are not recognized in print or for which the student has no meaning), you know which words to teach for sight recognition and which to teach for meaning.

Collecting Data on Metacognitive Strategies What you are looking for in assessing metacognitive strategies is students' reasoning about how they get meaning as they begin to read, what they do during reading when something goes wrong, and how they reflect on what they read after reading. While your students will not talk about processes like you do, their self-reports reveal whether they have an understanding of how to use knowledge about how the reading system works. For instance, you can ask students as they begin to read, "What are you thinking right now? What is it you are trying to do?" Also, after reading when students are trying to draw conclusions or to determine the theme, you can ask, "How are you trying to figure this out? What are you thinking in order to figure this out?" Students' self-reports about their thinking provide the window into the mind that allows you to decide whether or not students are metacognitive about the strategies they employ.

To illustrate more fully, consider how you can assess your students' use of fix-it strategies during reading. When a reader's predictions about text meaning are confirmed, the text processing continues smoothly. However, when the predictions are not confirmed, the reader stops and says, "Oh, oh, this doesn't make sense" or "Oh, oh, something's wrong here." At this point, the reader must become strategic. That is, the source of the difficulty must be located and an appropriate strategy applied to fix the blockage so that text processing can proceed. To monitor whether students use fix-it strategies, you can listen to their oral reading. When a blockage is encountered, ask students to talk out loud about fixing the blockage. In the course of this assessment, you are trying to answer four questions:

1. Does the reader recognize when a blockage to meaning occurs and stop to figure out what is wrong?

2. Once recognized, can the reader determine the source of the difficulty?

3. Can the reader identify the source of difficulty as one that can be fixed by reference to what is right there on the page? through search and think? or on your own?

4. Once the source of the difficulty has been located, can the reader apply an appropriate fix-it strategy? For instance, if the source of difficulty is a word unrecognized in print, can the reader retrieve a context strategy, a structural analysis strategy, or a phonics strategy to analyze and identify the word? Such assessment helps you determine the reader's ability to monitor his or her reading performance and to retrieve and apply fix-it strategies as needed. As a result, you can decide whether you need to emphasize strategies and, if so, which ones.

If enough text is read, students will eventually encounter a variety of blockages which, in turn, will allow you to observe their repertoire of fix-it strategies. However, this is a time-consuming procedure and, for diagnostic purposes, it is sometimes more efficient to assess strategy usage in more isolated tasks.

For instance, if you want to determine whether your students have strategies for decoding words not recognized in print, you can build brief assessments that check each of the three ways (context clues, structural analysis, and phonics) of analyzing unknown words. To determine whether your students can analyze using context clues, given them sentences with missing words and ask them to predict the missing word; to determine whether they can analyze using structural analysis, give them unrecognized words that can be identified through known prefixes and suffixes; to determine whether they can analyze using phonics, give them nonsense words containing known phonic elements and ask them to pronounce them. In each case, you should have the students talk out loud about their analysis so you can determine whether or not a strategy is being correctly applied.

You can also build informal assessments to determine whether students are metacognitive about comprehension. For instance, you can create examples that are similar to the passage about *rotation* in Chapter 3, in which you deliberately cause a certain prediction to be made initially, knowing that students will change it as they read further. Ask students to read a text orally, noting whether they look back when the blockage is encountered. Since you have intentionally included syntactic and semantic cues that can be reexamined during the look back, ask students to explain what cues are being used and how the predictions are being made. This technique gives you another check on students' overall awareness of their need to monitor meaning getting and gives you insight into their use of syntactic and semantic cues.

You can also create informal devices to assess students' ability to get and to go beyond the author's meaning. For instance, you can ask a student to read a sentence such as the following one.

> After the dance, I was unable to smile because Mary, who *was* my friend, played a despicable trick on me.

A variety of strategies are useful for getting the author's meaning in this sentence. Readers can use the comma after *dance* and commas setting off the phrase "who *was* my friend," as well as the italicized *was* to figure out what the sentence means. The meaning of the verb *unable* can be figured out from its root and prefix; and the words *after* and *because* are key words, the former because it signals a chronological relationship and the latter because it signals a cause-effect relationship. The meaning of *despicable* can be figured out using other words in the sentence. By asking students to explain how they get meaning from sentences such as this, you can assess their use of various kinds of strategies. Similarly, you can provide samples of various kinds of text and have students talk out loud about how they used their experience to get the author's meaning. For instance, a paragraph such as the following might be used.

> The camel and his driver were stumbling across the desert. They had not seen an oasis for days. The sun was low on the horizon on the fourteenth day when the driver croaked, "I see on." But he really didn't. It was just a mirage.

After this is read, ask a classification question such as: "Into what category would you put the words *camel, desert, oasis,* and *mirage*?" A question designed to elicit inference from gist might be: "Why did the driver want to find an oasis?" A question designed to elicit inference based on relationships might be: "At what time of day did the driver think he saw an oasis?" A post-reading question requiring the drawing of a conclusion might be: "What caused the driver to think he saw an oasis?" Finally, to determine the ability to make judgments, you might ask: "What do you think the driver could have done to prevent this situation from happening?"

To find out whether students can go beyond the author's meaning, you must ask questions that require them to create meaning beyond what the author intended to communicate. For instance, for the sentence about the dance you might ask students how people ought to respond when friends play tricks on them, and for the paragraph about traveling in the desert you might ask students whether mirages are real or imagined or to judge whether a word such as *stumbling* is an accurate descriptor for what camels are likely to do. By listening to students' answers to these questions and to their explanations of how they figured out the answers, you can assess whether they possess strategies for going beyond an author's meaning.

Collecting Data about Content Goals

To assess your students' ability to understand various kinds of text, you need to listen to them read functional and recreational text appropriate for their developmental level. In third grade, for instance, you might listen to students read expository materials such as social studies texts, directions for games, sections of the newspaper, and simple encyclopedia entries, and you might listen to them read narrative text such as children's realistic fiction, narrative poetry, fantasy, and fables.

To assess your student's comprehension of functional and recreational texts, follow the same procedure described earlier for determining comprehension of graded oral reading paragraphs. First, give your students an opportunity to retell or summarize the selection; then ask specific questions about the facts, concepts, or relationships that were omitted in the retelling. If your students demonstrate understanding of the various types of expository and narrative text typically found at that level, they are "healthy" regarding the content goal. If comprehension gaps are found in the reading of certain types of text, instructional assistance must be provided. Use the examples provided in Chapter 6 to compare your students' performance with the normal developmental progression.

Using a Diagnostic Kit

Collecting data about your students' achievement of the three goals requires considerable time and effort. However, the effort can be reduced if you make yourself a diagnostic kit containing the materials you need. Such a kit is described in Figure 11.3. You will find this kit useful in assessing all your students. Even when your class has mainstreamed students (see Chapter 20) or students with special language problems (see Chapter 21), you will be able to use this. Students with special problems are basically no different in reading from other students: You still need to find out what their instructional reading levels are and how they are doing relative to the goals of reading. A diagnostic kit will be useful in assessing all students.

FIGURE 11.3 Material Needed to Collect Diagnostic Data about Reading

I. Attitude goals

  A. Interview probes
  B. Check list for observing students
  C. Interest inventory and other forms students can complete

II. Process goals

  A. Routine skills
    1. Linguistic units
      a. Word recognition
        (1) Graded list of high utility words
        (2) Grade oral reading paragraphs
      b. Vocabulary
        (1) List of words from the text that may be unknown
    2. Language conventions
      a. Sample of various types of text
      b. Interview probes designed to get students to talk out loud about what they are doing
      c. Observations of their use of language conventions

  B. Metacognitive strategies
    1. Sample graded paragraphs for students to read
    2. Interview probes to use with these paragraphs to get students to talk out loud about what they do before reading, during reading, and after reading
    3. Materials for assessing specific strategies
      a. Sentences in which unidentified words are signaled by various context clues
      b. Sentences in which unidentified words are signaled by structural analysis
      c. Nonsense words containing phonic elements to be tested
      d. Sentences and paragraphs that cause blockages and in which there are syntactic and semantic cues for removing the blockage
      e. Sentences and paragraphs containing explicit syntactic cues (typographic cues, structural units, and key words) and semantic cues (context)
      f. Samples of various types of text
    4. Interview probes designed to get students to talk out loud about how they use their prior knowledge to get meaning

III. Content goals

  A. Functional text
    1. Various kinds of functional text appropriate for students' stage of developmental reading growth
    2. Questions designed to determine students' comprehension of the particular kind of text

  B. Recreational text
    1. Various kinds of recreational text appropriate for students' stage of developmental reading growth
    2. Questions designed to determine students' comprehension of the particular kind of text.

SUMMARY

Reading groups are useful because they help you deal with the wide variety of ability levels found in virtually all classrooms. Differences of ability occur because of differences in students' verbal learning and perseverance, which, in turn, cause students to move through the developmental stages of reading growth at varying rates of speed. Teachers provide for student differences by using ability groups, in which students are grouped by ability to perform the task being learned, and collaborative groups, in which students are grouped heterogeneously to work together temporarily on a specific task. Generally, collaborative groups are used when teaching attitude goals; ability groups are used when teaching process goals and content goals. To form groups, you must collect appropriate data on your students. Collaborative groups, for instance, require data on which students work well together; ability groups require data on each student's level of performance on the task to be taught. Once groups are formed, you should be prepared to continue collecting data on students' attitudes, processes, and abilities to understand content, which will change as the year progresses.

SUGGESTED ADDITIONAL READINGS

BAUMANN, J. F., & STEVENSON, J. A. (1982). Understanding standardized reading achievement test scores. *Reading Teacher, 35*(6), 648–654.

BAUMANN, J. F., & STEVENSON, J. A. (1982). Using scores from standardized reading achievement tests. *Reading Teacher, 35*(5), 528–532.

BLACK, J. K. (1980). Those "mistakes" tell us a lot. *Langauge Arts, 57*(5), 508–513.

BRECHT, R. D. (1977). Testing format and instructional level with the informal reading inventory. *Reading Teacher, 31*(1), 57–59.

BRISTOW, P. S., PIKULSKI, J. J., & PELOSI, P. L. (1983). A comparison of five estimates of reading instructional level. *Reading Teacher, 37*(3), 273–280.

CALDWELL, J. (1985). A new look at the old informal reading inventory. *Reading Teacher, 39,* 168–173.

FORELL, E. (1987). The case for conservative readers placement. *Reading Teacher, 41,* 857–862.

HALLER, E., & WATERMAN, M. (1985). The criteria of reading group assignments. *Reading Teacher, 38*(8), 772–781.

HELTON, G. B., MORROW, H. W., & YATES, J. R. (1977). Grouping for instruction: 1965, 1975, 1985. *Reading Teacher, 31*(1), 28–33.

HU-PEI AU, K. (1977). Analyzing oral reading errors to improve instruction. *Reading Teacher, 38*(1), 46–49.

JOHNSON, M. S., & KRESS, R. A. (1965). *Informal reading inventories.* Newark, DE: International Reading Association.

LANG, J. B. (1976). Self-concept and reading achievement: An annotated bibliography. *Reading Teaching, 29*(8), 787–793.

MARSHALL, N. (1983). Using story grammar to assess reading comprehension. *Reading Teacher, 36*(7), 616–620.

MCKENNA, M. C. (1983). Informal reading inventories: A review of the issues. *Reading Teacher, 36*(7), 670–679.

OMOTOSO, S. O., & LAMME, L. L. (1979). Using wordless picture books to assess cross cultural differences in seven year olds. *Reading Teacher, 32*(4), 414–419.

PFLAUM, S. W. (1979). Diagnosis of oral reading. *Reading Teacher, 33*(3), 279–284.

ROSER, N., & HOLMES, B. (1987). Five ways to assess readers' prior knowledge. *Reading Teacher, 40*, 646–649.

VALENCIA, S., & PEARSON, P. D. (1987). Reading assessment: Time for a change. *Reading Teacher, 40*, 726–733.

WIXSON, K. K., ET AL. (1984). An interview for assessing students' perceptions of classroom reading tasks. *Reading Teacher, 37*(4), 346–352.

WOOD, K. (1988). Techniques for assessing students' potential for learning. *Reading Teacher, 41*, 440–447.

WULZ, S. V. (1979). Comprehension testing: Functions and procedures. *Reading Teacher, 33*(3), 295–299.

RESEARCH BASE

FARR, R. (1969). *Reading: What can be measured?* Newark, DE: International Reading Association.

JOHNSTON, P. (1983). *Reading comprehension assessment: A cognitive basis.* Newark, DE: International Reading Association.

JOHNSTON, P. (1984). Assessment in reading. In P. D. Pearson (Ed.), *Handbook of reading research* (pp. 147–184). New York: Longman.

WIXSON, K., & LIPSON, M. (1986). Reading (dis)ability: An interaction and perspective. In T. Raphael (Ed.), *Contexts of school-based literacy* (pp. 131–148). New York: Random House.

12 How to Modify Basal Text Prescriptions

GETTING READY

Once you form your reading groups, instruction can begin. It is at this point that you turn to basal reading textbooks. What you do with the basal—whether you make professional adaptations or simply follow prescriptions like a technician—is especially important. This chapter describes how it is possible to modify basal text prescriptions, thereby remaining in metacognitive control of instruction. Adapting the basal prescriptions is a critical next step in organizing for instruction once you have formed reading groups.

FOCUS QUESTIONS

- What are the strengths and weaknesses of the basal reading textbook?
- How can you modify basal text grouping patterns?
- How can you modify basal text units?
- How can you modify basal text lessons?
- How can you modify basal text seatwork?

STRENGTHS AND WEAKNESSES OF BASALS

This chapter helps you avoid teaching like a technician by showing you how to organize your time so that the three major goals of reading can be accomplished despite the constraints posed by basal textbooks. You must first have a literate environment in place, as described in Chapter 10. Then you must know what the strengths and shortcomings of basal texts are and how to compensate for these while capitalizing on the strengths. This chapter provides a plan for doing so.

As noted in Part 1, the basal textbook has many appealing characteristics. Its sequential lessons provide a structured progression in which the gradually increasing difficulty of each level expedites the process of grouping students according to ability; the prescriptions in the teachers' guide provide valuable suggestions for teaching; the reading selections are written to appeal to students at that level; and the accompanying workbook practice pages provide numerous activities to keep students occupied. The overall impression is that an entire reading program is contained right there in the materials, and that all a busy teacher has to do is follow the prescriptions to ensure that students achieve all the goals of reading. It seems to be so, but it is not. Despite appearances, the comprehensiveness of the basal program is an illusion. There are three reasons for this.

Basals Deemphasize Attitude Goals Although basal texts prescribe many different kinds of activities, they do not give equal treatment to the three reading goals. While most basal text programs discuss the need for developing concepts and positive responses to reading, they actually allocate very little instructional time to this goal. They may suggest activities, but they provide little to help teachers incorporate these suggestions into the busy school day. Even when the basal contains good suggestions about developing attitude goals, it gives other tasks priority, leaving little time for attitude development. For instance, most basals place more emphasis on reading the selections (content goals) and on completing skill activities (process goals) than on attitude goals.

Basals Emphasize Skills, Not Strategies At first glance, the basal seems to place heavy emphasis on process goals. There are many suggestions in the teacher's guide for developing skills, but most basals emphasize mastery and automaticity, not reading strategies to be consciously applied when meaning is blocked.

Typically, a skill page in the workbook requires answer accuracy. Seldom are students asked to explain when the skill would be useful in reading text, what situation might occur for which this skill would be useful, how to use the skill strategically when encountering such a situation, or what mental steps to follow when applying the skill in real situations. In short, neither knowledge about how reading works nor strategic application of skills receives much emphasis in a typical basal lesson.

Basals Emphasize Content, Not Process Basal texts emphasize content goals. Typically, the first part of a lesson focuses on the story. The lesson begins with an introduction to the story, a discussion of new vocabulary words, the establishment of purpose-setting questions, and the assignment of the pages to be read. No mention is made of how the reading system works or of how to get meaning from the text; instead, teachers provide students with background and a "mind set" about the content of the selection. After students read the story, the teacher usually quizzes the students in a question-and-answer period. Because these questions focus on what happened in the story, the teacher is checking the students' understanding of the story content, not their understanding of how the reading system helped them get meaning from the text or how strategies were applied when meaning broke down.

Many of the suggested instructional activities in basals are directed at answers to comprehension questions. However, the answers are isolated from the process one uses to get the answer. Consider the order in which basal lessons are typically organized. The first step is to teach the story selection; the second step is to teach the several skills recommended in that section of the teacher's guide, usually by assigning workbook pages. Seldom is there an explicit connection between the story selection and the skills to be taught. In fact, skills are typically taught only in the context of the workbook; seldom are they connected to the reading selection in the basal text.

A more logical instructional system would be to recast the targeted skill as a strategy and connect it to the reading selection. As part of the preparation for reading the story selection, for instance, you could recast a skill as a strategy as described in Chapter 8 and teach it in the expectation that it will be used immediately when reading the story. In that way, you provide students with a rationale for why the strategy is being taught, illustrate how it can be used strategically in reading the story, and get students to apply it as they read the story. The emphasis is on application, not learning in isolation, so rather than having skills isolated to the workbook pages, you show that they are tools for immediate application in real text.

Thus, while you may sometimes get the impression that basal textbooks are complete reading programs, this is not really the case. If you simply follow prescriptions of the basal program, you end up emphasizing the content of reading selections and skill practice unrelated to the selections. You do not get to put much emphasis on attitude goals (even though these may be recommended by the basal teachers' guide) or on direct explanation of how the reading system works.

MODIFYING BASAL TEXT READING GROUPS

Teachers who rely on the basal textbook generally conduct reading instruction in small ability groups. Some goals are better taught in large group situations, however. This is the first way in which you can modify basal textbook prescriptions.

The development of accurate concepts and positive responses associated with attitude goals is particularly applicable to large group instruction. You can do language experience activities with the entire class, especially when the whole class has participated in a field trip, a school assembly, or other special event. The special event provides the stimulus for creating a written message. In creating this message, you develop concepts about the message-sending properties of reading, the author-reader relationship, the similarity between constructing meaning when reading and composing meaning when writing, and so on. Similarly, you can have book-sharing activities involving the entire class. During such sessions, you can develop positive attitudes toward reading by modeling, by pointing out how certain books stimulate particular emotional responses, by noting students who are particularly appreciative of literature, and so on.

You will also find large group instruction useful for developing certain process goals. You can teach mini-lessons about how the reading system works: Whenever there is a spare 5 minutes between activities, show students how knowledge about the reading process can help them determine the author's intended meaning. Or use such times to let students show how they constructed meaning in their own reading, or allow students to work together to resolve conflicts about the meaning of particular text passages. Finally, there are times during the school day when you may want the whole class to read the same piece of text, thereby developing content goals in a large group.

There are several advantages to such large-group instruction. First, it moves reading outside the context of the basal textbook. In doing so, you help students learn that reading fits into virtually all situations. Second, large group instruction provides the opportunity for students of varying ability levels to contribute. In contrast to small reading groups, which tend to foster elitism because they are formed on the basis of ability, large group instruction puts good and poor readers together. Finally, you will often find large group instruction to be a relaxing change of pace from the routine of daily reading groups. You can manage large groups more easily because all students are working on a single task rather than some working with you and others working independently at their seats.

Because basal text grouping patterns dominate programs in today's classrooms, teachers sometimes overlook the potential of large group instruction for developing important reading goals. To ensure a broad and comprehensive program, however, you should use large groups to develop goals basal textbooks tend not to emphasize. Also, as specified in Chapter 11, you should make use of collaborative groups.

MODIFYING BASAL TEXT UNITS

A "unit" in most basal textbooks is comprised of several selections grouped together in the book. These groupings often reflect a content theme. For instance, a basal text may have units of five stories each, with the theme of the first unit being courage, the second sports, and so on. Although the length of units and the way they are tied together vary from one basal text series to another, virtually all basals group selections into units.

Each lesson in a unit typically includes a selection to be read and skills or strategies to be taught. In most basals, the selection is taught first, followed by the skill or strategy. This tends to isolate the skill or strategy from the selection. You can rectify this by reorganizing the instructional sequence so that the skill or strategy is taught before reading the selection. In this way, the skill or strategy can be used when reading the story.

Accomplishing this reorganization is a two-step process. First, you must survey the basal prescriptions for the whole unit, reorganize these prescriptions according to the three major goals of reading, and identify which specific

Large-group reading instruction provides the opportunity for students of varying ability groups to work together. (David Strickler/Monkmeyer Press)

skill or strategy prescription goes with which goal. Second, you must decide which skill or strategy to teach with each story.

The first step is necessary because there is seldom any clear relationship among the skills or strategies taught in a particular unit and what is needed to read the selections. A phonics skill on the initial *ch* digraph may be presented in the same unit with a skill on predicting outcomes. Not only are these skills not related in any obvious way, but also the basal selections in the unit do not have any unknown *ch* words or call for predicting outcomes. In short, there is seldom a compelling reason to learn the skill or strategy.

To impose a more sensible organization on the unit, we recommend you list all the goals the basal prescribes for the unit, organize these into the three major reading goals, delete prescriptions that ought not to be taught or that do not relate to the three major goals, and add any other needed goals that the basal text may have neglected. After you have categorized all the prescribed and additional skills and strategies by goal, group together the items that go together. For instance, in the category of process goals, you would group all the routine skills together, all the initiating strategies together, all the during-reading strategies together, and all the post-reading strategies together. When you finish this categorizing, you know precisely what to teach in each of the three major goal categories and, within each category, you have lists of specific curricular tasks that go together. You can then state these as objectives (see Chapter 13). Figure 12.1 illustrates the steps in accomplishing such a reorganization of basal content.

Once you have identified the objectives to be taught in a basal unit, you must decide which objective goes with which selection. This often means you must move a skill or strategy from its place in the basal and teach it with a different story. For instance, it is not unusual for a basal textbook to prescribe a lesson on figuring out word meaning through the use of prefixes without having any prefixed words in the accompanying selection. Consequently, you cannot use that particular selection as a place to apply what was learned about prefixes, so you must move the prefix lesson to another place in the unit where there *is* a selection containing prefixed words. By matching objectives and selections, you ensure that goals will be taught in the context of their application in real reading rather than in isolation. This adds a dimension of meaningfulness, makes the instruction sensible, and, consequently, helps motivate your students.

MODIFYING BASAL TEXT LESSONS

Once you have organized a unit of instruction so that specific objectives are matched to specific selections, you are ready to organize individual lessons. The first step is to decide whether you are trying to achieve a content goal, a process goal, or an attitude goal, since each one has its own organizational scheme. Because you normally use indirect instruction with language experience and personalized reading to develop attitude goals, you generally limit your use of the basal to achieving content and process goals.

A Content Lesson Format If you decide to have students focus on the content of the selection, you organize the lesson using the six steps of the directed

---

FIGURE 12.1   Steps in Reorganizing Basal Text Prescriptions

Step 1   List all the objectives prescribed by the basal.

Step 2   Group these objectives into three categories according to the three major reading goals (attitude, process, content).

Step 3   Delete objectives that do not reflect any of the three major goals.

Step 4   Add any objectives that the basal fails to prescribe.

Step 5   For each of the three categories, group together similar objectives (put all phonics objectives together, all comprehension strategies together, etc.).

Step 6   Examine the lists and state an objective for each task. These are your objectives for the unit.

---

reading lesson: Introduce the story by activating appropriate background experience and introducing the new vocabulary words; set purposes for reading the selection; have students orally or silently read the selection; discuss the selection with students in terms of the set purposes; teach the prescribed skills; and bring the lesson to a close by summarizing the content or by involving students in an enriching activity. Throughout, your focus is on developing understanding of the content of the selection.

A Process Lesson Format If your objective is to develop a process goal, an eight step modification of the DRL sequence, called the modified directed reading lesson, is used: Introduce the selection and cite how it is an example of a place to use the strategy to be learned; introduce the strategy to be learned; model how to do the thinking associated with the strategy; mediate students' acquisition; set purposes for reading the selection with an emphasis on applying the strategy that was learned; have students orally or silently read the selection; discuss the content of the selection and how students used the strategy while reading the selection; and bring the lesson to a close. Throughout, you focus on developing understanding of a process goal and its application to content. This is in contrast to the DRL, which focuses on developing understanding of what went on in the selection in isolation from process; the MDRL focuses on making connections between how students make sense of text and how they apply that understanding in the story.

Using the Two Formats Figure 12.2 illustrates the similarities and differences in the two forms of the directed reading lesson. Both lesson sequences are examples of direct instruction. You decide at the outset (by reference to the unit plan) what process or content goal to teach with a particular basal selection. You use a DRL format to directly assist your students if content is the goal or an MDRL format to directly assist your students if process is the goal. It is as if you are saying:

> I know something about what is to be learned here, and I'm going to share it with you so you can learn it. I'm not going to keep secret what I know about it, nor am I going to make you figure it out by yourself as we go along. Instead, I'm going to make it as clear as possible so you can put it to work in this story and in other things that you read.

Both lesson plans require you to make decisions. If the intent is to develop a content goal, you must decide how to guide your students in activating appropriate background experience, on how to develop meaning for new words, and on how to ensure that the content is understood. To make these decisions, use your understanding of how readers tap into various knowledge sources to comprehend: knowledge of words, of topic, of purpose, and of text structure. You introduce vocabulary, tell your students what the topic of the story or selection is, state the author's purpose in writing it, and cue students to distinctive features of the text structure. Your intent is to help

FIGURE 12.2   Two Forms of the Directed Reading Lesson

Standard DRL (content lesson format)	Modified DRL (process lesson format)
Step 1 Introduce the selection (activate schemata and special vocabulary).	**Step 1** Introduce the selection as a focus for a strategy to be learned.
	Step 2 Introduce the knowledge or strategy to be taught.
	Step 3 Model how to use the knowledge or strategy.
	Step 4 Mediate student acquisition of the knowledge or strategy.
Step 2 Set purposes for reading the selection (for content understanding only).	**Step 5** Set purposes for reading the selection (include application of the knowledge or strategy as well as understanding the content).
Step 3 Have students orally or silently read the selection.	**Step 6** Have students orally or silently read the selection.
Step 4 Discuss the selection (for content understanding only).	**Step 7** Discuss the selection both in terms of the content and in terms of application of the knowledge or strategy.
Step 5 Teach the skills.	
Step 6 Bring closure to the lesson (by summarizing content only).	**Step 8** Bring closure to the lesson by summarizing both the content and the use of the knowledge or strategy.

students activate their prior knowledge and to make initial predictions about meaning based on what they know about the topic, author purpose, and cues provided in the text structure (such as titles, subtitles, headings, illustrations, etc.). By getting students to activate appropriate knowledge and to predict on the basis of that knowledge, you get them ready to comprehend the content of the selection. Consequently, in planning the DRL you guide students regarding the words, the topic, the purpose, and the text structure.

Your decisions are somewhat different when you are developing process goals. Despite the fact that the first step in both types of lesson is nearly identical, in process lessons the intent is to identify a need for the strategy or skill being taught by establishing that it will be used in that selection. In the second step, you make a brief statement, which answers three important

In teaching content goals, teachers stress students' understanding of topic, purpose, and text structure. (Robert Bawden)

questions for the students: What skill or strategy will they be learning? Where will they use the skill or strategy? (In this case, state exactly where they will use the skill or strategy in the basal selection they are about to read, as well as other similar but more removed situations where they could use it in the future.) What must they pay attention to in order to learn the skill or strategy? Answers to these three questions are keys to the learning objective, and one of your most important instructional tasks is to get your students to attend to the specific keys so they can learn easily and well. This step in the MDRL, then, is a brief but explicit statement that lets students tune in to the skill or strategy to be learned.

The third step is to model the skill or strategy being taught. You say, "Here, let me show you how it's done." Then, using a sample piece of text from the basal selection or one similar to the basal selection, you explain the thinking you do in using the skill or strategy. Your modeling gives your students information they need to use the skill or strategy themselves. Consequently, you do not omit or gloss over the steps. However, no matter how explicitly and thoroughly you model, your students must be given opportunities to try out the skill or strategy and to adapt it to their own mental processing. Consequently, the fourth step is for you to provide additional text passages similar to those used for modeling and to tell your students, "Do as I did." In short, students follow your model in explaining how they use the skill or strategy. At first, you provide lots of support in the form of cues and directives but, gradually, you remove such aids as students adapt and personalize the use of the skill or strategy. This is a critical stage in the instructional sequence since it is your students' responses at this stage that reveal misunderstandings about how the skill or strategy works. If misunderstandings become evident, you must spontaneously provide explanations to eliminate the confusion and put the student back on the right track. That is why this step is called "mediating student acquisition"—you form a connecting bridge between the student and the goal. Whether students learn to use the skill or strategy often depends upon your sensitivity in performing this mediational or bridging role.

Once students understand how to use the knowledge or strategy, go to the fifth step and assign the basal selection for practice. You set two purposes for reading the basal selection: Give your students content purposes associated with getting the meaning in the text; and ask them to apply to the selection the skill or strategy they have learned. In the sixth step, have students begin reading the selection together, usually silently but sometimes orally (especially in the primary grades). After they have read the selection, guide the seventh step, the discussion, talking with students about the content of the story and about how they applied the newly taught skill or strategy. Finally, in the eighth step you close the lesson by summarizing both the content of the selection and the process that was taught.

Ultimately, of course, you must ensure that students apply the skill or strategy in settings outside the basal textbook. Your real purpose in teaching reading is to help students become independent readers of real world materials. This purpose cannot be adequately achieved if students think reading strategies are only used in basal textbooks. Consequently, your task is not done until students can apply the knowledge or strategy in natural or "outside of school" text. Details for planning and teaching DRL and MDRL lessons are provided in Chapter 13.

MODIFYING BASAL TEXT SEATWORK

Seatwork in most classrooms consists of work sheets. Students are given workbooks, ditto sheets, or practice sheets supplied by the basal text publisher or the publisher of supplementary materials. In most classrooms, students' seatwork time is longer than the time they spend in the reading group. Consequently, even if you provide excellent instruction for 20 minutes in a reading group, what your students do in the 40-minute seatwork time is likely to have even greater impact. If your students spend more time on practice sheets than on reading text, they will most likely conclude that reading is more like work sheets than like books.

To combat this interpretation, you must use alternative kinds of seatwork.

You should supplement the usual drill and practice kind of seatwork with activities such as the following: free reading of self-selected books, journal writing, illustrating language experience stories, paired oral reading, games, listening activities, creative drama, letter writing, gathering information from outside reading sources, and others. The point is that you are not limited to using only the seatwork provided by the basal; in fact, you must be creative enough to initiate alternative seatwork if your students are to conclude that reading is a meaningful activity.

SUMMARY

Basal textbooks are useful as tools to help you organize your reading instruction. However, they also have many serious weaknesses, particularly in the way they develop attitude and process goals. Consequently, as a professional decision maker, you must modify basal text prescriptions to capitalize on their strengths while minimizing their weaknesses. You can do so by using large groups and collaborative groups as well as the ability groups prescribed by the basal; by modifying the sequence of basal text units to ensure that skills and strategies are taught with reading selections that call for the use of the skill or strategy; by modifying the basal lesson sequence so that the skill or strategy is taught before it is to be applied in the story; and by employing seatwork that is more representative of what literate people do than the typical basal text seatwork.

SUGGESTED ADDITIONAL READINGS

BAUMANN, J. F. (1984). How to expand a basal reader program. *Reading Teacher, 37*(7), 604–607.

BLANTON, W., MOORMAN, G., & WOOD, K. (1986). A model of direct instruction applied to the basal skills lesson. *Reading Teacher, 40*, 299–305.

CHARNOCK, J. (1977). An alternative to the DRA. *Reading Teacher, 31*(3), 269–271.

GOURLEY, J. W. (1978). This basal is easy to read—or is it? *Reading Teacher, 32*(2), 174–182.

GREEN-WILDER, J., & KINGSTON, A. (1986). The depiction of reading in five popular basal series. *Reading Teacher, 39*, 399–402.

PIERONEK, F. T. (1980). Do basal readers reflect the interests of intermediate students? *Reading Teacher, 33*(4), 408–415.

REUTZEL, D. R. (1985). Reconciling scheme theory and the basal reading lesson. *Reading Teacher, 39*, 194–197.

SCHMITT, M., & BAUMANN, J. (1986). How to incorporate comprehension monitoring strategies into basal reader instruction. *Reading Teacher, 40*, 28–31.

SWABY, B. (1982). Varying the ways you teach reading with basal stories. *Reading Teacher, 35*(6), 676–680.

RESEARCH BASE

DOLE, J., ROGERS, T., & OSBORN, J. (1987). Improving the selection of basal reading programs: A report of the Textbook Adoption Guidelines Project. *Elementary School Journal, 87*(3), 283–298.

DUFFY, G., ROEHLER, L., & PUTNAM, J. (1987). Putting the teacher in control. Basal reading textbooks and instructional decision making. *Elementary School Journal, 87,* 357–366.

DURKIN, D. (1981). Reading comprehension instruction in five basal reading series. *Reading Research Quarterly, 16,* 515–544.

SHANNON, P. (1983). The use of commercial reading materials in American elementary schools. *Reading Research Quarterly, 19,* 68–85.

13 | How to Plan and Teach Lessons and Units

GETTING READY

Getting organized for reading instruction involves many tasks. You must organize a literate environment, collect and organize data to form reading groups, and establish control over the basal reading textbook. Of all the organizing you do, however, planning is particularly crucial. This chapter describes how you can organize reading lessons and reading units using both indirect and direct instruction.

FOCUS QUESTIONS

- Why are instructional objectives so important?
- What is the purpose of each of the three parts of an instructional objective?
- Why are units important in organizing instruction?
- Why are lessons important in organizing instruction?
- What are the decisions you must make to plan indirect lessons?
- What are the decisions you must make to plan direct lessons?
- What is the purpose of a task analysis?
- Why must teachers consider the subtleties of instruction as well as the lesson format?

OBJECTIVES: THE CORNERSTONE OF PLANNING

When teachers are asked what task requires most of their time, they often respond with "planning." Planning of individual lessons and units requires your attention and effort all year long. It is crucial because it directly affects the quality of instruction.

Regardless of whether you plan lessons and units using indirect or direct instruction, the most important thing you can do is clearly state your objectives. For instance, you should know precisely what attitude, process, or content goals you are trying to achieve. When you do, your lessons have a focus. You know what you are trying to accomplish and, because you do, your students are better able to accomplish this. Consequently, for any lesson you teach, you should always be able to answer the questions: "Why am I doing this? What is the goal I am after? What should my students be doing differently after this lesson?"

Stating Objectives

A good instructional objective is a carefully structured statement. It has three parts, which are described in the following sections.

Student Behavior The first and most important part of an objective is a description of what students will be able to do after successful instruction. If you are teaching an attitude goal such as appreciation of free verse poetry, you might want your students to voluntarily select free verse poems for sharing with the class, something they do not now do. The objective might be, "The student will voluntarily select free verse poems to share with the class." If you are teaching a process goal such as the use of prefixes to figure out the meaning of unknown words, you might want students to tell you both the meaning of the unknown prefixed word and the process used to figure out its meaning. So the objective might be, "The student will state the meaning of previously unknown prefixed words and the thinking used to determine the meaning." If you are teaching a content goal such as reading a history chapter for information about the causes of the Civil War, the objective might be, "The student will read the chapter and state the three causes of the Civil War cited by the author." In each case, you create a descriptive statement of what students should be able to do after instruction. The targeted student behavior must be observable so that after the lesson you can determine whether or not your students are doing what you intended.

The Situation The second part of a good instructional objective specifies the situation where what is learned will be used. In reading, this means you must specify a real reading situation, since you want students to use what you teach when they are reading on their own. The real reading situation for the poetry objective is when students have the opportunity to voluntarily select poems to share with the class. Consequently, when you add the situation to your objective, the following statement of desired student behavior results: "Given a display of free verse poetry in the classroom, the student will voluntarily select free verse poems to share with the class." You are saying that the situation where the intended learning will be observed will be when students voluntarily read free verse poetry during class from the display provided. If, however, you want students to read free verse poetry during free time at home, then you must specify home reading as the situation that best indicates an appreciation of free verse poetry.

In a prefix lesson, you might want students to use prefixes to figure out the meaning of unknown words when reading books of their choice. Consequently, the situational part of your objective might be: "Given self-selected texts in which unknown prefixed words are encountered, the student will state the meaning of the unknown words and the thinking used to determine the meanings." Here you are saying that it is not good enough that students use prefix knowledge on workbook pages or ditto sheets; you must see them using the strategy with self-selected text to be satisfied that the desired learning has occurred.

In a lesson on the causes of the Civil War, you might amend your objective to read, "Given the history textbook and a study guide that helps locate passages about the causes of the Civil War, the student will read the chapter and state three causes of the Civil War cited by the author." Here you are saying that the desired learning should occur when students are asked to read the textbook.

The Criterion The third part of a good instructional objective is a statement of how well or how often students have to do a task for you to accept it as learned. In the case of appreciating free verse poetry, you might be satisfied with one reading of free verse. Consequently, the objective could be stated as follows: "Given a display of free verse poetry in the classroom, the student will voluntarily select at least one free verse poem to share with the class." In the case of the prefix strategy, you would not usually feel comfortable with only a single completion. Therefore, the objective might be stated: "Given self-selected text in which unknown prefixed words are encountered, the student will state the meaning of the words and the thinking used to determine the meanings on at least five occasions." For the content objective, you may decide that since a study guide has been provided the student should identify all three causes. Consequently, the objective might be stated: "Given the history textbook and a study guide that helps locate the passages dealing with the causes of the Civil War, the student will correctly state the three causes cited by the author."

To summarize, the hallmark of effective instruction is your awareness of the goal you are seeking. Specifically, the goal or objective focuses the unit or lesson, both for you and for your students. The best way to specify the goal is to state what you want students to be able to do, the situation in which it should be done, and the criterion that will make you confident that it has really been learned. With objectives clearly stated, a unit or lesson is off to a good start.

IMPORTANT ASPECTS OF UNIT PLANNING

Instructional units serve one primary purpose: to bring meaningful cohesion to a series of lessons. To achieve this function, two major conditions must be met.

First, a unit must have a theme that helps students tie learning together. The theme may be suggested by the basal textbook, but is usually determined by you on the basis of student interests. If your students are interested in animals and there are animals in each of the basal text selections, you could establish an animal theme; if your students are interested in building something, you can establish a theme about building. In any case, the theme cuts across reading selections and focuses on content—that is, the theme focuses on what the selections are about as they relate to students' interests.

Second, a unit must have a culminating activity. There should be an activity toward which students are working during the unit and that marks the end of the unit. Of course, this activity must reflect the theme. If the theme is animals, the culminating activity must somehow involve animals met in the unit, such as sharing stories they have written about animals; if the theme is building, then the culmination should be about building something, preferably things that were read about in the selections, such as models of bridges they read about. The theme and culminating activity provide an essential unitary characteristic that promotes instructional cohesion. Students perceive that their lessons are tied together in sensible ways, rather than being a series of isolated tasks.

Within this framework, you teach the reading goals selected for the unit. For instance, if the theme and culminating activities involve animals, the attitude, process, and content goals selected for the unit are taught within the framework of animals. Your students are motivated because the context provided by the theme and culminating activity reflect their interests; that is, they perceive the activities to be worthwhile so they learn the reading goals better.

To plan a unit, it is useful to follow a format such as that shown in Figure 13.1. Before planning individual lessons, develop the overall unit plan. After the unit is planned, plan individual lessons for each separate day.

The elements of unit planning described here should be combined with the modifications of basal units as described in Chapter 12. That is, imposing theme and culminating activity as described here is combined with reorganizing basal prescriptions as described earlier. The two result in clearly organized goals and objectives (from modifying the basal) and motivated students (from being taught within the context of a theme and a culminating activity).

LESSON PLANNING USING INDIRECT INSTRUCTION

In indirect instruction, you structure the environment and assign activities for students to interpret in ways that lead them to specific goals. Your role tends to be less intrusive than in direct instruction, and the activities you assign to your students take priority. Hence, the lesson planning format for indirect instruction revolves around an activity.

Ultimately, when students are engaged in indirect instruction they work

FIGURE 13.1   Unit Plan Format

1. Goals and objectives
   - What attitude, process, and content goals and objectives are students to learn during the unit?

2. Theme
   - What theme will capture students' interests and impose unity on the series of lessons?

3. Introduction and motivation
   - How will the purpose of the unit be presented?
   - How will students be motivated?

4. Unit schedule
   - How many days will the unit take?
   - What will be achieved each day?

5. Culminating activity
   - How will the unit be ended?
   - What will be done to bring closure and a sense of wholeness to the unit?

6. Evaluation
   - How will you determine whether the goals and objectives were achieved?

---

independently with little assistance from you. However, as noted in Chapter 4, instruction can be thought of as a continuum from direct to indirect. At the extreme, indirect instruction means no intervention from you at all. However, there are many times (especially when activities are being introduced) when instruction is indirect because your students learn some goals incidentally, but direction from you is nevertheless evident. This type of lesson is described here.

There are three major steps in the planning format for indirect instruction. First, involve students in an activity. Usually, this activity is associated with the literate environment, but it is chosen because of its potential for leading students to the specific goal identified in the objective. Second, discuss the activity with students. This discussion focuses students' attention on the desired goal, although you refrain from being overly directive. Finally, involve students in a second activity. This follow-up activity is related to the first one and gives students the opportunity to further develop what was the focus of the discussion.

This three-step format—activity-discussion-activity—is typical of many lessons based on indirect instruction. For instance, you can use uninterrupted sustained silent reading to develop positive attitudes toward reading and the concept that reading is enjoyable and rewarding. During the course of a week

Although indirect instruction often looks spontaneous, it is actually carefully planned. (Robert Bawden)

or more, the USSR activity often follows the three-step format: The activity is the reading; periodically you hold informal discussions with your students about the books they or you are reading with the intent of focusing them on positive responses and on the concept that reading is enjoyable and rewarding; and after the discussion, your students return to the reading activity.

Similarly, the typical language experience lesson is often organized around the three-step format. You may want to develop the twin concepts that reading and writing are related and written text conveys an author's message. To do so, you organize the first activity, a field trip to the fire station (perhaps in conjunction with a social studies unit on community helpers). On returning from the field trip, you discuss with your students the desirability of thanking the firemen for their help, shaping the discussion so students understand that their message can be effectively communicated through writing. You then move to the next activity, in which your students dictate a note of thanks, which you record on a sheet of language experience paper and then send to the firemen. Again, the three-step format of activity-discussion-activity has guided your organization of indirect instruction.

Analyzing Planning Decisions

Indirect instruction is deceptive. It often looks spontaneous and inventive. Teachers who use indirect instruction well are often labeled creative, meaning that others admire their ability to be so innovative on the spur of the moment. However, most good indirect instruction is not entirely spontaneous; it is planned. There is creativity, but it is found not in the teacher's ability to think on the spot so much as in his or her ability to make plans. To illustrate the kinds of planning decisions that must be made, let's examine a sample lesson that has some characteristics of indirect instruction. The steps are outlined in Figure 13.2.

Assume you are teaching a second grade class. You have observed that students in this class do not make predictions using text structure and that they have difficulty seeing the relationship between reading and writing. You want to change this situation by teaching story structure. The common **story structure** consists of an introduction that includes setting, main character, and problem; events related to the problem; and resolution of the problem.

Your first decision is to make instruction more indirect than direct because the goals you are after are conceptual and are best achieved through environmental experiences. Also, you are influenced by the fact that almost all the students in the class need to achieve these conceptual goals, so you use a large-group setting. Because you want your students to have experiences that cause them to associate reading with predicting and with writing, and because large-group instruction seems most efficient, you think more in terms of indirect instruction than direct instruction.

Your second decision involves translating the goals into an objective. You want students to understand that reading stories involves predicting based on typical story structure and that reading and writing are related. You translate these goals into observable student behaviors that can be stated as objectives. If you could observe your students writing a story in which they used story structure to create the meaning, this would be evidence that both goals were being achieved. Therefore, you state the objective as follows:

FIGURE 13.2   Decisions to Make in Planning Indirect Instruction

1. Decide to be more indirect than direct in achieving the outcome.

2. Specify the goal or objective.

3. Decide upon the three-part format of activity-discussion-activity.

4. Decide what you will say or do to facilitate the goal at each of the three major points of the lesson.

5. Assess your success in achieving the desired goal.

"Given the opportunity to write a story, students will write their own story using a story structure similar to the story the teacher read to them." The story writing is the behavior reflecting the targeted goals; the situation is that it should be modeled on the story that was read to them; and the criterion implied is that writing a single story will be an indication that learning has occurred.

Your third decision is to identify what happens at each step of the three-step format. The first step, the activity, is to read your students a story that uses a common story structure. The second step is to discuss with your students the various parts of the story structure and how they can use these parts to predict meaning and how, if the reader uses structure to predict meaning, the writer can use it to build meaning. The last step is another activity in which your students use the first story as a model to create a new story.

Fourth, you face a series of decisions about each of the three steps of the lesson. Step 1 involves selecting an appropriate story and deciding how to introduce it to your students. In selecting the story, you must be sure that it will be enjoyable for second grade students and that it reflects the structure employed in most stories. Consequently, you may select a book such as Mercer Mayer's picture and words book called *There Is a Nightmare in My Closet*. Second graders love it and it follows the familiar story structure of setting, character, problem, a series of events relating to the problem, and a resolution of the problem. In introducing the story, you decide to read it once for enjoyment and then to read it again during the discussion to point out the story parts.

To expedite identification of the story parts, step 2, you decide to show your students the pictures most closely associated with a particular part of the story, decide on key statements you must make to ensure a smooth discussion, and decide on any support materials (chalkboard illustrations, handouts, etc.) that might help achieve the goals. Once the story parts are identified, you prepare students for writing by modeling how the same story parts guide an author who is writing a story like Mayer's.

For step 3 of the lesson, you invite your students to use the same story parts to create a story like Mayer's. To ensure that the task does not become overwhelming and therefore frustrating, you give each student a booklet. On each page, you have written a component of story structure to guide the students (the first page is for *setting*, the second for *character*, the third for *problem*, etc.). Further, you elicit a story idea from each student before they begin writing, thereby ensuring that no one is left without a story to write.

At the conclusion of the lesson, you assess its success by determining which students attained the performance specified in the objective. Those students who wrote their own story using the story structure have achieved the conceptual understanding that reading involves predicting and that there is a strong relationship between reading and writing.

You might have a follow-up lesson that emphasizes the interrelated nature of reading and writing by having your students read the books they have written to younger children. Your first decision regarding this lesson involves choosing indirect instruction. Since the goal of having students better understand the interrelated nature of reading and writing involves developing a concept about reading and writing, indirect instruction seems appropriate. You state the objective in the following way: "Given a self-authored story, the student will read the story to younger children." The three-part lesson format for indirect instruction would consist of the following: students read their own stories; you discuss with them how to introduce their stories to younger children; and students introduce and read their own stories to younger children. You can then have students evaluate how the reading went and how well they read their story to the younger children.

LESSON PLANNING USING DIRECT INSTRUCTION

When using direct instruction to achieve process and content goals, you assume a much more overt instructional role. You define the task for students through verbal mediation; that is, you directly and explicitly explain to your students how to use a reading strategy or how to extract content from the text. Hence, the lesson planning format for direct instruction for process goals focuses on using a strategy to make sense out of text; the lesson planning format for direct instruction for content goals focuses on the information the student is to extract from the text.

With direct instruction, teachers carefully explain what students must do to accomplish a task. (Courtesy of Michigan State University)

Planning Direct Instruction for Process Goals

There are eight steps for planning direct instruction of process goals. They are described in the modified direct reading lesson presented in Chapters 4 and 12 and outlined in Figure 12.2.

When you teach a process goal, you want students to consciously use their knowledge. To develop such metacognitive awareness of story structures, for instance, use the MDRL and state the objective something like this: "Given an appropriate basal text, the student will state how story structure was used to make predictions about meaning in each of five different stories." In short, you want your students to state how they used story structure to predict meaning in five different basal text stories so you can determine if they are metacognitively aware.

Once you state the objective, begin planning the lesson using the MDRL. The first step is to select a basal text story in which story structures can be applied. Introduce the story by giving your students background information that activates their prior knowledge about the topic of the story, that develops new vocabulary associated with that topic, that gets them thinking about the author's purposes for writing the story (whether it is to inform, to entertain, to provide a moral lesson, or whatever), and that establishes what will be applied while reading the story. In this case, it is conscious use of story structures to predict meaning.

In the next section of the lesson, tell your students explicitly what they will be learning, where in the basal text selection they will apply it, and what they must attend to in order to learn it. This introductory step requires that you do a task analysis. A **task analysis** is just what the name implies: it is an analysis of the task being taught. Its purpose is to arm you with specific information about what to tell your students about how to perform the process goal (i.e., using story structures to predict meaning).

A task analysis has three parts, as can be seen in Figure 13.3. The features and sequence identified in the task analysis become the mental process (or thinking) you want students to consciously apply when using knowledge to make sense of text. Using our current example, the goal is the conscious use of story structure to make predictions about what will happen in a story; the language principle is the common story format; the features are the elements of the story structure; and the sequence might be identifying the story part, noting the information contained there, and using that information along with general information about the topic to predict what will happen next.

Once you have introduced knowledge of story structures, you should model its use. This is a crucial step since it is during modeling that you actually show students how good readers consciously apply structural knowledge to make predictions. While you might use visual aids and other devices at this stage, the best way to model is by explaining your own thinking processes. When teaching story structures, for instance, select a sample story and start by saying, "When reading this story, I first look at setting, characters, and problem. I see that it is about . . . ." In short, you make explicit the mental process identified in the task analysis by showing your students exactly how

FIGURE 13.3   Task Analysis

Goal
What is the goal I am after? What do I want my students to be able to do?

Critical features
What do readers pay particular attention to as they do this?

Sequence
What sequence do readers follow in thinking through the task and achieving the goal?

Result: A mental process, consisting of features and sequence, which students can use as a starting point when trying to do what you are trying to teach them to do.

you use it. In so doing, you ensure that your students have a model to follow as they attempt to use the knowledge. They are not left to figure it out for themselves. This is referred to as **mental modeling.**

In the next step, you mediate students' acquisition of the learning objective by providing guided practice. Mediation includes much assistance at first, with a gradual lessening of this assistance as students begin to catch on. For instance, you will initially provide students with many statements to direct their use of the knowledge or strategy, as well as cues and highlighting (such as underlining or pointing to particular elements) to assist them in thinking through the process. Gradually, you withdraw the cues and statements until your students are thinking with no assistance.

In teaching story structure, for instance, you will give students sample stories and ask them to use story structures to predict meaning and to explain how they do so. Initially, you may point to each of the three major story parts and make prompting statements regarding the next step in making predictions. As students do their thinking out loud, you listen for knowledge of story structures and provide assistance whenever they exhibit confusion regarding its use. Gradually, you provide less and less assistance as your students begin using the mental process without assistance.

Once students demonstrate an understanding of how the knowledge is used, guide them in applying it to the basal story that was introduced at the beginning. In a story structure lesson, for instance, you will not only talk to students about the content of the story they are reading but will also tell them that the story follows the same three-step format they just learned about and that they should use the thinking process they just practiced to make predictions about content while reading the story. Then you have students read the story with these two purposes in mind.

In the case of story structures, you may wish to combine the reading and the discussion by having the story read in sections corresponding to the major story parts and, as students finish each section, discuss with them their predictions about what will happen next. In any case, monitor their application of what was taught, and then close the lesson by having them summarize both the story content and the way story structures were used to predict that content.

Once your students have successfully applied the process goal to a basal story, you must still transfer the learning to other settings. For instance, remind students to use the knowledge of story structures when doing uninterrupted silent sustained reading and when reading textbooks. You can also use other activities in the literate environment to accomplish transfer. A particularly useful technique is to have your students write their own stories using a story structure. This not only reinforces the knowledge taught but also strengthens their understanding of the reading-composing relationship.

As can be seen, teaching story structures by direct instruction is significantly different from teaching story structures in a more indirect way. The planning format used for direct instruction of process goals is different, requiring careful task analysis, explicit teacher explanation and careful teacher mediation and guidance throughout. Figure 13.4 illustrates the steps for deciding the progression of the instructional sequence for process goals.

Planning Direct Instruction for Content Goals

The lesson format for direct instruction of content goals is the directed reading lesson, not the modified directed reading lesson, because when teaching content goals, you are less concerned with whether students understand how they get meaning. Instead, you simply want to make sure students understand the message.

To illustrate, let's go back to the process lesson on story structures described above. A content lesson involving the same story focuses on the story, not on how to use story structure to predict meaning. You might ask questions about the story in a sequence paralleling the story structure. However, your objective is that your students learn the content, not story structure.

Content lessons are also different from process lessons in the kind of direct instruction provided. In a process lesson, you make visible the thinking processes used to make sense out of text. In the story structure illustration, for instance, the lesson focused on how thinking about story structure can affect comprehension. In a content lesson, however, you focus on the topic, the author's purposes, and the information to be gleaned from the text. The intention is that your students will demonstrate understanding of information in the story or selection.

Although the lesson plan format for content and process lessons is similar in this first step, subsequent steps differ greatly. In an MDRL for process goals, you carefully explain how the targeted reading strategy works and how it is to be applied to the story. In a DRL for content goals, however, you move directly to the story, carefully stating the purposes for reading the selection (the value of the information contained in the text) and providing

FIGURE 13.4   Decisions to Make in Planning Direct Instruction of Process Goals

1. Assess to determine whether students need to learn the knowledge or strategy.

2. Decide whether to use direct or indirect techniques.

3. State the learning as a specific instructional objective.

4. Do a task analysis of what you want the student to be able to do.

5. Select a text in which the knowledge or strategy can be used.

6. Select examples to be used for your own modeling and for student practice.

7. Decide on the substance of what you will say and on the sequence of the lesson, following the eight-step format for direct instruction of process goals (MDRL).

8. Assess your instruction and decide whether it was effective.

whatever study aids (guides, notes, summaries) students might need. The differences continue as your students read and discuss the text. In an MDRL, the discussion deals with how the reading strategy was used to make sense out of the selection, whereas in a DRL the discussion deals with the pertinent information in the text. Similarly, the lesson closure differs. In a content lesson, only the content is summarized; in a MDRL, both the content and the strategy used to understand the content are summarized. Figure 13.5 illustrates the decisions to make in planning direct instruction for content goals.

To summarize, direct instruction for content differs greatly from direct instruction for process despite similarities in the lesson plan format. To be effective, you must first decide if you are developing an understanding of content or an understanding of process. Only when this decision is made should you proceed with planning and conducting the lesson.

Analyzing Planning Decisions

Like all good instruction, direct instruction requires careful planning, whether the goal is process or content. You must have a clear concept of the intended goal and must have the techniques and examples to be used firmly in mind. This does not mean that direct instruction involves no spontaneity on your part; on the contrary, unanticipated student responses frequently require you to spontaneously modify your lesson plans. Such interactive decision making is only effective if you carefully make the preceding planning decisions. The better prepared you are, the more likely it is that you will be able to spontaneously create good responses to unanticipated happenings.

To illustrate the planning decisions in direct instruction of process, assume once again that you are teaching a second grade class. You note that

FIGURE 13.5   Decisions to Make in Planning Direct Instruction of Content Goals

1. Decide whether the selection is worth reading.

2. State an objective for the content knowledge you want students to learn.

3. Analyze what the students need to know about the words, topic, purpose, and text structure in order to get the content knowledge.

4. Decide how you will aid students in using the words, topic, purpose, and text structure to get the content knowledge.

5. Decide the sequence of the lesson and what you will say in the lesson.

6. Decide how you will evaluate whether the lesson has been a success.

prefixes is one of the skills suggested by the basal text being used by one of your groups and students in that group cannot figure out the pronunciation of an unrecognized prefixed word. Since your assessment indicates a need for instruction, you make your first decision: You decide to teach prefixes.

Second, you decide which of the three major goals you are after and what kind of instruction to use. Since you want your students to use prefixes to repair blockages to meaning caused by unrecognized words, you are teaching a process goal. Since strategies are better taught by direct than by indirect instruction, you decide to use direct instruction.

Third, you decide to state the goal as an instructional objective. In this case, you state your objective as follows: "Given a text containing unrecognized words having a known root prefixed by *dis-* or *un-*, the student figures out how to say the unrecognized word and explains the thinking used to figure out the word in each of the five samples of real text."

The fourth decision is to do a task analysis of how readers think through the process of figuring out the pronunciation of unknown words having prefixes. You know the goal is to consciously apply a strategy to pronounce unrecognized prefixed words; the language principle is that new words can be built by adding prefixes and suffixes; a sequence to follow in identifying a prefixed word could be identify the root, identify the prefix, separate the two, pronounce each separately, pronounce them as one word, and see if the word makes sense in the sentence.

The fifth decision is to select a text that will give your students a real opportunity to apply the strategy. Usually, basal text stories are used, although you must ensure that the basal selection does indeed contain prefixed words that your students might not recognize so there is really an opportunity to apply the strategy. If there is no text situation and you teach it in isolation, students may never learn to apply it to text.

Sixth, collect examples that can be used when explaining the strategy. There must be examples you can use for modeling and examples students can use to try out the strategy. Not only must there be enough examples, they must all be ones which reflect the critical features of the strategy.

Seventh, decide what to say during the course of the lesson. Since direct instruction is heavily dependent upon your ability to explain things, it is necessary that you plan what to say. This does not mean that you must write out everything you will say ahead of time. It *does* mean, however, that you think carefully about what needs to be said, make notes about the sequence of your explanation, decide on key statements, on what to display on the chalkboard, on what material (if any) students should have in hand during the explanation, and so on. It is helpful to use the MDRL format to guide your thinking in this regard. Example 13.1 illustrates what a carefully stated lesson in prefixes looks like when it follows this format and shows how a teacher might talk through each step.

Finally, assess the effect of your instruction and decide whether you were successful or not. Did your students learn to use prefixes? Do they exhibit the behavior specified in your objective? In this regard, it is sometimes useful to interview students following instruction. If, after your lesson is over, students can answer the questions "What were you learning to do? When would you use it in real reading? How do you do it?" you have probably been instructionally successful.

The decision patterns are similar when teaching a content goal. However, rather than starting with a skill contained in the basal, you start with a selection that needs to be read. Your first decision is whether this selection is worth reading. You then decide why it is worth reading, and develop an objective describing what student behavior will be when the targeted content has been learned. Instead of doing a task analysis as you would with a process goal, you analyze what knowledge sources (words, topic, purpose, and text structure) the student might use to get meaning from the text. On the basis of this analysis, you decide what learning aids to provide your students to ensure that they get the targeted content. Such aids might take the form of an explanation or could be paper-and-pencil aids such as study guides that focus students on the right section of the text or on certain relationships being developed by the writer. In any case, decide how you will talk to students during the lesson. Finally, as with the process lesson, decide how to evaluate the success or failure of the lesson.

To summarize, direct instruction is *not* a matter of planning an instructional script and then reading it to students. It is a carefully developed, well-structured, and explicit effort to achieve particular curricular goals with the particular group of students you are teaching at the moment. Careful planning is essential for two reasons. First, teaching students how to make sense from text is a complex and difficult task. If you do not think carefully about it, the instruction can become jumbled and confusing. Second, all instruction demands that you be able to respond spontaneously during instruction to your students' unanticipated responses while still maintaining an instructional focus on the intended goal. Such focused spontaneity is not possible unless careful planning has been done beforehand. Consequently, good planning is crucial to effective direct instruction.

PLANNING FOR THE SUBTLETIES OF INSTRUCTION

The foregoing suggestions for planning lessons are important and practical. However, good lesson planning is not simply a matter of following a format. Instruction requires subtle distinctions and decisions, some of which are described below.

Lesson Length

Many people think of lessons as confined to a definite length of time, usually a single class period. However, lessons are seldom started and finished in one day. What is planned for either direct or indirect instruction often extends over several class periods, even if everything goes perfectly.

In reality, however, things seldom go perfectly. No matter how well you plan, something always needs improving. Consequently, a lesson plan initiated one day will often need to be modified overnight and presented again in order to clarify points of confusion. Often the second day of instruction will begin with a review of the first day and, depending on the review, will either remain at the first phase of the lesson or move on to the next phase. Lesson plans are not permanent documents. They are constantly being tinkered with, modified, adjusted, and improved to meet the needs of your students. This tinkering requires careful attention and subtle decision making.

Introducing the Lesson

Direct instruction requires that students be told what the lesson is about at the outset. However, when the targeted goal is the use of a strategy, three factors complicate the seemingly simple task of introducing the lesson.

First, there is the difficulty of translating skills into strategies. It is easier to introduce a lesson on main idea by saying, "Today, we are going to learn *about* main ideas" rather than saying, "Today, we are going to learn *how to figure out* the main idea the author is trying to convey." The distinction is subtle, but crucial. If your students are to learn how to be strategic readers, you must emphasize strategic thinking, not knowledge about the skill.

Second, although it is easier to think in terms of separate and isolated lessons, in actuality lessons cannot be isolated from one another. Instead, each lesson is a minor variation of earlier ones. All share certain characteristics: the goal of sense making, active student thinking, student use of text and prior knowledge to predict, and student confirmation or rejection of predictions based on whether the result makes sense in context. Consequently, you make better progress when you emphasize common themes instead of teaching isolated lessons. Again, the difference is subtle, but critical.

Third, being a good reader means understanding where and when to use the strategies that have been learned; application is crucial. Hence, you should specify when a strategy is to be used in real reading. Rather than saying that a strategy "will make you a better reader," it is better to start with

EXAMPLE 13.1   Sample Lesson for Direct Instruction of Process Goals: Teaching Prefixes as a Strategy for Pronouncing Unrecognized Words

1. Introducing the basal text lesson

"Today we are going to read a story about a monkey that lived in the zoo. How many of you have been to the zoo? What do you see at the zoo? We are going to read about the monkeys that lived in the zoo and the special problem a monkey named Clyde had with his brothers and sisters. Now in this story there are some hard words that you have never had before. Here's one right here [*shows students*]. Here's another [*shows students*]. I'm going to teach you a strategy for figuring out these words and others like them so that, when you come to them in the story, you will be able to figure them out yourselves and go right on finding out about what happens to the monkey."

2. Introducing the strategy

"Sometimes when you are reading you run into a word you don't recognize, like the words I just showed you which are in the story we'll read today. Because you don't recognize it, you can't understand the story. So we need to stop and figure out the word. Today I'm going to show you how to figure out unrecognized words that have prefixes on them. At the end of the lesson, you will have a strategy for pronouncing in your basal text story or in other books you read those unrecognized words that begin with the prefix *dis-* or *un-*. This strategy will help you figure out the pronunciation of prefixed words so you can continue getting the author's meaning despite these hard words. In order to do this, you need to look for the root word, then look for the *dis-* or *un-*. Then you separate the two, pronounce each one separately, then say the prefix and the root together."

3. Mental Modeling

"I'll explain how I figure out words like these. You'll do this in a moment, so pay attention to the way I figure these words out. Let's say that I'm reading along in my basal story and I run into the word *unhappy*. If I've never seen this word before, I say to myself, 'Oh, oh. I need to figure this word out if I'm going to continue getting the author's meaning.' So I stop, look at the word and think about what strategy I can use to make sense out of this word. I see that it is a prefixed word, so I think about a prefix strategy. I find the root [*circles it*]. I separate the root from the prefix [*draws a line between them*]. Then I pronounce the prefix—*un-*. Then I pronounce the root—*happy*. Then I say the two parts together—*unhappy*. Then I put the word back into the sentence in the story to make sure it makes sense. Now let's review what I did. You tell me the steps I followed, and I'll list them up here on the board. Susie, what did I do first? Yes, first I . . . [*writes on board*] . . . then I . . . [*writes on board*] . . . , [etc.]."

4. Mediating students' initial attempts to apply the strategy using directives and cues

"Can you use my strategy to figure out unrecognized words? Let's try one and I'll help you. Let's assume that you are reading your story and you come to this unknown word [*writes* dislike *on the board, circling the prefix and root and drawing a line between them*]. Let's see if you can use the strategy I used to figure out this word. You have two things to help you: the steps in the strategy listed on the board here [*points*] and the circles and lines in the word you're trying to figure out here [*points*]. Mary, show me how you use the strategy to figure out this word." [*Mary responds by starting with the recognition of a break in meaning getting caused by an unknown word and by going through the steps of the strategy aloud, ultimately identifying the word as* dislike *and checking to see if it makes sense in the sentence.*]

• Interaction with questions and faded cues

"Okay. That was good because you thought about how to figure out words that begin with the prefix *dis-* or *un-*. Now let's see if you can do the same thing when I give you less help. I'm going to erase from the board the steps of my strategy, and you see if you can use a strategy of your own that is like mine. And when I

EXAMPLE 13.1   continued

put our word [*writes* unkind *on the board*], I'll just circle the prefix and root but leave off the dividing line [*circles prefix and root*]. Now, Sam, what would you do first to figure out this word? Can you show me how you'd figure out the word?" [*Sam responds by just pronouncing the word, says* unkind.] "You said the word correctly, Sam, but I don't know whether you were doing the thinking correctly. What did you do first? Talk out loud so I can hear how you figured that word out." [*Sam responds, stating the steps he used.*] "That's good, Sam. You stated the steps you used to figure out the word correctly. This strategy doesn't work all the time, because some of our words look like words with prefixes but really aren't." [*Illustrates the word* under.] "See if this word can be pronounced using our prefix strategy." [*Leads students through the process showing them where the strategy doesn't work and why.*]

● **Interaction with fewer cues**

[*Continues to elicit responses from the students, but gradually phases out the amount of assistance until the students are doing all the thinking without help and are figuring out the prefixed words independently. Provides other nonexamples, such as* unless, *having students state whether the strategy works and why.*]

● **Interaction with supportive feedback and no cues**

"Okay. Now before I give you practice in doing this alone, let's make sure we all know how to figure out words like these." [*Has students tell how they figure out prefixed words when no cues are provided. Also provides nonexamples for contrast.*]

5. Setting purposes for reading the basal selection

"Now we are going to read the story about the monkey named Clyde. We talked about the fact that Clyde had a problem with his brothers and sisters and we want to find out what that problem was and whether you have had similar problems in your house. There are some hard words in this story, which you haven't seen before. When you come to these words, say to yourself, 'Oh, oh. I'm going to have to figure this word out.' Then see if your prefix strategy will work, and, if the hard word does have a prefix, use what we learned about figuring out prefixed words to figure out the word in the story."

6. Silent or oral reading

[*Students read the story. The reading may be oral in primary grades but will almost always be silent reading in the middle and upper grades.*]

7. Discussion

[*Leads a discussion in which questions are posed about both the content and the application of the prefix strategy while reading the story. The intent is to assess whether students understood the content and the application of the prefix strategy.*]

8. Lesson closure

[*Closes the lesson by having students summarize what happened in the story and how the prefix strategy was used to help understand the story. May also do some kind of culminating activity, enriching activity, or broadened language experience activity at this stage as a means for bringing closure to the lesson. The closure should also include a statement such as the following.*] "All right. Now that you have successfully used the prefix strategy to figure out hard words in the basal text story, we have to be sure to use it in other things you read. What other things do you read where you could use this strategy? What if you ran into an unknown word when reading in your USSR book? Could you use this strategy in that situation? Can you tell how you would use the prefix strategy in reading a newspaper?"

a passage from real text, illustrate how one might lose the gist of such a passage, and state that "this strategy will help you fix situations like this when they happen to you." Again the distinction is subtle, but essential.

Showing Students How

All lesson plan formats include a section in which you explain and demonstrate what is being learned. Your explanations must reflect three subtle distinctions.

First, keep the desired goal firmly in mind. For instance, if the object is to teach a strategy, you must not get sidetracked into emphasizing the story's content. Explanations must focus on the process of understanding the strategy, not on the content itself. This is a subtle distinction because process can never be totally separated from content so we often end up emphasizing story content. Note what happens in the following lesson where a main idea strategy is being taught, but student responses indicate that they do not understand how to figure out the main idea. The teacher uses a paragraph about bears hibernating in the winter to reexplain.

T: Let's talk about animals that hibernate. You know what hibernate means, right? What does *hibernate* mean?

S: [*inaudible*]

T: Okay, animals that sleep through the winter, right? Now, what are some animals that might hibernate?

S: A bear.

T: Okay, a bear.

S: Rabbit.

T: Rabbit.

S: Fox.

T: I'm not sure about all the animals. Squirrels, okay. But don't you see squirrels out in the winter?

S: Yeah.

S: Yeah.

T: Then are they hibernating?

S: No.

S: Yeah.

T: Maybe they do. I don't know. Maybe that is something that I should check out, too.

At this point, the teacher realizes that she is not teaching students a strategy for figuring out main idea but is focusing on story content about animals that hibernate. She tries to shift to a process focus—that is, to the strategy for figuring out main idea. She generates the following nonexample:

T: Okay, let's say we were talking about those animals that hibernate and I said, "Oh, many, many animals sleep through the winter. Some of the animals are bears. Bears hibernate in caves." And I talk about bears, but then all of a sudden I say, "Fish swim in the sea."

S: How do fish hibernate in that cold water?

T: I didn't say they hibernate. I said "Fish swim in the sea." "Birds fly south." Is that about animals that hibernate?

S: No.

S: Yeah.

T: No. So, would this be included in my paragraph?

S: No.

T: No. So, what is a main idea? A main idea is a group of sentences that do what?

S [*in chorus*]: Hibernate.

Despite this teacher's best efforts, instruction failed because she slipped into discussing the content of the story when she should have continued to emphasize how to figure out the main idea. Maintaining a focus on the intended goal is the crucial component of effective instruction.

A second subtlety in lesson explanation involves showing students how to do something. Because reading is an invisible mental process, it cannot be demonstrated like a swimming instructor demonstrates a new stroke. Instead, you must make visible the thinking that led to the answer. To do this, say aloud the mental steps you perform when using the strategy (or that you have analyzed to be the steps a novice would need to use). Such thinking out loud models the thinking you want students to do. Hence, it is helpful to say, "When *I* use this strategy, I think first about the important words. For instance, in this paragraph, I read along and identify these words as important. Then I . . . ." In so doing, your students can initially "do as the teacher does" when employing the strategy. Such modeling is an essential part of explanation. Without it, your students may not know how to begin the task.

A third subtlety in making effective explanations requires that you not be too prescriptive. No one knows precisely how humans process information. The best that you can do is to analyze your own thinking, show your students what you do, and encourage them to adapt your model to their style and needs. Allowing for student adaptation is the key. Your model must be descriptive, not prescriptive. Say, "Here is a way I think about this problem.

Now I want to see if you can use my demonstration to help you solve similar problems." Don't say, "Here is *the* way to do this; you must employ it as I do."

Mediating Student Acquisition

A major part of a process lesson is the interactive phase, sometimes called **guided practice.** It is here that you attempt to move your students gradually to the point where they can use strategies independently. As in the other sections of the lesson, subtle verbal distinctions are crucial.

Explanation implies that a teacher does all the talking. However, when you do that, learning does not occur. There must be a gradual transition from teacher modeling to student control, and you must carefully judge how quickly or slowly to effect this transfer. Moving too quickly leaves students unclear about what to do; moving too slowly is boring. In order to control this transfer process, probe for how students get their answers, emphasizing mental processing rather than answer accuracy. For instance, when you direct a student to the main idea of a paragraph, it is better to ask, "How do you know what the main idea is?" than to ask "What is the main idea?" If your students show understanding of how to use the strategy, the lesson can progress; if they do not, more explanation is needed.

If student responses indicate a misunderstanding of the strategy, you must spontaneously generate a reexplanation. Such reexplanation is difficult because it requires instant decision making. In the following illustration taken from a lesson on main ideas, the teacher reads a paragraph to the group, then proceeds as follows.

T: Now, of these three titles, which one would be the best main idea? Mary?

S: A trip downtown.

T: Okay, John, what do you think?

S: The new shirt.

T: Bob, what was your choice?

S: The new shirt.

T: Joan, what about you?

S: A trip downtown.

At this point, it is clear that her students have not understood the teacher's explanation. The situation calls for an elaboration or reexplanation of how one figures out the gist of a paragraph. Instead, the teacher says:

T: I think the girls decided on a trip downtown and the boys like the new shirt. Mainly, what was the story about?

S: A trip downtown.

S: Getting a new shirt.

T: Getting a new shirt, wasn't it?

The teacher *does* try to elaborate by referring to what the story was mainly about. However, she is not explicit. Compare it to the following spontaneous reexplanation.

T: We seem to have some confusion. The main idea is the author's major message in the paragraph. Look at the paragraph here on the chalkboard. What words did we say were important in this paragraph? Sam, can you read them?

S: Store, shirt, buy, long-sleeved, downtown mall.

T: Good. Now, the topic of all these words—that ties them together—is what? Mary?

S: They're all about a new shirt.

T: Good. The new shirt is what it's about. That's the topic. Now I've got to think about what the author's major message is regarding the new shirt. So I think to myself, "What does the author want me to understand about the new shirt? What is his main message to me?" To do that, I think of how these words and sentences can be combined into a message. When I think about them together, it's more than just a new shirt. Let's combine them together like this [*writes on the board*]. What message ties all these words together? John?

S: It's about how to buy a new shirt.

T: Right. There are many words in paragraphs, but we have to decide what the main message is—what idea ties it all together. How did you know what ties this paragraph together, John?

S: I looked for words that would tell me what the topic was and then thought about what the author wants me to understand about the topic—about the shirt.

This spontaneously generated reexplanation is more helpful than the first sample because it's more explicit. This difference, though subtle, is crucial.

It is not unusual to use various kinds of highlighting to focus student attention on salient features of the strategy. For instance, you may use the chalkboard and underline key words, draw arrows from one meaning relationship to another, circle particular structures, or write out steps to help students learn to use the strategy. However, you must ensure that your students learn the intended goal, not the cues and prompts (such as your underlining or the steps in the procedure). You can be very explicit about salient features, steps, and sequences but, in the process, unintentionally make reading into a mechanical activity of rote memory rather than a strategic, sense-making activity.

Practice

All lesson plan formats call for practice, and all practice calls for repetition of a task to make it habitual. Here, again, the subtleties are crucial. An important consideration in the practice part of the lesson is in choosing the proper form of practice. Most teachers use workbooks or ditto sheets. However, these tend to emphasize artificial reading tasks. Since your object is to get students to use strategies in reading real text, we recommend that practice occur in guided reading of real text—for example, the basal text selection, the social studies text, library books, or some other real reading material. Then the learning can be practiced in contexts similar to where it will ultimately be used.

Another important decision involves the nature of the activities assigned students. In traditional basal instruction, students are asked to read and answer questions and are then assigned grades based on the number of correct answers. When teaching reading strategies, however, you are more interested in the thinking processes students go through to get the answer than in the answer itself. Good practice activities, therefore, call for repetitive use of the *thinking* involved. The goal is thoughtful, not automatized, application.

A third decision regarding practice involves the student behaviors you choose to reward. Since you want to develop a strategic approach to text, you should praise students for "knowing how they know." There is a fine distinction between being praised for thinking strategically and being praised for getting the right answer. The most effective instruction praises the former.

Transfer to Real Reading

Application is the most neglected part of all lessons. When teaching for strategic reading, application requires more than an opening statement about a strategy's usefulness or a general reminder of the possibility of applying it to a basal story. Application must include a genuine reading situation where, once a meaning breakdown occurs, students can be guided through their storehouse of strategies, select the appropriate one, fix the difficulty, and continue processing text. The subtlety here involves knowing how to help students recognize when a strategy is called for, how to access the proper one, how to use it in a real situation, and how to determine whether the strategy worked or not. This part of a teacher's explanation is perhaps more crucial than any other.

To summarize, using lesson plan formats helps guide the planning of indirect and direct instruction. These provide a structure that aids your decision making as you plan. However, good instruction also involves fine distinctions that you must anticipate. If you follow the lesson plan formats as a rote procedure, your instruction will be boring and ineffective. If, however, you use the lesson formats as a guide and think about the subtleties of the task, your students, and the intended application to read text, your instruction will be more successful, more interesting, and relevant.

SUMMARY

The essence of instruction is its intentionality. That is, instruction is designed to develop specific objectives through direct instruction, indirect instruction, or a combination thereof. To achieve intentionality, you must state objectives for both long-term units that build cohesive networks of understandings and for individual lessons that develop specific goals. The objective should not only state what the student should be able to do and how well, it should also state the situation and conditions under which it is to be done. If your instruction is to be mainly indirect, decisions revolve around the three steps of indirect lessons; if your instruction is to be mainly direct, decisions revolve around the eight steps of the modified directed reading lesson when teaching a process goal and around the directed reading lesson when teaching a content goal. For either kind of instruction, you must do a task analysis to decide where to direct your students' attention. However, instruction is a fluid, complex enterprise. You must be prepared with lesson formats but also must be prepared to make spontaneous subtle distinctions and adjustments as you teach.

SUGGESTED ADDITIONAL READING

ALLINGTON, R. L., & STRANGE, M. (1977). The problem with reading games. *Reading Teacher, 31*(3), 272–274.

ATWELL, A. A., & RHODES, L. K. (1984). Strategy lessons as alternatives to skill lessons in reading. *Journal of Reading, 27*(8), 700–705.

DAVEY, B. (1983). Think aloud: Modeling the cognitive processes of reading comprehension. *Journal of Reading, 27*, 44–47.

DUFFY, G., & ROEHLER, L. (1987). Improving reading instruction through the use of responsive elaboration. *Reading Teacher, 40*, 514–521.

DUFFY, G., & ROEHLER, L. (1987). Teaching reading skills as strategies. *Reading Teacher,* 414–418.

DUFFY, G., ROEHLER, L., & HERRMANN, B. A. (1988). Modeling mental processes helps poor readers become strategic readers. *Reading Teacher, 41*.

GAMBRELL, L. B. (1980). Think-time: Implications for reading instruction. *Reading Teacher, 34*(2), 143–146.

GUTHRIE, J. T. (1982). Teacher effectiveness: The quest for refinement. *Reading Teacher, 35*(5), 636–638.

GUZZETTI, B. J., & MARZANO, R. J. (1984). Correlates the effective reading instruction. *Reading Teacher, 37*(8), 754–758.

ISAACS, M. L. (1979). The many facets of language arts: Helps and handbooks for lesson planning. *Language Arts, 56*(5), 577–580.

JOHNS, J. L. (1982). Does our language of instruction confuse beginning teachers? *Reading Psychology, 3*(1), 37–41.

KITAGAWA, M. M. (1982). Improving discussions or how to get the students to ask the questions. *Reading Teacher, 36*(1), 42–45.

RILEY, J. D. (1979). Teachers' responses are as important as the questions they ask. *Reading Journal, 32*(5), 534–537.

SADOW, M. W. (1982). The use of story grammar in the design of questions. *Reading Teacher, 35*(5), 518–522.

SHAKE, M. C., & ALLINGTON, R. L. (1985). Where do teachers' questions come from? *Reading Teacher, 38*(4), 432–438.

RESEARCH BASE

DUFFY, G., ET AL. (1987). Effects of explaining the reasoning associated with using reading strategies. *Reading Research Quarterly, 22*(3), 347–368.

PEARSON, P. D. (1985). Changing the face of reading comprehension instruction. *Reading Teacher, 38*(8), 724–738.

ROEHLER, L., & DUFFY, G. (in press). Teachers' instructional actions. In R. Barr, M. Kamil, P. Mosenthal, & P. D. Pearson (Eds.), *Handbook of reading research*, 2nd ed. New York: Longman.

How to Manage Reading Instruction | 14

GETTING READY

More than any other single thing, the scarcity of time makes classroom teaching difficult. There are many things to do and not enough time in which to do them. Consequently, time is your most important instructional resource.

To get the most from the time you have, you must manage it well. Expert teachers manage reading instruction in three ways: they allocate time to reading, they assure effective activity flow, and they ensure sustained student engagement in tasks. This chapter develops each of these three management techniques.

The hard truth of teaching is that you can do all the organizational steps specified in previous chapters—create a literate environment, assess students' abilities, adapt the basal, and plan good lessons—and still be ineffective if you cannot get your students on task and keep them there. Consequently, management is crucial to getting organized for instruction.

FOCUS QUESTIONS

- What can you do to ensure that enough time is allocated to reading?

- What techniques can you employ to achieve smooth activity flow?

- What can be done to make sure that students remain engaged in tasks?

ALLOCATING TIME TO READING

In most classrooms, reading period occurs first thing each morning and lasts for an hour or an hour and a half. Typically, all this **allocated time** is taken up by basal text instruction. Usually a teacher meets with three or four reading groups during this time, teaching one group while the other groups do seatwork.

To develop all three goals of reading, however, you must think more broadly about how to allocate time for reading. Because reading permeates all aspects of the school day, you can integrate reading instruction into other school activities; that is, reading goals can be achieved during times other than the hour or hour and a half planned for reading. In the area of attitudes, for instance, you can develop conceptual understandings about the communication function of reading in conjunction with any subject matter; you can develop concepts about the reciprocal nature of reading and writing during a writing period; and you can develop positive responses to reading at any point in the school day when you are sharing stories and poems. Similarly, you can teach certain process goals about how the reading system works from a social studies or science textbook as well as from a basal reader. Finally, you can develop content goals anytime a text is used. In short, reading goals can be developed all day long.

Likewise, you can integrate other school content into reading time. Students can read science materials as seatwork during the reading period, read stories and poems during reading group time, and share quality books in collaborative student groups as seatwork while you work with another reading group. You can arrange for direct and indirect instruction to occur simultaneously. For instance, while you directly instruct one reading group, other reading groups can be engaged in indirect instructional activities.

Accomplishing such integration, however, requires careful year-long planning. You must identify when certain goals will be developed, and you must consciously allocate instructional time for reading beyond the usual hour or hour and a half. For instance, you must examine the year-long lan-

Reading goals can be achieved while sharing stories. (George Bellerose/Stock, Boston)

guage arts or social studies curriculum and decide when objectives in those areas can be integrated with reading goals. Integrating reading with other content areas does not occur by accident; you must consciously plan instructional time to make the integration happen. By doing so, you create more instructional time for reading.

Another way to create more reading time is to look for **nook-and-cranny time** in the school day. All school days have "dead spots" of 5 to 10 minutes duration. It may be a transition from one activity to another or a short period of time between two special teachers or any other time that is too short to start a formal lesson. These nooks and crannies of time are gold mines for you if you are looking for extra reading time. For instance, these are good times for sharing and other activities designed to develop concepts and positive feelings. Similarly, these short periods of time are useful for direct instruction about how certain words convey emotional connotations, how to make predictions about what meaning is being communicated, or how to get content meaning from various kinds of texts.

PLANNING FOR EFFECTIVE CLASSROOM ACTIVITY FLOW

Successfully engaging students on tasks demands a smooth flow of classroom activity. Smooth **activity flow** depends on the physical arrangement of your room, the patterns you use, and your behaviors in managing academic content.

Physical Arrangement

If you plan to use both large- and small-group instruction and have an average sized room, then space becomes a problem. Many teachers find that the traditional rows of seats take up too much space, and they use seating clusters instead. Other teachers use a large rug in the middle of the room for whole-group instruction and have students sit at independent learning centers around the edges for beginning and closing exercises. There are many ways to physically arrange a classroom. The only limitations are the dimensions of the room and your creativity. Some teachers are very elaborate and use portable screens, old furniture, large floor pillows, and hanging screens as part of the physical setting. Some simply move the existing furniture. Others organize the room into a noisy half (interaction areas, physical activity areas, and small-group instruction areas) and a quiet half (listening centers, reading centers, and study areas). Whatever the arrangement, when teaching small groups you should place yourself where you can see the entire room. This allows you to monitor students who are not in the group and to help students in the small group remain attentive. Figure 14.1 shows two ways to create space by organizing classroom desks. Organizing student desks into rows, as in Plan 1, uses up too much floor space; space for learning centers and other activities is created by eliminating rows, as in Plan 2.

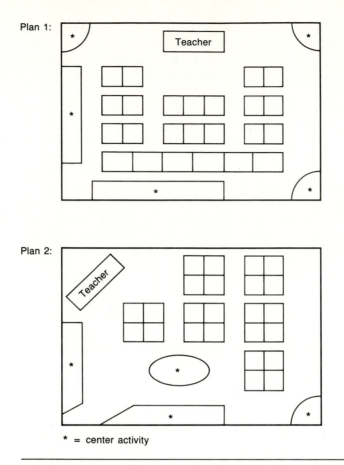

FIGURE 14.1   Creating Space by Organizing Classroom Desks

Patterns

When teachers work with a reading group, students not in the group must work independently. If students are to work independently, you must firmly establish patterns or routines on which both you and the students agree. For instance, if you want your students to complete a workbook page or a practice game independently during the reading period, you should provide them with a pattern of steps to follow. It is vital that students understand these patterns and use them frequently enough to acquire habits that operate without your direct supervision. You must develop patterns for independent activities, safety valve activities, procedures, and interaction between teacher and students.

Independent Activities Students who are not in the participating reading group will require **independent activities**. While you teach a small group, the other students work by themselves on activities such as reading for pleasure, applying and practicing skills, reading basal stories, completing science or social studies assignments, creative writing, or practicing oral and written language skills. They can complete these independent activities as individual seatwork or at centers located in various spots within the room.

Assume that you want to develop a classroom library and reading center for your students' independent activity when they are not in a small group. You need to make decisions about where to put these, what types of books to include, what types of furniture to use, and what patterns will govern its use. You might bring in shelves that are easily accessible to your students, a piece of carpeting or rug to mark the reading center, several bean bag chairs, and several large pillows for comfortable reading. You could file books on shelves alphabetically or by interest areas (mystery books, horse stories, stories of today's world, and so forth). The patterns you develop for using the reading center may include considerations such as: Where can your students read in the room? How are books to be returned? How long can a student stay in the center? Can your students return to their seats whenever they wish? Are there follow-up activities? Can your students choose whether to work in the center or at other places? You need to decide on these patterns and then have students practice them until they become routine. Giving attention to such detail may seem mundane, but it is crucial to the success of independent activities.

Safety Valves Once you create independent activities for your students to pursue while you are teaching small groups, you must be prepared for them to finish their assignments at varying times. Some will get done before you finish with a reading group, and if you have not anticipated this, disruptions may result. Consequently, you should plan safety valves that your students can fall back on when they finish their independent work early.

Safety valves usually take the form of learning centers or activities in which your students can participate at any time. They are different from independent activities because they do not change daily, they are not always associated with ongoing academic work in the classroom, and students think they are fun. Appropriate safety valves include recreational reading, writing in journals, vocabulary games, phonics games, chess or backgammon, art centers, or anything else that appeals to both you and your students. The important thing is that they can be completed with little assistance from you. You will, of course, need to establish with students the patterns to follow in using safety valves.

Procedural Patterns **Procedural patterns** include routines on how to start, change, keep track of progress, and stop. You should carefully establish each of these patterns.

You use **how-to-start patterns** to get initial information, such as directions and opening procedures, to your students. One way to handle this is to provide students with mailboxes, each containing directions for the period and other needed information. You can duplicate these directions on ditto sheets to minimize preparation time. The direction sheets tell your students what to do first, second, and so on. Using such a technique saves time and gets students engaged more quickly. For nonreaders, how-to-start procedures can make use of color. A manila folder that has been folded to form a pocket can hold needed materials color coded to correspond to different centers. Numbered clothespins could also be used. The intent is to keep your students well informed about procedures so they get on task as quickly as possible. Students can go to their mailboxes, pick up their directions and needed materials, return to their designated places, look at their directions, and begin. Transition time is minimized and instructional time is increased.

After how-to-start patterns are developed, **how-to-change patterns** are required. The options here are as varied as your preferences. Activities can be changed on a signal from you or when students have completed an activity. If you want students to change activities independently, one of your problems will be unfinished activities. For some activities, such as reading or ditto sheets, interruption poses little problem. However, an independent activity involving complicated steps (art projects, science experiments, and so forth) may create a problem. You can circumvent this by offering independent activities that can be interrupted during the reading period only. However you decide to change activities, your students need to know the patterns for change and to be able to implement them independently.

Once the reading period has started and is running smoothly, you need a way to keep track of students' activities. There are many ways to keep records efficiently. A good record-keeping device should not be bulky or cumbersome. It should require little time or effort to record your students' progress, and it should provide an immediate picture of where each student is in relation to desired reading goals. It should also assist in the development of reading groups. Further, it should allow you and your students to see progress. The things to remember are that it should be manageable in size and easy to use, while providing a good visual image of your students' progress relative to your goals.

A record-keeping device we have used with success consists of graph paper and a looseleaf notebook (see Figure 14.2). Arrange your students' names down the side of the paper and make divisions across the top for each of the three major goals. Within each square in each curricular category, list the objective for that outcome. As objectives are assessed, taught, retaught, practiced, or applied, note it in the squares for that objective. Keep the notebook handy to record events or behaviors as they occur, and inform students of the patterns for keeping track of progress.

Contracts are also useful for keeping track of reading progress. You and your students develop a contract, which may vary in length of time for completion (several days, a week, etc.). The completed contract is an individual record of what each student intends to complete, and it can be placed in each student's folder.

Whatever techniques you use, students should keep as many of their own records as possible. This eases your time problem and gives students a continued awareness of their own progress.

Finally, it is also important to establish patterns for putting away mate-

	Attitudes			Process					Content	
	Reading as communication	Reading as a tool	Positive response to reading	Language conventions	Linguistic units	Strategies: initiating predictions	Strategies: during reading	Strategies: post-reading	Functional text	Recreational text
Mary										
John										
Sue										
Frank										
Allen										

FIGURE 14.2   Sample Record-Keeping Device

rials, storing incomplete activities, and handing in completed activities at the end of the reading period. This requires that you teach all your students where various materials belong and what kinds of filing systems and storage arrangements are used. You need to develop such **how-to-stop patterns** before fully implementing a reading program.

Interaction Patterns **Interaction patterns** include procedures for socialization among students and between you and your students. Socialization is an important factor in any elementary school classroom and it occurs with or without your forethought. In order to make socialization work, you need to develop patterns for it.

There is no single way to manage interaction in the classroom. Major guidelines are that you establish some sort of patterns and that you adjust these patterns for particular students and situations. One way to regulate interaction is to divide the classroom into a noisy half and a quiet half. All verbal communications occur in the noisy half, leaving the quiet half relatively noise free. Some teachers, because of personal preference or special circumstances, confine social interaction to a designated center where their students go to talk, or to a communication center, such as a listening center or a drama center, where interaction has a set purpose.

Regardless of the interaction patterns you establish, there will never be enough for some students. Establishing times for written interaction can help alleviate this difficulty. For instance, each person in the room may have a mailbox where messages can be left, thereby allowing all members of the class to interact via letters or notes. The patterns specify when mail can be left and when you and your students can pick up and read mail.

After you have developed interaction patterns for independent activities, you must develop interaction patterns for small-group instruction. Efficient reading instruction depends upon a smoothly operating group. You should identify a section of the room as the small-group learning area where students know to come quickly and with any needed materials. You also should have your materials ready and be prepared to instruct. Finally, just as you need a way to get independent activities started, you need a way to start small-group instruction. The use of some sort of signal is often helpful.

Many teachers find that the use of a buffer helps minimize interruptions during small-group instruction. A **buffer** is another adult or a student who handles unanticipated situations while you are teaching a group. Ideally, the buffer would be a trained paraprofessional or teacher's aide, but it could also be a volunteer parent. The buffer could also be a high school student who has been released from school to help with such duties. Another source is students from higher grades in the same school. Finally, the buffer can be a student assistant from your own classroom. Responsibilities include handling minor problems such as unexpected interruptions and directions for assignments, supervision of practice activities, participation in learning games, listening to students read aloud, completing assessment activities, correcting papers, and generally providing any kind of nonprofessional classroom assistance.

To summarize, when establishing patterns, it is important that you be clear and consistent about expected behaviors. This requires careful planning. It is also important to remember that your students have a much more difficult time unlearning a pattern and then learning a new one than learning one initially. Once you set a pattern, it becomes a permanent part of a classroom routine. Make sure that the patterns you start are the ones you want. It will be necessary to give students much directed assistance early in the school year (including models, walking students through the patterns, talking over modifications, and dress rehearsals), but this assistance will diminish as they get used to the patterns. Once patterns are established, you can begin instruction with confidence that your students will be engaged on task.

MANAGING THE ACADEMIC CONTENT OF READING

Before instruction starts, you must make certain decisions about managing the reading content. The following six decision areas are particularly important:

1. Your lessons should focus on academic content.

2. You need to be aware of your students' personal concerns.

3. You need to accurately assess skill levels and provide learning tasks of appropriate difficulty.

4. You need to know how to focus attention.

5. You need to know how to provide appropriate challenges.

6. You need to help your students be responsible and cooperative.

First, you should keep the instructional focus on targeted academic content during a lesson. If it is a process lesson, keep the focus on the process; if it is a story being read for enjoyment, keep the focus on the content of the story; if it is a lesson on developing a concept of reading, keep the focus on that concept. This means that you must resist students who try to steer you into discussions of other topics. If you want students to learn what the lesson is designed to teach, you must keep the focus on that content.

Second, you need to be sensitive to your students' personal concerns. The focus may be on academic content, but students' personal concerns need to be woven into lessons. For instance, when a lesson is on tornadoes, and students live in an area where tornadoes occur, you should be aware of their related worries.

Third, you need to determine your students' instructional level (see Chapter 11) and create learning tasks that challenge them intellectually. You must know which curriculum goal you are working on and where your students are with regard to that goal. For instance, if the goal is to develop an understanding that reading involves making predictions and confirming or modifying those predictions, and your students have never worked on this goal, assume that they are at an initial learning phase. If they have worked on this goal in previous years, estimate whether they are still in the initial learning phase or in a subsequent one and if they need more presentation, just practice, or guided application. In any case, the more precise you can be in assessing needs, the easier it will be to match instructional activities to student developmental levels and thereby ensure a high degree of task engagement.

Fourth, you must know how to focus your students. Knowing what your students attend to depends on knowing what their personal concerns are. To focus their attention, you must have the targeted goal clearly established in your mind. If the goal is a memory task, focus the students' attention on the salient features; if the goal is a procedural task, focus students' attention on the procedural steps, and so on. Once you know what the goal requires, you need to focus students on that.

Fifth, you need to provide appropriate challenge for your students. If they can do a task without assistance, there is no challenge. If they cannot do the task even with appropriate assistance, then the challenge is too great.

Providing the appropriate challenge means selecting a learning task with which your students need some assistance but which is not so hard that it is frustrating.

Finally, you need to cultivate student responsibility and cooperation. The ultimate goal of schooling is to have all students responsible for their own behaviors and actions. Classrooms characterized by responsible behavior naturally create an optimum environment for learning. Similarly, each member of a group is affected by the other members. Cooperative behaviors allow a group to make decisions and move ahead. Anything you do to promote group decisions and cooperative behavior helps create optimum conditions for achievement.

ENSURING SUSTAINED STUDENT ENGAGEMENT

Allocating time to the three major curricular outcomes is fairly easy; keeping students on task is harder. Younger students will become engaged just because you want them to, but older students rarely do so. In both cases, it is difficult to keep students engaged once instruction has started. The following discussion of teacher behaviors that encourage continued **student engagement** is divided into those behaviors that apply to all or most teaching situations and those that relate to specific problems.

General Teacher Action

Six general teacher behaviors help maintain student engagement on task. First, you should make students accountable for all work, whether it is completed independently or in groups. Once work has been assigned, it should be completed. If they are not held accountable for completing their work, students find other things to do. This means that you must correct and provide feedback for all academic work assigned in the classroom. Attention to student accountability helps ensure engaged time on task.

Second, you should ensure all students are not only attentive but actively involved during instruction. It is not enough to have their eyes on you. In order to keep their attention, you must actively involve them in thinking, observing, doing, listening, speaking, reading, or writing. The hardest activities to sustain are thinking, listening, and reading. After students have thought for a moment or two, or listened or read for a short time, allow them to speak or write. Continued active involvement requires opportunities to both receive information (listen, observe, or read) and express information (speak, act, or write). Younger children can sustain only short periods of receiving and giving information, while older children can sustain their involvement for longer periods of time.

Third, seatwork should include both activities you have assigned and student-choice activities. Seatwork can be completed either individually, in pairs, or in small groups. The activities assigned can vary from the practice of newly learned skills, to applying activities, to reading and writing, to informal assessment activities. In any case, variety is important.

Students should be held accountable for all assigned work. (RH Photo by Peter Vadnai)

Fourth, you should adjust the pace of instruction to the needs of your students. For both high-aptitude and low-aptitude students the pace should be brisk enough to keep their attention, but not so brisk that they become frustrated and stop attending. You can expedite pacing by breaking instruction into small steps that students can easily understand. Clarifying the purpose or the usefulness of a lesson also encourages a brisk pace because your students understand why they are doing a task.

Fifth, you should ensure high success rates for your students. Generally, success rates should be above 80 percent. All students, but particularly low-aptitude students, must have high success rates in order to maintain a high level of perseverance. Students persevere and remain on task when success is high; as the failure rate increases, they get discouraged and their engagement diminishes rapidly.

Finally, you should give your students frequent opportunities to respond. Students need to speak, write, or do in order for learning to occur. Frequent response opportunities encourage their learning because it is through these responses that you determine their understanding and provide the positive feedback that solidifies learning.

To summarize, you can increase your students' engagement on tasks by holding them accountable, involving them, providing a variety of seatwork, ensuring brisk pacing, ensuring success, and having frequent responses.

Specific Teacher Action

You will use many of these general teacher behaviors whenever you teach. However, some teacher behaviors relate only to specific problems of student engagement.

Helping Students Become Engaged To help students become engaged, you must get their attention. You can do this by using verbal statements, written statements, or some type of an attention-getting device such as an object or a figure drawn on the board. Once your students are attentive, you can establish procedures for the activity. It may be necessary to have students remain in their seats, to form a large circle on the rug, or to complete the activity in small groups at learning centers. Whatever procedures apply, students need to know them early in the activity.

You can also promote student engagement by providing thorough, lucid directions for the task they are to complete. Most elementary students can keep only a limited number of things in their minds at one time. This means that you can give only three or four directions at a time; otherwise, some of your students will be unable to complete the work without help. Therefore, it is sometimes necessary to provide directions for the first half of a task and then for the second half, or to provide written directions to supplement oral directions. Remember, however, that written directions are more easily followed when they reflect a pattern of behavior that is familiar. By providing directions within the limits of the students' memory capacity and according to established classroom patterns, you help promote student engagement.

How teachers distribute materials can also effect engagement. If you pass out materials before you provide directions, the chances are good that some of your students will pay more attention to the materials than to you. Many problems can be avoided if by giving directions first, then distributing materials.

After everyone knows what is to happen and what their role is, students need a signal to begin the activity. Although you can simply tell them to begin, an established signal helps ensure that all students will begin at the same time.

Once started, you can enhance engagement by ensuring that students' personal needs have been considered. For instance, are the activities pleasant ones from the students' point of view? Do they understand your rationale for the lesson and concern for their work? Is there variety in the activities, and are there opportunities for your students to express themselves about the lesson content? Are student concerns heard and clarified? Are you reinforcing appropriate student behavior? By attending to personal needs such as these, you help ensure sustained student engagement on tasks.

Question asking also helps your students become engaged because it allows them to demonstrate their understanding of the lesson and to be attentive during it. For instance, if you are teaching a content goal, you should ask questions to activate knowledge about the topic of the story; if you are teaching a process goal, you should ask questions to activate knowledge about the target strategy. Questions serve a dual role by helping students become engaged and preparing them to focus on the lesson content.

In summary, initial student engagement is enhanced if you get their attention, given thorough, lucid directions before distributing materials, signal when to begin, consider their personal needs, and ask questions to focus their attention on the lesson.

Helping Students Sustain Engagement Just as there are things you can do to help students become engaged, there are others that help students maintain that engagement. This requires sensing a pending break in the activity flow and doing something to prevent its occurrence. A teacher who lacks this sensitivity allows a break to occur and then has to restore the activity flow. Obviously, when a teacher can prevent such breaks students will learn more because they will be engaged longer.

There are a number of teacher behaviors that help maintain activity flow. One relates to the steps within the lesson. You should break lessons into small steps to keep the cognitive demands within the capabilities of your students. The size of the steps varies with the age and aptitude of your students and must be adjusted to their needs.

Another teacher behavior is to look for signals that a group is not working well together and to deal with the potential problems quickly, before activity flow is disrupted. Often a student's body posture signals that off-task behavior is about to occur. Similarly, students' eyes or the type of noise coming from a group signals a need for your assistance. When you are alert and can assess a group's problem before a disruption occurs, you can solve problems without a break in activity flow.

You can also prevent breaks in activity flow by letting students know what to do with completed work. If everything has to pass through your hands, valuable instructional time will be lost. If your students have to ask you what to do with their work, activity flow is broken. Established patterns for turning in work and recording the results aid in sustaining activity flow.

Your use of humor and affection can also help sustain engagement because it releases the tension associated with concentration, fear, and insecurity. Students who are working hard benefit from a moment of humor, as do students who want to work hard but do not quite understand the task and those who experience a high degree of anxiety during a lesson. Make sure that your humor is funny to all students, however. Sarcasm can make a situation worse, as can laughter directed at a particular student. Similarly, you must use affection wisely. All students need to know that they are important, but artificial affection is quickly spotted and is usually counterproductive. Honest affection makes everyone feel good and aids in developing feelings of belonging.

You can also help sustain student engagement by monitoring involvement in lessons. Everyone, but especially low-aptitude readers, needs to be checked and receive appropriate feedback. Regardless of the focus of the lesson, the only way to determine students' understanding is to monitor their responses. This monitoring helps sustain engagement on task. While monitoring, you can move near potentially disruptive students and use nonverbal signals—a lifted eyebrow or a finger on their lips—as a way to head off disruptions. Redirection away from inappropriate behavior and toward the expected behavior, reinforcement of appropriate behavior, removal of potential distractions, and assisting students who are showing signs of frustration are other ways of combating disruptions.

Your interactions with students also help sustain engagement. When you stop to talk with students, you should talk about the activity at hand. If a group of students are completing a task about favorite books, you should talk about that assignment. If you are taken off task by discussing something else, that too creates a break in engagement, a situation that is often hard to repair.

Your sensitivity to students' constraints also helps sustain engagement. This includes sensitivity to intellectual limits, where the content demands more than your students can deliver; to emotional limits, where the content is so unrelated that your students have no interest in learning; to concentration limits, where no matter how exciting the lesson is your students have been attending for too long. Teachers who are sensitive to the constraints of their students' learning abilities can use that knowledge to stop lessons before a break in the activity flow occurs.

Sustained engagement is also aided by planned, brief breaks. Few people can concentrate on a task for long periods without an opportunity for the brain to rest. Therefore, breaks are necessary if your students are to sustain attention to the lesson. Long breaks, however, allow students to become involved in something entirely new, so short breaks are better. They allow for rest while minimizing chances that attention will wander.

In summary, it is important to remember that students will vary in their ability to remain engaged. A room that is uncomfortable will shorten the time of engagement, as will an exciting upcoming event or hunger. High motivation and interest will lengthen it. The trick is to use what is known to be successful in sustaining high engagement rates while also being sensitive to your students' needs.

STEPS IN CREATING A MANAGEMENT SYSTEM

This chapter focuses on how to enhance student engagement during lessons. However, the organization and management of a reading program requires the melding of many little pieces. It is a difficult task, but the following guide offers structured assistance. You can adapt this guide in developing your own personalized management system.

Before the opening of school and the assignment of your students

1. Using the three goals of reading instruction as a guide, develop curriculum goals for the year.

2. Within each curriculum goal, collect and categorize activities for assessment, instruction, practice, and application.

3. Develop a teacher resource file for oral reading, independent reading, interest grabbers, independent activities, safety valves, guided application (basals, other commercial activities), room arrangements, and others.

4. Collect and categorize children's books and other printed material by interest and general reading levels to be used for independent reading, grabbing interest, and guiding application.

5. Develop student activity card files for learning centers, independent activities, safety valves, and interest grabbers.

6. Collect and develop informal and formal assessment tools, including graded oral-reading paragraphs, games, and interest inventories.

7. Develop a general pattern for reinforcement that can be adjusted after you know your students.

8. Develop patterns for how-to-start procedures.

9. Develop patterns for how-to-change procedures.

10. Develop procedures for keeping track of students.

11. Develop patterns for the optional activities (independent activities and safety valve activities).

12. Develop patterns for how-to-stop procedures.

13. Develop patterns that allow for interaction among teacher and students.

14. Develop the general role of the buffer and the steps in training the buffer.

15. Develop your philosophy about approaches (basals, language experience, and personalized reading) to reading instruction and how the three outcomes can be integrated into your philosophy. What balance will strike in developing these three outcomes?

Before the opening of school, after you have been assigned to a classroom

1. Continue to develop curriculum goals and activities for the three outcomes of reading instruction. Collect source books, activity cards, assessment tools, materials for instruction and application, and lists of recreational books. Develop procedures for the various patterns for the buffer, and refine your philosophy of reading instruction.

2. Develop a floor plan for the physical arrangement of your classroom.

3. Make an inventory of the materials and facilities you have for the coming school year.

After the school year begins

1. Implement instruction for developing attitude outcomes.
2. Implement patterns for procedures and interactions.
3. Implement independent activities and safety valves.
4. Implement the role of the buffer.
5. Evaluate progress so far, including patterns and procedures.
6. Determine the reading preferences of each student.
7. Initiate plans for students to begin developing their own lifelong reading habits.
8. Administer the informal and formal assessment devices for year-long needs.
9. Implement instruction for developing process and content outcomes.
10. Evaluate the progress of your reading program to date.

Continued growth and evaluation

1. Continue to develop materials, ideas, sources, a library, patterns, and a teaching style.
2. Be alert for ways you can vary safety-valve activities as the year progresses, and be alert for new ideas and materials. Try not to alter established safety valve patterns.
3. Continue to evaluate the ongoing reading program. Are your expectations reasonable? Are patterns developing as expected? Are positive attitudes and an understanding of reading being established? Are content outcomes being achieved? Are you implementing and maintaining the reading program as successfully as you want?

SUMMARY

Management—making the most of the time you have—is a crucial component of effective reading instruction. There are many specific techniques to use to increase time for reading by looking beyond the allocated reading period. By establishing routine patterns for enhancing activity flow in the classroom and by employing procedures to ensure that your students' attention to tasks is sustained you can achieve maximum student engagement time.

SUGGESTED ADDITIONAL READINGS

BURNS, M. (1981). Groups of four: Solving the management problem. *Learning, 10,* 46–51.

CASTEEL, C. P. (1984). Computer skill banks for classroom and clinic. *Reading Teacher, 38*(3), 294–297.

CHERNOW, F. B., & CHERNOW, C. (1981). *Classroom discipline and control: 101 practical techniques.* West Nyack, NY: Parker.

EMMER, E., EVERTSON, C., & ANDERSON L. (1980). Effective management at the beginning of the school year. *Elementary School Journal, 80,* 219–231.

FLEET, A. C., HURST, A. W., & MACKAY, M. E. (1976). Expanding the classroom with study areas. *Reading Teacher, 30*(1), 33–38.

FORGAN, H. W. (1977). *The reading corner.* Santa Monica, CA: Goodyear.

KLEIN, M. L. (1979). Designing a talk environment for the classroom. *Language Arts, 56*(6), 647–656.

MORRIS, R. D. (1979). Some aspects of the instructional environment and learning to read. *Language Arts, 56*(5), 497–502.

NEVI, C. N. (1983). Cross-age tutoring: Why does it help the tutors? *Reading Teacher, 36*(9), 892–898.

WELCH, F. C., & HALFACRE, J. D. (1978). Ten better ways to classroom management. *Teacher, 96,* 85–86.

WOOD, K. D. (1983). A variation on an old theme: 4-way oral reading. *Reading Teacher, 37*(1), 38–41.

RESEARCH BASE

ANDERSON, L., EVERTSON, C., & BROPHY, J. (1979). An experimental study of effective teaching in first grade reading groups. *Elementary School Journal, 79*(4), 183–223.

ANDERSON, L., EVERTSON, C., & EMMER, E. (1980). Dimensions in classroom management derived from recent research. *Journal of Curriculum Studies, 12,* 343–346.

BROPHY, J. (1983). Classroom organization and management. *Elementary School Journal, 83,* 265–286.

BROPHY, J., & PUTNAM, J. (1982). *Classroom management* (Occasional Paper No. 50). East Lansing: Michigan State University, Institute for Research on Teaching.

DOYLE, W. (1986). Classroom organization and management. In M. Wittrock (Ed.), *Handbook of research on teaching* (3rd ed.) (pp. 392–431). New York: Macmillan.

KOUNIN, J. (1970). *Discipline and group management in classrooms.* New York: Holt, Rinehart & Winston.

Part 4

Conducting Instruction at Various Grade Levels

Earlier sections of this book provided information designed to help you construct general understandings about the reading curriculum and how to organize for instruction. However, since reading instruction differs in specific ways depending on the grade level being taught, this general information must be augmented. The four chapters in this section offer specific guidelines about how to conduct reading instruction when you teach preschool or kindergarten (Chapter 15), primary grades (Chapter 16), middle grades (Chapter 17), or upper grades (Chapter 18).

15 | Teaching Preschool and Kindergarten Reading: Readiness Stage

GETTING READY

To teach a preschool or kindergarten class, you must adapt what you have learned in earlier chapters to students who, for the most part, do not yet know how to read. This chapter helps you do this. It describes language instruction for the readiness stage and provides a general background, the major curricular emphases, and instructional activities to help you develop the intended curricular goals.

FOCUS QUESTIONS

- What special problems are associated with teaching reading to pre-readers?

- How are attitude goals developed in preschool and kindergarten?

- How are process goals taught in preschool and kindergarten?

- How are content goals developed in preschool and kindergarten?

- How are reading and writing integrated at the readiness stage?

- What does a typical preschool and kindergarten instructional day look like?

OVERVIEW OF PRESCHOOL AND KINDERGARTEN READING

There has been much debate in recent years about how and whether to teach reading in preschools and kindergartens. On one side of the debate are those who argue that emphasis should be limited to socialization in which children are taught the personal and social responsibilities associated with going to school behavior. Here, the major instructional activity looks much like play, and the expectation is that children will learn reading goals incidentally while engaging in socialization activities. On the other side of the debate are those who argue that preschool children can and want to learn to read, and, therefore, schooling at this level should emphasize formal, systematic reading instruction.

Although the debate still rages in some quarters, most educators have settled on a middle-ground position. In this position both socialization and reading are included, but reading instruction receives less formal emphasis. "Less formal" does not mean there is an absence of direct instruction; in fact, both direct and indirect instruction are found in good preschool and kindergarten programs. It does mean there is less emphasis on the trappings of formal education: Basal text reading groups are seldom found in kindergartens or preschools; similarly, the use of readiness workbooks, although more prevalent than basal texts, is generally frowned upon. Instead, teachers provide students many opportunities to expand background experiences, to communicate about these experiences, to use listening and speaking, to perceive reading and writing as exciting and useful activities, and to understand the graphic nature of written language.

The readiness stage is actually a broad introduction to language. It seldom looks like the formal "book learning" associated with the basal text

At the readiness stage, teachers provide many opportunities for speaking and listening. (John R. Maher/EKM-Nepenthe)

TABLE 15.1 Instructional Emphasis at the Readiness Stage

OUTCOME	INSTRUCTIONAL EMPHASIS	MAJOR INSTRUCTIONAL ACTIVITY
Attitude goals		
Concepts about reading	Reading is talk written down What you are reading was written by someone Reading is for enjoyment Reading is for getting information	Indirect instruction using language experience and USSR activities
Positive responses to reading	Reading is exciting Reading is satisfying Reading results in knowledge	Indirect instruction using language experience and USSR activities
Process goals		
Routine skills Vocabulary	Discuss experiences that employ new words Emphasize concrete words	Direct instruction of word meanings
Word recognition	Develop print awareness related to recognizing words instantly Develop letter and word awareness	Direct instruction of letters and words Direct instruction in how to use knowledge sources of listening and comprehension
Metacognitive strategies Initiating strategies	Activate background knowledge of content using picture and title Use story structure and author purpose to make predictions	Direct instruction of strategies in listening situations Direct instruction of how to use story structure to make predictions when listening to recreational text

reading instruction found in first grade and above, but teachers do structure a learning environment that broadly emphasizes communication. Because most children at this level cannot yet read, communication is mostly oral and the emphasis is on speaking and listening. Content goals focus almost entirely on listening to the teacher and other adults read texts for functional and recreational purposes; process goals stress how comprehension works in listening situations; and positive attitudes toward reading are often created when students listen to a teacher read good children's literature. The major encounter with written text at the readiness stage is through language experience stories, and reading skills focus on students' awareness of print and the graphic nature of reading. Table 15.1 summarizes the instructional emphasis at the readiness stage.

TABLE 15.1 continued

OUTCOME	INSTRUCTIONAL EMPHASIS	MAJOR INSTRUCTIONAL ACTIVITY
During-reading strategies		
Monitoring strategies	Monitor accuracy of predictions Monitor fluent sense making	Direct instruction of monitoring skills in listening situations

Fix-it strategies	Recognize disruption in sense making while listening
	Access strategies to solve the problem
	  Word recognition
	  Vocabulary
	  Author's meaning
	  Beyond the author's meaning
	Determine which strategy is needed
	Implement the strategy
	Verify repair of sense making
		Direct instruction of fix-it strategies for listening comprehension

Post-reading strategies		
Organizing strategies	Recall what's important through story structure (beginning, middle, end)	Direct instruction of recalling story structure in listening comprehension
Evaluating strategies	Judge real or make believe	Direct instruction in listening comprehension
Content goals		
Recreational	Get meaning from story narratives that the teacher reads orally	Directed listening activity
Functional	Get meaning from simple expository text that the teacher reads orally	Directed listening activity

DEVELOPING ATTITUDE GOALS

Since many children first encounter reading and writing in preschool and kindergarten, their attitudes are often determined by what happens to them there. At this level, then, the most important goal is to create experiences that will develop accurate concepts and build positive feelings about reading and writing.

Two concepts—the message-sending nature of reading and the potential rewards of reading—are fundamental to reading success, and you should strongly emphasize them at the preschool and kindergarten levels. First, develop the understanding that language is a communication system, with both reading and writing as parts of the system, because it is crucial for students to understand that what they read is a message from someone else; it is like an oral mssage except that it has been written down. Second, show students that reading has an important role to play in their lives, that constructing meaning from text can be both functional (provides information and helps solve problems) and recreational (brings enjoyment and enriches lives).

You should also place heavy emphasis on developing positive feelings about reading. Your students should be involved in activities that help them see that reading is exciting, is satisfying, and results in new knowledge. Conversely, if their initial encounters with text are boring, frustrating, or of little personal use, students will develop negative feelings. The importance of creating positive responses cannot be overemphasized.

Creating a Literate Environment

A strong literate environment is crucial to the success of preschool and kindergarten programs. Meaningful activities and communication should play an integral role. The intent, as it always is with the literate environment, is to create an atmosphere that encourages students to engage in representative literacy activities.

Make sure the physical environment in your classroom includes tangible evidence of the importance of communication. Emphasize listening, reading picture books, writing, and language experience stories. Maintain a room arrangement that promotes communication, and have displays in the room that celebrate the products of individual and collaborative communication efforts. Your classroom's physical environment should clearly show that participants engage in important and exciting activities that require them to communicate.

Much of the physical environment of a classroom is a reflection of the intellectual environment you create. If you plan and promote exciting class projects, students will be engaged in meaningful activities. If you set the expectation that students will work collaboratively on these projects, real communication will result. Similarly, a good social-emotional environment in the classroom promotes student collaboration and sharing, thereby maximizing opportunities for communication and developing targeted concepts and responses about language.

Hence, it is through a literate environment that you create the atmosphere, activities, and interactions that preschoolers and kindergarteners associate with literacy.

The Major Instructional Approach

At the readiness stage, the major instructional approach is language experience. By engaging students in collaborative writing based on common experiences, you highlight several reading concepts: the communication function of written language; the writer-reader relationship; and the relationship among listening, speaking, reading, and writing. In addition, creating real text about meaningful experiences is exciting and satisfying for preschoolers and kindergarteners and does much to build positive feelings.

Preschool and kindergarten teachers spend much time developing language experience stories with students. Since these stories are based on real experiences, it is important to organize common experiences that are worth writing about. For instance, you might plan field trips to places of interest in the community, have students share their most exciting experiences with each other, and plan special classroom events, such as guest presenters, parties, and plays. Children's literature that is read aloud in the classroom can also be an effective source of language experience stories since it can be the genesis for student written stories.

Once you have selected an experience, you can use it as an occasion for message sending and receiving. For instance, before visitors to the classroom arrive, you and your students can write invitations, write signs directing the guests to their seats, create posters depicting classroom activities, and write stories for display. Once the activity is over, students may write thank-you notes, keep journals, create summaries, generate a report to parents, or write a newspaper that chronicles the events and experiences. You can represent in collaboratively developed language experience writing any kind of text associated with the real world. Through participation in these activites students develop the concepts and responses that are the foundation for continued growth in reading. The lesson shown in Example 15.1 shows how to incorporate language experience activities into the readiness stage.

EXAMPLE 15.1   How to Develop Positive Attitudes

Background	You want to develop the concept that reading is talk that has been written down. You decide to do so by involving students in a language experience activity.
Activity 1	Arrange a field trip to the fire station, city hall, or some other community agency. Prepare students for what they are to learn on the trip.
Discussion	In the classroom after the trip, discuss what was learned. Direct students to the need to thank the people who provided the information. Point out that you could speak your thanks if you saw them, but since you probably will not see them, you can send a note.
Activity 2	Work with students to write a thank-you note on chart paper. As the note is composed, point out that what they say can be written down, and that what is written down can be read by the receivers of the thank-you note.

ACTIVITIES TO DEVELOP ATTITUDE GOALS

Here are some useful preschool and kindergarten activities to supplement development of positive attitudes toward reading.

1. Have students write short letters to classmates that are mailed and then delivered by a child who plays the role of a postman. The children can then read the letters they have received. Emphasize the concept that reading and writing are communication tools.

2. Using the special kinds of animal or adventure stories that children are interested in, encourage them to collect or print words essential for reading and enjoying their particular interests. List these words in a special book to develop positive responses toward reading.

3. Show pictures of some of the same things your students draw, such as a dog or an airplane. Say, "These pictures tell a story. Do you know what this picture is?" Call on a child as you point to the picture. After the correct response is elicited, ask another child, "What is this picture?" When all the picture details have been discussed, ask more general questions, such as "What do you think they are doing? Have you ever seen an airplane land? Where did you see it? Was anyone you know in it?" These questions help students develop the concept that pictures and words convey information.

4. Use the covers of children's books for a game. Have students sit in a circle, then hold up a cover and have the students guess what the story is about if it is new, or tell about it if it is familiar. Call on several children to get a variety of stories and ideas. Picture postcards, magazine pictures, and travel pictures may all be used if old covers are not available. The concept that reading is both enjoyable and informational is developed while also developing predicting skills.

5. Have students write or dictate their own stories, which you type in primary type. They may then read their stories and exchange them with other students. These stories may be bound into books. This helps students develop positive attitudes toward reading.

6. Have students read simple poetry. They should read it over until it becomes easy for them, developing the idea that language is fun.

7. Feltboard characters provide an excellent vehicle for storytelling. Using a feltboard and teacher- or student-made characters from books, have students talk about the books they have read. This develops positive attitudes about reading.

8. Puppets are as much fun to make as they are to operate. A large packing box or a table turned on its side can serve as the stage. Kindergarteners enjoy making small drawings of characters introduced in picture books or

storytelling sessions and then pasting them on pencils or sticks to use as puppets. The concept of what reading is, as well as positive attitudes toward reading, is developed.

9. Have students write their own concept books (what is round, what is heavy, what is loud, and so on); this will develop positive attitudes toward reading.

TEACHING PROCESS GOALS

Process goals help students understand routine skills that are applied automatically and metacognitive strategies that are consciously applied. Since most preschool and kindergarten students are unable to read text independently, the process goals taught at this level are preparatory in nature.

Routine Skills

In preschool and kindergarten, you teach students routine skills associated with language conventions and linguistic units in two ways. First, you use language experience activities to teach about the conventions of print in our language. When constructing language experience stories, point out the top-to-bottom and left-to-right sequencing of language, that spoken words can be represented by written words, that they can tell where a word ends because there is a space, that a spoken sentence can be represented as a printed sentence, and that there are certain conventions (capital letters and periods, for instance) that signal when a sentence begins and ends. Help students learn that words are made up of letters and teach them these letters. At first, preschoolers and kindergarteners can see no sense in how letters are formed and have difficulty visually discriminating such letters as *u* and *n*, *w* and *m*, and *d* and *b*. It is important that you show them how the system of discrimination among letters works. A sample of how to teach such language conventions in preschool and kindergarten is provided in Example 15.2.

Second, you need to increase vocabulary. All students need a large store of word meanings they understand in oral language. Most children come to school with an oral vocabulary of approximately 4,000 words, but they need many more to be successful. In preschool and kindergarten, you need to provide many opportunities for students to hear about, experiment with, and interact with words. **Concept books** are one good way to do this. Students can brainstorm things that are round, square, soft, hard, and so on, and then you can introduce other words that fit into that category. Drawings and pictures of new words that fit the category can be put into books. Whenever you introduce new words, it is important that you be as concrete as possible.

Teachers often overestimate children's capacities for understanding the words they use in oral language. They assume that because students say the

---

EXAMPLE 15.2   How to Teach Visual Discrimination

Background	Your students continually confuse the letters *b* and *d*. You decide to teach them how to visually examine the letters.
Lesson Sequence	
Introduction	Point to examples of the letters they are confusing in the story you have been reading to them. Indicate that being able to read the story themselves requires their being able to tell the letters apart and that you are going to show them how to do that.
Modeling	Explain the way you visually examine print to tell letters apart. In the case of *b* and *d,* visual examination emphasizes left-to-right orientation, with the "stick" of the letter being encountered first in *b* and the "ball" of the letter being encountered first in *d.*
Interaction with students	Give students several opportunities to distinguish *b*'s from *d*'s in text. Give them considerable help in the early stages as they talk out loud about how they are visually examining the letters, and gradually reduce this assistance as they demonstrate a consistent pattern in their visual examination.
Closure	Return to the text you have been reading to them. Point out the letters again, and have them use their strategy to visually examine the letters and to distinguish between them.
Desired Outcome	Given printed text, students will use the conventional ways of visually examining text to distinguish letters.

---

words, they share the adult meaning for it. For instance, a group of kindergarteners were discussing an upcoming parents' night. All of them entered the conversation about how to best prepare for the event. Yet, when it came time to write invitations to their parents, the children did not understand that parents were their mothers and fathers. They used the word *parents,* but they did not share the adults' meaning.

Function words, such as *not, same,* and *or,* are particularly crucial since preschoolers and kindergarteners need these words to operate successfully in school. When teaching the meanings of these words, it is important to do so within the students' physcial world by using language modeling. Modeling use of function words such as *not, same* and *or* during instruction might be as follows: "Who is sitting down? Who is *not* sitting down? Is the rabbit the *same* as the table? Is the desk the same as the floor *or* is it different?" A sample of how to teach vocabulary in preschool and kindergarten is provided in Example 15.3.

EXAMPLE 15.3   How to Teach Vocabulary

Background	Your students understand that many words can be grouped as round, but they seem to be confusing round with square. You decide to teach them distinctions between round and square.
Lesson Sequence	
Introduction	Explain that you are going to show them how to decide whether a picture fits with something round or square by hightlighting corners and no corners.
Modeling	Use concepts books for *round* and *square*. Go through the books naming each entry and modeling how you use corners to determine if it is round or square.
Interaction with students	Give students many opportunities to decide if a picture should be placed with one concept or the other. Have them verbalize how they made their decision. Gradually reduce assistance as they demonstrate their understanding.
Closure	Return to the concept books and have students draw new pages. When they have completed their drawings, have them explain to each other or to you why the drawings fit in one concept book or the other.
Desired Outcome	Given spoken words that stand for something round or square, students will categorize words according to which fits each grouping.

Metacognitive Strategies

At this level, three categories of metacognitive strategies are taught, mostly in listening situations: initiating strategies, during-reading strategies, and post-reading strategies. Each is discussed below. Study strategies are not used at this stage.

Initiating Strategies The initiating strategies include activating prior knowledge of topic, story structure, and author's purpose. At the preschool and kindergarten level, messages are presented orally, not in print. Activating prior knowledge depends on the topic of the reading selection and what students already know about it. Begin by providing statements and asking students questions about their prior experiences with the topic. For instance, in preparing for a lesson on mail deliverers as community helpers, you would provide statements and ask questions like: "We have people who deliver mail. Do you know how mail is brought to your houses? Have you ever seen or talked to the people who bring the mail? Let's see what all of us know about mail carriers."

To activate prior knowledge, you might begin by reading text to your students and showing them how understanding the words, topic, purpose, and text structure helps to figure out meaning. For instance, you might read a story about a mailman and then talk about (1) how the words in the story provide clues to the topic, (2) how recognizing the topic (or what is talked about) triggers thinking about that topic and predictions based on what they already know, (3) how the purpose (having fun or getting information) makes them listen for certain things, and (4) how their general knowledge of stories helps them predict what will happen next in this story. Although it is a listening situation, the process of getting the meaning is very similar to that used when reading. Consequently, when students get to formal reading, they will already be familiar with this strategy. Example 15.4 illustrates how to structure such a lesson in preschool and kindergarten.

During-Reading Strategies The during-reading strategies are monitoring and fix-it strategies. Since preschoolers and kindergarteners do not actually read when first learning how to monitor text or when learning their first fix-it strategies they use listening situations and simulated situations involving language experience stories.

At the readiness stage, monitoring involves simply listening to a story to see if it makes sense. When reading a story to your students, stop periodically, have students recall what has just happened, and ask them if that makes sense. In this way you provide many opportunities for students to realize that reading and listening are sense-making processes. Eventually you want students to tell you when the story does not make sense. When this occurs, text monitoring has begun.

At the readiness stage, the most emphasized fix-it strategy relates to vocabulary—what to do when students encounter a word unknown in meaning. You do this by using listening situations to teach students how to use oral context to predict a word that is unknown or left out. For instance, play games with them in which they have to complete sentences such as, "When I went to the store, my mother told me to buy a pair of _____." Or have students predict words that will fill certain slots in sentences such as, "The _____ went to the fair." In this case, a defensible noun would have to be used, whereas in "I saw a horse in _____ barn," a defensible article or adjective would have to be used; and so on. By engaging students in such exercises you help them learn that language is a sense-making activity, and they develop a solid foundation for using context to figure out unknown words. The thinking process used by readers is similar to that used by listeners, so listening instruction becomes a preparation for reading. Example 15.5 shows how to teach oral context.

Another strategy emphasized at the readiness stage relates to word attack or word analysis (or decoding), particularly as it relates to phonics. In order to use phonics to figure out unknown words encountered in print, students

EXAMPLE 15.4   How to Use a Listening Situation to Teach an Initiating Strategy for Getting Meaning

Background	As part of getting your students ready to read, you want them to be aware of how to get meaning—how to make predictions about meaning based on our knowledge of the words, topic, purpose, and type of text. You use a listening activity to develop the goal of activating prior knowledge.
Lesson Sequence	
Introduction	After reading a story to students, discuss what happened in the story. Ask them how they know what the story means. Tell them you are going to show them how readers and listeners get meaning from stories.
Modeling	Read sections of the story orally and explain what you think of as you hear the first group of words, how hearing those words causes you to predict a topic, how your knowledge of the topic causes you to expect certain things, how your understanding of the author's purpose and the normal pattern of stories gives you clues to where the story is going, and how these predictions continue to be refined as you hear more of the story.
Interaction with students	Using other story samples, have students do as you did. At first, give them much assistance as they try to talk out loud about their thinking while processing text. Gradually diminish this assistance until the students can make predictions about meaning without assistance.
Closure	Read another story having the students explain what happened and how they know what the story meant.
Desired Outcome	Given oral text, students can explain how they use knowledge of the words, topic, purpose, and type of text to make predictions about meaning.

must know letters, must be able to distinguish one letter sound from another, and must be able to associate the correct letter sound with the correct letter in print. Some preparatory work for using phonics occurs in the preschool years and much of it occurs in kindergarten. Most teachers introduce phonics by creating simulated situations in the language experience stories that have been written with students. For instance, while reading a language experience story, you might say to a student, "Let's pretend that you didn't know this word. When you came to it, you would have to stop and try to figure it out. How could you use what you know about the sounds of letters to figure out this word?"

EXAMPLE 15.5   How to Teach Oral Context Clues for Getting Meaning

Background	As part of your effort to get students ready to read, you want them to know how to use context to predict what unknown words mean, but you must teach this strategy in an oral situation.
Lesson Sequence	
Introduction	Select a story to read to the students. Pick a word the students are not likely to know and present it to them. Tell them you are going to teach them how to figure out such words as they listen to the story.
Modeling	Read aloud a section of the story that contains the word. Explain how you used the other words in the sentence and your own background knowledge to figure out the unknown word.
Interaction with students	Present to students other difficult words embedded in context. Have them talk out loud demonstrating how they used the other words and their experience to predict the meaning of the unknown word. Give them much help initially, but gradually diminish this help as you go along.
Closure	Read the story aloud. Afterward, discuss the story content with them. Discuss how they used their strategy to figure out word meaning while they were listening.
Desired Outcome	Given a listening situation, students will use context to figure out the meaning of unknown words.

These situations must be simulated because most children in the process of creating the story will learn the words in a language experience story as sight words, meaning that they no longer have to figure them out. The simulation, however, will help prepare them for figuring out unknown words when they encounter them in their reading at the initial mastery stage. Having children combine this sounding technique with the context strategy just discussed provides an even stronger preparation for reading since the two strategies in combination are a powerful and efficient way to figure out words unknown in print. Example 15.6 provides an illustration of how to prepare students for phonics.

Post-Reading Strategies The post-reading strategies are organizing and evaluating content. The organizing content strategy taught at the preschool and kindergarten level is recalling what is important through use of simple story structures (beginning, middle, and end). This means that you signal where

EXAMPLE 15.6   How to Teach Letter Sounds

Background	As part of your effort to get students ready to read, you want them to know letter sounds. Then if they enounter a word they do not recognize in print, they can use initial consonant sounds together with context to predict the unknown word.
Lesson Sequence	
Introduction	Using a story you have read orally, point out the words and show students how the words begin with letters they know by name. Say that if they know the sound letters make, they can begin to say the words on the page and that you are going to teach them those letter sounds.
Modeling	For each letter in turn, demonstrate how you point at the letter and simultaneously say its sound.
Interaction with students	Have students do what you did (point to each letter in turn and say the sound). At first provide much assistance by pointing to the letter and saying the sound with the students. Gradually reduce such help as the students begin associating the sound with the letter.
Closure	Return to the story. Point out the words that begin with the letter sounds. Have students use those sounds and the context of the sentence (which you can read orally) to predict what the word is.
Desired Outcome	Given a word unrecognized in print, students will use the initial letter sound and the sentence context to predict what a word is.

the beginning, middle, and end sections are in stories and discuss each section with students in terms of what happened. At the readiness stage it is not important to be concerned with what constitutes the sections of the story; it is more important that students understand the stories have beginning, middle, and ending sections and that important information is found in each section. A more refined level for organizing content occurs at later stages. Example 15.7 illustrates how to structure a lesson on organizing oral content in preschool and kindergarten.

The major emphasis in evaluating content at this stage is judging stories to be real or make-believe. This strategy is developed in terms of your students' background experiences. It is not important that every story be judged real or make-believe; it is important that preschoolers and kindergarteners understand that some stories present information in ways that could

EXAMPLE 15.7   How to Teach Organizing Content

Background	Your students try to remember everything, or they remember only the last things they heard about in stories. You decide to teach them how to organize story information by remembering what happened in the beginning, middle, and end sections of a story.
Lesson Sequence	
Introduction	Read a story orally. Note for the students where each section is started and completed as you read.
Modeling	Explain that it is helpful when organizing story information to remember it in terms of the beginning of the story, the middle of the story, and the end of the story. Read each section and demonstrate how you remember the important information in that particular section. Then demonstrate how to organize important information based on where it is in the story.
Interaction with students	Give students several opportunities to remember information by organizing it in terms of the story structures of beginning, middle, and end. Start with single sections and gradually move to entire stories. As students demonstrate their understanding and use of this strategy, gradually reduce your assistance.
Closure	End the lesson series with another story. Point out the beginning, middle, and ending sections and have students use their strategy to organize information for remembering.
Desired Outcome	Given oral stories, students will organize story information by remembering the content found in the beginning, middle, and end of stories.

really happen and other stories do not. Your students judge stories real or make-believe based on what their background experiences tell them could or could not really happen. Example 15.8 illustrates how to structure a lesson on evaluating content taken from oral stories.

ACTIVITIES TO DEVELOP PROCESS GOALS

In preschool and kindergarten many of the activities to develop process goals are created by the teacher and focus on language conventions and linguistic units associated with word recognition and vocabulary. Certain commercial materials may be used (such as word games, work sheets, and so on), but the bulk of the activities grow naturally out of the communication activities being

EXAMPLE 15.8   How to Teach Evaluating Content

Background	Your students do not understand how to judge stories as real or make-believe. You decide to teach them how to judge whether a story is real or make-believe when it is read to them.
Lesson Sequence	
Introduction	Read a story that could happen based on students' backgrounds. Note and discuss those events that could really happen. Repeat the process using a story with events that couldn't really happen.
Modeling	During discussion, explain and demonstrate how to decide if events are real or make-believe. Continue to model by demonstrating how background experience signals whether a story is real or make-believe. Repeat the process using a make-believe story.
Interaction with students	Give students several opportunities to judge whether a story is real or make-believe. Start with real stories, move to make-believe stories, and then intermix both types. Gradually diminish your assistance as students demonstrate they can judge stories as either real or make-believe based on their background experiences.
Closure	End the lesson series with stories that are either real or make-believe. Have students judge whether stories are real or make-believe.
Desired Outcomes	Given orally read stories, students will judge story content as real or make-believe based on their background experiences.

pursued in the literate environment. Here are some activities you can use to supplement your teaching of process goals in preschool and kindergarten. Be cautioned that these are practice activities to be used after students understand how the various process goals are to be used in real reading.

1. Cut an oak tag into cards of handy size, such as 3″ by 5″, and have students paste on them pictures cut from old books, magazines, and newspapers. Under each picture print the word or phrase that tells about the picture and print the same word on the reverse side of the card. This helps students associate printed symbols with pictures (language convention).

2. Use an activity like bingo. Give each player a card marked off into 12 square blocks. In each block a sight word has been printed. On a small

pack of cards, each the size of a block, words have been printed. Show the cards one at a time. The student whose card has the displayed word raises her or his hand, pronounces the word, points to it, is given the small card, and places it over the appropriate word. The first student to cover a line of words in any direction is the winner. This helps students learn to recognize words at sight (linguistic units).

3. Have all the words your students learn put into their vocabulary book, *My Word Book*. Students may illustrate this book or cut pictures from other sources and paste them under each word. This helps students build meaning vocabulary (linguistic units).

4. Labeling is a worthwhile device only if it is made meaningful. Label toys students bring to class; label shelves in the classroom closet to indicate places for various supplies. Label children's hooks in the wardrobe and encourage children to learn the names of their classmates. Use complete sentences when labeling—for example, "This is a Tonka truck." This helps students learn to recognize words at sight (linguistic units).

5. Write jumbled sentences on cards or on the board and have your students reassemble the sentences. This helps students search for meaning that makes sense and left-to-right directionality (language conventions). Examples:

> baby down slid
> a puppy black and white spots had

6. Place phrase cards along the blackboard ledge. Read one of these phrases and ask a student to go to the board and pick out the phrase that was read. Then have the student read the phrase to the class. This helps students recognize words at sight (linguistic units).

7. Give students several phrase cards based on a story they have read. Write on the board a question that can be answered by one of the phrase cards. Ask all students who think they have a phrase that answers the question correctly to raise their hands. Ask students to first read the question from the board and then the answer from their card. Write the answer on the board and then write another question to be answered as before. Example: *Charlotte's Web,* by E. B. White, provides phrases such as *Charlotte and Wilbur, at the fair, in the barn,* and so forth. A question could be "Wilbur and Charlotte lived _____?" or "Charlotte said good-bye to Wilbur _____?" This helps students develop recall for what is read.

8. Place a large box filled with small objects or pictures before your students. Arrange printed word cards corresponding to the objects or pictures along the blackboard ledge. Have students close their eyes and draw an object or picture, for which they must then find the corresponding word. This helps students recognize words at sight (linguistic units).

9. Number a large cardboard clock face from 1 to 12 and fit the clock with a large moveable hand. Print and number twelve words or phrases either on the blackboard or on a large sheet of paper. Call on a student to spin the hand, see the number at which it stops, then read the corresponding printed word or phrase. This helps students recognize words at sight (linguistic units).

10. Prepare cards with black and white drawings of objects that have a characteristic color. Print directions under the objects are such as, "This is a ball. Its color is blue." Because the picture is black and white, you will know your students can read the colors.

11. Show a picture to a group and have students discuss either the main idea, the figures in the foreground or background, or the colors. Occasionally ask specific questions, such as, "What is the little boy holding in his hand? Where do you think he is going?" Some students may be able to make up a short story of two or three sentences about the picture, while the others listen for the sequence of ideas. This helps students develop comprehension.

12. Have students learn sequencing of common activities by dividing a large sheet of oak tag into four or six squares and putting a picture showing one part of an action sequence into each square. Put the same pictures on small cards cut the same size as the squares on the large card. Ask students to take the small pictures and assemble them in a sequence that tells the same story as that on the large sheet. This helps students develop understanding of sequencing (language conventions).

13. Have students learn letter memory of upper and lower case letters (linguistic units) by giving them sheets prepared with short rows of letters. Tell students to circle either the capital or the small letters.

AAaa   aaaA   AAAa   aaaA

BBBB   BBBB   bbbb

CCC   Ccc   ccC   CCc   ccc   cCC   CCC

DdD   DDd   ddd   DDD (etc.)

14. Have students fish for sight words. Fold word cards and pin the open ends together with a large straight pin. (Take care to use steel pins, or hairpins, because a magnet will not pick up ordinary pins.) Place the cards in a container. Have students use a piece of string attached to a small magnet to pull out one of the "fish." If they can read the word on the card, they may keep it; otherwise it must be thrown back. Keep records of the number of words correctly read each day. This helps students learn words at sight (linguistic units).

15. Place pictures of objects that rhyme on the blackboard: pictures of a *pie* and *sky*, a *hand* and *sand*, and so on. Point to the first picture and ask

what it is. "Yes, it is a *pie*. Who can find another picture that rhymes with *pie*?" This helps students develop auditory discrimination (linguistic units).

16. Say, "We are going to play a new guessing game today. This little boy is Bill." Point to a picture or to a child whose name is Bill. "He lives on a high _____. Who can tell me where Bill lives? It is a word that sounds like *Bill*. Yes, it is a *hill*. Bill likes to sit on the window _____. Yes, *sill*. Who can give me another word that sounds like *Bill* and *sill*?" This helps students develop auditory discrimination (linguistic units).

17. Perform or have a student perform a short series of acts, such as tapping on the desk, lifting a book, and then picking up a piece of chalk. Ask students to replicate the acts performed to develop auditory memory and sequencing (language conventions).

18. Have students practice letter recognition by playing the game concentration. Use six different letters at one time with each letter on two separate cards. Place the 12 cards randomly on the table, letter side down. Students find the pairs and keep each pair they find. This develops memory for letters (linguistic units).

19. Have students use concentration to recognize sight words. Follow the same procedure as in Activity 7. This develops memory for words (linguistic units).

20. Use recorded sound patterns in which each pattern is repeated. Direct students to listen to a sound pattern, stop the recorder, repeat the pattern, start the recorder, and check their accuracy. This develops auditory discrimination (linguistic units).

21. Play the airport game with students using a game board, a toy airplane, and someone to give the oral sound patterns to each child in turn. If the child reproduces a sound correctly, he or she moves the airplane one space down the runway. As each plane reaches the end it may be flown briefly. The same technique can be used in reverse to return the airplanes to the hangar. This develops auditory discrimination (linguistic units).

22. Play a game in which students pair off and then take turns clapping two sound patterns to each other. This develops auditory discrimination (linguistic units). The partner must respond to each pair of sound patterns by identifying them as the same or different. Determine the winner either by recording the number each child gets right or by adapting the game to a game board such as the one described in Activity 10.

23. Play the game monkey hear, monkey do, using pairs of players and a game board. Have one child clap or say a sound pattern and tell the partner to mimic it. If the partner is correct, he or she moves forward one space on the game board. Auditory discrimination is developed (linguistic units).

24. Play a dot-to-dot game, using any connect-the-dots picture. Pair students and have one say letter sound patterns. Tell the other to mimic it and, if correct, to connect as many dots in the picture as there are letter sound units in the pattern. This develops memory for letter sounds (linguistic units).

25. Play a remembering game in which one student says a word, the next student repeats it and adds another word, the third student repeats the first two words and adds a third, and so on. Continue until one student cannot remember the sequence. The object is to develop memory for words (linguistic units).

26. During story time or reading time, purposely distort some word in the story by leaving off its first sound. Stop and say, "Oh, I didn't say that word correctly! What should I have said?" Do this during any daily oral activity. This develops predicting skills.

27. Have students bring to class pictures cut from magazines, with each picture or series of pictures showing something that has the same sound at the beginning, end, or middle. This develops readiness for phonics (linguistic units).

28. Bring in a group of magazine pictures, and direct students to tell what each picture shows and to sort the pictures according to the common beginning, middle, or ending sounds. For instance, all the pictures that begin with the same sound heard at the beginning of *kite* go in one pile, all the pictures that begin with the same sounds heard at the beginning of *top* go in another pile. This helps students learn phonics (linguistic units).

29. Spread a group of pictures on the floor. Have students point to a picture that has the same sound heard at the beginning, end, or middle of the word you say. This helps students discriminate among sounds (linguistic units).

30. Play games with students that follow this pattern: "I'm thinking of something on your desk that begins with the same sound heard at the beginning of the word *pig*. What am I thinking of?" You may also adapt this activity to middle and ending sounds. This helps students use phonics in combination with predicting (linguistic units).

31. Divide a shallow box into four squares. Place a key picture in each of the top two squares. Provide students with a group of pictures, and tell them to sort the pictures and place them in the square beneath the picture that has the same sound at the beginning, middle, or end. This helps students learn to categorize while also developing phonics (linguistic units).

32. Make a shutter device out of tagboard in which the opening of the shutter can be controlled. Insert a card that has the letter to be learned at the

left, followed by a picture of an object beginning with this sound. Open the shutter to reveal first the letter and then the picture. Have students form the letter sound with their mouths and blend that sound into the picture name as it is exposed. This helps develop phonics as a word analysis strategy (linguistic units).

33. Give each student a group of pictures, some of which begin with the letter to be worked on and some of which do not. Hold up a letter card and direct students to hold up any picture they have that begins or ends with the sound of that letter. This helps develop phonics (linguistic units).

34. Give students a group of letter cards. Have each student take turns saying the letter name and a word beginning with the letter, as in, "I have a letter. *Money* begins with the letter *m*."

DEVELOPING CONTENT GOALS

As previously mentioned, much preschool and kindergarten language activity is oral, and this is especially true of content goals. Because your students cannot read yet, you teach listening comprehension of functional and recreational text. Consequently, what becomes a reading activity at the higher grades is often a listening activity at the readiness stage.

Many students receive their first formal introduction to recreational and functional text at the preschool and kindergarten level. Students should begin to understand the content of simple narrative text and simple expository text that you read to them. In both cases the selections should be simple in structure because this is typically your students' first formal encounter with text. Listening comprehension is emphasized because students have not progressed to the point where they can read independently.

Directed Listening Activity

Since your students listen rather than read at the preschool and kindergarten levels, you will often use the directed listening activity (DLA). This is similar to the standard directed reading lesson (DRL) used with many basal texts (see Chapters 4 and 12). The difference, of course, is that the DRL is used with written text, whereas the DLA is used with listening activities.

The DLA works like this. Before you read to your students, introduce the topic to activate their background knowledge and develop the meaning of unknown words. With this background established, specify what your students are listening for (set the purpose). Then begin reading, stopping periodically to remind students what they are listening for. After the reading, hold a discussion in which everyone shares what they learned, focusing primarily on the purposes that were set at the beginning. Finally, close the lesson by having students summarize what was learned and by engaging them in an activity that applies (or enriches) this learning.

A directed listening activity helps kindergarteners focus on text content. (Robert Bawden)

The DLA can be used to guide your students' listening of either recreational or functional text. For instance, if you are reading students a story, you can activate schemata about the setting and the problem encountered in the story, cite the purposes for listening, and hold a discussion after the story to share what was learned about the established purposes. If you are reading a functional text, you can activate schemata related to that topic, establish the purposes, and hold a discussion about those purposes. In both cases student listening is guided and, as a result, there is a greater chance that the content will be understood. An illustration of how to use the DLA is provided in Example 15.9.

Preschoolers and kindergarteners create both functional and recreational text as part of their language experience activities. For instance, language experience activities that result in written invitations, lists of activities the class pursued, or a recipe are all examples of functional text. Similarly, language experience activities that result in stories or poems are recreational text. However, it is seldom necessary for teachers to guide students' understandings of these texts. Because students create them, they understand them. They have strong backgrounds for the words used, the topic, the purpose, and the text structure. As a result they comprehend the content without guidance.

EXAMPLE 15.9   How to Use a Directed Listening Activity for Content Goals

Background	You are reading a story to your students. You want to be sure they understand what happens to the main character and why it happens. To ensure they get this content, you guide their listening using a directed listening activity.
Lesson Sequence	
Introduction	Tell students what you are going to read them. Discuss the setting and the circumstances surrounding the story and elicit student prior knowledge. Identify any words they may not have heard before and explain their meanings.
Set purposes	Specify the particular things you want students to listen for.
Oral reading	Read the story and be sure students are listening for the right information.
Discussion	Discuss what they found out about the purposes set at the beginning.
Closure	Have students summarize what was learned and/or have them use what was learned in a subsequent activity.
Desired Outcome	Given a text that is read orally, students will be able to discuss the story in terms of the specific purposes set.

ACTIVITIES TO DEVELOP CONTENT GOALS

Almost any occasion when you read functional or recreational text to children can be used to develop content goals. Here are some activities to supplement your teaching of content goals in preschool and kindergarten.

1. Have a news corner for announcements or for news pertaining to students themselves, such as "We are going to the market tomorrow." This leads to an understanding of uses of functional information.

2. Place interesting pictures with an explanatory word or two about them in very simple language on the bulletin board. You may also use colorful book jackets from children's books, which develop the understanding that reading is recreational.

3. Use bulletin boards to show all the enjoyable elements of books such as adventure, excitement, and laughter.

4. Use concept books that have been written by the students as functional texts for other students. Concepts can include the following: What is round? What is soft? What is exciting?

5. Use puppets to act out information that has been read to students.

INTEGRATING READING AND WRITING

One of the advantages of the language experience approach is the way it dramatizes the integration of reading and writing. In fact, when students are creating language experience charts and stories to read, they are engaged in writing. You can use these occasions for language experience to develop positive feelings about writing as an activity. While actually producing the written text associated with language experience, you can demonstrate process goals such as how writers use the conventions of language to signal meaning to readers, how authors monitor the text they are producing, and how they use certain techniques to focus, reorganize, and clarify their meaning. Regarding content goals in writing, you can use language experiences to model how decisions are made in the planning stage about whether the writing is to be functional or recreational and what meaning is to be conveyed.

As important as language experience is, however, it is not the only time that preschool and kindergarten students engage in writing activities. Very young children enjoy what they call writing even though we might call it doodling. They will sometimes draw a picture of something and put a lot of squiggles on the page, which they describe as "a story I have written." This preliterate writing is an important part of learning to write. You can use these activities to build important concepts about writing, what people use it for, and how it works, as well as to build positive feelings toward writing.

Writing is an integral and important part of the preschool and kindergarten experience. It is evident both in the language experience activities and in the pretend writing that students engage in at this age. Both kinds of writing activities are important to reading because they provide additional experience with written language that, in turn, strengthens students' desire and ability to use written text.

There are many ways to integrate the various language modes in preschool and kindergarten. One of the most effective is to teach a unit that carries over several days and develops a variety of objectives. Warm-up activities are used to get things started; focusing activities direct attention to the specific task; reading-writing activities include reading or writing, or a preparation for or follow-up to the reading or writing activity. The culminating activity is the unifying, closing activity students are working toward, and assessment is using the data collected to determine the effectiveness of the instruction. The sample unit that follows is designed to develop students' awareness of the postal system.

SAMPLE TEACHING UNIT: Postal Awareness

LEVEL
Preschool and kindergarten, readiness stage

OBJECTIVES

1. To become familiar with mail transportation.

2. To become aware of the structure and function of letter writing.

3. To write letters to parents and to address envelopes.

DAY 1

Warm-up activity: Bring a letter to class from a parent or several parents telling about something they like about the class. Discuss how exciting it is to get mail. Read the letter to the class.

Focusing activity: Discuss the letter and lead a discussion to the point where the students decide they want to invite their parents to a tea or coffee.

Reading-writing activity: Construct a group letter telling where and when the parents should come. Read the letter together.

Assessment: During the letter-writing process, assess students' knowledge about the form of a friendly letter. Directly teach the form to those students who need it.

DAY 2

Reading-writing activity: Print the letter to parents neatly, using letter form.

Assessment: Assess students' ability to print letters and words found in letters. Directly teach penmanship skills to those students who need it.

DAY 3

Warm-up activity: Using an overhead or an opaque projector, present a model envelope like the one that will be used to send the letter to parents.

Focusing activity: Directly teach how to address an envelope.

Reading-writing activity: Students practice on sample paper (same size as an envelope) how to address an envelope to their parents.

Assessment: Assess students' ability to address an envelope. Note whether students know their address.

DAY 4

Focusing activity: Discuss the purpose and structure of the postal system.

Reading-writing activity: Address the envelopes. Take the letters to the mailbox and mail them.

DAY 5

Reading-writing activity: Draw the steps the students' letters will go through in the process of being delivered. Have them predict when the letters will arrive. Have them verify the arrival.

Note: A trip to the post office would be appropriate at this time.

DAY 6
Warm-up activity: Brainstorm with students about all the interesting things they've been doing in class.

Focusing activity: From the brainstorming list, select activities to show parents during the coffee or tea.

Reading-writing activity: Decide how to show parents work, songs, plays, and so on.

DAY 7
Focusing activity: With the students' help, decide what refreshments will be served at the coffee or tea.

Reading-writing activity: The results of the discussion can lead to reading recipes to make whatever is served; measuring the ingredients to be used; and cooperatively serving refreshments.

DAY 8
Culminating activity: The coffee or tea with parents.

Assessment: Assess the success of the coffee or tea. Did the parents enjoy it? Did the students successfully show the parents what they have learned? Did the letters arrive at their homes? Were the reading and writing uses successful? Was information conveyed?

ADDITIONAL INTEGRATED READING AND WRITING ACTIVITIES

Here are some additional activities to supplement your integration of reading and writing in preschool and kindergarten.

1. Provide pictures from magazines and have students write titles to them. Put pictures and titles on display for all to read.

2. Read a *Weekly Reader* to students and do the writing activities suggested there. This is usually completed as a group activity.

3. Have students write and illustrate a group story. Place the words and pictures on a roll and show them as a television program. Have students read the words as they appear on the "screen."

4. Have students create class stories after field trips. Place the stories in a travel folder and refer to them for future trips or for review.

5. Have students create concept books such as: what is trying, what is big, what is old, and so on. Each student creates a page with a sentence and an illustration.

6. Have students create a collage with a theme such as happy, sad, excited. Once the collage is created, have the class create a poem such as "Happiness is _____," "Sadness is _____," and so on. Display the collage and poem for reading and enjoyment.

7. Begin an alphabet book for each student with a page for each letter. Add appropriate pictures of illustrations to each page throughout the school year.

8. Read *The House that Jack Built*. Discuss the book's repetitive pattern. Discuss other content. Write a group story using the repetitive pattern.

9. Using a story such as *Jack and the Beanstalk* read the story to the point where Jack wakes up the golden harp. Insert into the story the harp saying, "You are as noisy as _____." Discuss with your students what things are *noisy*. Have each student create an ending to the sentence. Read the revised story with each student's insertion.

CHARACTERISTICS OF AN INSTRUCTIONAL DAY

Of all the levels of elementary school, preschool and kindergarten have the most distinctive characteristics for three reasons.

First, almost all public preschools and kindergarten are half-day rather than full-day sessions. Consequently, the total daily allocated time for instruction is typically between 2½ and 3 hours. This characteristic has several consequences. For you, it usually means two completely different classes in a day, one in the morning and one in the afternoon. This poses a real problem since much language instruction should be individually tailored to students' needs, but when you have 50 to 60 students each day, it is hard to keep track of their individual needs. In terms of planning for individual development, more preparation time is required for the preschool and kindergarten teacher than for teachers at the higher levels.

A second distinguishing characteristic of instruction in preschool and kindergarten is the dominance of playlike activities. Because children at this age cannot read and are not yet socialized into the behaviors associated with traditional schooling, you cannot give them traditional seatwork tasks that require independence and good work habits. Instead, find a variety of shorter activities, most of which are fun, such as story sharing, games, and creative drama.

The third distinguishing characteristic of preschool and kindergarten is the absence of designated periods for reading, mathematics, and social studies. Although these subjects are taught at this level, the allocated instructional time is divided by activities (manipulative objects, animals, children's literature, and so on), with each activity often calling for the integrated use of reading, mathematics, and social studies. This allows teachers to focus on activities that relate to students' real experiences. It also offers the option of brisk pacing, a crucial aspect of teaching at this level since preschool and kindergarten children have relatively short attention spans and must have a variety of activities in a relatively short period of time.

The instructional day in preschool and kindergarten is unlike that found at any other grade level. Students do not sit at desks, they do not have reading groups in the traditional sense, they seldom use basal readers, the activities often look like play time, and many different kinds of activities are squeezed into a relatively brief half-day period. Even though the school day looks quite different, teachers at these levels are teaching to the same three goals as teachers at the higher levels and are striving to lead students to the same ultimate outcome.

SUMMARY

Reading instruction at the preschool and kindergarten level provides the foundation for literacy. A special problem at this level centers on whether to have formal reading instruction or to focus on socialization. A balance of these two forms is recommended to ensure a broad introduction to communication. Attitude goals are developed through the literate environment where students are engaged in important and exciting tasks involving sharing, cooperation, and collaboration. Process and content goals are also taught within the literate environment, primarily with language experience activities, during which students learn about conventions of print, vocabulary and word recognition strategies, and about stories and simple texts. The reading-writing connection is also stressed. The typical instructional day looks different than at other elementary grades: Subjects are not differentiated, the instructional tasks are more playlike, and oral language and listening are emphasized.

SUGGESTED ADDITIONAL READINGS

ALLEN, R. V., & ALLEN, C. (1976). *Language experience activities.* Boston: Houghton Mifflin.

ANSELMO, S. (1978). Improving home and preschool influences on early language development. *Reading Teacher, 32*(2), 139–143.

BAILEY, M. H., ET AL. (1982). Preparation of kindergarten teachers for reading instruction. *Reading Teacher, 36*(3), 307–311.

BURRIS, N. A., & LENTZ, K. A. (1983). Caption books in the classroom. *Reading Teacher, 36*(9), 872–875.

CAZDEN, C. (1985). Research currents: What is sharing time for? *Language Arts, 62,* 182–188.

COMBS, M. (1984). Developing concepts about print with patterned sentence stories. *Reading Teacher, 38*(2), 178–181.

CROWELL, D., KAWAKAMI, A., & WONG, J. (1986). Emerging literacy: Reading-writing experiences in a kindergarten classroom. *Reading Teacher, 40,* 144–151.

DEGLER, L. S. (1979). Putting words into wordless books. *Reading Teacher, 32*(4), 399–402.

ELLERMEYER, D. (1988). Kindergarten reading programs to grow on. *Reading Teacher, 41,* 402–405.

ELLIS, D. W., & PRESTON, F. W. (1984). Enhancing beginning reading using wordless picture books in a cross-age tutoring program. *Reading Teacher, 37*(8), 692–698.

EVANS, J. R., & SMITH, L. J. (1976). Psycholinguistic skills of early readers. *Reading Teacher, 30*(1), 39–43.

GAMBY, G. (1983). Talking books and taped books: Materials for instruction. *Reading Teacher, 36*(4), 366–369.

GOODALL, M. (1984). Can four year olds "read" words in the environment? *Reading Teacher, 37*(6), 478–482.

HALL, M. (1976). Prereading instruction: Teach for the task. *Reading Teacher,*

HOFFMAN, S., & FILLMER, H. T. (1979). Thought, language and reading readiness. *Reading Teacher, 33*(3), 290–294.

JOHNSON, T. D. (1977). Language experience: We can't all write what we can say. *Reading Teacher, 31*(3), 297–299.

KAISEN, J. (1987). SSR/Booktime: Kindergarten and first grade sustained silent reading. *Reading Teacher, 40,* 532–537.

LARRICK, N. (1976). Wordless picture books and the teaching of reading. *Reading Teacher, 29*(8), 743–746.

LASS, B. (1982). Portrait of my son as an early reader. *Reading Teacher, 36*(1), 20–28.

LESIAK, J. (1978). Reading in kindergarten: What the research doesn't tell us. *Reading Teacher, 32*(2), 135–138.

MARTINEZ, M., & TEALE, W. (1987). The ins and outs of a kindergarten writing program. *Reading Teacher, 40,* 444–451.

REIMER, B. L. (1983). Recipes for language experience stories. *Reading Journal, 36*(4), 396–401.

SIPPOLA, A. (1985). What to teach for reading readiness: A research review and materials inventories. *Reading Teacher, 39,* 162–167.

WEEKS, T. E. (1979). Early reading acquisition as language development. *Language Arts, 56*(5), 515–521.

WISEMAN, D. L. (1984). Helping children take early steps toward reading and writing. *Reading Teacher, 37*(4), 340–344.

ZIRKELBACH, T. (1984). A personal view of early reading. *Reading Teacher, 37*(6), 468–481.

RESEARCH BASE

BRUNER, J. (1979) From communication to language: A psychological perspective. In V. Lee (Ed.), *Language development.* New York: Wiley.

CALKINS, L. (1980). Children learn the writer's craft. *Language Arts, 57,* 2.

MASON, J. (1984). Early reading from a developmental perspective. In P. D. Pearson (Ed.), *Handbook of reading research* (pp. 505–544). New York: Longman.

RESNICK, L., & WEAVER, P. (1979). *Theory and practice of early reading.* Hillsdale, NJ: Erlbaum.

Teaching Primary Grade Reading: Initial Mastery Stage   16

GETTING READY

First and second grade are important to literacy development because it is here that most students first receive formal reading instruction. If they are well taught in first and second grade, reading success often follows; if they are poorly taught in these grades, a cycle of failure is initiated that sometimes persists for a lifetime. This chapter focuses on teaching reading at the initial mastery stage. It provides a background for primary grade reading instruction, describes the major curricular emphases, and provides specific instructional activities to help you develop the intended curricular goals.

FOCUS QUESTIONS

- What special problems are associated with teaching primary grade reading?
- How are attitude goals developed in the primary grades?
- How are process goals taught in the primary grades?
- How are content goals developed in the primary grades?
- How are reading and writing integrated at the initial mastery stage?
- What does a typical primary grade instructional day look like?

OVERVIEW OF PRIMARY GRADE READING

Teaching grades 1 and 2 places special demands on teachers. Both the students and the curriculum are unique. The students are unique because they are newcomers to formal reading instruction. They may have received reading readiness of the kind described in Chapter 15 while in kindergarten, but few have actually read a book on their own. It is not until first grade that students become conscious of learning reading skills or strategies, and it is then that students often form lasting impressions about what reading is. Primary grade students are at a particularly sensitive stage in their academic careers. Primary grade teachers, like kindergarten teachers, must make special efforts to provide experiences that develop positive attitudes and accurate conceptions of reading. The development of such attitude goals is a major effort in grades 1 and 2.

There is a second curricular focus in first and second grade: It is decoding—figuring out what the printed squiggles on the page say. This is because, although reading is a matter of getting meaning, the first task readers face is graphic—interpreting the letters and words on the page. Therefore, primary grade reading instruction emphasizes letters, their sounds, techniques for recognizing printed words instantly, and strategies for figuring out unrecognized words. Comprehension instruction is not neglected, however. It continues to be taught in the listening mode until students can decode words.

The tension that exists between the need to develop attitude goals and the need to develop decoding ability is a particularly difficult aspect of primary grade reading instruction. The experiences you provide your students result in concepts and feelings that stay with them for a lifetime, so you must emphasize the sense making, meaning getting, and communication aspects of reading. At the same time, you must emphasize decoding—the letters, the sounds of letters, individual words, and other linguistic units and language conventions that govern how print represents oral language. This conflict often means that first and second grade teachers overemphasize decoding and neglect attitudes. Most basal textbooks have a relatively heavy emphasis on word recognition, which reinforces this inclination.

Your unique challenge when teaching primary grade reading is to create positive and accurate experiences with real reading and language while simultaneously providing a solid foundation in how to decode. The first and second grade reading curriculum reflects this conflict, as seen in Table 16.1, which illustrates the instructional emphasis at this level.

DEVELOPING ATTITUDE GOALS

Attitude development is crucial at the initial mastery stage of developmental reading growth. Positive attitudes result from positive experiences that help students build accurate concepts of what reading is and positive feelings about reading activities. Specifically, we want first and second graders to develop the concepts that reading is a message from an author to a reader, an enjoyable pastime, and useful for getting information as well as feeling excited, satisfied, and fulfilled about reading.

Creating a Literate Environment

In the primary grades, your intent is to establish a literate atmosphere that emphasizes comprehension while it simultaneously supports a curricular emphasis on letters and words.

In the physical environment include special centers to display recreational books, lounging areas for relaxed reading, displays of children's writings and language experience stories, collections of class-written books, clusters of messages, and objects that have been labeled and tagged. Because labeling should feature words in context rather than words in isolation, a chair would not be labeled "chair" but "This is a chair."

Organize the intellectual environment by planning for many genuine reading and writing opportunities. You and your students can engage in language experience activities to construct, send, and receive messages. You want to establish the expectation that you and your students will engage in meaningful reading, that you will model this reading by leading your students in language experience activities, and that your students will be given choices of both topic and activity.

Organize the social-emotional environment by emphasizing working together. This, in turn, encourages communication and interaction with oral language, which supports literacy development.

In creating a literate environment in grades 1 and 2, then, you make a deliberate effort to have students conceptualize reading as a meaning-getting activity that is an integral part of language, and to instill feelings about reading that will motivate them. You highlight the prominent role of language in the physical environment, you stimulate engagement in real language through the intellectual environment, and you encourage genuine language interactions through the social-emotional environment. In addition, you emphasize the graphic code because you display printed words everywhere and frequently refer to its relationship with oral language.

Instructional Approaches

In the primary grades, you will make heavy use of the language experience approach to develop attitude goals. Look for opportunities to create text to illustrate to your students that reading is a message from an author to a reader. Similarly, create language experiences to illustrate that reading is enjoyable and can convey information. Such activities also get your students excited about reading.

Make use of personalized reading activities to develop positive feelings about reading. Usually, these activities take the form of uninterrupted sustained silent reading or some other kind of free reading activity. Even though first and second graders are just beginning to learn to read, you can nevertheless involve them in reading books of their choice. Such books may include picture books with words, wordless books, and student-authored lan-

TABLE 16.1 Instructional Emphasis at the Initial Mastery Stage

OUTCOME	INSTRUCTIONAL EMPHASIS	MAJOR INSTRUCTIONAL ACTIVITY
Attitude goals		
Concepts about reading	Reading is a message written by an author	Indirect instruction using language experience and USSR activities
	Reading is for enjoyment	
	Reading is for information	
Positive responses to reading	Reading is exciting	Indirect instruction using language experience and USSR activities
	Reading is satisfying	
	Reading results in knowledge	
	Reading satisfies curiosity	
Process goals		
Routine skills		
Vocabulary	Build vocabulary through discussion of vicarious and direct experiences	Direct instruction of words
	Emphasize concrete words	
Word recognition	Identify words at sight	Direct instruction of words
	Recognize words easily confused	
	Fluent recognition of sight words in connected texts	
Metacognitive strategies		
Initiating strategies	Activate background knowledge of content using predicting	Direct instruction of initiating strategies
	Activate prior knowledge of how the reading system works using story structures, expository structures, and author's purpose	
During-reading strategies		
Monitoring strategies	Monitor for unrecognized words, for unknown words, for fluent sense making and accuracy of predictions	Direct instruction of monitoring strategies

guage experience books. By organizing such personalized reading activities for your students, you help them develop the concepts that authors write to convey messages to readers and that reading can be done for enjoyment and for information. Similarly, such self-selected reading helps your students feel excited and satisfied about what they are reading.

Lessons associated with language experience and personalized reading are organized in the three-step format for indirect instruction described in

TABLE 16.1   continued

OUTCOME	INSTRUCTIONAL EMPHASIS	MAJOR INSTRUCTIONAL ACTIVITY
Fix-it strategies	Recognize disruption in sense making while reading or listening	Direct instruction of fix-it strategies for comprehension

	Access strategies to solve the problem
	   Word recognition
	   Vocabulary
	   Author's meaning
	   Beyond the author's meaning
	Determine which strategy is needed
	Implement the strategy
	Verify repair of sense making	

Post-reading strategies		
Organizing strategies	Recall what is important by story and text structure Classify words and phrases Determine main idea of expository text	Direct instruction of organizing strategies
Evaluating strategies	Distinguish between reality and fantasy	Direct instruction in making judgments
Content goals		
Recreational	Get meaning from story narrative texts Get meaning from various literature genres Use listening comprehension in recreational text	Directed reading lessons using basal text selections
Functional	Get meaning from simple expository texts Use listening comprehension in functional text	Directed reading lessons using basal text selections

Chapter 13 (activity-discussion-activity) and make use of collaborative groups as described in Chapter 11. For instance, assume that you want your students to feel knowledgeable as a result of reading (positive response) and to understand that reading involves receiving a message from a writer (concept of reading). After you decide to develop these goals through indirect instruction using a language experience activity, you might plan and conduct a lesson like the one shown in Example 16.1. Such indirect instruction helps first and

Building positive attitudes about reading and writing is critical at the initial mastery stage. (Courtesy of Michigan State University)

second grade students feel knowledgeable as a result of reading (they know how to make applesauce) and helps them understand that reading involves a writer who has a message to send (they were the writers with a message of thanks to send to the apple farmer).

ACTIVITIES TO DEVELOP ATTITUDE GOALS

Here are some useful first and second grade activities to supplement development of positive attitudes toward reading.

1. Develop a continuing contact with the expressive writing of skilled authors so students have the opportunity to develop appreciation of literature.

2. Place interesting pictures with a word or two about them in very simple language on the bulletin board. Colorful book jackets from children's literature are also good bulletin board material. Such bulletin boards help develop positive attitudes.

3. Have students read or recite favorite poems to help develop positive attitudes toward reading and language and to stimulate further reading of poetry by the group.

EXAMPLE 16.1   How to Develop Positive Attitudes

Background	You want to develop the concept that reading and writing are related aspects of language communication. You decide to do so by involving students in a language experience activity.
Activity 1	Arrange to take the class on a field trip to a farmer's apple orchard where students are shown how apples are grown, harvested, and marketed.
Discussion	In the classroom after the trip, organize students into collaborative groups, have them discuss what they saw and learned in the trip, have each group develop a thank-you note to the farmer, and then work with the whole group to combine the ideas into a single thank-you note.
Activity 2	Have students read a recipe for making applesauce, and then engage them in actually making applesauce from the apples picked at the orchard.

4. Hold informal conferences with students to stimulate continued reading, using both student-authored books and library books. This helps set expectations that reading is enjoyable.

5. Plan a field trip to the public library to develop positive attitudes about the lively world of books.

6. Develop a class book in which each student has one page to review his or her favorite book. Each page should include a brief statement of what it is about, why it is a favorite, and the title and author. Encourage students to include an illustration of the best part.

7. Pair students and let each pair read to each other from books they choose. A buddy system is a good way to encourage students to use library books.

8. Have each student write or dictate a story that is typed in primary type. Have students read their stories and exchange them with other children. Bind these stories into books and place the book in the classroom or school library. This helps develop positive feelings about reading.

9. Have students read and dramatize conversation, and then write the conversation for them to read. This develops the concept that reading is talk written down.

10. Trace or draw cutouts of favorite characters from illustrations. Use these drawings to provide a constantly changing population of book friends in displays.

11. Draw life-sized figures of favorite characters on mural paper and display them in the classroom or hall. First and second graders like to draw the animals they have read about including Paddington, Curious George, and other well-known book characters, and it helps them develop positive attitudes toward reading.

12. Make a class list of favorite books in chart form to offer students an opportunity to express their interests and preferences. Revise the list periodically as the children's tastes and interests develop.

13. Create a library corner. Responsibility for management can be a buffer's role. Include fairy tales, poetry, picture books, and concept books in the selections.

14. Introduce new books to the class. Tell what is special about each new book to help students develop an interest in them.

15. Model reading and writing often for your students. If students never see adults read or write, they are not likely to value reading and writing. What you do is just as important as what you say. Let students see you writing notes to friends, business letters, and expressive stories and poems to share. During nook-and-cranny time, read aloud what you have written and ask students to comment on your writing. Let students be a part of your revision process for all types of writing.

16. Encourage students to write for free samples and information. Many books and magazines include sections that list companies and addresses. This develops the concept that reading is a useful tool.

17. Be alert to occasions when students can be involved in writing and reading activities such as adding notes at the end of letters to parents, making and sending holiday and birthday cards, writing notes to friends, and drafting school notes for parental signature. When such occasions are used in these ways, students are encouraged to build accurate concepts about what literate persons do when they know how to read and write.

TEACHING PROCESS GOALS

Two process goals are emphasized in the primary grades: routine vocabulary and decoding skills and metacognitive strategies for figuring out unknown words.

Routine Skills

In the primary grades you will spend much time teaching your students about words and the role words play in reading. Your first emphasis should be on vocabulary—developing meanings for words. You do this in two ways: teach specific word meanings and teach about words. In the former, determine what words your students do not know by asking them to use specific words in sentences. If students cannot, provide either direct or vicarious background experiences as a conceptual base, then develop the distinguishing characteristics of the concept, using examples and nonexamples and, finally, ask students again to use the word correctly in a sentence. Example 16.2 illustrates how to teach word meaning.

When you teach *about* words in the primary grades, focus mainly on the fact that words can have multiple meanings. For instance, the word *strike* can be associated with unions, clocks, baseball, bowling, fishing, and matches. The correct meaning in a particular sentence depends upon the context of the message in which it is embedded. In a sentence about bowling, *strike* means one thing; in a sentence about unions, it means another. You want your primary grade students to know that words have multiple meanings and that the "correct" meaning is determined by the context of the message.

It is also important to teach first and second graders to be automatic in identifying words in print. When a reader instantly identifies words, the reading is smooth and uninterrupted. To achieve fluency, most words should be sight words. That is, they must be firmly embedded in the reader's memory, and when they appear in the text, they must be identified immediately and without conscious effort. Efforts to build your students' sight word vocabulary begin with the print awareness tasks (letter naming, visual discrimination, and visual memory) described in Chapter 15. Once students can discriminate among letters and words and remember their visual form, you can teach individual sight words. Normally, you teach first the most utilitarian words, such as *a, the, in, are, is,* and other high frequency words because they are essential for students to read real text. The list provided in Figure 7.1 shows examples of high utility words.

Also among the first sight words to teach are those which are less utilitarian but which appear in the particular text to be read. For instance, if the text is about going to school, teach sight words such as *school, teacher, desk,* and *chalkboard.* As students recognize more and more words, begin teaching easily confused sight words. It is not uncommon for primary grade students to confuse words that look alike. They may say *was* for *saw, where* for *there, them* for *then.* Such miscues are not disastrous when reading for meaning since the reader will detect the dissonance, look back, and make a correction. However, repeated miscues of this kind disrupt fluency and should be corrected. Some students confuse *was* and *saw* because they examine the words from right to left instead of from left to right; some confuse *where* and *there* because they fail to discriminate the initial letter; and some confuse words such as *after* and *father* because of hasty and partial visual examination. As students progress through the grades, they learn more and more sight words. You decide what words to teach your students by examining the next selection your students will read and by determining which of the words used in a particular selection need to be taught. Examples 16.3 and 16.4 show how to teach sight words.

EXAMPLE 16.2   How to Teach Vocabulary

Background	To increase your students' vocabulary, you decide to introduce the new words in conjunction with a text about trains being read in class. You decide which words need to be taught by asking students to use a word in a sentence. If the word is used correctly, students have a concept for the word; if it is used incorrectly or not at all, students do not have a concept for the word.
Lesson Sequence	
Introduction	State what word meaning is to be learned (diesel locomotive) and why it is important to have a meaning for the word at this time (in preparation for reading a selection on trains).
Background experience	Discuss students' real experiences or provide a vicarious experience for diesel locomotive as a basis for identifying the concept's distinguishing characteristics.
Developing characteristics	Illustrate the conceptual characteristics of the word using a chart such as the following:

What is it?
(part of a train)

What are some nonexamples
(a steam locomotive)
(a caboose)
(a diesel truck)

↑
← **diesel locomotive** →
↓

What is it like?
(it pulls the train)
(powered by diesel fuel)
(big)

What are some examples?
(the one we saw at the train station)
(the one in this picture)

	Engage students in a discussion of the distinguishing characteristics of *diesel locomotives*.
Closure	Have students use the word in a sentence. Then assign guided reading in which the new word appears.
Desired Outcome	When students encounter the word in real text, they will have an accurate mental picture of the word and will be able to use this knowledge to construct the author's message.

Metacognitive Strategies

Three categories of metacognitive strategies receive emphasis at the initial mastery stage: initiating strategies, during-reading strategies, and post-reading strategies.

EXAMPLE 16.3   How to Teach Sight Words

Background	You want your students to recognize words by sight. To decide which words need to be taught as sight words, note which frequently appearing words are not instantly recognized or anticipate which words in the text to be read are not known as sight words. Be sure students have concepts for *letter, word, first, last, top, bottom, left, right, alphabet, sight word,* and *instantly* if you intend to use these words when teaching sight words.

Lesson Sequence

Introduction	Show students a text they are going to read and tell them what words they are going to learn to recognize instantly, so that they can read the story fluently. Tell them they must understand both the visual form (what it looks like) and the "name" of each word. Show students where they will encounter the words in the text they will read.
Modeling	Print the words in phrases on cards. Present the cards one at a time. Point to the phrase, say it, and use it in a sentence.
Interaction with students	Have students do what you did (point to the phrase, say it, and use it in a sentence). Write a sentence containing the word on the back of the card, underlining the sight word. Then have students read the sentence containing the word, read the underlined sight word, write the sight word, and say it. Repeat this procedure (with variations) until students instantly recognize the word.
Closure	Have students demonstrate which sight words they have learned by flashing them the words and having them name them. Also have students state why it is important to know these words at sight and when these words will be used in the story to be read. Then guide the reading of the story that contains these new words.
Desired Outcome	When reading text, students will instantly recognize the words in print and will be able to state why it is important to instantly recognize such words.

Initiating Strategies The initiating strategies are activating prior knowledge for topic, text structure, and author's purpose.

Activating prior topic knowledge at the primary level involves helping students bring to a conscious level what they know about a topic. This can be accomplished with concrete objects, representations of objects such as illustrations or pictures, and teacher-student conversations. For instance, if

EXAMPLE 16.4   How to Teach Easily Confused Sight Words

Background   Your students confuse *was* and *saw* when reading. You want them to examine the word carefully for its distinctive visual, or graphic, characteristics. Be sure students have concepts for *letter, word, first, last, top, bottom, left, right, alphabet, sight word,* and *instantly* if you intend to use these words in your teaching.

Lesson Sequence

Introduction   State which two words are to be learned, why they are being taught together, your evidence that the student is indeed confusing the words, and why it is important to fluent reading that they not be confused. In the case of *was* and *saw,* students must be sure to visually examine the word from left to right.

Modeling   Present the two words simultaneously on separate cards. Point to each word, say its name, and use it in a sentence. Then show how *was* and *saw* do not look alike when you read them from left to right. Model moving across the page from left to right, encountering the first letter, visually examining the word from first letter to last letter, and saying the word.

Interaction with students   Have students do what you did (move across the page from left to right, visually examine the word from first letter to last letter, and say the word). Present the word repeatedly in various phrases and sentences and have students visually examine the word and say its name until the two words are no longer confused.

Closure   Have students state which words they have learned, what they have learned about visually examining words which will prevent similar miscues in the future, and when they will use what they have learned in real text. Then guide reading that contains these easily confused words.

Desired Outcome   When reading text, students will instantly recognize look-alike words that were previously confused and will be able to state how to visually examine such words to avoid confusion.

---

the topic is how to care for pets, rabbits in particular, there are three ways to activate background knowledge. First, you can have a live rabbit to activate what students know and generally provoke conversation. Second, you can use films, filmstrips, or pictures, which are not as stimulating, so you will have to provide more statements and questions. Third, you can simply talk about rabbits; here you provide statements and questions as the way to activate prior knowledge. Conversation alone does not stimulate students as much as concrete objects or their representations, but it can be effective if you provide information and ask questions that are tied to your students' background experiences about rabbits and pet care. Statements broaden students' range of background activation while questions narrow it, so use statements interspersed with questions. Rather than simply asking your students what they know about how to take care of rabbits, combine statements and questions as follows: "People have kept animals as pets throughout history. Rabbits are sometimes kept as pets. Think about what you know about rabbits as pets. Do you have a pet rabbit? Do you know someone who has a rabbit as a pet? Let's see what we know about rabbits as pets."

Not only is it necessary to activate what students know about topic, it is also necessary to activate what they know about purpose and text to predict initial meaning. From the very beginning, give students real text to read and teach them directly that reading involves making predictions about the meaning of text. Show them how knowledge about an author's purpose helps us predict the message, and how the text structure itself can be used to predict an author's message. For instance, during nook-and-cranny time or when guiding students' reading of stories, you may discuss how to decide whether an author's purpose is one of entertaining or informing and to use this knowledge to help predict the meaning; and teach them to use their knowledge of story structure to predict what will happen next. Your aim is to make your students aware of how they use their knowledge of purpose and text to construct meaning so they can be in control of the meaning-getting process. Example 16.5 illustrates how to structure such a lesson.

During-Reading Strategies The during-reading strategies include monitoring and fix-it strategies related to decoding. Primary age students have had experiences with monitoring strategies and fix-it strategies in oral situations in kindergarten (see Chapter 15). As they learn to decode words, they move these strategies into printed texts.

Monitoring is crucial for early reading. Even though instructional emphasis is on development of word recognition, your students need to understand that reading is accomplished only when the text makes sense. This is difficult for many students to understand because so much instructional time is spent on decoding. You can help students with this problem by continuing to emphasize monitoring during orally presented stories and by teaching them how to monitor when using printed materials. You want your students to understand that text that does not make sense is a problem to be solved. They monitor to see if it does make sense—to see if there is a problem.

Because of the emphasis in primary grades on words, fix-it strategies focus on what to do when you come to a word that you do not recognize at sight. This category of fix-it strategy is sometimes called word attack or word analysis because when you do not instantly know a word, you must attack it or analyze it to figure it out. There are three major ways for figuring out unrecognized words.

First, teach students to use context to predict an unrecognized word. For

EXAMPLE 16.5   How to Use Text Structures to Predict Meaning

Background	You have recently read two books to the class about hermit crabs, one written as a narrative text that gives a hermit crab human characteristics and another written as expository text that provides factual information about hermit crabs. You decide to use nook-and-cranny time to help students understand how different text structures can be used to make predictions.
Lesson Sequence	
Introduction	Initiate a discussion about the two books with a purpose-setting statement such as, "Let's see how these two books are organized differently and how that helps us predict meaning.
Modeling	Show how the narrative follows a story structure and that you can predict what will happen next if you know the parts of a story. Show how the expository text structure helps you predict meaning and how you used these knowledge sources to predict the author's message.
Interaction with students	Using other narrative and expository texts, have students follow your model and describe how they used text structure to construct meaning.
Closure	Summarize the discussion by having students state what they have learned about how to use text structure to construct meaning.
Desired Outcome	When reading text students should be able to predict the author's message and explain how they used text structures to help make their predictions.

instance, if students do not recognize the printed word *engine* in the sentence, "The airplane's engine stopped and it crash-landed in a field," they can use their knowledge of airplane crashes to predict that the unknown word is either *engine* or *propeller*. This strategy is the most efficient way to solve word recognition problems because it is fast and it emphasizes meaning getting. For instance, even if a student predicts *propeller* in the example above, the essential meaning of the message remains intact. Consequently, teach your first and second grade students to turn first to the strategy of contextual prediction when they encounter words they do not know. Even before formal reading begins, teach your students to supply endings for oral sentences such as, "I went to the store and bought a pound of _____" or "I went to the store and bought a pair of _____." Later, require more difficult predictions, such as filling in the blanks in an exercise like the following:

...

The elephant went around the circus _____, performing his tricks and entertaining the _____. He did not seem very happy. _____ master was whipping him and he _____ slowly through one trick after another.

Examples of the various kinds of context are provided in Chapter 7.

Your instruction in context emphasizes monitoring meaning getting so readers know when they encounter an unrecognized word and so they first use context to identify the word. Later, when they have also learned to use phonics and structural analysis to figure out unknown words, teach your students to combine these methods with context clues. In the airplane example, if you teach first and second grade students to use context in combination with phonics they would not predict that the unknown word is *propeller* because, although it makes sense in the sentence, propeller does not begin with the letter *e*. Consequently, the reader searches for a word that both makes sense and fits the phonic and structural constraints of the unknown word (see Example 16.6).

Second, teach students to figure out unrecognized words using structural analysis. This involves teaching them to examine an unknown word for structural meaning units and root words which, when broken apart, make it easier to figure out what the word is. For instance, when readers encounter the unknown word *unneeded*, they can separate the root word *need* from the prefix *un* and from the inflectional ending *ed* and pronounce each part in turn. This strategy is more efficient than phonics because it focuses on meaning units rather than on sound units and because it is faster than phonics (there are normally fewer meaning units in a word than sound units). However, for it to be useable, the unknown word must contain structural units. In teaching structural analysis, you progress from the most common structural units to the less common ones. Consequently, instruction begins with analyzing compound words, then common inflectional endings (such as -s, -ed, and -ing), contractions, common prefixes and suffixes, less common prefixes and suffixes, and Greek and Latin roots. A list of common structural units is provided in Figure 7.3.

Teach your students to examine unknown words for recognizable structural units, to break the units apart, to pronounce the units in turn, and to check the results with the sentence context to see if the word makes sense. To use this strategy, readers must be aware of the various kinds of structural units so they can recognize them and they must not confuse structural analysis with syllabication (which is analysis by sound unit or phonics, not analysis by meaning unit). Also, your students must not confuse structural analysis with "looking for the little word in the big word," which does not always work (sometimes it does, as when one looks at the *at* in the unknown word *chat*, and sometimes it does not, as when one looks for the *at* in the unknown word *father* or the unknown word *plate*). Structural analysis is illustrated in Example 16.7.

Third, teach your primary grade students phonics. Teach them the sound of each of the letters (or letter combinations) and how to blend those sounds together to pronounce an unknown word. In the word *umbrella*, for instance,

EXAMPLE 16.6   How to Teach Context Clues as a Strategy for Figuring Out Unrecognized Words

Background	When students encounter an unrecognized word in print, you want them to first use context as a means for figuring out the word. You decide to teach them the language principle that words in any text are related through meaning and through syntactical relationships. Be sure students have concepts for *predict, identified words, unidentified words, context,* and *relationships* if you intend to use these words when teaching context.
Lesson Sequence	
Introduction	State what kind of reading problem you are trying to fix, the specific kind of context strategy to be used, why context is a preferred strategy, and the situation in which it will be used. Stress the need to look at the particular syntactic and meaning relationships between the unknown word and the known words around it. Show students where the strategy will be used in text to be read.
Modeling	Present an example in which you encounter an unknown word when reading. Explain how you encountered the problem while reading, how you decided to use context to fix it, how you examined the context for the particular syntactic or meaning relationship you are teaching, how that relationship gave you clues to what the unidentified word was, how you tested the predicted word to see if it made sense, and how, if it did fit the context, you then continued reading for meaning.
Interaction with students	Give students similar examples of text containing unknown words and have them explain as you did. At first, provide directives in the form of verbal and visual cues to aid students, but gradually phase these out in successive attempts as students become more successful. Be prepared to explain again and remodel if students are confused about how to use the strategy.
Closure	Have students state what they have learned, when it will be used, and the mental process one goes through when using it. Then assign guided reading in which the context strategy can be used in real text.
Desired Outcome	Given real text and a blockage in getting the meaning caused by a word unknown in print, students will use a context strategy (or a context strategy combined with other kinds of cues) to figure out the unknown words, remove the blockage, and continue with meaning getting.

EXAMPLE 16.7   How to Teach Structural Analysis as a Strategy for Figuring Out Unrecognized Words

Background   When students encounter a word unknown in print which has a root and affixes, you want them to use such structural elements as an aid in identifying the word. You decide to teach the principle that the meaning of many English words are changed by adding prefixes, suffixes, and inflectional endings. By separating these affixes from the root, an unrecognized word sometimes becomes recognizable. Be sure students have concepts for *prefix, suffix, inflectional endings, roots,* and *structural analysis* if you intend to use them when teaching structural analysis.

Lesson Sequence

Introduction   State what kind of reading problem you are trying to fix and the specific kind of structural analysis to be used to fix it. Describe when this strategy would be used, and state that students must attend to the affix in question and separate it from the root. Show students where the strategy will be used in text to be read.

Modeling   Present an example in which you encounter an unknown word when reading. Explain how you decided to use structural analysis to fix this blockage, examined the unknown word for the affix in question, separated the affix from the root, pronounced the two separate parts, pronounced them together, tested the newly pronounced word to see if it made sense, and continued reading if it did make sense.

Interaction with students   Give students similar examples of text containing unknown words that have structural units. Have them explain their mental processing in figuring out the word. Assist them at the early stages with verbal and visual directives, but gradually diminish these as students demonstrate success. Reexplain and remodel as dictated by the quality of student response.

Closure   Have students state what they learned, when they will use it, and how to do it. Assign guided reading containing unknown words to which structural analysis can be applied, and have students use the strategy in this real reading situation.

Desired Outcome   Given real text and a blockage in getting the meaning caused by an unknown word composed of structural units, students will use structural analysis (in combination with context) to figure out the unknown word, remove the blockage, and continue with meaning getting.

teach students to divide the word into parts (um-brel-la) and to pronounce each part by saying the letter sounds individually and then blending them together. Students will say the short *u* and the consonant *m* to get *um;* the consonant blend *br,* the short *e* and the consonant sound for *l* to get *brel;* and the consonant sound for *l* and the schwa sound to pronounce the unaccented final syllable *la.* Then they say the three parts one after another, blend them together, and identify the unknown word (assuming that the reader's pronunciation is accurate enough and that *umbrella* is a word they have heard or used before).

You can see that phonic analysis often requires more time and effort on the reader's part than either context or structural analysis. Consequently, phonics is the least efficient of the strategies for attacking unknown words. Also, it is sometimes inaccurate since, unless you know virtually all there is to know about phonics, you may produce an approximation of the unknown word rather than an exact reproduction of the actual pronunciation. Finally, phonics is difficult to teach because there are so many letter sounds, letter-sound combinations, generalizations, and exceptions to be learned. Despite these disadvantages, however, phonics is an important word attack strategy because almost all words can be pronounced (or pronounced almost the way they are supposed to be said) by using phonics. When a sentence does not provide enough context clues to make an accurate prediction about a word, and the word does not contain meaning units for structural analysis, readers can turn to phonics in the expectation that a reasonable facsimile of the word's pronunciation will result. For this reason, it is important to spend considerable time teaching primary grade students to use phonics to attack and sound out unknown words.

Begin instruction in the prereading stage with emphasis on auditory discrimination of sounds and letter-sound associations (see Chapter 15). Teach your students the various sound elements, beginning with single consonant letter sounds, consonant blends and digraphs, letter substitution in common phonogram patterns (such as substituting initial consonants in *mat, bat, fat,* and *sat*), short vowel sounds, long vowel sounds, vowel combinations, vowel generalizations, and syllabication. As students progress through the grades, more and more of these phonic units are presented. Place your emphasis on examining words for specific phonic elements (to determine, for instance, whether the unknown word *chow* should be attacked as c-h-o-w or as ch-ow), breaking the word apart by these units, applying the appropriate sounds to the units, pronouncing the separate sounds, blending them together, and checking to see if the resulting pronunciation makes sense in the context of the sentence. See Example 16.8 for an illustration of how to teach phonics as a strategy in the primary grades.

To be good readers, students must first understand the relationship between sight words and word analysis. Most words in any given text must be recognized at sight. In fact, the rule of thumb used by most teachers is that unless 95 percent of the words are sight words, a text is too difficult. Only the 5 percent that are not instantly recognized should require word attack

EXAMPLE 16.8   How to Teach Phonics as a Strategy for Figuring Out Unrecognized Words

Background	When an unrecognized word cannot be figured out using context or structural analysis, you want students to use phonics. You decide to teach the language principle that alphabetic letters and phonogram units have assigned sounds that can be blended together to approximate the sound of the unknown word. Be sure students have concepts for *letters, words, sounds, first, last, middle, same, different, blending, phonogram,* and *phonics* if you intend to use these words when teaching phonics.

Lesson Sequence

Introduction	State what kind of reading problem you are trying to fix, the specific phonic element to be used, and when it will be used. Tell students to look at the visual form of the phonic element and its associated sound. Show students where this strategy will be used in text to be read.
Modeling	Present an example in which you encounter an unknown word while reading. Explain about how you decided to use phonics to fix the blockage, how you examined the word to find the phonic elements you knew how to use, how you supplied the appropriate sound and blended it with other letter sounds, how you tested the approximation that resulted to see if it made sense, and how you then continued reading if it did.
Interaction with students	Give students similar examples of text containing unknown words made up from the phonic element being taught. Have them explain the mental processing they used to figure out the word. Assist them at the early stages with verbal and visual cues, but diminish these gradually until they are doing the task independently. Be prepared to reexplain and remodel if student responses indicate confusion.
Closure	Have students state what they have learned, when they would use it, and how to do it. Assign guided reading containing unknown words to which phonics can be applied and have students use the strategy.
Desired Outcome	Given real text and a blockage to getting the meaning caused by an unknown word composed of known phonic elements, students will figure out the word using phonics (in combination with context) and continue with meaning getting.

using context clues, structural analysis, and phonics. Students must monitor their own word identification as they read. They must determine if they recognize a word visually, if they require word attack skills, and if so, how to select the appropriate strategy. Strategy use must be preceded by self-monitoring. Good reading ultimately demands that readers use these strategies in combination—they use visual characteristics, contextual meaning, structural units, and phonics because using them together is more efficient than using them separately.

Word recognition, then, involves, a four-step procedure. First, the reader examines the word visually and tries to identify it as a sight word. If that does not work, the reader turns to context and tries to predict the unknown word by reference to meaning cues. Then, the unknown word is examined for structural units and, if they are present, these are used in combination with context to figure out the word. Finally, the word can be sounded out and the pronunciation confirmed by reference to the sentence context (if it makes sense, it is probably the right word). As you introduce each of these four procedures, teach your students to use them in combination.

Post-Reading Strategies The post-reading strategies are organizing and evaluating content. During the initial mastery stage, these strategies are emphasized more than they were at the readiness stage.

Organizing content is a strategy that becomes increasingly important as first and second graders learn how to recognize words. For organizing content, the major strategy taught at this level is recalling what's important through use of simple story structures and text structures. This means that students need to recognize where the beginning, middle, and end sections are in stories and texts and then each section as a way to organize content. You need to teach your students how to do this. Example 16.9 illustrates how to structure a lesson on organizing content of narrative texts, or stories.

In the initial mastery stage students continue to evaluate the content of narrative and expository texts as real or make-believe but it is taught when students are reading, not listening, as was the case in kindergarten. You want your students to judge whether or not information they read could really happen. It is not important that every story students read be classified real or make-believe. Students judge stories and texts based on what their background experiences tell them could really happen or could not happen. Example 16.10 illustrates how to structure a lesson on evaluating content after reading narrative or expository text.

Role of the Basal

Basal textbooks emphasize many process goals and, therefore, frequently are the basis for process instruction in primary grades. However, you should be cautious about basing your process instruction on the basal in grades 1 and 2.

First, what the basals recommend is not necessarily what needs to be taught. For instance, only a few current basal texts recommend much instruc-

EXAMPLE 16.9   How to Teach Organizing Content

Background	Your students have been organizing content for listening situations. You decide to teach them how to organize information from stories and texts that are read by remembering what happened in the beginning, middle, and end sections.
Lesson Sequence	
Introduction	Have students read a story or text. Direct them to read the beginning section and stop, the middle section and stop, and the ending section and stop. You signal each section.
Modeling	Explain that it is helpful when organizing information that has been read to remember it in terms of the beginning, middle, and end sections. Explain that the usefulness of organizing content by beginning, middle, and end sections helps the memory process and makes it easier to remember it at a future date. Be specific about the future use of the strategy. All students read each section, and you demonstrate how you remember information in a particular situation. Then demonstrate how to organize information based on where it is in the story or text.
Interaction with students	Give students several opportunities to remember story or text content through use of the beginning, middle, and end sections. Start with single sections and gradually move to entire selections including both narrative and expository texts. As students demonstrate their understanding and use of the strategy, gradually reduce your assistance.
Closure	End the lesson series with another selection. Point out the beginning, middle, and end sections and have students read the selection and use their organizing strategy to remember information.
Desired Outcome	Given narrative and expository texts that are read by students, students will remember information by organizing it into beginning, middle, and end sections.

tion in using prior knowledge, purpose, and text structure in combination to construct meaning. Similarly, not all basals have carefully structured programs of word meaning and sight word vocabulary; others do not make a distinction between instant word recognition and word analysis; still others teach word analysis techniques as skills to be memorized rather than as strategies to be consciously applied; and still others put a priority emphasis on phonics (rather than context) as a word attack technique.

Second, your intention in teaching process goals is that your students

EXAMPLE 16.10   How to Teach Evaluating Content

Background	Your students may already know how to judge stories they listen to. You decide to teach them how to judge stories or texts as real or make-believe when they read them.
Lesson Sequence	
Introduction	Have students read a narrative or expository text that is real. Then have them read a make-believe selection. Note and discuss the events that make each selection real or make-believe.
Modeling	During discussion, explain and demonstrate how to decide if events are real or make-believe by using background experiences.
Interaction with students	Give students several opportunities to judge whether a selection is real or make-believe after it has been read. Gradually diminish assistance as students demonstrate they can judge selections as real or make-believe based on their background experiences.
Closure	End the lesson series with narrative and expository texts that are either real or make-believe. Have students judge whether the selections they read were real or make-believe and then support their decisions.
Desired Outcome	Given stories that students have read, students will judge selection content as real or make-believe based on their background experiences.

will *apply* process knowledge when reading real text. Most basal texts, however, make only minimal attempts to transfer skills from the instructional context of the workbook to the application context of real books and stories. In fact, many basals do not even recommend that skills taught in a particular lesson be applied in the reading of that lesson.

Consequently, you should modify basal text prescriptions to ensure that what needs to be taught is indeed taught and that what is taught is actually applied by students to real text. The recommendations made in Chapter 12 should be used to guide your decision making when making these modifications.

ACTIVITIES TO DEVELOP PROCESS GOALS

Here are some activities you can use to supplement your teaching of process goals in first and second grade. The activities at this level tend to focus on words because this is a process emphasis in primary grades. Be cautioned, however, that understandings about words are best developed within a literate environment and that these activities should not be used in isolation from real reading situations.

1. Hold up familiar objects to elicit descriptive words such as *round, heavy, square,* and so forth. As the object is shown, ask questions such as: "What is this? What shape is it?" You may also use pictures. This helps develop oral vocabularies, which are essential for reading success.

2. When students begin to read, they need to recognize certain words for directions. This includes such concepts as *same, different; smaller, larger; big, bigger, biggest; up, down; circle, underline; left, right.* Games are good for this purpose. For example, to develop correct ideas for *left* and *right,* have students play the game "Simon says, turn left, turn right." Or have them dramatize or give directions as they say the nursery rhyme "Jack and Jill."

   Activities 3 through 12 can be used to help students develop sight words.

3. Make up racing games in which students progress in the race by pronouncing at sight the words to be learned. For instance, construct an auto racing course and divide the track into equal-sized squares. Give each student a toy racing car. Using a pack of cards upon which are printed the words you want the class to learn, flash one word to each student in turn. Students who pronounce a word instantly move their racing car one square closer to the finish line. Students who are unable to pronounce the word do not move their car. The first student to get his or her car to the finish line wins.

4. Help students construct self-help references for the words they find difficult. For instance, each student can be provided with a 3″ by 5″ file box and a supply of file cards. Have students write difficult words on a file card, and glue a picture or other aid to the card to help remember the word. Tell students to refer to the file frequently to study the words and to remind themselves when they are unable to identify words in reading.

5. Place the words to be learned at sight on the chalkboard. Send one student into the hall, and have another go to the board and point to one of the words. Tell the rest of the class to pronounce the word to be sure that all the students know it. Then bring the first student back into the room and tell him or her to guess the target word. Have the student point to one word and say, "Is it _____?" The student continues this way until the word is identified.

6. Construct ladder games in which a paper ladder leads to a place where a reward of some kind is waiting. For instance, the ladder can lead to the upper branches of a paper apple tree that has many paper apples on

it. Each rung of the ladder has a sight word attached to it. Tell students to instantly pronounce the word on each rung of the ladder to reach the top. The reward is knowing all those words. Other rewards can be used, such as a real apple or a check on a progress chart.

7. A multitude of games for building sight words can be based on the idea of a trip. This trip may be a reconstruction of the adventures of some famous story character (such as Peter Rabbit), it may be a trip that the students are actually going on, or it may be a trip that is completely imaginary (such as a trip to the moon, a trip to a distant city, and so on). In any case, construct a game board and draw the path to be followed in reaching the destination as well as the hazards to be overcome along the way. Each student progresses on the trip by correctly pronouncing the words that are flashed. The first student to complete the trip wins the game.

8. Play a fishing game in which students are given a pole constructed of a stick and a string with a magnet tied to the end. Place paper fish with sight words printed on them in a box or in some other object that will serve as a pond. Attach a paper clip to each fish. Have students drop their line into the pond until the magnet attracts the paper clip on a fish. They pull the fish out and get to keep it if they can correctly pronounce the word printed on its side. Each student tries to increase the number of fish caught each time the game is played.

9. Make nine packs of ten cards each. The nine packs represent the nine holes of a golf course, and the word printed on the cards are the words to be learned at sight. Shuffle the cards and tell the player to put the pack for the first hole face down on the desk. Have the student turn each card over in turn, pronounce it, and go on. Every time a word is incorrectly pronounced, put a mark on the score card. The number the student gets wrong on the first hole (first pack of cards) is his or her score for that hole. Have student continue in this manner through the nine packs of word cards, trying to get as low a score as possible. Encourage students to keep a record of their scores so they can note their progress in mastering the course. Construct new courses offering new challenges as new words need to be learned.

10. Put some sight words on cards, placing a numerical value from 1 (low) to 3 (high) in the upper right-hand corner of each card in accordance with its degree of difficulty in being remembered. For instance, *dinosaur* is a fairly easy word for learners to identify and would only be given a value of 1, but *the* is very difficult for young students to recognize and would be given a value of 3. Students take turns drawing the cards, reading the words, and noting their scores. If they pronounce the word correctly, their score is the numerical value noted on the corner of the card. Each student tries to increase the number of points each time the game is played.

11. Play a treasure hunt game in which some packets of ten or more word cards are hidden around the classroom. Give each student the first packet and direct students to read each word. Have students go through the words as quickly as possible and try to get to the last card that tells them where the next packet is hidden. They go to that packet and repeat the process. The final packet directs them to a spot where each student will receive a reward for having completed the game.

12. Play a variation of the television game concentration. Place the words to be learned on cards and put them face down on the table. Tell students to try to remember where there are two cards exactly alike and to pick up matching pairs. As students turn over each card, they must pronounce the word on the card. If they succeed in picking up a card that matches the first word, they get another turn. All students try to increase the number of pairs each time the game is played.

13. Help students write headlines to develop an understanding of how reading works. Popular first and second grade books may lead to such headlines as "Dinosaur Missing from Museum," "Fish Saves Family," or "Sharing Is Fun." This helps students learn to focus on main ideas.

14. Read three or four lines of a story not known to your students, and have them create an ending. Later have students compare their version with the original. This activity helps students learn to predict.

15. Play a game in which you (or a student) start off with a word, such as *Wilbur*. Ask the next student to add a new word. Continue the game with each student adding a word until a complete story sentence about the initial word is given. This game shows how the reading-writing system works.

16. Line up a series of objects for students to see. Tell them to look carefully and to remember the objects from left to right. While their eyes are closed, you (or a student) shift the order of one or two objects, then ask some of the other students to recreate the original order.

17. Present the following to students orally or in written form:

      Sugar is sweet, but pickles are _____?
      A jet is fast, but a bicycle is _____?
      The clouds are above; the dirt is _____?

This type of procedure helps students with comparisons and relationships. For example:

      Bread is made by a baker; boats are made by a _____?
      A dog runs on its legs, but a car moves on its _____?
      In the morning the sun rises; at night the sun _____?

18. Once students develop a sight word vocabulary, you can use those words to create written sentences and ask students to provide the missing word. If students cannot yet read independently, you can do the same thing as in a listening activity by putting the sentences on tape or having them spoken by another student, an aide, or you. This helps develop skill in using context clues.

19. Read a paragraph to students and state that you will stop reading every once in a while and hold up a letter card. Direct them to keep the paragraph in mind, to look at the letter on the card, to think of the sound associated with that letter, and to say a word that both begins with that letter sound and fits the sense of the paragraph. This helps develop using context and phonics in combination.

20. Play games that require students to use both context and sound-symbol connections. For instance, direct them to listen to a sentence such as, "I went to the store and bought a mouse, a _____, a _____, and a _____." Hold up a letter card to indicate the beginning letter of each word required to fill the missing spaces. Students expand the sentence by adding words that begin with the letter sounds you show.

21. Group students in pairs. Give each pair a supply of letter cards. Let each take a turn in making up a sentence in which one word is left out. One student must hold up the beginning letter of the missing word at the appropriate spot in the sentence, while the other uses the sense of the sentence and the sound-symbol connection of the letter card to guess what word goes in the space. After correctly identifying the missing word, that student must make up a sentence. This helps students use context clues and phonics in combination.

22. Give students riddles in which the context supplies only a minimum outline of the missing word. For instance, you could provide the sentence, "The swimmer dived into the _____." Elicit student responses and encourage a variety of answers, such as water, pool, lake, river, and so on. Then place a letter card (such as the letter w) at the left of the blank space and say, "What word must now go in the blank space?"

23. Use context activities to develop structural analysis. Provide students with sentences in which one word is missing and give them a choice of a root word or a root plus its structural ending to fill the space. For instance, a sample sentence might be, "The two (boy, boys) went to the store." Students choose the correct word to fill the blank, pronounce it, and tell why that word is the correct one. This helps students learn to use context clues and structural analysis in combination. Caution: The successful use of this technique presupposes that students already know orally the correct form of the word. Certain dialects will not contain many of these inflected and derived forms of words. Teach these as oral responses prior to the activity.

24. It is sometimes helpful to reverse the decoding process. That is, ask students to create words with prefixes and suffixes, or to compound words. Print the known words and word parts on separate cards, scramble them up, and have students choose a card. Then have the student choose another word card that goes with that word, making it either a prefixed word, a suffixed word, or a compound word. Be sure to have students pronounce each word they have created.

25. To help develop structural analysis skills, make a chart or a work sheet in which root words or parts of compounds are listed down the left side and suffixes or the second part of the compound are listed down the right side. Attach strings to the words on the left-hand column and direct students to connect the string with the suffix or other part of the compound listed at the right to make a new word.

26. Make up crossword puzzles in which only compound and/or prefixed and suffixed words can be used as answers.

27. Play a card game in which each player is dealt cards with root words written on them. Place the rest of the deck, with prefixes and suffixes on the cards, in the center of the table. Have students take turns drawing cards from the deck to try to match the drawn card with one of the root words to form a new word. If they can do so, they lay the two cards down together and pronounce the new word. If students draw a card they cannot use, it is put back on the bottom of the pile. The first player to get rid of all his or her cards is the winner.

28. Plan activities in which students must complete a series of sentences using the same root word in each. For instance, you might provide them with the root word *play* and tell them to use it with suffixes to complete the following sentences (see caution in Activity 2).

    He is a baseball _____.
    She is _____ in the game.
    Yesterday he _____ football.
    When she _____ she is happy.

29. Make a shutter device out of tagboard so that you can control the opening of the shutter. Insert a card that has the letter to be learned on the left and a picture of an object with the beginning sound of that letter on the right. Open the shutter to reveal first the letter and then the picture. Have students form the letter sound with their mouths and blend that sound into the picture name as it is exposed. This helps develop phonic skills.

30. Use the same device as described in Activity 29, but this time insert a picture first, then the letter, then the picture again. Have students say the picture name, then its beginning letter sound, and then blend that sound into the picture name as it is exposed the second time.

31. Use flash cards containing the letters to be learned. Flash a letter to students and direct them to respond with a word that begins (or ends) with that letter sound. This helps students develop phonic skills.

32. To help your students connect letters and sounds, display pictures of common objects (dogs, money, and so on) with the letter the object begins with printed at the left. Encourage students to use these pictures when trying to remember the sound of a particular letter.

33. Make a box and label it with a large printed form of the letter you are teaching. Place in the box pictures and objects whose names begin (or end) with the letter to be practiced. Direct students to reach into the box, draw out a picture or object, name it, and tell what letter it begins with. Make sure students look at the letter on the box while saying the object's name.

34. For students who need to review a number of letters and their sounds, modify Activity 33 by putting several letters on the outside of the box and placing objects that begin with all these letters in the box. The students then draw an object, name it, and point to the letter on the box that begins the object's name.

35. Give each student a group of pictures, some of which begin with the letter to be worked on and some of which do not. Hold up a letter card and direct students to hold up any picture they have that begins (or ends) with the sound associated with that letter. This helps develop phonic skills.

36. Using a flannelboard or a pocket chart, place a letter card to the left and a row of three pictures to the right. Two of the pictures should begin with the sound associated with the letter and one should not. To help develop phonic skills, direct students to select the beginning sound of the two pictures that begin the same.

37. Make a bulletin board or a large chart showing the letters to be learned in one part and in the other, next to each one and under a flap, a picture whose name begins with the sound associated with that letter. When students cannot remember the sound of *m*, for instance, they can go to the bulletin board, look under the flap next to *m* and say, "Oh, the sound of *m* is what we hear at the beginning of *money*" (or whatever the picture is under the flap).

38. Make a tagboard chart with the letters to be learned listed down one side and pictures beginning (or ending) with the sounds of these letters listed down the other. Attach pieces of string to the letters, and have students who need help with phonics connect the string from each letter to an object that begins with its sound.

39. Provide students with a number of letters. Play a game in which you say, "I see a letter whose sound we hear at the beginning of the word *money*.

What letter do I see?" Tell students to hold up the proper letter card, look at it, and say, "*Money* begins with the letter *m.*"

40. Make a set of picture cards for each letter sound. Teach students to play a card game in which several cards are dealt to each player. Tell students to pair picture cards beginning with the same letter sound. Have each player take turns asking their partner "Do you have a picture card beginning with the letter *m?*" If a student has such a card, he or she gives the picture card to the student requesting it and then has the opportunity to draw a card from the student's hand in return. Tell students to keep track of the number of pairs they possess.

41. Give students a group of letter cards. Tell each student to take turns saying, "I have a letter. *Money* starts with the sound of my letter. What letter do I have?" The student who responds correctly is the next one to select a letter.

42. To help review phonics, play a dramatization game with students in which you hold up a letter card and ask them to act out something that begins with the sound of that letter. Tell those who are not acting to guess what begins with the letter sound being dramatized.

43. To develop student use of context clues and ending sounds, use activities in which you provide the student with a key word and a sentence in which one word is missing. Direct them to supply a word to fill the blank. This word must rhyme with the key word. For instance, give the key word *cat* and the sentence, "Hit the ball with the _____." Students must supply and pronounce the word *bat*.

44. Play games in which you start with a common spelling pattern (phonogram) written on the board. To help develop phonic skills, students change either the initial or final letter, substitute another, and pronounce the new word. The next student must change it again and pronounce the new word. The pattern of words might look something like this:

cat is changed to *bat*
bat is changed to *bag*
bag is changed to *bad*
bad is changed to *had*
had is changed to *has*

45. Have one student write on the chalkboard a word illustrating a common phonogram pattern. He or she must then pronounce the word and make up a sentence using that word. Tell the next student to go to the chalkboard, change either the initial or final consonant in the word, pronounce the new word, and use it in a new sentence. At first, you may want to accept any sentence students produce. As they become more skillful, however, modify the activity to have them produce successive sentences that are related to each other and that tell a story so that students are

using phonics and context clues in combination. For instance, the sentences might proceed in this manner:

The *cat* is in the house.
He is sleeping near the *bat*.
A man put the cat in a *bag*.
He must be a *bad* man.

46. Make word cards using words incorporating common phonogram patterns you have been working on. Include also a number of cards that have the word *changeover* written on them (meaning that the phonogram pattern may be changed). Deal each student five cards. Tell one student to start by laying down any word card and naming it. The next student must lay down and name a card in his or her hand that has the same phonogram. If the student cannot play because he or she does not have such a word, he or she must draw from the deck until finding a word that fits or drawing three cards. When the *changeover* card is drawn, the student can play that and name any word with a different phonogram pattern. The first person out of cards wins the game.

47. Play a variation of crazy eights by making a deck of 40 cards that have printed on them words containing the phonogram patterns you have been working on. Make six cards with the numeral 8 on them. Give each student four cards, and place the rest of the cards in the center of the table. Tell the first student to lay down a card that contains the same word element or an 8 card. If students have neither a word card that fits nor an 8 card, they must draw a card from the deck. The first person out of cards is the winner.

DEVELOPING CONTENT GOALS

Ultimately, the ability to read is measured by noting how much of the content of particular texts is understood by the reader. Teaching to these goals begins in the primary grades and builds from the listening comprehension activities initiated in preschool and kindergarten (see Chapter 15).

Both recreational and functional texts are used at the primary level. Recreational texts are usually short stories with a simple story structure. Typically, they include a character, a setting, a problem the character must solve, a brief series of incidents relating to the character's problem, and a resolution of the problem. Many stories of this type appear in primary grade basal textbooks. However, primary grade recreational reading is not limited to basal text stories. Trade books (picture books and easy-to-read stories) and magazines (*Jack and Jill, Humpty-Dumpty*) are also read recreationally.

The predominant functional texts in grades 1 and 2 are simple expository articles conveying factual information. These are usually brief and straightforward, following a format of introduction-body-conclusion. Many times such functional text will be presented as a story; that is, expository text about animals may convey factual information by personifying an animal and telling a story about it. Some functional text of this kind is found in basal textbooks, and examples are also found in current events magazines and newspapers designed for use by primary grade students (such as *Weekly Reader* and *Scholastic Magazine*).

In first and second grade, you want students to comprehend the content of both kinds of text. Plan your instruction to guide students to acquisition of content.

Directed Reading Lesson

As noted in Chapter 15, instruction in comprehending the content of recreational and functional text begins in preschool and kindergarten when virtually all comprehension is listening comprehension. The major technique to guide listening comprehension is the direct listening activity. In grades 1 and 2, you will continue to develop listening comprehension using directed listening activities.

After your students develop a sight word vocabulary and an accurate concept of reading, however, you can begin to guide students' reading of recreational and functional text using the directed reading lesson. The DRL can be used with either recreational or functional text. In either case, you clearly communicate the purpose of the reading before beginning. If you involve students in this step, you will guarantee more student involvement in the reading (and, hence, more comprehension) while also establishing the importance of having clear purposes for reading. Example 16.11 illustrates how to use a directed reading lesson with a basal text selection.

Role of the Basal

It is important to make connections between process goals and content goals. Process goals should not be taught in isolation; in fact, the lesson format for teaching process goals (the MDRL) begins with discussion of the selection to be read for content. Consequently, there are times when both process and content are taught together, with the intention of helping students apply process knowledge while reading for content information.

Part of your responsibility is to decide whether you are teaching a particular lesson only for content knowledge or whether you are trying to help your students consciously use process knowledge. If the lesson is to ensure comprehension of content, you can use the directed reading lesson as described in Example 16.11; if the lesson is for applying process knowledge to content, use an MDRL.

Both forms of the DRL are typically used with basal textbooks. That is, you can use basal text selections to teach content goals alone or to teach how process knowledge is applied to content. In either case, however, you must override the basal text prescriptions, make a decision about why you want to

EXAMPLE 16.11   How to Use a Directed Reading Lesson for Content Goals

Background	You want your students to read the next selection in the basal textbook, and you want to make sure they comprehend the content. You guide the reading using the steps of the directed reading lesson. At the primary grade level, the selection to be read will almost always be a narrative text.
Lesson Sequence	
Introduction	Introduce the story in a manner designed to activate the students' prior knowledge about the topic or problem encountered. Extend students' schema for the topic or problem by teaching the meaning of new words that appear in the story, using a technique similar to that described in Example 16.2. When appropriate, also activate student knowledge about text structure and how this knowledge is used to predict meaning.
Purpose-setting	There are many ways to comprehend a story. You may wish students to focus on certain causal relationships, on how story problems are reflected in real life, or on broad themes. To ensure that students are focusing on the type and level of comprehension you intend, state the purposes for reading the selection and point out the author's purpose for writing the selection. Then tell how these two purposes are compatible.
Reading	Have students read the selection. At the early primary level this reading will often be oral, since students may not yet know how to read silently. Also you may ask students to discuss the story in sections as it is being used.
Discussion	Follow a question-answer format for the discussion. Base questions on the purposes stated at the outset and guide the discussion to ensure that students comprehend the story in the intended way.
Closure	Have students review what was learned from the selection, particularly in terms of the purposes set earlier. Usually you will also plan some type of follow-up activity that will extend and enrich the content knowledge. Frequently such follow-up activities involve writing or otherwise emphasize how reading and writing are integrated.
Desired Outcome	Students will be able to state what current knowledge has been gained from reading the selection.

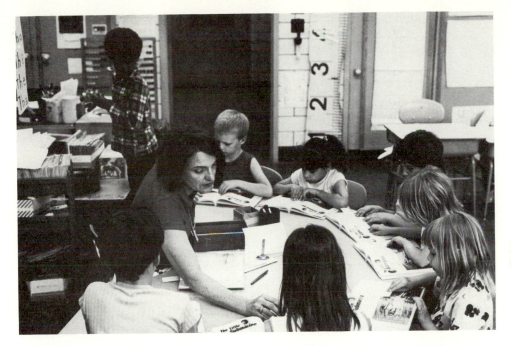

Teachers must decide whether they are teaching a lesson for content knowledge or for process goals. (Susan Lapides/Design Conceptions)

use the selection, and then plan the lesson to achieve that objective. By making such decisions, you maintain cognitive control of instruction.

ACTIVITIES TO DEVELOP CONTENT GOALS

Here are some activities you can use to supplement your teaching of content goals in first and second grade. The suggestions are not extensive because instructional activities for content goals depend on your choice of text. Thus your task is not to collect activities but to use different kinds of text.

1. Have students find an action picture in a newspaper or magazine. Have them discuss how the picture helps develop the information in the text.

2. Have students cut out questions in the weekly reader newspaper. Tell them to exchange questions and then provide answers. Have students compare answers given by the newspaper to their own.

3. Have students choose an advertisement that intrigues them. Have them discuss what might have happened before the ad was placed, then have them discuss the uses of advertisements.

4. Have students read aloud particularly the "most interesting" or "most exciting" parts of a story. This helps them develop and comprehend the meaning of recreational text.

5. Have students sell some toys they no longer want. Have them examine some ads for toys and then write an ad that will help sell the toys. This will illustrate the functional use of newspapers.

6. Discuss a news article. Divide the class into groups of four or five and have each one recount the article. Have them rewrite the article as if they had been an eyewitness. Members of the group then share their stories with one another.

INTEGRATING READING AND WRITING

The language experience approach provides endless opportunities for you to integrate reading, writing, and oral language. Such integrated activities help primary grade students develop positive attitudes about both reading and writing. During an integrated unit where students first read and then write their own books, an understanding of the reading and writing systems can be directly taught and used while they are involved in activities leading to content goals (such as finding out how the local government works). When integrated activities are used, time is not only used efficiently but also is used effectively since integrated instruction more closely represents the writing and reading in everyday life. Following is an example of one integrated language unit.

SAMPLE TEACHING UNIT: Allocating Time

LEVEL
First and second grade, initial mastery stage

DAY 1 OBJECTIVES
1. To identify behaviors that lead to task completion.

2. To develop taking turns in discussions.

3. To orally express ideas.

4. To increase behaviors that assist in completion of work.

Focusing activity: Set the purpose that the tortoise has correct behavior for completing work. Read aloud the story "The Tortoise and the Hare."

Thinking-speaking activity: Discuss the outcome of the race, why the tortoise won, how we can act like a tortoise or a hare, who we'd rather be like, consequences of being a tortoise or a hare, etc. Make use of opportunities to assess listening skills, taking turns, and oral expression.

Thinking-speaking activity: Have students "try on" the behaviors discussed in the previous activity. As the story is read, have students act out the behaviors next to their seat or in more open space. Discuss tortoise behaviors seen during the story.

Assessment: Record the behaviors that were discussed. Note both expressive and receptive behaviors. Record students who orally communicated ideas and took turns. Note students who need instruction in skills and teach them.

DAY 2 OBJECTIVES
1. To become aware of time.

2. To estimate time needed for a task.

Warm-up activity: Review the behaviors of the tortoise that led to completing the race. Introduce a tortoise bulletin board. Have pictures of desired behaviors. Have students label the pictures and put them on the bulletin board.

Focusing activity: Decide how long it takes to complete some unit of work. Have students close their eyes and estimate how long a minute is. Have students raise their hands when they think a minute is up. Discuss whether a minute is longer or shorter than was thought. Decide on the time needed to do an activity, and discuss whether it takes longer or shorter than we thought. Estimate the time needed to do the first independent task.

Reading-writing activity: Give students a reading-writing task and record the time used. Check to see if the estimate was correct. Discuss why the estimate was correct or incorrect. Repeat this sequence of estimating time and then doing a task until students are fairly accurate. Use a clock and a timer to help set times. As students complete their tasks, have them place a tortoise figure with their name on it on the tortoise bulletin board next to the behaviors they most exhibited.

Assessment: Note those students who were accurate in estimating time and those who need further assistance. Reteach those needing assistance.

DAY 3 OBJECTIVES
1. To use the following steps in completing a task: listen, look at what needs to be done, check understanding, do the task, check over work, and give self-praise.

2. To follow oral directions.

Warm-up activity: Discuss how well time estimating is going. Review behaviors that lead to task completion and add any additional behaviors to the tortoise bulletin board. Act out those behaviors.

Focusing activity: Introduce a chart of the steps needed to finish a job. Uncover step 1: Listen to what you need to do.

Thinking-speaking activity: Give students simple oral directions such as, "Go to the blackboard. Sit up straight." etc. Start with one direction and increase to two or more. Have the students give each other directions.

Assessment: Note students who are following directions and those who need further assistance. Reteach those who need assistance.

DAY 4 OBJECTIVE
1. To use the following steps in completing a task: listen, look at what needs to be done, check understanding, do the task, check over work, and give self-praise.

Warm-up activity: Discuss what a scout for a wagon train does. Have students act like scouts.

Focusing activity: Review step 1 of the chart. Uncover step 2: Look at what you need to do. Then uncover step 3: Check understanding. Discuss why we need to be like scouts.

Thinking-speaking activity: Play a game in which you present a number of objects on a tray. Have students observe and then close their eyes. Remove an object. Students observe the tray and decide what was removed. Put the tray away and ask students to list all the items that were on it. Have students state the purpose of the activity to verify understanding.

Assessment: Note which students were successful and not successful in observing. Provide other activities for those that were not successful.

DAY 5 OBJECTIVE
1. To use the following steps in completing a task: listen, look at what needs to be done, check understanding, do the task, check over work, and give self-praise.

Warm-up activity: Discuss the first three steps. Note the number of tortoise figures on the bulletin board beside each behavior. Estimate the time for the next activity.

Focusing activity: Uncover step 4: Do the task. Then uncover step 5: Check your work. Discuss how to work, being a good worker, finishing the job, etc. Emphasize doing a job right rather than fast. Discuss how to check over work, what to check for, i.e., any unanswered questions, right answers, etc.

Thinking activity: Have students use the steps in independent work.

Assessment: Note students who are successful and unsuccessful at following steps and give further assistance to those who need it.

DAY 6 OBJECTIVES
1. To complete the first five steps in working through a task.

2. To listen to a story.

3. To visualize behaviors that are like an ant or the tortoise.

Warm-up activity: Review the work behaviors by having students act them out. Include specific behaviors from the tortoise bulletin board.

Focusing activity: Review steps 1 through 5. Discuss how it feels to finish and know you've done a good job. Uncover step 6: Tell yourself you did a great job. Read the story "The Grasshopper and the Ant."

Thinking-doing activity: Discuss how the grasshopper would do his work if he were in the room and what the ant would do. Then ask students if they would be like ants or grasshoppers. Have students draw pictures of themselves being an ant or a grasshopper. Label the pictures.

Culminating activity: Have students give self-praise by pinning a good job badge on themselves as they complete a task using the six steps.

Assessment: Note the students who still need help on task estimating and task completion.

ADDITIONAL INTEGRATED READING AND WRITING ACTIVITIES

Here are some additional activities to supplement your integration of reading and writing in grades 1 and 2.

1. Provide pictures from magazines and other sources. Have students discuss what led up to the events in the pictures. Have students write a story about an event. Put their stories in books to be added to the classroom or school library.

2. Have students write riddles and place them in riddle books to be read during free time or nook-and-cranny time.

3. Have students share a story and retell it in a rebus. Example:

    Three little _____s built _____s.

4. Write comparison books with a variety of comparisons. Examples:

    As big as a _____, as little as a _____.
    As warm as _____; as cold as _____.
    As light as _____; as heavy as _____.

    Books for each set of comparisons can be added to the classroom or school library.

5. Have students discuss a sport they are knowledgeable about, such as soccer, tennis, or swimming. As a group, have students write one line about how it feels to play, then one line about how it feels to watch.

6. Have students think like a vendor at a baseball or football game. Discuss how vendors might sell their products, then have students write a chant about selling them. During nook-and-cranny time, have students read their chants.

7. Have students select their favorite story and rewrite it in playscript. Ask other students to read the new stories, with each person taking a character role.

8. Have students select their favorite food and create the recipe for its preparation. Place all recipes in a book, duplicate it, and send each parent a copy to be read and enjoyed.

9. Have students create recipes for a "good kid" cookie. Discuss all the important ingredients by starting with the statement, "A good kid is _____." Have students write individually or in groups their recipes for a "good kid" cookie.

CHARACTERISTICS OF AN INSTRUCTIONAL DAY

First and second grade reading instruction has a number of unique characteristics. One of the most obvious is the heavy allocation of time. In most primary grades, there are two designated times for reading instruction, one in the morning and another in the afternoon. This allocation of extra instructional time for reading is another example of how crucial reading is at this level.

Another distinguishing characteristic is the way in which time is used. Time tends to be allocated in large blocks: It is more typical to find reading being conducted for 1½ hours than for the 50 minutes we normally associate with instructional "periods." Moreover, most first and second grade teachers do integrate reading with the other language arts. Hence, reading periods normally include listening comprehension, writing, language experience activities, oral sharing of ideas and experiences, creative drama, and teacher reading, as well as the typical basal text activities normally associated with reading instruction.

This difference in time usage reflects the curricular emphasis in the primary grades. Because attitude goals are so important at the primary grade level, you plan many diverse activities to develop language concepts and positive responses. This diversity is also a reflection of the shift from listening comprehension to reading comprehension, which accompanies the move from the readiness stage to the initial mastery stage.

Another distinctive characteristic is the self-contained instructional day in which one teacher is responsible for teaching virtually all subjects. Primary teachers usually place more emphasis on the classroom library than on the school library, do much more of their own art and music instruction, and integrate such activities into on-going reading instruction.

First and second grade often have a highly integrated curriculum that includes many diverse activities with little evidence of different subjects being taught. Within this framework, reading is heavily emphasized. However, the emphasis is not just on skills—it is also on developing conceptual understanding about language and positive responses. Consequently, instruction in first and second grade is dominated by language, in that all modes of communication (listening, speaking, and writing, as well as reading) are in evidence.

SUMMARY

While comprehension is always a priority in reading, teachers in grades 1 and 2 place a relatively heavy emphasis on attitude and decoding. A particularly difficult aspect of teaching in the primary grades is the need to develop well-rounded conceptions of reading while also emphasizing word-level skills and strategies. To achieve this balance, teachers place heavy emphasis on creating a literate environment and on using language experiences to develop attitude goals; they also use directed reading lessons and modified directed reading lessons with a basal textbook to develop content and process goals. Typically, primary grade reading instruction integrates reading instruction with general language activities and includes two allocated instructional times, one in the morning and one in the afternoon.

SUGGESTED ADDITIONAL READINGS

BRIDGE, C. (1979). Predictable materials for beginning readers. *Language Arts*, 56(5), 503–507.

BRIDGE, C. A., WINOGRAD, P. N., & HALEY, D. (1983). Using predictable materials vs. preprimers to teach beginning sight words. *Reading Teacher*, 36(9), 884–891.

CARR, K. S. (1983). The importance of inference skills in the primary grades. *Reading Teacher*, 36(6), 518–522.

CUDD, E., & ROBERTS, L. (1987). Using story frames to develop reading comprehension in a 1st grade classroom. *Reading Teacher*, 40, 656–663.

DYSON, A. H. (1982). Reading, writing and language: Young chidren solving the written language puzzle. *Language Arts*, 59(8), 829–839.

EEDS, M. (1985). Bookwords: Using a beginning word list of high frequency words from children's literature K–3. *Reading Teacher*, 38(4), 418–423.

FOWLER, G. L. (1982). Developing comprehension skills in primary students through the use of story frames. *Reading Teacher*, 36(2), 176–184.

FRIEDMAN, S. (1985). If you don't know how to write, you try: Techniques that work in first grade. *Reading Teacher*, 38(6), 516–521.

FRIEDMAN, S. (1986). How well can first graders write? *Reading Teacher*, 40, 162–167.

GIPE, J. P. (1980). Use of relevant context helps kids learn new word meanings. *Reading Teacher*, 33(4), 398–402.

HEALD-TAYLOR, B. G. (1984). Scribble in first grade writing. *Reading Teacher*, 38(1), 4–8.

HEALD-TAYLOR, B. G. (1987). How to use predictable books for K–2 language arts instruction. *Reading Teacher*, 40, 656–663.

MANNING, M., MANNING, G., & HUGHES, J. (1987). Journals in 1st grade: What children write. *Reading Teacher, 41,* 311–315.

MILLER, R. (1982). Reading instruction and primary school education. *Reading Teacher, 35*(8), 890–894.

RASINSKI, T. (1988). The role of interest, purpose and choice in early literacy. *Reading Teacher, 41,* 396–401.

SPACHE, E. B. (1982). *Reading activities for child involvement* (3rd ed.). Boston: Allyn & Bacon.

SPIEGEL, D. L. (1978). Meaning-seeking strategies for the beginning reader. *Reading Teacher, 31,* 772–776.

STAUFFER, R. G., & CRAMER, R. (1968). *Teaching critical reading at the primary level.* Newark, DE: International Reading Association.

RESEARCH BASE

BARR, R. (1984). Beginning reading instruction: From debate to reformation. In P. D. Pearson (Ed.), *Handbook of reading research* (pp. 545–608). New York: Longman.

CALFEE, R., & DRUM, P. (1986). Research on teaching reading. In M. Wittrock (Ed.), *Handbook of research on teaching* (pp. 804–849). New York: MacMillan.

CLAY, M. (1972). *Reading: The patterning of complex behavior.* Auckland, New Zealand: Heinemann.

Teaching Middle Grade Reading: Expanded Fundamentals Stage 17

GETTING READY

If things go well in grades 1 and 2, young readers come to grades 3 and 4 with accurate conceptions and positive feelings about reading, an understanding of how to handle words, and an understanding of how to use topic, purpose, and type of text to predict an author's message. Grades 3 and 4 expand these fundamentals. This chapter describes how third and fourth grade teachers teach reading. It describes the characteristics, curricular emphases, and instructional techniques needed to teach reading in the middle grades.

FOCUS QUESTIONS

- What particular characteristics are associated with teaching middle grade reading?
- How are attitude goals developed in the middle grades?
- How are process goals taught in the middle grades?
- How are content goals developed in the middle grades?
- How are reading and writing integrated in the middle grades?
- What does a typical middle grade instructional day look like?

OVERVIEW OF MIDDLE GRADE READING

The middle grades represent the bridging years between learning the fundamentals of reading (the initial mastery stage) and applying these fundamentals in a variety of specialized content areas (the application stage).

Hence, third and fourth grade reading instruction expands on fundamentals taught in grades 1 and 2 in preparation for the greater reading demands in the upper grades.

Because of the middle grades' bridging function, the reading curriculum is unique. Emphasis on attitude goals shifts from helping students build accurate concepts and positive feelings about reading to helping them build accurate concepts and positive feelings about themselves as readers; emphasis on process goals shifts from print to comprehension; and emphasis on content goals shifts from simple narrative stories and simple expository text to a variety of literature and expository texts.

As the curriculum shifts, instructional emphasis also shifts. For instance, group language experience activities, which are relied on heavily in the primary grades, give way to individual language experience activities and more collaborative grouping; direct instruction shifts to metacognitive comprehension strategies and fluency; and teachers guide reading using techniques that are more complex than the standard directed reading lesson. The relative emphasis in curriculum and in instructional activities in the middle grades is shown in Table 17.1.

The bridging function of grades 3 and 4 provides a special challenge for teachers. Because different students progress at different rates, virtually every child in grades 3 and 4 is at a different point in crossing the bridge from beginning reading to upper grade reading. Some are still trying to make sense out of the print, while others are eagerly demanding more challenging texts. This diversity is a major instructional challenge in teaching third and fourth grade.

DEVELOPING ATTITUDE GOALS

Developing positive attitudes is always a major outcome of reading instruction because, without good attitudes, students are unlikely to become literate people. The heavy attitude emphasis in the primary grades continues at the middle grade level. There is continued development of concepts about the communicative nature of reading and its recreational and functional purposes. There is also continued emphasis on making reading exciting and satisfying. But the greatest emphasis at the middle grade level is on helping students perceive themselves as readers with a lifelong habit of reading.

Creating a Literate Environment

The literate environment in grades 3 and 4 must encourage students to become involved in real reading. You can do this by designing the physical environment of your middle grade classrooms so that it looks like a place where literate people live and work. Make sure you have a room library consisting of a large selection of children's books (about three or four books per student, representing a variety of genres and topics). Be sure the library is prominently located, attractively decorated, and comfortable looking (some teachers use throw pillows and beanbag chairs to entice students to settle down with a book) to create the image that reading is a natural part of life in your classroom. You can reinforce this by arranging other aspects of your physical environment, for instance, by including a variety of projects that require written directions and student writing. Your physical environment will thus communicate that your classroom is an exciting place where literate people read books of their choice.

Also create an intellectual environment to stimulate many reading and writing activities. Set up the room library, encourage various projects and written communications, establish collaborative groups to exchange ideas, and generally establish the expectation that your students will participate in language in real ways. These expectations are an intellectual stimulation that promotes development of goals. Similarly, arrange the social-emotional environment to help students perceive themselves as readers and develop the habit of reading. Create an environment where students work together, usually in collaborative groups. Because reading and writing are a natural part of such cooperative learning situations, it is easier for your students to develop the desired concepts and responses.

Instructional Approaches

Basal textbooks play a relatively minor role in developing attitude goals in the middle grades. Rather, you should use language experience and personalized reading activities to promote attitude goals.

Personalized reading plays a particularly heavy role in the middle grades. Uninterrupted sustained silent reading (USSR) is an integral part of every[a] instructional day. In addition, look for other ways to involve students in free reading. You can place a heavy emphasis on sharing books, and use collaborative groups to plan and organize puppet shows, skits, creative drama, simulated newcasts, and other non-book reporting activities. These kinds of activities help your students see themselves as readers and promote the reading habit.

Language experience also plays a role in the middle grades. In contrast to the primary level, however, much of the language experience at this level is individual rather than group work. Have your students use their reading experiences as the basis for writing an imaginary story or use a field trip as the basis for writing a poem, for instance. You, of course, create the opportunities for such writing and encourage your students to make use of the experiences that are present. However, instead of a jointly produced language experience story, such as those typically found in the primary grades, have individuals do the writing.

These efforts are not necessarily unstructured. Indeed, you can use the three-step format for indirect instruction (see Chapter 12) to give these activ-

TABLE 17.1 Instructional Emphasis at the Expanded Fundamentals Stage

OUTCOME	INSTRUCTIONAL EMPHASIS	MAJOR INSTRUCTIONAL ACTIVITY
Attitude goals		
Concepts about reading	Reading is communication between writer and reader Reading is predicting meaning Reading is sense making Reading is a tool	Indirect instruction using projects, language experience, USSR activities, and writing
Positive responses to reading	Reading is exciting Reading is satisfying Reading results in knowledge Reading satisfies curiosity Reading is a source of power	Indirect instruction involving projects, language experience, USSR activities, and writing
Process goals		
Routing skills		
Vocabulary	Build vocabulary through direct study of words associated with content being studied Emphasis shifts from concrete words to multiple meaning words, homonyms, synonyms, antonyms, and other special categories of words	Direct instruction of words
Word recognition	Recognize a wide variety of words instantly and fluently	Direct instruction of words using basal text recommendations
Metacognitive strategies		
Initiating strategies	Active prior knowledge of content using predicting	Direct instruction of initiating strategies

ities some structure. For instance, this format might be used to plan and conduct a lesson like the one shown in Example 17.1. Such instruction is designed to help students derive a sense of empowerment from reading while also building the concept that reading is a useful tool.

ACTIVITIES TO DEVELOP ATTITUDE GOALS

Here are some activities you can use to supplement development of positive attitudes in the third and fourth grade.

TABLE 17.1   continued

OUTCOME	INSTRUCTIONAL EMPHASIS	MAJOR INSTRUCTIONAL ACTIVITY
	Activate prior knowledge about how different types of text and author's purpose to help make initial predictions about meaning	
During-reading strategies		
Monitoring strategies	Monitor for unknown words, for un-recognized words, for fluent sense making, and for accuracy of predictions	Direct instruction of monitoring strategies

Fix-it strategies	Recognize disruption in sense making
	Access strategies to solve the problem
	  Word recognition
	  Vocabulary
	  Author's meaning
	  Beyond the author's meaning
	Determine which strategy is needed
	Implement the strategy
	Verify repair of sense making
		Direct instruction of fix-it strategies for comprehension

Post-reading strategies Organizing strategies	Recall what is important by recognizing different types of text structure (stories, articles, poems, letters), classifying sentences, and determining main idea	Direct instruction of organizing strategies
Evaluating strategies	Judge content of message by author's word usage • denotative and connotative words	Direct instruction of evaluating strategies

1. Have students act as evaluators for first and second grade books to help middle graders develop a positive attitude toward reading. Ask students to present their evaluations to first and second graders.

2. Present radio shows using a tape recorder. By writing, reading, and speaking favorite stories, students develop the concept of the integrative nature of language.

3. Use quiz shows, patterned after "What's My Line?" or "Jeopardy" or "Wheel of Fortune" or "I've Got a Secret," to help middle grade students

TABLE 17.1 continued

OUTCOME	INSTRUCTIONAL EMPHASIS	MAJOR INSTRUCTIONAL ACTIVITY
	Judge content of message by completeness of content development	
Study strategies		
Locational strategies	Use book strategy of table of contents and glossary to locate information	Direct instruction of study strategies
	Use library strategy of card catalog to locate books by title or author	
	Use reference source strategy of dictionary to find word meanings	
	Use graphics strategy of simple bar and line graphs to gain meaning	
Study habits	Follow written directives involving three or more parts	Direct instruction of study habit strategies
Rate strategies	Develop a slow pace for careful reading and a fast pace for skimming	Direct instruction of rate strategies
Organizing strategies	Use semantic maps to organize content	
Remembering strategies	Use summarizing to remember content	
Content goals		
Recreational	Getting meaning from various types of narrative text	Directed reading lessons
	Understanding various literary devices used by authors	
Functional	Getting meaning from expository texts found in content area textbooks	Guided reading of context area texts

become acquainted with book characters. This type of activity helps develop the concept that reading is life captured in print.

4. Use newspaper and magazine articles about children's books, authors, or illustrators to stimulate development of a positive attitude toward reading. Have students bring these articles to class for discussion.

5. Use collaborative group reporting of children's literature to provide an opportunity for comparisons and contrasts of similar books. Use books

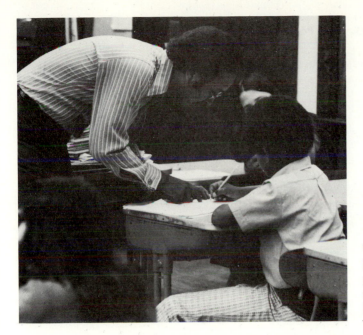

Written communication is emphasized at the expanded fundamentals stage. (Burt Glinn/Magnum Photos)

about animals, family life, periods of history, etc., as the basis for these discussions. Such discussions stimulate student interest in books.

6. Use feltboard characters to provide an opportunity for storytelling and development of positive attitudes. Ask students to develop and present their favorite stories to younger children.

7. Put questions in envelope pockets on the bulletin board to help students develop a positive attitude toward reading. Label an envelope "Who Am I?" and put in clues about popular characters. Label another "Where did it happen?" and include clues about events in various books. Tell students to add their own questions about books they have read.

8. Have students make bookmarks illustrated with "the part I liked best" or "my favorite character." They make lasting momentoes of enjoyable reading experiences and help to develop positive attitudes toward reading.

9. Have students make a video of a book by illustrating and connecting scenes from the book. The series of scenes, rolled on a wooden rod, may be passed through a frame cut from a box. You can also use an opaque projector. Such activities help students develop positive feelings about reading.

10. Use student-developed book jackets, illustrations, or advertising posters to illustrate a book that has been read. These make excellent bulletin board displays and develop positive attitudes toward reading.

EXAMPLE 17.1   How to Develop Positive Attitudes

Background	You want to develop the feeling that reading makes one feel empowered. You establish a situation in which students are unable to do what they want to do because they lack information.
Activity 1	As part of the literate environment, establish an activity that the students very much want to pursue, such as setting up an aquarium. Although you know they do not have enough information to complete the task, allow them to work on it. When frustration occurs because they lack the necessary information, initiate a discussion.
Discussion	Discuss the problem with the students and identify the lack of information as the source of the frustration. Help them locate the needed information in reference books. Point out that reading provided them with the power to complete a task that had previously frustrated them.
Activity 2	Have students return to the original activity and complete it.

11. Have students illustrate maps to show a character's travels or the area encompassed by a story. These offer a good way of sharing a book. Historical fiction books are especially effective.

12. Have students conduct interviews on selected topics with an adult or students from upper classes. Use them in activities where positive attitudes toward reading are being developed.

13. Have students prepare and make appeals before another class on behalf of school or community drives that can be related to selected reading topics.

14. Have students correspond with hospitalized children and adults. Have them share interesting information about reading topics and favorite books. This helps develop the concept of the interrelatedness of language as well as positive feelings about reading.

15. Have students take characters from books such as *Charlotte's Web* or *Pippi Longstocking* and rewrite the story in a setting suitable to the present. This activity promotes the concept of integrated language usage.

16. Have students write and then display a letter from one character in a book to another. Suggest they tell about something that might have happened had they both lived at the same time and place. Such activities help students learn to appreciate reading.

17. Have students create a magazine for the classroom by compiling voluntary artwork and writing projects completed during reading. Publish the magazine for classroom distribution to help students learn to value reading and its communicative function.

18. Hold a book fair. This opportunity to share a wide variety of books is an ideal device for getting middle grade children involved in book reviewing. Have students assume responsibility for reviewing important books before the fair, and ask representatives to travel to other classes to review the books before the exhibit. Students then use the reviews as guides for locating at the fair books that may be of particular interest to them.

19. Have students take responsibility for reviewing Caldecott Award winners for the primary grades. Have them present these reviews orally.

20. Keep a library corner, complete with bulletin board display. Such access to books helps develop positive attitudes toward reading. Relate themes for the displays to popular authors (Cleary, Wilder), genres of books (realistic fiction, mysteries, informational), or topics (animal, sports).

21. New books in the classroom library deserve recognition. A few well-chosen words about selected books will help build student interest and will keep the books circulating.

TEACHING PROCESS GOALS

Because the middle grades are bridging years, process goals are emphasized. There is a continued emphasis on the routine skills of knowing word meanings and sight words and on the metacognitive strategies of knowing how to use prior knowledge and strategies to remove word level blockages when getting meaning from text. In addition, however, middle grade reading emphasizes fluency and fix-it strategies to repair breaks in comprehension. Also, study skills are introduced in the middle grades. In short, middle grade teachers must continue the development of primary grade goals, begin placing special emphasis on metacognitive comprehension strategies, and introduce new strategies for study that will be emphasized in the upper grades.

Routine Skills

In the middle grades, there is less emphasis on the routine skill of sight words. Students progressing at a normal rate should have a large store of sight words, which should increase as they practice and use words that appear frequently in their texts. You do not need to focus on the learning of sight words, but sight word development does continue.

Do continue to emphasize vocabulary development, however. Within vocabulary instruction you continue to build meaning for many words, helping students understand the characteristics, properties, and examples for these words and how various words fit together into categories. You should continue to emphasize words that are useable: Ask yourself whether your students will need the words five years from now. If the answer is yes, teach the meanings of those words in instructional situations that actively involve students. Also continue vocabulary development through use of context clues for multiple meaning words, structural analysis, and understanding and using synonyms, antonyms, and homonyms, so that students become independent in figuring out word meaning.

In addition, emphasize fluency in the middle grades; that is, how smoothly and accurately students interpret meaning of text. If your students read a text with no hesitations or miscues and use intonation patterns consistent with the text's meaning, they are reading fluently. If, on the other hand, they read in a slow, choppy manner with many errors and poor intonation patterns, they are not fluent.

Fluency is a concern in both oral and silent reading. However, it is emphasized instructionally in oral reading situations because the easiest way to observe fluency is to listen to your students read out loud. You can then observe exactly where in the text the fluency began to break down and you can generate hypotheses regarding both causes and appropriate corrective instruction. However, you can also assess fluency during silent reading by timing students. If, for instance, your third and fourth grade students take much longer to silently read a particular text than you do, you can assume that their fluency is not good.

Poor fluency is often associated with poor sight-word recognition because when students instantly recognize all the words in a selection, they tend to read it fluently. Similarly, fluency is associated with general language competence because it is reasonable to assume that students who have limited oral-language backgrounds, who have limited exposure to oral reading, or who have recently learned English as a second language would find it difficult to be fluent.

When such problems are the cause of fluency difficulties, the remedy is straightforward. If unfamiliar words cause readers to hesitate, teach the needed words as sight words before assigning text reading. If inadequate general language competence is the problem, establish a strong oral language program that includes frequent listening to oral reading and frequent participation in other forms of oral language (see also Chapter 20).

Many times, however, students are not fluent even though there is no difficulty with sight words or with general language ability. Such students need direct instruction on how to be fluent. Begin such fluency instruction with the concept that authors expect their text to have a certain sound when read—that it should sound the way it would be said. In order to "say" the text properly, one must know what it means. Therefore, to be fluent a reader must understand the author's message; if it does not sound right, it probably is not the message intended by the author. Monitoring of the meaning, then, is the first instructional emphasis in helping nonfluent readers become fluent.

You can aid monitoring for fluency by encouraging students to think about intonation patterns when reading. For instance, encourage them to read as the author would say it. Then show them how to draw lines under clusters of words that should be "said together," and how to change boundaries of such word clusters until the text sounds right. Similarly, help students improve their fluency by teaching them to attend to the typographic cues embedded in the text, particularly the punctuation cues. These cues are direct aids to intonation and, hence, to fluency.

Another frequently used technique is **repeated readings.** To use this technique, have students first read a text for understanding. Then direct them to read it aloud again and again until it sounds the way they would say it. This technique works because it sets the expectation that reading should sound like real language and because it challenges students to strive for natural sounding reading until it becomes almost second nature to them.

Fluency is a major process goal at the middle grades. It is closely tied to comprehension since appropriate voice intonation depends on understanding the meaning of the text. An example of how to teach fluency is illustrated in Example 17.2.

Metacognitive Strategies

At the expanded fundamentals stage, metacognitive strategies expand into four categories. In the initiating reading category are strategies for activating prior knowledge for topic, text, and purpose. During-reading strategies emphasize monitoring and fix-it strategies for getting the author's meaning. Postreading strategies emphasize organizing and evaluating knowledge. The fourth category—study strategies—includes locational strategies, rate strategies, organizing strategies, remembering strategies, and study habits.

Initiating Strategies In the middle grades, initiating strategies include activating knowledge of topic, text structures and purposes of both the author and the reader.

Activating background knowledge for topic involves helping your students bring to a conscious level what they know about a topic. The best way to accomplish this continues to be using concrete objects, such as animals or people, or representations of objects such as films, pictures, and drawings, as described in Chapter 16. Whether concrete objects or representations are used, it is important to also use teacher statements to activate student prior knowledge and to ask questions as the way to initiate talk. For instance, in a lesson on developing friendship, you might activate your students' prior knowledge as follows: "Having friends is an important part of third graders' lives. We need to know how to make friends. Think about the times you have made friends. Remember what you did that seemed to help. Let's see what we can remember. Who wants to be first?"

It is also important to continue developing strategies about using prior knowledge to make predictions. During the expanded fundamentals stage,

EXAMPLE 17.2   How to Develop Fluency

Background	Some of your students read in a choppy, hesitant manner despite knowing the words at sight and having strong language backgrounds. You want to help them develop fluency.
Lesson Sequence	
Introduction	Set a purpose for orally reading a particular text; for instance, plan to have students read a book to a group of first graders. Explain that they must read fluently so the first graders will enjoy their reading. Give examples of fluent reading and nonfluent reading.
Modeling	Explain how the meaning of a passage signals what the intonation should be. For instance, say, "This is a dangerous situation. The story character must be scared. I need to read it like I'm scared." Then read it that way.
Interaction with students	Give students sample pieces of text and ask them to do the same kind of thinking that you did. At first, help them by pointing out what is happening and how that helps us say it. Gradually diminish the amount of help until students are independently making decisions about how to say the text passage.
Closure	Have students apply what they have learned about fluency to the text they are to read to the first graders. Guide their practice of the oral reading, and then have them read to the first grade.
Desired Outcome	When reading a text, students will monitor the meaning of the text and use this meaning to decide how to say the words in the text.

continue to give students real text to read and show them how knowledge about topic, purpose, and type of text all combine to help readers predict the meaning being conveyed. Since this is introduced in the primary grades, in the middle grades it often takes the form of a reminder. Nevertheless, you must be conscious of the need to keep meaning getting in the forefront and to continuously illustrate for your students how various knowledge sources can be used to predict what an author is conveying.

During-Reading Strategies   This category contains strategies to monitor reading and to fix meaning blockages. Although students were introduced to monitoring their reading in primary grades and have probably developed a beginning understanding of it, the middle grades especially emphasize monitoring. Students learn to monitor for words unrecognized in print, for words unknown in meaning, for what the author means, and for meaning beyond the author's intention. That is, readers check themselves to make sure they know what each word says, they know what each word means, they know what the author means, and they can make critical judgments and conclusions that go beyond the author's meaning.

To enhance monitoring, teach students to see if the text is making sense— to determine whether the anticipated meaning is what actually emerges while reading. In the course of such monitoring, readers occasionally become aware of something that does not make sense or that is unanticipated. At these times, most readers first look to see if there are words they did not say correctly; then they look to see if they have the appropriate meaning for each word; then they look to see if they understand the author's meaning; and finally they check to see if the judgments they are making about the author's meaning are appropriate in light of what the author is saying.

If the problem is a word they did not say correctly or an incorrect word meaning, then the word recognition and vocabulary strategies developed in Chapter 7 and emphasized in the primary grades (see Chapter 16) are accessed and applied. However, if the problem is the author's meaning or judgments that go beyond the author's meaning, comprehension strategies are accessed and applied. Example 17.3 illustrates one way to teach monitoring for the author's meaning.

When the problem is the author's meaning, it is helpful to look back at the typographic cues (punctuation, italics, bold print, etc.), or for key words or word elements (prefixes, suffixes, etc.), or for certain context clues. These cues are all visible in the sense that they are right there on the page. By looking for visible cues, a reader may note that the author's meaning can be determined by attending to a previously ignored comma, a misread prefix or suffix, the sequence of key words, or a missed relational word such as *finally*, *since*, or *but*. Example 17.4 illustrates one way to teach students to use such visible cues to determine an author's meaning.

Similarly, you can help your students understand an author's meaning that is not explicitly stated. Readers search for clues and infer what has been implied but not stated. They look inside themselves for knowledge they already have that can be combined with clues to make inferences. For instance, readers can often determine the gist of a written message by classifying, that is, by grouping together similar words or ideas and using them to infer the meaning. Readers use their own prior experience with similar situations to predict an author's implied meaning. And readers make inferences about relationships in text (chronological, causal, compare-contrast, etc.). By thinking of a similar situation from their own experience and determining the similarities between it and the text situation, they combine the text clues with their related prior knowledge and infer the author's meaning. Example 17.5 illustrates one way to teach students to use prior knowledge to determine meaning implied by the author.

Strategies for making judgments that go beyond the author's meaning require critical thinking. These strategies are described in Chapter 18.

EXAMPLE 17.3   How to Teach Students to Monitor Predictions

Background	You want your students to monitor their sense making when reading and to look back to generate new predictions when meaning getting breaks down.
Lesson Sequence	
Introduction	Using a basal text selection the students are to read, locate an ambiguous passage that might generate an erroneous prediction. State that you are going to show them how to check meaning and to generate new predictions until a sensible one is found.
Modeling	As you read, explain your thinking to students. Model your continuous monitoring of the meaning in light of your initial prediction, your puzzlement when the prediction no longer fits the subsequent text, your looking back for clues, your examination of these clues to produce new predictions (such as words have multiple meanings or reversals in the usual word order), your generation of a new prediction, and your testing of this prediction in the text.
Interactions with students	Give students examples of ambiguous text so they can do as you did. Have them explain their thinking so you can evaluate it. Gradually reduce the help you provide until students are generating new predictions without assistance.
Closure	Return to the basal text selection. Set the purpose for reading the selection, including the reminder to use the strategy for generating new predictions if they encounter situations where their initial prediction is not confirmed.
Desired Outcome	When reading text, students will monitor their meaning getting, will look back when sense making breaks down, and will use clues to generate new predictions.

Post-Reading Strategies Organizing and evaluating content are both post-reading strategies taught in the middle grades. Organizing content is important because this is where students restructure text information and store it in long-term memory for future use. This helps counter rote memory and simplifies the process of understanding and remembering through conscious grouping and storing. The major strategy to teach your students is based on purposes for reading. If the purpose is to find answers to predictions, then the information to remember is organized by the predictions; if the purpose is to remember sensory details, then the information could be remembered by organizing information by senses. Teach your students to organize around whatever the purpose is. Example 17.6 illustrates how to structure a lesson on organizing content according to purpose.

EXAMPLE 17.4   How to Teach Students to Use Visible Cues for Comprehension

Background	You want your students to know how to look for meaning through visible cues embedded in the text. For instance, when they lose track of the story sequence, they do not know that you can look for key words used by the author.
Lesson Sequence	
Introduction	Find a basal text selection in which the author uses visible cues to sequence, such as *first, next, then,* and *finally.* Tell students you will teach them a look-back strategy to use if they lose track of the story sequence.
Modeling	Show students how, after losing track of story sequence, you look back for key words. Explain what you think about as you encounter the problem, as you search for cues, and as you find the cues.
Interaction with students	Provide a series of similar textual examples for students and have them do as you did (determine story sequence by using key words). Provide help at first, but gradually phase out assistance as students' explanations provide evidence they understand how to use the strategy.
Closure	Have students read the basal text selection. Have them use the key word strategy if they lose track of the sequence.
Desired Outcome	Given a real text containing sequential events signaled by key words, students will be able to use key words as a strategy for determining story sequence.

The second post-reading strategy is evaluating content. A specific strategy taught in the middle grades is judging content by author's word choice. Teach your students to consider the purpose of written materials and the text structure used, and to then judge if the words used are appropriate. Your students should not consider all words that carry meaning but select words that seem to be important. Such words might be repeated often or might have extensive definitions, descriptions, or explanations within the text. Example 17.7 illustrates how to structure a lesson on evaluating content by author's word choice.

Study strategies is a new set of metacognitive strategies emphasized for the first time in grades 3 and 4. Up to now, students have focused on learning how to read. During the middle grades, the emphasis moves gradually to reading to learn. Accordingly, middle grade students are introduced to study strategies. However, the greatest instructional emphasis on study strategies occurs in the upper grades. Consequently, they are discussed in detail in Chapter 18.

EXAMPLE 17.5   How to Teach Inferencing

Background	You want your students to use invisible knowledge from their prior knowledge of the topic to make inferences.
Lesson Sequence	
Introduction	Use a basal text selection that poses questions requiring students to draw inferences. Note the need to answer such questions at the outset, and state that you are going to show them how to answer these kinds of questions.
Modeling	Using the basal selection, explain the thinking in making inferences. Show how you attend to the clues in the text while also thinking of situations from your prior knowledge which are similar. Talk about how you relate the text clues to your own prior experience and use it as a basis for drawing inferences about what the author is implying.
Interaction with students	Using similar text passages, have students follow your model in drawing inferences. Provide much help initially, but gradually reduce this assistance. Be sure you have students talk out loud to determine whether they are using a viable strategy.
Closure	Have students read the basal text selection, using their strategy to answer questions that require drawing inferences.
Desired Outcome	Given a real text to read, students will use their prior knowledge and text cues to answer questions that require drawing inferences about meaning authors imply but do not explicitly state.

Role of the Basal

Most process strategies are taught in conjunction with basal textbooks. However, teachers must use considerable caution in following basal prescriptions for two reasons. First, most basal texts do not present comprehension strategies as they are presented in this book. The reason is that most basals reflect only research that has long been accepted by the buying public to whom they must sell the books. Since the strategies presented here reflect current research findings, they are not always found in basal texts. What is often found instead is reference to the more traditional "skills" of comprehension, such as main idea, cause-effect relationships, looking for details, and so on. Consequently, you must modify the prescriptions of the basal text and recast them as strategies (see Chapter 12).

Second, as has been previously mentioned, most basal textbooks tend to

EXAMPLE 17.6   How to Teach Organizing Content

Background	Your students have been organizing content of narrative and expository texts by the beginning, middle, and end sections. You decide to teach them how to organize information from books by focusing on purpose.
Lesson Sequence	
Introduction	Have students read a book selection after the purpose is set. The purpose is to compare and contrast two positions. Proceed with the lesson using small segments of text.
Modeling	Explain that when organizing text information it is helpful to remember it in terms of purpose. Explain how this strategy is useful when we need to remember information that is read. Describe generally how they will use the strategy in the future. Demonstrate specifically how you remember text information about the two positions discussed in the particular text being modeled.
Interactions with students	Give students opportunities to organize text information according to different purposes. Start with simple purposes and gradually move to more complex purposes. As students demonstrate their understanding and use of the strategy, gradually reduce your assistance.
Closure	End the series of lessons with another text. Have students read the selection and use their strategy of organizing text information by purpose as a way to remember.
Desired Outcome	Given selections that are read, students will remember text information by organizing it according to purposes set.

isolate process goals, teaching them in association with workbook and ditto sheets. Seldom are the "skills" of comprehension applied to real text. Consequently, you must make the necessary modifications so that strategies are taught in real contexts.

In sum, while you will teach most comprehension strategies in direct instruction situations employing basal textbooks, you must be prepared to modify basal text prescriptions regarding comprehension, both in terms of *what* strategies to teach and in terms of *how* to teach them.

ACTIVITIES TO DEVELOP PROCESS GOALS

Here are some instructional activities you can use to supplement your teaching of process goals in third and fourth grade. Be cautioned that these activ-

---

EXAMPLE 17.7   How to Teach Evaluating Content through Word Choice

Background	Your students already know how to judge the selections they read as real or make-believe. You decide to teach them how to evaluate content by analyzing word choice.
Lesson Sequence	
Introduction	Establish what the author's purpose was for writing the selection (to inform, to entertain, to persuade, etc.). Have students note words that seem important.
Modeling	During discussion of the selection, explain and demonstrate word choice using words you think are important. Demonstrate whether you think the author used an appropriate word and explain why. Explain that this strategy is particularly useful when reading persuasive writings, such as advertisements or editorials. Be specific about when students will use the strategy.
Interactions with students	Given students many opportunities to judge whether author's word choice is appropriate according to the purpose. Gradually diminish your assistance as the students demonstrate they can judge author's word choice.
Closure	End the lesson series with another selection. Have students judge the author's word choice and then have them support their decisions.
Desired Outcome	Given selections that have been read, students will state how the author's word choice was designed to influence the meaning obtained from the text.

---

ities are best used within a literate environment and that they should not be used in isolation from real reading situations.

1. Draw a runway with a hangar at the end of it. Divide the runway into sections on which are printed new words. Pair students and give each an object representing an airplane. Have the game begin with both planes in the hangar. Tell the first player to spin and move the number of spaces that the spinner signals if he or she can use each word correctly in a sentence. Have the players take turns until one plane reaches the end of the runway. Such activities help students build vocabulary.

2. Have students select an article from a newspaper and list all the pronouns in it. Then have them write the nouns the pronouns refer to beside each pronoun. This helps students use pronouns to determine an author's meaning.

3. Use exercises in which students replace words with synonyms. Encourage students to supply another word that means about the same thing. Group discussion can judge the appropriateness of the synonyms. This helps students use different words in determining author meaning.

4. Teach word opposites. One way to discriminate a concept is by knowing not only what it is but what it is not. Activities with word opposites help students develop vocabulary.

5. Encourage students to associate words with mental pictures of that concept. Let them draw or describe their mental pictures to help create meaning for words.

6. Have students note on 3″ by 5″ cards the word meanings they have learned and the key characteristics and/or synonyms they have created. In this way you not only build meaning vocabulary but also a synonym source for use in writing assignments.

7. Have students work in pairs with concrete objects. Tell one student to manipulate the objects and make a sentence. Tell the other student to change the word order in the sentence. Then have the first student put the sentence back in correct order. This helps students become sensitive to how syntactic order influences meaning.

8. Use exercises in which you present a string of words orally. Tell students to create sentences using those words. Determine appropriateness by correct positioning of the words to communicate a meaning.

9. Use the "telegram" technique. Direct students to read a paragraph and decide what words could be omitted without losing the meaning. Explain that they are going to send the paragraph as a telegram and will have to pay for each word. What is left will be the main idea and essential supporting details. This helps students learn to summarize.

10. Make "stand-up" paragraphs. They can be fun and they can teach skills for comprehending both the main idea and details. Select a student to stand in front of the class and think up a key topic sentence. (This might have to be supplied at first.) Tell other members of the class to think up details that elaborate on the topic sentence. As each adds an important detail, have the child stand behind the student who made the topic sentence. The paragraph becomes a row of students starting at the front of the room. When all the "sentences" have taken their places, have them repeat their sentences one after the other and then construct the paragraph. Don't be afraid to have sentences rearranged or even omitted if they do not belong.

11. Have students find five words with prefixes or suffixes in a newspaper or magazine, and then have them write new sentences using each one of them. This helps students focus on how meaning can be changed through structural analysis.

12. Have students combine simple, known words to create either real compound words or invented compounds, then discuss the new concept created when two simple words are made into one compound word. This helps students focus on meaning.

13. Put words on the chalkboard that signal certain meaning relationships (such as cause-effect) and have students think up sentences using these words. This helps students understand the role certain words play in signaling meaning.

14. Say words or show objects to students and ask them to tell how they are alike in meaning or which one does not belong. This helps students learn to look for common meaning and to classify.

15. Have one student call out a category (such as *groceries*) and another student supply as many things that would go in that category as possible. This helps build classification skills.

16. Select a well-written informational paragraph. Put the paragraph's individual phrases on the chalkboard, and direct students to examine each phrase and use their classifying skills to write the overall theme. Example:

> Brush teeth regularly
> Bath frequently
> Eat well-balanced meals
> Get enough rest
> Get regular exercise

> Main idea: good health habits.

17. Have one student create a sentence and another change one word or phrase to indicate a change in meaning.

18. Provide unpunctuated sentences for students. Have them punctuate each sentence several times, each time communicating a different meaning by using different punctuation. Then have students read each sentence, using the correct intonation according to the punctuation supplied and describing how the meaning changed.

19. Before directing students to read a selection, set a purpose by asking them how many things they can learn while reading. Direct students to keep a tally while reading, with each mark standing for something learned. This helps focus students on meaning getting.

20. Before reading a selection from a textbook or reader, put the following purpose-setting formula on the board: Who? Where? When? How many? What happens? Ask students to use this formula as a guide in their reading. Such a guide invariably will result in increased comprehension and helps students learn the importance of setting purposes for their reading.

21. Have students find five examples of connotative words. Tell them to group words according to where they found them (newspaper editorial, news article, magazine article, and so forth). Discuss the relationship between the words and their source, and how the words influence the reader's interpretation of the author's meaning.

22. Have students choose two sports writers, then analyze and discuss the structure each writer uses in writing stories about sporting events. Let students try to develop their own sports articles based on such structures.

23. Begin a sentence with a function word. Have students complete the sentence using words appropriate to the relationship signaled by the function word. Example:

> The book is on ——————————————————————.
> Because Tommy was late ——————————————————.

p. 310 —

DEVELOPING CONTENT GOALS

In the middle grades, students begin reading various types of text, and content goals become more complex. In terms of recreational text, third and fourth grade students will not only read increasingly complex stories but also will read biographies, autobiographies, plays, poems, diaries, cartoons, and riddles, as well as folk literature, fantasy, realistic fiction, and humorous stories.

Functional text also becomes more complex. In addition to simple expository articles typical of primary grade reading, third and fourth grade students encounter content area textbooks; that is, textbooks dealing with academic fields. Middle grade students are expected to comprehend this more complex material.

Techniques that Promote Comprehension

The directed reading-thinking activity (DRTA) can be used to help students achieve content goals in the middle grades. It has the advantage of helping students develop the habit of making predictions. An example of how to teach using the directed reading-thinking activity with recreational text is provided in Example 17.8.

The DRTA can also be used with functional text. You follow the same format, but instead of making predictions about what is going to happen in the story or to the main character, focus predictions on expository information. For instance, in a text about the pyramids of Egypt, your students would examine the text, note the clues in the form of titles, headings, subheadings, photographs, and so on, and then make predictions regarding what they are going to learn about pyramids.

Another guidance technique that you will find particularly useful when teaching content goals with functional text is **survey, question, read, recite,**

EXAMPLE 17.8   An Example of How to Use a Directed Reading-Thinking Activity to Ensure Comprehension of Recreational Text

Background	You want your students to read the next selection in the basal text, and your major objective is that they comprehend the content of the story. You decide to use a directed reading-thinking activity.
Lesson Sequence	
Introduction	Provide a story introduction designed to activate students' background knowledge about the topic, the purpose, and the text structure. Teach new vocabulary as needed.
Purpose-setting	Direct students to survey the selection, examining illustrations, headings, and other clues to story content. Have them use these clues to make predictions about what they are going to encounter in the story. List their predictions on the board, then direct them to read the story to see if their predictions were accurate.
Reading	Have students read the selection for the story content and check their predictions.
Discussion	Discuss the story content and the accuracy of students' predictions.
Closure	Review the content of the selection. You may wish to follow up the story with an enriching activity that calls for using the knowledge gained from the story.
Desired Outcome	Students will be able to state what has happened in the story selection.

and review **(SQ3R),** a five-step process designed to recall text information. It works like this. First, you direct your students to survey the material to be read, noting titles, headings, subheadings, pictures, and other clues to text content. Next, have them list questions they should be able to answer after reading the text. They can get the questions from you or from the end of the chapter, but it is best to have students formulate their own questions by turning what they surveyed into questions. For instance, a text on the pyramids of Egypt might include a subheading such as "The Pyramids: An Engineering Marvel" which you teach students to turn into a question such as, "Why are the pyramids an engineering marvel?" Once questions are listed, have your students read text to answer the questions. When they finish reading, have them look at the questions again and answer them. Finally, if they cannot answer one or more questions, tell them to go back into the text, review it, and then try again.

SQ3R is a very systematic technique and works well for many of the same reasons as the directed reading-thinking activity. It involves readers in establishing purposes for reading; it allows them to get a feel for the text through an initial survey; it encourages confirming or disconfirming predictions embodied in the questions; and it promotes the habit of checking to make sure that predictions have indeed been confirmed. An example of how to use SQ3R is provided in Example 17.9.

The middle grades, then, strongly emphasize content goals. There is particular emphasis on more complex forms of recreational and functional text. These are bridging experiences from the relatively simple content goals at the primary level to the increasingly more complex and diversified reading demanded in the upper grades.

Role of the Basal

Basal textbooks are often an excellent place to teach and apply techniques such as DRTA and SQ3R. Middle grade basals typically include a variety of recreational and functional text. If your major goal is for students to compre-

---

EXAMPLE 17.9   How to Use SQ3R to Ensure Comprehension of Functional Text

Background	Your students are reading a selection from a science textbook on photosynthesis. To help them understand this difficult scientific content, you decide to guide their reading with SQ3R.
Lesson Sequence	
Survey	Activate students' experience with leaves and trees, and elicit their conceptions of how trees get food. Have students look over the chapter to determine what the text is about.
Question	Have students examine the headings, subheadings, illustrations, and end-of-chapter discussion points. Have them pose a question for each. These questions become the purpose setters for reading the chapter.
Read	Have students read the chapter to determine the answers to their questions.
Recite	Discuss their answers for each of the questions.
Reread	For questions that have not been answered, direct students to the appropriate place in the text and have them try to answer it again.
Desired Outcome	Students will remember and recall the important information in the text.

hend these samples of text, then you should use DRTA and SQ3R with these selections.

The important thing to remember about using basal texts, however, is that they serve two purposes: they contain samples of recreational and functional text that you can use for teaching content goals or for applying process goals. Consequently, you must consciously decide whether you are using a particular selection primarily as an application of a process goal or as a selection to be comprehended because of its inherent content value. Both are important, but you must know when you are teaching for one goal and when you are teaching for another.

ACTIVITIES TO DEVELOP CONTENT GOALS

Unlike attitude and process goals, for which you can specify a variety of activities, the activities for content goals are limited because specific activities depend on the text you use. Consequently, you must decide on the particulars of the activity once you have selected the text. Here are some activities you can use to supplement your teaching of content goals in third and fourth grade.

1. Have students sell a book to the class as a novel way of presenting an oral report. Tell the reader-salesman to convince the rest of the class that the book is the best book of its kind.

2. Use a book tree to develop both functional and recreational reading. As a book is read, label a leaf on the tree with the title and author, and place it on the functional or the recreational side. The goal is to keep the tree balanced in terms of number of leaves.

3. Use pantomime to share the content of a story that has proved especially popular with the class. One or more students can put on the pantomime while the rest of the class tries to guess who or what the performers represent and/or the type of content represented.

4. Use puppets, which are as much fun to make as they are to operate, as an excellent way of sharing content. Make puppets using clay or paper-mâché for the heads and simple cloth squares for the bodies.

5. Construct mobiles in the form of major characters from a story. You can also use settings or illustrations of the major content as a display.

6. Make dioramas and shadow boxes to illustrate content from a book. Again, either recreational or functional books can be the basis. Have students indicate their purpose for reading the book.

7. Have students make a miniature stage setting with pipe-cleaner figures to describe part of the information learned from a book. Have them display the stage setting and figures and give a two-minute talk explaining the content they represent and why they were selected.

Third and fourth graders are expected to do more individual creative writing. (Elizabeth Crews)

8. Have students write using the patterns employed in favorite books. Mercer Mayer's books can lead to original stories, Rudyard Kipling's *Just So Stories* can be used to generate fanciful explanation, the poems on color in O'Neil's *Hailstones and Halibut Bones* can stimulate poems about sounds, smells, and so on.

9. Have students turn to the food advertisements in a newspaper and pick four items they would want for dinner. Write down how much each of these items will cost and the total food costs for preparing dinner.

10. Using advertisements, have students find at least seven things they drink. Have them note their favorites and the cost for a week's supply.

11. The class or school newspaper should have a good feature section devoted to children's books. The sections can classify books as recreational or functional and highlight their novel aspects. Have a different theme for each issue, such as Pioneers, Life in Other Lands, Science Fiction, Magic and Fantasy, Biography, Natural Science, etc. The class or classes responsible for this section ought to concentrate on novel ways of stimulating interest in the books presented.

12. Use original posters, illustrations, or book jackets to illustrate the contents of a book. These become excellent displays and can be used also to develop positive attitudes to reading.

13. Illustrate maps to show a character's travels or the area encompassed by a story as a novel way to show the content of a book. This helps students decide whether to read the book for entertainment or information.

14. Draw murals to depict either functional or recreational content, and include sample book titles associated with the content.

15. Have the class publish booklets about various subjects (science, ecology, World War II). Tell contributors to do research and then write their portion of the booklet.

16. Have students present a "You are There" show where they enact the content of a book they have read.

17. Have students present a talk show and interview the central characters of a book they have read.

INTEGRATING READING AND WRITING

There are many opportunities to integrate subject matter and the various language modes when teaching the middle grades. The following sample unit is one example.

SAMPLE TEACHING UNIT: Egyptian Mummies

LEVEL
Third and fourth grade, expanded fundamentals stage

OVERALL PURPOSE
Students will learn about the rituals of ancient Egypt and compare them with rituals of today by gathering information through reading, listening, and interviewing.

OBJECTIVES
1. To generate questions to ask a museum curator after reading about Egyptian mummies.

2. To enact the ritual and the subsequent discovery of tombs after gathering information about the burial ritual.

3. To list the personal artifacts students would choose to have with them as the Egyptian "kings" did, and to share with the class why those objects are important.

4. To paint a time line of important events in students' own lives, and to represent each class member in the time line, as if it were a picture inside a pyramid.

5. To infer from the objects found in Egyptian tombs what life was like in that time.

6. To discuss what objects have been placed in well-known American time capsules, and to create a time capsule representing their time.

7. To research and write reports about death rituals in different cultures, and present them orally to the class.

DAY 1

Warm-up activity: Using a model of a mummy, a film strip about mummies, or pictures of mummies, motivate students to develop questions about mummies. Place the questions generated on a blackboard. Stimulate students with the following questions or comments: "What is a mummy? How many people have seen a mummy on television? In a museum? Who knows how mummies were preserved? Are mummies created today? How do our burial procedures differ from those of the Egyptians?"

Assessment: Assess group knowledge about mummies and students' ability to generate and state questions.

Focusing activity: Read aloud and show pictures from an appropriate book on Egyptian mummies. Tell students to listen and observe so they will be able to answer questions (information gathering) that have been generated in the warm-up activity, and perhaps generate additional questions.

Reading-writing activity: Have students discuss questions that can be answered from the text. Tell them to list questions that should have been asked. After the discussion, classify questions into answered and unanswered categories. Have students generate sources for answering the unanswered questions (library, museum, guest speaker, etc.).

Assessment: Assess students' knowledge about mummies, ability to develop and state questions, and knowledge of where to go for information. Teach these skills to students who could not develop questions or locate information.

DAYS 2 & 3

Warm-up activity: Using the questions generated in the prior lesson, have students play the game, pick and seek. Place each question on a card and have enough cards with duplicate questions so that each student will have at least one question to sort. Tell students to decide where to look for the answer to the question on their cards. Have a student stationed at each location (library, *Mummies Made in Egypt*, museum, speaker, etc.) to verify the choice. By the end of the activity all questions are classified for further research.

Focusing activity: Have library researchers go to the library to gather information about the art, artifacts, pyramids, rituals, etc. of the ancient Egyptians and the process of mummifying and burying their Pharaohs, as well as the discovery of such famous tombs as that of Tutenkhamen.

Reading-writing activity: Have students share the information found in the library with one or more students acting as recorders during the discussion. Have the recorders write a report of the discussion that will be shared and verified by their classmates.

Assessment: Assess students' knowledge about ancient Egypt, some students' abilities to record and report an oral discussion, and all students' abilities to participate in oral discussions. If a skill lesson for locating information was taught previously, it could be checked during the focusing activity.

DAY 4
Warm-up activity: Have students read the written record of the previous day's discussion and alter or approve it. Give each student an approved copy of the written record.

Focusing activity: Have students revise and update the questions generated for the guest speaker. New questions can also be generated at this time.

Reading-writing activity: Have groups of four or five students interview another student who is role playing a guest speaker knowledgeable about ancient Egypt. Tell students to check their own knowledge of ancient Egypt and the validity and form of their questions. Have students give their questions to the guest speaker.

Assessment: With the students, assess their knowledge of ancient Egypt, the ability to record and report oral discussions, and the skill of interviewing. (If a skill lesson had been taught earlier on questions, it could be evaluated during the focusing activity. All needed skills should be taught.)

DAY 5
Warm-up activity: Have students brainstorm all the words they can think of that relate to ancient Egypt. Then tell them to classify words according to the questions prepared for the guest speaker. Have them put words that cannot be classified under a question in a separate group.

Focusing activity: Give each student the responsibility of asking one question. Then have the speaker present knowledge of ancient Egypt.

Reading-writing activity: After the oral presentation, have students ask their questions individually. Encourage additional questions. Have students write an answer to their question. Duplicate questions and answers, and give them to each member of the class.

Assessment: Evaluate knowledge of Egypt (brainstorming or written answers to questions), ability to classify, skill in careful listening, skill in interviewing.

DAY 6
Warm-up activity: Have students list the sources of information (book presented in class, library, speaker, etc.), and how they can use each source to locate knowledge about Egyptian burials.

Focusing activity: Have students sort and discuss their questions and answers about burials in ancient Egypt.

Reading-writing activity: Have students select parts to play in re-enacting the burial of an Egyptian king and the later discovery of his tomb. Some students may be artists who create jewelry, others may be embalmers, others discoverers, etc. Then have them enact the ritual, using the information they have gathered. After the tomb in the pyramid is secured, have the contemporary discoverers find the tomb and carefully dismantle it, telling of the artifacts they find.

Assessment: Assess students' ability to classify, recall information about Egyptian burials, and dramatize Egyptian burials.

DAYS 7 & 8

Warm-up activity: Have students create their own time line with 12 inches of string and five cards. Have each student select five important events in his or her life and put one event on each card. Hieroglyphics may be used, but the pictures should tell a story to people who might find them many years later. Tape each card on the line in sequential order so that each student has a time line (informing). Have students read each other's time lines.

Focusing activity: Discuss how the kings of Egypt, like the students themselves, had five important events in their lives. Discuss how those events could be illustrated with hieroglyphics. Lead the discussion to Egyptian burials of the kings where personal artifacts as represented in the time lines might be buried with them.

Reading-writing activity: Have students list the personal artifacts they would choose to have buried with them if they were kings of Egypt. Share these lists with other classmates. Discuss the similarities and differences among the items selected, as well as their implied values. Do not allow students to criticize each other's selections. Have students orally compare and contrast the artifacts and picture they would have in their tomb with the artifacts found in the tomb of King Tut.

Assessment: Assess students' ability to sequence events and enumerate similarities and differences of items selected for burial with King Tut's burial.

DAY 9

Warm-up activity: Brainstorm items that have been discussed so far in the unit and that people would consider important. List items by people.

Focusing activity: Tell students that in a way the Egyptian tombs are like time capsules. Identify a local time capsule (i.e., cornerstone of a school, church, or courthouse) that has been opened recently, or a famous time capsule such as the one on top of the John Hancock Building in Chicago. Ask: "How do the items included in these time capsules reflect their society? What items would you put in a time capsule to reflect your society for those who open it in 100 years?"

Assessment: Assess classification skills, justified choice skills, and abilities to recall, inform, and imagine.

Culminating activity: There are many rituals in every culture, and they are usually different across cultures. Have students form small groups to research and write reports about ritualizing a death in different cultures throughout history (including America today). Have each group of students give a report orally to the class.

ADDITIONAL INTEGRATED READING AND WRITING ACTIVITIES

Here are some additional activities to supplement your integration of reading and writing in grades 3 and 4.

1. Provide pictures of action. Have students discuss what might have happened earlier to cause this action. Have students write a story of the events that led to the action. Have students read the stories to each other or to younger students for enjoyment.

2. Have students write riddles and place them in riddle books to be read during free time.

3. Have students share a book about a spaceship. Ask: "If you could turn your chair into a spaceship, what would you do?" Have students write their answers.

4. Have students read a well-known story (fairy tale, tall tale, etc.). Then have them discuss how the story would change if it were told from another point of view, for example, Hansel and Gretel from the witch's view, Paul Bunyan from the Blue Ox's view, *It's Like This Cat* from the cat's view. Have students write a new version of the story from a different view.

5. Have students discuss what new inventions might occur in the future. Have them illustrate their invention and write a paragraph to explain its use. Place a compiled book in the classroom library. Examples: automatic surfboard, robot hairdresser, a plane-boat-helicopter, an automatic comb, a pencil that knows all the answers.

6. Have students discuss nicknames such as Slim, Bones, and Speedy. Have them select a nickname and write a paragraph on how that person got the name. File paragraphs in the writing center to be used in future stories.

7. Have students read a humorous story such as those about Pippi Longstocking or Amelia Bedelia. Have them select one incident and create a cartoon strip for it. Share the cartoon strips with another class.

8. Have students create a What If book. Include topics such as: What if there were no cards? What if you were the teacher? What if you were

asked to travel on the space shuttle? What if you were invited to the White House to receive a bravery award? What if you were asked to show the Queen of England around your school? Have the students create either a book for the class or their own book. Share books with other classes or schools.

9. Have students create a Liar's Club with a "biggest whopper" award. Tell students to write about topics such as heroic deeds, family, travel, funniest event, strangest event, etc. Publish all whoppers in the classroom newspaper. Publish the winners in the school newspaper.

10. Have students think like a football player, getting ready to begin a play. Have them write what the player would say to a player on the other team. Have students write what the player's response would be. Keep dialogues for future stories.

CHARACTERISTICS OF AN INSTRUCTIONAL DAY

Because the middle grades are bridging years between the primary and the upper grades, the instructional day takes on some characteristics associated with both. For instance, in many schools third and fourth grade retain the self-contained classroom arrangement typically found in first and second grade. That is, your students remain with you all day, rather than having different teachers for different subjects as is typically the case in the upper grades. At the same time, however, the middle grades do make a sharper distinction between subjects taught in school than the primary grades do. While the school day at the primary grade level is primarily devoted to language (especially reading), reading is but one of several subjects taught in the middle grades. For instance, most middle grades have a reading period, another period for language arts other than reading (usually emphasizing writing but including elements of listening and speaking), another for mathematics, another for social studies, and another for science, with "special" subjects (such as art, music, and physical education) taught once in a while (often by specialists in these areas). Hence, the school day in third and fourth grade is often a combination of the self-contained classroom unit found in the typical primary grade and the subject-by-subject arrangement found in the typical upper grade.

Time allocation in the middle grades is different from that found in the primary grades: Reading is only taught once a day in most third and fourth grades. Also, it is often harder to integrate the various language arts in the middle grades because of the shift in emphasis to specific subjects. There is a tendency to teach only reading during reading period, only social studies during social studies period, and so on. This is regrettable, of course, since all these "subjects" offer opportunities for genuine communication using all the language modes. The best third and fourth grade teachers do strive to integrate subject matter that promotes genuine language uses. In their classes you will find students reading for content goals during social studies, being reminded of how to apply certain fix-it strategies during science, reviewing reading content while doing mathematical story problems, being shown how certain reading strategies can be converted into writing strategies, and so on.

Also typical of the middle grades are attempts to involve students in individual reading and writing efforts. Because students in first and second grade are just beginning to read, many of their activities are group oriented and result in group products. The language experience story is one example. In the middle grades, however, the emphasis shifts to individual efforts and individual products. Third and fourth graders are expected to do much more independent silent reading and individual writing. This does not mean that there is no place for groups in the middle grades. Indeed, many of the individual projects designed to develop attitude goals are preceded by collaborative groups in which students help one another before working alone. Similarly, process and content goals are often initiated in the basal text reading groups and then move to individual work.

The middle grades retain many of the characteristics of the primary grades while also adapting some of the characteristics students will encounter when they get to fixth, sixth, seventh, and eighth grades. Although reading usually becomes a separate subject that gets taught in a certain time slot, teachers strive to integrate it into the other subjects, thereby requiring students to be involved in real language activities.

SUMMARY

The middle grades are a bridge from learning how to read in the primary grades and using reading to learn in the upper grades. During these years, the instructional emphasis is on comprehension. Third and fourth grade teachers typically rely on directed reading lessons and modified directed reading lessons to develop content and process goals, although every effort is made to also develop attitude goals through the literate environment and to integrate reading instruction with instruction in other content areas. Generally reading instruction at this level occurs during a single time allocation designated as the reading period.

SUGGESTED ADDITIONAL READINGS

ALLINGTON, R. L. (1983). Fluency: The neglected reading goal. *Reading Teacher*, 36(6), 556–561.

ARNOLD, R. D., & WILCOX, E. (1982). Comparing types of comprehension questions found in fourth grade readers. *Reading Psychology*, 3(1), 43–49.

BABBS, P. J. (1984). Monitoring cards help improve comprehension. *Reading Teacher*, 38(2), 200–204.

BAKER, D. T. (1982). What happened when? Activities for teaching sequence skills. *Reading Teacher*, 36(2), 216–218.

BECK, I. L., & MCKEOWN, M. G. (1983). Learning words well—A program to enhance vocabulary and comprehension. *Reading Teacher*, 36(7), 622–625.

BERGQUIST, L. (1984). Rapid silent reading: Techniques for improving rate in intermediate grades. *Reading Teacher*, 38(1), 50–53.

CHAPMAN, J. (1979). Confirming children's use of cohesive ties in text: Pronouns. *Reading Teacher*, 33(3), 317–322.

COHEN, R. (1983). Self-generated questions as an aid to reading comprehension. *Reading Teacher, 36*(8), 770–775.

CROWHURST, M. (1979). Developing syntactic skill: Doing what comes naturally. *Language Arts, 56*(5), 522–525.

FARRAR, M. T. (1984). Why do we ask comprehension questions? A new conception of comprehension instruction. *Reading Teacher, 37*(6), 452–456.

FRICK, H. (1986). The value of sharing stories orally with middle grade students. *Journal of Reading, 29*, 300–303.

HOFFMAN, J. V. (1979). Developing flexibility through reflex action. *Reading Teacher, 33*(3), 323–329.

KIMMEL, S., & MACGINITIE, W. (1985). Helping students revise hypotheses while reading. *Reading Teacher, 38*(8), 768–771.

KOSKINEN, P., & BLUM, I. (1986). Paired repeated reading: A classroom strategy for developing fluent reading. *Reading Teacher, 40*, 70–77.

MARTINEZ, M., & ROSER, N. (1985). Read it again: The value of repeated readings during story time. *Reading Teacher, 38*(8), 782–786.

MCGEA, L., & RICHGELS, D. (1985). Teaching expository text structure to elementary students. *Reading Teacher, 38*(8), 739–749.

MCINTOSH, M. (1985). What do practitioners need to know about current inference research? *Reading Teacher, 38*(8), 755–761.

MCKEOWN, M. G. (1979). Developing language awareness or why *leg* was once a dirty word. *Language Arts, 56*(2), 175–180.

MOLDOFSKY, P. B. (1983). Teaching students to determine the central story problem: A practical application of schema theory. *Reading Teacher, 36*(8), 740–745.

REUTZEL, D. R. (1985). Story maps improve comprehension. *Reading Teacher, 38*(4), 400–404.

SMITH, M., & BEAN, T. W. (1983). Four strategies that develop children's story comprehension and writing. *Reading Teacher, 37*(3), 295–301.

STAUFFER, R. G., & HARREL, M. M. (1975). Individualized reading-thinking activities. *Reading Teacher, 28*(8), 765–769.

TAYLOR, B. M. (1982). A summarizing strategy to improve middle grade students' reading and writing skills. *Reading Teacher, 36*(2), 202–205.

WONG, J. A., & HU-PEI AUK, K. (1985). The concept-text-application approach: Helping elementary students comprehend expository text. *Reading Teacher, 38*(7), 612–618.

WOOD, K. D., & ROBINSON, N. (1983). Vocabulary, language and prediction: A prereading strategy. *Reading Teacher, 36*(4), 392–395.

RESEARCH BASE

GARNER, R. (1982). Resolving comprehension failure through text lookbacks: Direct training and practice effects among good and poor comprehenders in grades six and seven. *Reading Psychology, 3*(3), 221–231.

GORDON, C. J., & BRAUN, C. (1983). Using story schema as an aid to reading and writing. *Reading Teacher, 37*(2), 116–121.

MASON, J. M. (1983). An examination of reading instruction in third and fourth grades. *Reading Teacher, 36*(9), 906–913.

SAMUELS, S. J. (1979). The method of repeated readings. *Reading Teacher, 32*(4), 403–408.

SCHWARTZ, R., & RAPHAEL, T. (1985). Concept of definition: A key to improving students' vocabulary. *Reading Teacher, 39*(2), 198–205.

18 | Teaching Upper Grade Reading: Application Stage

GETTING READY

The upper grades are significant because it is here that students move from elementary to middle school or junior high school and take a major step toward eventual adulthood. Students are moving further from learning how to read to using their reading abilities to learn in other content areas. This stage of reading growth is called the application stage—students apply what they know about reading to the learning of content subjects. This chapter describes the difficulties of teaching reading at this level and makes suggestions to help you overcome them.

FOCUS QUESTIONS

- What are the unique difficulties of teaching reading in the upper grades?
- How are attitude goals developed in the upper grades?
- How are process goals taught in the upper grades?
- How are content goals developed in the upper grades?
- How are reading and writing integrated in the upper grades?
- What does a typical upper grade instructional day look like?

OVERVIEW OF UPPER GRADE READING

The shift from middle grade reading to upper grade reading is almost as dramatic as the shift from kindergarten to the primary grades for four reasons.

First, the move to fifth, sixth, seventh, and eighth grade often means a physical move from one school building to another. Typically, American students attend an elementary school for grades 1 through 4 or 5 and then move to a middle school or a junior high school in grade 5 or 6. This change to a new, unfamiliar physical environment is dramatic for children, making it a significant time in their lives.

Second, the shift heralds important organizational changes in the way schooling is conducted. In elementary school, students typically have one homeroom teacher for most of the school day and receive almost all instruction from that person. In grades 5 through 8, however, the homeroom teacher is the person to whom students report at the beginning of the day, but they may receive instruction from as many as five or six other teachers over the course of the day. Hence, the organization of the school shifts from self-contained classrooms in which one teacher provides most of the instruction to a departmentalized setting in which specialists teach one subject to five different groups of students each day.

Third, the upper grades represent a dramatic psychological change for students. While the environment in the first four or five grades is consistent and stable, the environment in the upper grades is more diverse and requires much more flexibility. The upper grades are intentionally designed as a bridge from the lower grades to high school and, as such, are designed to ease students into high school behaviors. Nevertheless, the change is still a dramatic one for many students.

Finally, the upper grades have traditionally taken a different approach to curriculum and instruction, especially as it relates to reading. In fifth, sixth, seventh, and eighth grade reading is not a formal part of the curriculum, and typically there is no specialized reading teacher as there is for the subject areas. The assumption is that reading has been mastered from preschool to fourth grade and does not need to be emphasized thereafter. Recently, however, there has been a growing awareness of the need to continue reading instruction into the upper grades and to have subject matter teachers show students how to read the specialized materials associated with their content area. The basal text, however, is not as prevalent as it is in the earlier grades because reading is not normally taught as a separate subject.

All these characteristics make teaching reading in the upper grades a unique and challenging endeavor. The building is different, the school organization is different, the students themselves are at a unique psychological stage, and the context in which reading is taught is different. The result has often been that upper grade teachers feel a pressure unlike that felt by teachers at any other level. They are in a unique position between elementary school and high school, charged with bridging the gap from learning how to read to applying reading knowledge to the learning of specialized subject matter. The task is not an easy one.

Despite these differences, however, the overall instructional goal in reading remains essentially unchanged in the upper grades—to develop students who control their meaning getting as they read functional and recreational text. However, the context for reading instruction becomes the various content areas and their specialized texts. There is also a growing emphasis on critical reading (teaching students to make judgments about what is read), study skills (guiding the efficient handling of more complex reading materials), and content goals (providing guidance in reading difficult text).

These curricular emphases are reflected in the instruction found in the upper grades. The curricular and instructional emphasis in the upper grades is shown in Table 18.1.

DEVELOPING ATTITUDE GOALS

Because reading in the upper grades is so closely associated with reading in the content areas, attitude goals often receive less attention than they should. Teachers emphasize learning content, and they often assume that students' elementary years provided them with all they need to know about reading and with a positive attitude toward reading. Such is not the case. The development of concepts and responses that make for positive attitudes toward reading is still important in the upper grades.

One of the major tasks of an upper grade teacher is to maintain the earlier emphasis on positive attitudes. You do this by providing your students with reading experiences that reinforce both the conceptual understanding of reading and the positive responses developed in previous years. You should reinforce reading as a communication process, that it is a functional tool, and that it is a medium for enrichment and enjoyment. You ensure that reading is enjoyable so positive feelings develop.

Creating a Literate Environment

Because of academic departmentalization in grades 5 through 8, students encounter many classroom environments on any given day. Departmentalization makes it difficult for teachers to physically arrange their classrooms to stimulate literate activities when they switch rooms every period. They cannot establish a preferred physical arrangement because each classroom is the homeroom of a colleague.

Despite this limitation, you can create a literate environment by relying on intellectual and social-emotional characteristics more heavily. You can create a literate environment intellectually by involving students in meaningful reading and writing tasks and by setting the expectation that they will pursue those tasks in literate ways. To organize the social-emotional environment you can involve students in collaborative groupings that encourage intellectual diversity and cooperation in pursuing assigned language tasks. Some teachers counter the changing physical environment by creating posters that can be carried from classroom to classroom. Others put physical decorations in cartons and take them from room to room as they move.

Because upper grade teachers often specialize in a particular content area, the literate environment is frequently associated with that content. For instance, an eighth grade social studies teacher teaching a unit on the Civil War may involve students in examining real documents from that era and in drawing conclusions about how people in various parts of the country felt about the morality of the war. Although such reading tasks are closely associated with the content being studied, they nevertheless help students conceptualize reading accurately and feel positive about it. They are, in short, literate activities.

Instructional Approach

Upper grade teachers expedite attitude development by planning units of instruction that are characterized by a unifying project or culminating activity within a content area. Such projects can easily be done within the departmentalized organization typically found in the upper grades. Students in an English class studying various forms of free verse poetry may study them in preparation for creating a book of poetry. Students in a social studies class may study state government in preparation for holding a mock legislative session in their school. The unifying theme provides a meaningful and interesting context in which to learn content and promotes attitude development.

For the unit approach to help attitude development, you must choose projects that are motivating to students and necessitate learning some targeted content. Here are some sample project ideas you can use in fifth through eighth grade science, social studies, and mathematics classes as a culminating activity for an integrated unit of instruction.

SCIENCE AND SOCIAL STUDIES PROJECTS

1. After a current events unit where issues related to city, state or country have been discussed, have students list five changes they would make. Have students read each other's lists and create a class list.

2. After a science unit on health needs, tell students to select what they feel was the most important point, then to put this point in a poster. Place posters in prominent spots in the school.

3. After a unit on budgets, provide students with a budget, a family, and the local newspaper advertisements from grocery stores. Have students buy food for a week's time.

4. During election year have students conduct a mock election of those running for office.

5. After a science unit on ecology, have students select an important point and create an editorial to be placed in the class or school newspaper.

6. End a science unit on weather with daily written forecasts that includes maps. Record and graph the accuracy of the forecasts.

MATHEMATICS PROJECTS

1. After a travel unit, have students plan an itinerary for a motor trip in the United States. Given mileage and meal and hotel costs, have students develop the costs for the trip.

TABLE 18.1 Instructional Emphasis at the Application Stage

OUTCOME	INSTRUCTIONAL EMPHASIS	MAJOR INSTRUCTIONAL ACTIVITY
Attitude goals		
Concepts about reading	Authors have purposes for writing text; readers have purposes for reading text	Indirect instruction using projects, language experience, USSR activities, and writing
	Reading can clarify knowledge, feelings, and attitudes	
	Reading can expand knowledge, feelings, and attitudes	
	Reading is a valuable tool that meets needs	
Positive responses to reading	Reading is exciting	Indirect instruction involving projects, language experience, USSR activities, and writing
	Reading is satisfying	
	Reading results in knowledge	
	Reading is curiosity	
	Reading is a source of power	
Process goals		
Routine skills		
Vocabulary	Build vocabulary through direct study of words encountered in content area subjects	Direct instruction of vocabulary
	Emphasize abstract words	
Word recognition	Recognize a wide variety of words instantly and fluently	Direct instruction of word recognition
Metacognitive strategies		
Initiating strategies	Activate background knowledge of content using predicting	Direct instruction of initiating strategies
	Activate background knowledge about different types of text structures, author's purpose, and reader's purpose	
During-reading strategies		

2. After a unit on mapping, have students measure and map the school, the neighborhood, or their route from home to school.

3. After a unit on measurement, have students measure and record the weights of unknown rocks. Using the sizes and the weights, have students predict in writing the types of rocks they have.

TABLE 18.1   continued

OUTCOME	INSTRUCTIONAL EMPHASIS	MAJOR INSTRUCTIONAL ACTIVITY
Monitoring strategies	Maintenance Monitor for unknown words, for unrecognized words, for author's meaning, and for meaning beyond what the author says	Direct instruction of monitoring strategies

Fix-it strategies	Recognize disruption in sense making
	
	Access strategies to repair sense making
	   Word recognition
	   Vocabulary
	   Author's meaning
	   Beyond the author's meaning
	Employ strategies
	Verify repair of sense making
		Direct instruction of fix-it strategies for comprehension

Post-reading strategies		
Organizing strategies	Recall what is important by using knowledge of the different types of text structure, classifying paragraphs, and determining main idea Draw conclusions Summarize content	Direct instruction of organizing strategies
Evaluating strategies	Judge content of text in reference to prior experience Judge author's structuring of text in reference to content	Direct instruction of evaluating strategies
Study strategies		
Locational strategies	Use book strategies of table of contents, glossary, and index to locate information	Direct instruction of study strategies

Within units, use indirect instruction to develop particular concepts about reading and particular responses to reading. For instance, an English unit on newspapers may have as its culminating activity the publication of a student newspaper. During this unit, you may wish to develop the concept that newspaper editorials represent an attempt to persuade readers to the paper's view on some issue. To do this, you may plan a trip to the local

TABLE 18.1 continued

OUTCOME	INSTRUCTIONAL EMPHASIS	MAJOR INSTRUCTIONAL ACTIVITY
	Use library strategies of card catalogs and the Dewey Decimal System to locate information	
	Use reference source strategies of dictionaries, encyclopedias, atlases, thesaurus, etc., to locate information	
	Use graphics strategies of using graphs, charts, tables, etc., to locate information	
Study habits	Organize time	Direct instruction of study habit strategies
	Develop test-taking strategies	
Rate strategies	Develop scanning pace, skimming pace, and slow pace	Direct instruction of rate strategies
Organizing strategies	Develop note taking	Direct instruction of organizing strategies
	Develop outlining	
Remembering strategies	Maintain semantic map useage	
	Use SQ3R and variations	
Content goals		
Recreational	Get meaning from various literature genres	Guided reading
	Get meaning from various forms of narrative text	
Functional	Get meaning from text containing heavy conceptual loads	Guided reading
	Get meaning from expository texts found in content area textbooks	Guided reading
	Use QARs to get meaning from expository text	Guided reading

newspaper and a visit with the editorial writer. Your instruction would follow the three-step format for indirect instruction. An illustrative example is shown in Example 18.1.

ACTIVITIES TO DEVELOP ATTITUDE GOALS

Here are some activities you can use to supplement development of positive attitudes toward reading in fifth through eighth grade.

Upper grade teachers must maintain the earlier emphasis on positive attitudes toward reading. (Susan Lapides/Design Conceptions)

1. Have students sell a book to the class as a novel way of presenting an oral report and developing positive attitudes. Tell reader-salesmen to convince the rest of the class that the book they read is the best book of its kind.

2. Use index cards with brief summaries and reactions to books read independently. These can be a valuable asset to the class if other students are allowed to use them to get ideas for future reading.

3. Illustrate maps to show a character's travels or the area encompassed by a story. These offer a novel way of sharing all kinds of books ranging from historical fiction to realistic fiction.

4. Suggest that the school newspaper include a feature section devoted to children's books. The section might have a different theme for each issue, such as Science Fiction, Magic and Fantasy, Biography, Natural Science, etc. The class responsible for writing this section concentrates on novel ways of stimulating interest in the books presented.

5. Have students broadcast a book review, as if they were radio or television critics. Tape record the review, and have others listen and state whether or not they would like to read the book and why. This helps develop students' interest in reading.

EXAMPLE 18.1   How to Develop Positive Attitudes

Background	As part of a unit on newspapers, you want your students to learn that newspaper editorials are written by people trying to influence the reader to share the same viewpoint as the publisher of the paper. You can develop this concept indirectly.
Activity 1	Arrange to take students on a field trip to the local newspaper office. Schedule an interview with the editorial writer, and prepare students to ask questions about how the topics are chosen, why certain positions are taken, and what the writer's techniques are in composing the editorials.
Discussion	In the classroom after the trip, discuss what students found out about the editorial writer and the purpose of editorials.
Activity 2	Organize students into collaborative groups to analyze recent editorials written by the writer they interviewed and to draw conclusions about the persuasive nature of editorials. Then have students produce their own newspaper and include editorials. Establish an editorial policy to determine the positions to be taken by the newspaper, and assign someone the task of writing editorials that will convince others to share the views of students.

6. Have students write a script and produce a radio or television program about a favorite book. Have them present it to another group of students.

7. Have students develop and present commentaries about favorite books for a silent movie, a filmstrip, or a slide show. Have them use their own photographs or slides, if possible.

8. Have students write an imaginary letter from one story character to another. Have them tell about something that might have happened had they both lived at the same time and place. This helps students develop interest in reading about others in books.

9. Have students create "tall tales" like those they read. Have them write, illustrate, and share at least two of the tales they create. This activity helps develop interest in and appreciation for reading.

10. Have students identify comic strips that reflect contemporary social values, and have them discuss how comic strips relate to concepts of reading such as communicating messages, providing enjoyment, and so on.

11. Authors are important. Your students, especially by the upper grades, should begin to be aware of prominent authors. This awareness can lead

to discussion of various authors and comparisons of their works, which strengthens their concepts of reading and the author-writer relationship.

12. Have students discuss value-laden problems that appear in advice columns to develop the concept that language communicates shared values.

13. Have students write a letter to the editor that is constructively critical of the editorial position of the newspaper on some given issue. This develops the concept that language allows us to communicate.

14. When reading a story aloud to your students, have them keep a journal of the story as if they were a character in it, or simply have them record their reactions to the story. Periodically share the journals. This helps develop students' interest in recreational reading.

15. Have students draw a series of comic strips, basing them on a short story, fairy tale, or myth. This helps students develop interest in various forms of literature.

TEACHING PROCESS GOALS

One of the major tasks for teachers in grades 5 through 8 is to continue developing the process goals introduced in earlier grades. You will continue developing some routine skills, and you will continue to develop students' understanding of how to use various knowledge sources to make predictions, to monitor comprehension, and to apply fix-it strategies when text no longer makes sense. In addition, you will extend post-reading strategy instruction into the area of critical reading and heavily emphasize study strategies.

Routine Skills

Although you no longer place instructional emphasis on teaching sight words, students' sight word knowledge continues to grow independently. This occurs primarily because students read widely, and as they read they are exposed to words repeatedly; those words gradually become sight words. To expedite this process, you need to provide many opportunities for your students to read a wide range of texts.

Instruction in vocabulary development continues, for few relationships have been so clearly documented as the relationship between word meanings and reading performance. The more words your students know, the better they read. Continue developing word meanings and providing opportunities for students to use their new words in reading and writing.

Metacognitive Strategies

All four metacognitive strategies are emphasized in the upper grades: initiating strategies, during-reading strategies, post-reading strategies, and study strategies.

Initiating Strategies You will continue to emphasize how to activate background knowledge of topic and how to predict in the upper grades. For instance, you might help students activate prior knowledge of topic in preparation for a story on mummies by saying, "Today we have a video clip on mummies. I know many of you think of horror movies when I say mummies, and that's valid—there are often mummies in horror movies. However, today we're going to read about the process of mummifying people. Start thinking about what you know about mummifying people as we watch the video clip. Take notes on what you didn't know. Later, we will learn more from our reading selection." The important element is to start students thinking about the process of mummifying people.

During-Reading Strategies During-reading strategies are grouped into two categories: monitoring and fix-it strategies for word recognition, vocabulary and getting the author's meaning. The strategies in these categories are introduced and taught at earlier grade levels. They are maintained and reviewed in the upper grades, particularly in the reading of content materials in academic subjects such as English, social studies, science and mathematics.

Post-Reading Strategies Organizing and evaluating content are both post-reading strategies taught in the upper grades. Organizing content is important because this is where students restructure information found in texts and store it in long-term memory for future use. This strategy helps counter rote memory and starts the process of understanding and remembering through conscious grouping and storing. Teachers at this level continue to maintain the organizing strategies of classifying paragraphs, determining main ideas, and drawing conclusions developed in earlier grades.

Beyond these things, though, you should develop your students' critical reading. Critical reading involves making judgments about what is read, based on the knowledge that something is not necessarily true just because it appears in print and that writers sometimes compose text to persuade readers to do or believe something. Critical reading is taught throughout the grades, usually as a post-reading comprehension strategy, but it is emphasized more in the upper grades. Teachers want their students not only to make judgments but to be enthusiastic about what they agree with, to get angry at writers they disagree with, to feel justified about modifying positions with which they disagree, and so on. Hence, in the upper grades they not only help students make post-reading judgments as in earlier grades but also develop new concepts and responsible responses associated with critical reading.

For instance, you might focus on connotative language; that is, language that triggers emotional responses. Its opposite is denotative language, which refers to the use of neutral terms that tend to be objective in nature. To illustrate, saying that a person is slim is a use of denotative language; saying that the person is skinny is a use of connotative language. Calling a person proud has a positive connotation; calling a person arrogant has a negative connotation. Through skillful use of denotative and connotative language, writers subtly influence a reader's feelings about a person, topic, or issue. Consequently, plan instruction that familiarizes students with connotative language techniques and shows them how to make their own decisions about issues despite an author's choice of words. Example 18.2 illustrates how to do this.

A second way in which authors influence readers is through using a set

---

EXAMPLE 18.2   How to Develop Understandings about How Word Choice Influences Meaning

Background	You want students to reflect after reading on how authors choose words that influence readers' feelings about the topic at hand.
Lesson Sequence	
Introduction	Show examples of text in which authors have used emotion-laden, biased, stereotyped, or mood words to influence readers. Discuss the need to understand such words so that readers will not be unknowingly manipulated.
Modeling	Read sample pairs of sentences such as the following: He *quickly* put away his books. He *frantically* put away his books. Explain how the italicized word is objective and neutral in the first sentence and is emotion-laden and suggestive in the second sentence (it causes readers to associate haste and panic with the student). Discuss how you came to agree or disagree with the author's word choice, and how you decided for yourself about the issue at hand.
Interaction with students	Present a series of similar sentences such as: The *new* tool was on the table. The *new-fangled* tool was on the table. Have students do as you did, talking out loud about whether the italicized words are objective or are designed to trigger emotional responses and influence opinion.
Closure	Return to the examples you used in the introduction and have students use their understanding to determine whether the authors are trying to influence their thinking.
Desired Outcome	When reading real text, students will recognize when authors are using connotative language to influence them and will make objective post-reading decisions about the topic rather than being influenced by the author's choice of words.

FIGURE 18.1   Propaganda Devices

Glittering generalities General statements the exact meanings of which are not clear.

Bandwagon Statements that encourage one to follow the crowd.

Authority endorsement Statements in which an authority recommends use, i.e., company president, etc.

Hero endorsement Statements in which a hero or heroine recommends use, i.e., sports star, movie star, etc.

Plain folk Statements that identify a product or position with the average person.

Name-calling Statements that associate a product or position with something that is disliked or undesirable.

Wealthy endorsement Statements that associate a product or position with an exclusive, well-to-do group.

---

of techniques known as propaganda devices. These techniques, which are listed in Figure 18.1, are used to influence readers in much the same way as connotative language. You should make sure upper grade students are aware of these techniques as they read.

When teaching critical reading try to make your students aware that writers can use the language system to influence their feelings and opinions, and that good readers can recognize these techniques and avoid being unwittingly influenced. Consequently, teach your upper grade students the propaganda techniques writers use and how to make independent judgments about a writer's objectivity in presenting information.

Study Strategies Teachers in upper grades emphasize study strategies to handle students' unique study demands. The first category focuses on study habits. For study habits you teach your students to use their free time efficiently. Help them estimate available study time, prioritize study assignments, and make a time budget that distributes available time according to priorities.

A second category focuses on reading rate. Students who are falling behind everyone else may need to make more efficient use of their study time. Since the study load is typically light in elementary school and students are not routinely expected to spend their free time studying until they get to the upper grades, it is not unusual that this kind of problem arises. Upper grade students can learn to control the problem by using a variety of reading rates and by organizing their free time.

Using a variety of reading rates is not the same as speed reading. In fact, speed reading has no real place in the elementary reading curriculum because it is highly specialized and of limited use. Adjusting the rate of reading, however, is something all students can learn to do, and it is applicable to

EXAMPLE 18.3   How to Teach Students to Read and Study Efficiently

Background	In a class on various forms of written communication, you have asked students to read several different kinds of text in preparation for the next lesson. The kinds of text include encyclopedia articles, newspaper articles, fiction books, magazine articles, and speeches written by politicians. You want to help them study efficiently.
Lesson Sequence	
Introduction	In the reading assignment, make sure that each student gets at least two different types of text to read. Emphasize the need for reading both while also using study time efficiently.
Modeling	Demonstrate how to tie reading speed to the purpose for reading and to the difficulty of the material. Explain how to make this decision and how to think about reading rate as you read the text.
Interaction with students	Have students examine their texts and explain how they decide how fast to read and how they monitor their reading.
Closure	Have students use various reading rates when reading the various forms of written communication.
Desired Outcome	When students have assignments to read they will examine the difficulty of the text and the purpose of the assignment and then select an appropriate reading rate.

many content area reading situations. It involves teaching your students to read at a normal pace if the materials are easy and are being read for recreational purposes, at a slow pace if the materials are difficult and are being read for factual information, at a rapid, skimming rate when looking for a key word or key idea, and at a very rapid scanning pace when previewing material. By adjusting the reading rate to the purpose for reading and to the difficulty of the material, students can make much better use of their study time. To teach reading rates, you must explain to students that there are various rates, show them how to move their eyes more quickly across the page, and show them how to move at different rates depending on what they are trying to find out. Most important, you must provide practice in reading material at different rates. Example 18.3 is an example of how to organize a lesson on reading rate.

A third category of study strategies is locational skills, taught to help students locate information. For instance, students may need to find infor-

EXAMPLE 18.4   How to Teach Locational Skills

Background	Your students are completing a social studies unit on regions of the United States. Each student has volunteered to make an oral report on one particular region and what it is famous for. You help them understand how to get all the information they need from the social studies textbook.
Lesson Sequence	
Introduction	Discuss the task of locating in the textbook the information about specific regions of the country. Suggest that a quick way to answer the question "How am I going to find the information I need?" is to use the index.
Modeling	Model for students the mental steps you go through in using the index to find specific information about a topic. Explain what you are thinking at each step so they can do what you did.
Interaction with students	Give students tasks similar to the ones they will pursue in their reports on regions of the country. Have them demonstrate how they would do as you did to locate the information in the textbook.
Closure	Have students use the index to locate the information each needs to make the required oral report on regions of the country.
Desired Outcome	When faced with the need to locate specific information in a textbook, students will successfully use the index.

mation in a particular type of book, graphic material, or other reference information storage device typically found in libraries and other public agencies. When this occurs, they need to stop and think, "What do I know about finding information in this situation?" Locational skills are taught to answer that question.

Upper grade students need to learn a variety of locational skills in order to locate information efficiently. You should provide instruction in these strategies following the format for direct instruction. Example 18.4 illustrates how to teach one such skill.

The fourth category of study strategies is organizing. Organizing strategies help students put information into order; they include note taking and outlining. To illustrate, Example 18.5 provides a sample summarizing lesson.

The final category of study strategies is remembering. Remembering strategies help students recall information and include systematic reading

EXAMPLE 18.5   How to Teach Students to Organize Information Using Summarization

Background	In a class on the lives of famous American presidents, students have been assigned to read short biographies of selected presidents. You want them to organize the essential points by summarizing them.

Lesson Sequence

Introduction	When students have finished reading the biographies, set the purpose for summarizing by emphasizing the need to organize information into manageable chunks.
Modeling	Show students how you summarize the main events and themes in the life of persons they read about by putting all the details into categories and then labeling the categories.
Interaction with students	Have students demonstrate the same mental steps in summarizing what they have read. Have them explain their reasoning so you have a window into their thinking and can provide appropriate assistance if they get off track.
Closure	Use students' summaries as the next step in the unit on American presidents.
Desired Outcome	When students are trying to organize content information, they will summarize it using a strategy that calls for categorizing.

techniques such as SQ3R. Direct instruction can be used to teach these strategies.

Role of the Basal

Because reading is seldom taught during a separate period as it is in the earlier grades, reading in upper grades is integrated into the content areas and, sometimes, is associated with literature studies conducted in English class. As such, the prevalent textbook is not a basal reading text but, rather, a text for the content: a social studies text, a science text, a literature text.

Consequently, basal reading textbooks are found less frequently in the upper grades. Instead, when you teach reading strategies such as critical reading or study strategies, have students apply what they learn in a content area text rather than in a selection from a basal textbook. However, decision making is much the same. Use a modified directed reading lesson (MDRL) as you would in the lower grades, but apply it to a textbook instead of to a basal selection.

ACTIVITIES TO DEVELOP PROCESS GOALS

Here are some activities you can use to supplement your teaching of process goals, particularly critical reading and study skills, in fifth through eighth grade. Be cautioned that these activities should be used in conjunction with a literate environment and that they should not be used in isolation from real reading situations.

1. Have students compile a reading notebook containing excerpts from their reading that are unusually expressive. Have them use expressive language in their own writing as a way to increase their sensitivity to how word choice can influence meaning.

2. Have students compare the language of an editorial column with that of a news article on the same topic to increase understanding of the need to be critical when reading.

3. Have students find an article that arouses emotional response. Have them rewrite it in their own style as a straight newspaper article. This will help them understand how text can be used to influence readers.

4. Have students compare the quality of advertised goods by noting what is omitted from various ads. Note the use of propaganda devices.

5. Have students identify examples of technical vocabulary used in various types of articles (e.g., foreign policy, sports, business news) and the way this influences meaning getting.

6. Have students write an article persuading people to their point of view by using biased words and propaganda devices.

7. To help students with reading rate, give students an entire page from a newspaper. Have them find, as quickly as possible, an article about some subject you have discussed in a story. Time them. To increase their ability to quickly spot articles in which they are interested, have them select a subject and then list as many key words as possible for that subject to help them identify articles on it.

8. At the upper grade levels it is useful to study homonyms or pairs of words that sound and look alike but have different meanings. Present students with a list of words that are frequently confused. Develop the meanings and have students use the words in sentences. Give such words as: alleys, allies; aloud, allowed; bare, bear; board, bored; borough, burrow; bough, bow; bridal, bridle; cell, sell; break, brake; course, coarse; desert, dessert; except, accept; lose, loose; lesson, lessen; peace, piece; cue, queue; quiet, quite; receipt, recipe; rein, rain; sensible, sensitive; site, sight; tide, tied.

9. To develop sensitivity to word choice in conveying meaning, have students list words found in their reading which they think may some day disappear from our language. Examples: pullover, skillet. They may also list new words or phrases that have come into common use. Example: yuppie.

10. Have students locate and organize information from three or four authorities on a given subject and then list the various facts each advances to support his or her opinion. This combines the use of study strategies and critical reading.

11. Have students evaluate the reliability of articles by judging the source (e.g., the president said; the White House announced; an informed spokesman said; all Washington believes; etc.). Rank the reliability of the sources.

12. Have students pick an editorial and list all the persuasive language used. Have them write their own editorial for some subject covered on the editorial page.

13. Have students pick an editorial and list the following: The nature of the problem, facts supporting and contradicting the writer's position, and opinions supporting and contradicting the writer's position.

14. To help develop students' abilities to locate information using an index, give students a list of questions, in each of which one word is underlined. This is a key word. Have them draw two lines under another word in each question that would also be a key word to look for in an index. For example:

    What percentage of the industry in <u>Kentucky</u> is devoted to <u>coal</u> mining?

    What is the value of the annual <u>orange</u> crop in the state of <u>Florida</u>?

    Do the seasons affect the formation of <u>icebergs</u> in the <u>North Atlantic</u> Ocean?

15. Have students predict the response of a governmental official or agency to a current news event. Discuss why critical reading is important when reading such responses.

16. To develop students' use of a table of contents, have them open a book. Ask questions that may be answered from the table of contents, such as, "Is there a chapter in this book about mammals? On what page is the chapter? How many pages are there in the chapter?"

DEVELOPING CONTENT GOALS

Content goals are especially emphasized in the upper grades because the curriculum at this level focuses on content area subjects such as social studies,

Much upper grade reading is done in content area textbooks. (Burt Glinn/Magnum Photos)

English, and science. Indeed, the purpose of reading in these subjects is to understand and be able to answer questions about such content.

Since much of upper grade reading instruction occurs in subject area classrooms, it is often referred to as content area reading, from instruction provided by subject matter teachers to help students understand the content of textbooks being read in those areas. Content area reading, like content goals, can be divided into two major categories: recreational and functional. Recreational reading occurs mostly in English classes where students read and study literature, whereas functional reading occurs mostly in subjects such as social studies and science where students read textbooks loaded with factual information. In both types of classes, use various guided reading techniques such as DRL or DRTA to ensure that students comprehend their texts.

There are special problems associated with developing content goals in upper grade reading. For instance, when teaching literature in the upper grades, good authors use special literary devices, such as foreshadowing, flashbacks, symbolism, and allegory, and they employ special language forms, such as idioms, similes, metaphors, and onomatopoeia. These literary devices are best taught while reading literature. Example 18.6 illustrates what such a lesson might look like.

Similarly, when using functional texts, you can apply techniques such as

EXAMPLE 18.6   How to Teach Students to Interpret Literary Devices to Comprehend Content of Recreational Text

Background	The book *The Island of the Blue Dolphins* by Scott O'Dell contains many idioms that must be understood in order to understand the story. You decide to teach your students how to interpret idioms.
Lesson Sequence	
Introduction	After introducing the novel, point out in the text several examples of idioms (such as "night had fallen"). Tell students that the author uses several idioms in his story and that you are going to show them how to interpret idioms.
Modeling	Give several examples of idioms and model how you use your background experience and the context of the passage to interpret them figuratively rather than literally. Explain your thinking so that students have an opportunity to use your model when they try a similar passage.
Interaction with students	Provide several more examples of text containing idioms. Have students do as you did in figuring out what the idioms mean.
Closure	As students read sections of *The Island of the Blue Dolphins,* point out the idioms and have them interpret their meaning in the context of the passage.
Desired Outcome	Given an example of literature in which an author uses idioms, students will be able to interpret the author's meaning in that passage.

a DRL. However, the increased complexity of reading material in upper grades often means that additional guidance is needed. For instance, you can guide functional reading by teaching a technique called question-answer relationships, also known as QARs. Since much upper grade reading is guided by questions asked by authors and teachers, the QAR technique helps students decide where answers to various types of questions might be found. For instance, teach your students that answers can be found in a sentence on the page (right there) or in several sentences or paragraphs (think and search) or in your own prior knowledge (on your own). Hence, when faced with the task of answering questions in functional texts, students think about the question, its relationship to what is said in the text, and where to go to find the answer. A sample lesson on teaching the QAR technique to upper grade students is contained in Example 18.7.

You can also guide students' reading of functional text by giving them

EXAMPLE 18.7   How to Teach Students to Use QARs to Comprehend the Context of Functional Text

Background	In a science class on systems of the body, students have been directed to read a chapter in their science text and answer the questions found at the end of the chapter. You want your students to use question-answer relationships (QARs) as an aid for finding the correct answer.
Lesson Sequence	
Introduction	After the purposes of the science unit have been set, explain to students that they will more easily find the answers to the questions if they use a technique called QARs.
Modeling	Demonstrate how you identify whether the answer to a question requires one of three strategies: right there (because the answer is found right on the page), think and search (because the answer requires information from more than one sentence or paragraph), or on my own (because the answer is not in the selection but, instead, is found in the reader's own prior knowledge). Explain how you thought about the question, the information in the text, and where to find the answer.
Interaction with students	Give students samples of text and related questions. Have them explain how they looked through the information provided in the text and then decided how to answer the question. Gradually increase the complexity of the text material as students become more proficient at answering questions.
Closure	Have students apply their understanding of QARs in answering the questions at the end of the science chapter on systems of the body.
Desired Outcome	When required to answer questions about textual material, students will first analyze the question in terms of where the answer is to be obtained.

study guides. Study guides are precisely what the name implies: guides to the study of the material in the text. It is helpful for you to prepare your own study guides, gearing them to a particular chapter or text. For instance, if a science chapter on classifying animals is organized in a particularly complex way, provide a study guide that directs students to particularly relevant sections of the text. If a social studies text requires literal thinking at one point, requires thinking about implied relationships at another, and requires generalizations beyond the text at another, write a study guide that cues students to the kind of thinking required in each section. If you want your students to pay particular attention to certain charts and illustrations or certain sections of the text, write a study guide directing them to those particular materials. Study guides can take many forms: lists of questions; matching tasks; simple directions for what to do first, second, and third; complex charts that students must complete as they read. Whatever their form, their purpose is to help students comprehend functional text.

A third technique for guiding students' reading of functional text is using structured overviews, which are particularly useful for text that introduces many new words. (Figures 2.1 and 2.2 are a type of structured overview.) Structured overviews usually consist of a schematic diagram of the important words in the text and show how these words are related to each other. Such overviews enable students to preview and relate the major ideas that will be covered in their reading and thereby create expectations that are helpful in comprehending the text. Example 18.8 illustrates how to use structured overviews.

There are many modifications of QARs, study guides, and structured overviews that you can develop and use when teaching content subjects using functional text. All these modifications have one thing in common, however—they are all attempts by you to direct your students' comprehension of targeted content.

ACTIVITIES TO DEVELOP CONTENT GOALS

Here are some activities you can use to develop content goals in fifth through eighth grade.

1. Have students follow published weather reports for your location for an extended period and then try to account for them by applying meteorological theories found in relevant functional text. Have them try forecasting the weather.

2. Have students use functional text to identify examples of social and technological changes by comparing historical accounts of some event or activity with its contemporary counterpart. Some examples of issues that have persisted in American history include:

   Isolationism vs. foreign involvement
   How wealth is distributed
   Race relations
   Civil liberties
   Industrialization vs. conservation
   The balance of power between state and federal governments

3. Have students choose an item of current interest or concern and read a variety of functional and recreational text on it.

4. Have students collect folklore such as rope-jumping rhymes, mottoes,

EXAMPLE 18.8   How to Use Structured Overviews to Ensure Comprehension of Functional Text

Background	You want your students to read the appropriate chapter in the social studies textbook on the branches of the federal government and how the system of checks and balances works. You are concerned about the heavy conceptual load and decide to use a structured overview.
Lesson Sequence	
Introduction	Select the words in the chapter that represent the key concepts about how the branches of the federal government work, and arrange them into a network of concepts that shows the relationship of one concept to another and the relationship of these concepts to previously learned ideas. Encourage students to add related ideas from their own prior knowledge.
Modeling	While showing the structured overview, talk about the concepts, their relationships to each other, and how these concepts are the framework for the chapter to be read.
Interaction with students	As students begin reading sections of the chapter and encounter the various concepts in the structured overview, have them discuss how one concept is tied to another, how new information is added to old information, and how their prior knowledge is expanded.
Closure	After the chapter has been read, modify the structured overview to reflect the new ideas that emerged during discussion. Display this modified overview and discuss it as a means for summarizing the chapter.
Desired Outcome	Given a content area text on a given topic, students will understand the relationships among various key concepts.

counting out rhymes, legends, myths or folk songs related to the area as a way to develop understanding of various forms of recreational text.

5. To develop understanding of how to use functional text such as road maps, have students plan an automobile trip they would like to take. Use road maps to determine exact routes.

6. Have students use various forms of functional text to create travel brochures.

7. Analogous stories written in the manner of old favorites offer a challenge to older students and help them learn to use various forms of recreational

text. Edward Lear's nonsense limericks can lead to original limericks and Rudyard Kipling's *Just So Stories* to other reports on how something happened.

8. Hold panel discussions of various kinds of recreational text. Even though no two members of the panel may have read the same book, students can discuss stories in terms of problems faced by main characters. They can compare stories with one another and react in terms of the kind of solution presented in each story: Did the solution involve magic, accident, or effort on the part of the particular character who is being discussed? Would the students have handled the problem in a different way if they had been there? Why or why not? How is each solution different from (or the same as) solutions mentioned by other members of the panel?

9. As a way to broaden understanding of functional text, select a topic and search for original manuscripts, old page proofs, first editions of books, book jackets, taped interviews with authors and other interesting persons in the community, or any other documentation related to the topic. Have students write history from original sources.

10. Have students keep diaries about memorable historical experiences as if they had lived through the period being read about. Add the diaries to the functional text resources available for studying the topic.

INTEGRATING READING AND WRITING

Upper grade English, social studies, mathematics, and science teachers should involve students in writing activities associated with their content area. Most of the reading and writing that occurs in fifth through eighth grade is embedded in topical units from content areas. Social studies teachers may have units on the Civil War, on the development of laws, or on the relationship between geography and economics; science teachers may have units on simple machines, on electricity, or on photosynthesis. Although these units primarily focus on content goals associated with social studies and science, they also include reading and writing outcomes. This is because teachers intentionally structure their content area units to include reading and writing. Following is one example of such a unit. It was taught as a social studies unit, and it includes both reading and writing.

SAMPLE TEACHING UNIT: Resolutions of Conflicts

LEVEL
Fifth through eighth grade, application stage

OVERALL PURPOSE
To learn how conflicts can be resolved.

MATERIALS
Students read a book that focuses on conflict and resolutions such as *My Brother Sam Is Dead* by James Lincoln Collier and Christopher Collier (New York: Fourwinder Press, 1974).

DAY 1 OBJECTIVE
1. To recognize varying points of view in the story.

Warm-up discussion activity: Have students discuss their feelings about the book, especially those that relate to the characters.

Reading-writing activity: Have students categorize the feelings that were expressed and group those feelings according to various character's (father, Tim) points of view. Have students conclude with written statements of the varying points of view.

Assessment: Teach the students who cannot determine points of view.

DAY 2 OBJECTIVE
1. To develop a point of view.

Discussion activity: Sam's brother, Tim, was often asked to state publicly which side he was on. Using this as a springboard, tell the class to generate other areas of conflict with which they are familiar (weekend privileges, propositions to be voted on, school rules, etc.). For each topic provided, create an affirmative statement and a negative statement. Assign students to collaborative groups, one group taking the affirmative position, the other the negative position.

Collaborative group activity: Have students collaborate to develop their positions using examples and elaborations to support them.

DAYS 3 & 4 OBJECTIVE
1. To defend individual points of view.

Discussion activity: Have students discuss how Tim had to defend his point of view. Using the examples generated, instruct students in persuasive writing.

Strategy instruction: Instruct students in components of persuasive writing, i.e., persuasive writing contains a statement indicating the importance of the audience, examples and elaborations that support the positions, and an appeal for the audience to act on the position.

Writing-reading activity: Have students collaborate to write a position paper using the components of persuasive writing.

DAY 5 OBJECTIVE
1. To state how varying points of view created conflict in the story *My Brother Sam Is Dead.*

Discussion activity: Have students review the varying points of view and how that led to intrapersonal conflicts within the characters.

Reading-writing activity: Have students list the conflicts in the story *My Brother Sam Is Dead* and support each stated conflict with examples.

DAYS 6 & 7 OBJECTIVE
1. To develop strategies for resolving conflict.

Discussion activity: The story *My Brother Sam Is Dead* contains three types of conflict: intrapersonal conflicts within individuals who were torn between different points of view; personal conflicts among family members who believed differently; and national conflicts among those who wanted linkage with England and those who wanted to separate. Have students discuss these conflicts in terms of how people try to persuade others to their view. These include appeals to authority (credibility or power of the source), motivational appeals (needs, fears, etc. of the receiver), and substantive appeals (relations between phenomenon such as cause and effect, analogy, and deductive or inductive reasoning). For instance, on page 6 of the book, Sam's father said, "In my house I will decide what constitutes treason." His argument depends on his perceived authority. Center discussion around questions such as, When can conflict be handled by talk? How many of the conflicts in the book could have been resolved by talk? What parallel examples of national, intrapersonal, or interpersonal conflict can be identified? Which of these can be resolved through talk?

Culminating activity: Have students in collaborative groups write a scenario of a conflict they have observed. Have them include needed background information that explains the conflict. Then have students read the scenarios and try to resolve the conflict through role playing. Ask other students to observe the role play and assess the effectiveness of the resolution and to critique the ways used to resolve the conflict. Finally, have students brainstorm alternative methods of resolving conflicts based on the three methods of persuasion.

ADDITIONAL INTEGRATED READING AND WRITING ACTIVITIES

Here are some additional activities you can use to supplement your integration of reading and writing.

1. Provide pictures in which an emotion is clearly illustrated (exhaltation, anger, happiness, etc.). Have students discuss what events led to the emotion and then write a story that climaxes with this emotion. Have stories read in collaborative groups to judge if the story line is appropriate and to provide feedback about the best sections.

2. Have students write "think-pinks" (two one-syllable words that rhyme, such as *sad lad*) and provide definitions (What is an unhappy boy?). They make books with the questions on one page and the answers on the next page. "Thinky-pinkies" (two-syllable words) can also be written. (What

is an angry devil? A steamin' demon.) "Thinkity-pinkities" can also be written (What is an exact car accident? A precision collision.).

3. Have students read a mystery story, such as the one about Encyclopedia Brown (*Encyclopedia Brown and the Case of the Dead Eagles,* by Donald J. Sobal), either individually or in groups. Discuss different endings that could have occurred. Have students answer "what-if" questions. Have students write their new ending for the story.

4. Have students read a number of ghost stories (*The Haunted Trailer,* by Robert Arthur, *Ghost Story,* by Genevieve Gray, *Hix House,* by Betty Levine). Have them discuss what makes ghost stories scary and then write ghost stories using the results of the discussion.

5. Have students discuss sayings such as the following: Sometimes you get more by giving; It's better to give than to receive; The grass is always greener on the other side of the fence; You only get what you take for yourself. Have students select a saying and write a short critical essay about it. Then have other students read and critique the essay.

6. After sharing a book together, have students write a letter from one of the book's characters to another, describing what happened after the story ended. Example: Using the character Kit in *Witch of Blackberry Pond* (by Elizabeth Speare), a student might write to a cousin about what happened after the witch trial.

7. Have students create lists of things to do before they finish school. Compile the lists in a book and note when each item is completed. Add to the list when convenient.

8. Have students create poems and compile concrete poem books made up of poetry formatted to visually reflect the subject of the poem. Example:

                    m
                   erry
                 christma
               shappynewy
             earmerrychristma
           shappynewyearmerryc
                 h r i s
                 t m a s
                 h a p p
                 y n e w
                 y e a r

9. Have students place themselves in the role of a famous sports person (a tennis player, gymnast, runner, etc.) who drops their racket, falls off the parallel bars, or trips during the last 10 yards. Discuss what the player might do, think, and say. Have students write a poem using these circumstances.

10. Read the book *The King Who Rained*, then discuss figures of speech. Brainstorm figures of speech such as, I've got a frog in my throat, I'm a little hoarse (horse), I'm playing bridge, etc. Have students write and illustrate their own books and then read them to younger children.

CHARACTERISTICS OF AN INSTRUCTIONAL DAY

In the upper grades, school is usually departmentalized according to subject matter areas and students are often grouped by ability. Consequently, rather than spending all day with one teacher and a heterogeneous group of students, upper grade students see several different teachers each day and are often homogeneously grouped with other students of similar ability. All this is further complicated by the fact that in many school districts there is no formal reading instruction in the upper grades except for those students who are reading well below grade level. Each content area teacher provides instruction in the attitude, process, and content goals.

The unique characteristics of the upper grades greatly influences the reading instruction provided there. Because reading instruction is confined to content area textbooks, it is not unusual for both students and teachers to begin ignoring reading. However, if students are to move through the application stage of developmental reading growth and go on to the power stage, teachers must consciously integrate into their content instruction appropriate attitude and process goals.

SUMMARY

Upper grade reading instruction is often dramatically different from instruction at earlier levels. Not only are students in a new building, where they move from teacher to teacher rather than stay with one teacher all day, they often do not have a subject designated as "reading." Instead, upper grade content area teachers integrate reading instruction into the teaching of their content specialty, a technique referred to as content area reading. The focus, therefore, is on content goals, particularly as they relate to subjects being taught in the middle or junior high school. However, process goals continue to be emphasized, especially critical reading and study strategies, and attitude goals also receive emphasis. Since a typical instructional day in the upper grades is divided into separate periods for separate subjects, the hardest thing about teaching reading at this level is integrating reading instruction with content in ways that help students develop wholistic understandings about reading.

SUGGESTED ADDITIONAL READINGS

BARROW, L. H., KRISTO, J. V., & ANDREW, B. (1984). Building bridges between science and reading. *Reading Teacher, 38*(2), 188–192.

BERGQUIST, L. (1984). Rapid silent reading: Techniques for improving rate in intermediate grades. *Reading Teacher, 38*(1), 50–53.

CUNNINGHAM, P., & CUNNINGHAM, J. (1987). Content area reading-writing lessons. *Reading Teacher, 40,* 506–513.

DEGLER, L. S. (1978). Using the newspaper to develop reading comprehension skills. *Journal of Reading, 21*(4), 339–342.

DWYER, E. J. (1982). Guided reading in poetry: Combining aesthetic appreciation and development of essential skills. *Reading Psychology, 3*(3), 261–270.

FLOOD, J. (1986). The text, the student and the teacher: Learning from exposition in middle schools. *Reading Teacher, 39,* 784–791.

FREEMAN, R. H. (1983). Poetry writing in the upper elementary grades. *Reading Teacher, 37*(3), 238–242.

HELMSTETLER, A. (1987). Year-long motivation in the 8th grade "reluctant" class. *Journal of Reading, 31,* 244–247.

HOLBROOK, H. T. (1985). The quality of textbooks. *Reading Teacher, 38*(7), 680–683.

LANGE, J. T. (1983). Using S2RAT to improve reading skills in the content areas. *Reading Teacher, 36*(4), 402–404.

SMITH, L. B. (1982). Sixth graders write about reading literature. *Language Arts, 59*(4), 357–363.

STOTT, J. C. (1982). A structuralist approach to teaching novels in the elementary grades. *Reading Teacher, 36*(2), 136–143.

SULLIVAN, J. (1986). The Global Method: Language experience in the content areas. *Reading Teacher, 39,* 664–669.

THOMPSON, L., & FRAGER, A. (1984). Teaching critical thinking: Guidelines for teacher-designed content area lessons. *Journal of Reading, 28,* 122–127.

WIDMANN, V. F. (1978). Developing oral reading ability in teenagers through the presentation of children's stories. *Journal of Reading, 21*(4), 329–334.

WOOD, K. D., & MATEJA, J. A. (1983). Adapting secondary level strategies for use in elementary classrooms. *Reading Teacher, 36*(6), 492–496.

RESEARCH BASE

ANDERSON, T. H., & ARMBRUSTER, B. B. (1982). Reader and text—studying strategies. In W. Otto & S. White (Eds.), *Reading expository material.* New York: Academic Press.

ANDERSON, T. H., & ARMBRUSTER, B. B. (1984). Study skills. In P. D. Pearson (Ed.), *Handbook of reading research.* New York: Longman.

BROWN, A. L., CAMPIONE, J. C., & DAY, J. C. (1981). Learning to learn: On training students to learn from text. *Educational Researchers, 10*(2), 14–21.

GAYLOR, B., & SAMUELS, S. J. (1983). Children's use of text structure in the recall of expository material. *American Educational Research Journal, 20*(4), 517–528.

Part 5

Continued Professional Growth

One of the distinguishing characteristics of professionals is that they continue to learn and to grow. The four chapters in Part 5, provide suggestions for how you can continue to learn and grow as a teacher, thereby assuring your status as a professional. Four areas for continued growth are pinpointed: how to use computers, how to deal with language differences, how to handle special learning problems, and how to avoid burnout. When you finish these chapters, you should have an understanding of what it takes to maintain a sense of professionalism and vitality while working in the reality of classrooms.

19 | Uses of Computers in Reading and Writing Instruction

Michael L. Kamil

GETTING READY

In this chapter you will learn what a computer is, what it can do, and how it can and cannot, or should not, be used in reading and writing instruction. Examples of excellent applications of computers in reading and writing as well as some cautions are given, and a list of sources for information about computers and their uses in reading and language arts is provided.

FOCUS QUESTIONS

- What are the potential uses of computers in reading and writing instruction?

- How do computers work?

- How are computers being applied to classroom instruction in reading and writing?

- How do you evaluate computer software designed for use with reading and writing?

- How do you evaluate computer hardware?

- How effective are computers in instruction in reading and writing?

- What are some cautions to keep in mind when using computers for classroom reading instruction?

- What can you expect to be some future classroom uses of computers?

HOW COMPUTERS AFFECT READING INSTRUCTION

There are three distinct areas in which computers affect reading and writing instruction.

The first of these is the relatively new area of computer literacy. Traditionally, literacy has been conceived of as being wholly related to the ability to read and write. A new aspect of literacy evolved with the development of electronic computers (beginning around 1945) and microcomputers (around 1974), and now it is necessary to teach students about the uses of computers.

There has been little agreement on what constitutes computer literacy, just as there is dispute over definitions of conventional literacy. The major issue is usually whether or not computer literacy should include knowledge of how to use programming languages. It is often argued that knowledge of programming computers is analogous to learning arithmetic. That is, hand calculators make the mental performance of the mechanics of arithmetic obsolete, but the knowledge of how to do those operations is viewed as important for conceptual understanding. The proponents of programming as part of computer literacy often suggest that this knowledge is important to understanding computers even though the user may never apply that knowledge.

Other content of computer literacy includes familiarization with operating a computer, the uses one can make of computers, and the social consequences of computers.

Early definitions of computer literacy placed heavy emphasis on learning computer programming and the mechanics of operating computers. This seemed like an improvement over the lack of computers in schools for many years. However, current views of computer literacy stress the use of computers as tools for accomplishing tasks for which the computer is well-suited. In most educational settings this has come to mean using the computer for teaching or as a tool to accomplish other educational tasks.

Instructional Uses of Computers

The second area in which computers relate to language arts is that of using computers to deliver instruction for reading and writing. These uses can be further classified as computer-assisted instruction (CAI), drill and practice, simulations, and aids to instructional management. These are the uses that most people consider the heart of computer use in reading and writing, and they will be discussed in the following sections.

Computers as Tools for Reading and Writing Instruction

The third use of computers in reading and writing is as a tool for performing common tasks. The computer can be an extremely powerful writing tool when it is coupled with word processing software. While this is also an instructional use of computers, it is becoming more prevalent as an indispensable aid to composition. A word processing program can allow a student to revise, edit, correct, and manipulate text before printing a final copy. It can eliminate the repetitious work of manual copying to incorporate changes in a manuscript.

Another use of computers as a tool is for retrieval of information from centralized data bases. Many libraries have card catalog systems that can be accessed from a computer terminal. Commercial computer services, such as Dow Jones, Compuserve, and The Source, have on-line information banks that can also be accessed by appropriately equipped computers.

Before proceeding to examine the applications of computers in greater detail, it is important to consider what a computer is and what it can do. We will also consider the strengths and limitations of using computers for educational applications.

A BRIEF INTRODUCTION TO COMPUTERS

The question most often asked about computers is: What is a computer? This is also one of the most difficult questions to answer in terms that are meaningful to the average person. At the simplest level, it is easy to say that a computer is an automatic electronic device that processes information. However, there are few elements in that definition that make it easy for someone to incorporate the concept of computer into a familiar schema.

Computers process information that is stored electronically in codes. These codes are represented by *bits* (short for *bi*-nary dig-*it*), the smallest unit of information a computer can process. A bit can be thought of as something similar to a switch. That is, each bit is either on or off. Mathematically, this is represented as either a 1 or a 0. For most microcomputers, groups of 8 bits are used to represent a *byte,* often referred to as a computer "word." When the memory capacity of a computer is described as 48K or 256K, for example, the units are bytes of memory.

Every letter, number, or other symbol used in written English is assigned a code, called an ASCII code (for American Standard Code for Information Interchange). Each code is stored in a single byte. Every character displayed—including spaces, periods, etc.—has to be represented in a single byte of memory. Text storage uses up large amounts of memory; 64K of memory, without any other considerations (like information the program needs to handle the text and is stored in memory along with the symbol codes), could hold the equivalent of about 35 pages of typewritten text (assuming about 300 words to a page).

Components of Computers

Every computer must have a *central processing unit (CPU),* memory, and peripheral devices to allow information to be input to the computer and output from it. The CPU is like an executive, making decisions about how to handle information coming into and going out of the computer. It is the CPU that does the "real" work of the computer.

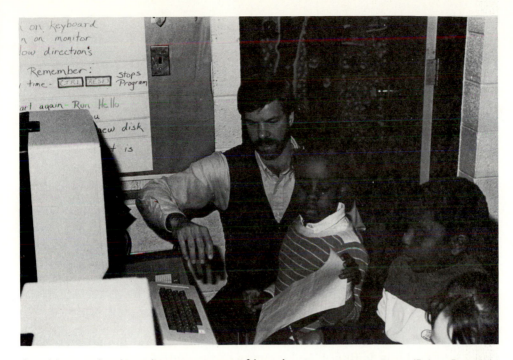

Good instruction is an important part of learning to use computers. (Robert Bawden)

Memory is generally divided into two sorts: RAM and ROM. *RAM* stands for random access memory. The contents of RAM are said to be volatile—they disappear when the power is turned off. The user of a computer can change the contents of RAM at any time and can tell the computer to read the contents or to write into any part of it. Conversely, *ROM* stands for read only memory. It is memory that cannot be changed and is nonvolatile: It always remains the same, even when the power is off. ROM memory is usually reserved for special instructions that the CPU needs, for example when the computer is first turned on.

When describing the memory size of a computer, it is customary to refer only to the RAM memory, since this is the only portion of memory that the user can control. When a computer has, for example, 64K of memory, it actually has 65,236 words or bytes of RAM memory. (K stands for 210, or 1024.) RAM memory is critical since it is the working memory of the computer. If a program cannot fit in the amount of RAM, it cannot be run on the computer.

The normal input device for microcomputers is a keyboard. Output is usually accomplished by a VDT or video display terminal. Other output devices can include printers, voice synthesizers (to allow the computer to be understood, for example, by someone who could not read), and a range of other machinery the computer can control.

To be really useful, the computer has to be connected to some sort of storage device, typically a tape recorder or a disk drive. With these storage devices any program can be stored and kept for use at a later time. When the computer is turned on, it can be instructed to read a program from one of its storage devices into RAM. After the program is loaded into memory, it can be "run." The storage capacity of tape and disk drives is very large—many programs can be stored on a single cassette or diskette. However, each of the programs stored on the diskette or tape must be small enough to fit into the amount of RAM available to the computer.

A printer is another important peripheral device that is often attached to computers. For a great deal of instructional computing, printed output (hard copy) is not often needed. However, when a student must be able to take along a copy of an assignment, work sheet, or even a composition, a printer is indispensable. There are two categories of printers, dot matrix and letter quality. *Dot matrix* printers are so named because they form each printed character by making impressions of appropriate dots in locations in a matrix. This accounts for some of the poor legibility in computer-printed text. The larger the number of dots in the matrix, the better the quality of the individual letters. Some of the newest dot matrix printers are almost indistinguishable from typed copy.

Letter quality printers often use *daisy wheels* to form the characters by impacting a ribbon with a wheel containing the individual characters. This is similar to the way in which typewriters operate, and the resulting print is usually indistinguishable from typed text. A recent development is the *laser printer.* These printers have the ability to print high-quality text and graphics very rapidly, much as a duplicating machine copies pages. The best laser printers produce print that is indistinguishable from typeset copy. These are relatively expensive and are just beginning to be found in school settings.

Some microcomputers come equipped with what is called a *hard disk* drive. This is a storage device that is similar to a diskette, but with far greater capacity. Floppy diskettes are so named because they can easily bend. Hard disks do not. They come in sealed cases, and the data stored on them are less likely to be subject to accidental loss. The major advantage of a hard disk is the amount of storage. While a floppy diskette can store from about 100K to over 1MB (1 million bytes) of programs or data, a hard disk has the capacity to store upwards from about 5MB (5 million bytes). Note that the smallest figure for a hard disk represents the equivalent of approximately 50 floppy diskettes.

Hard disks are relatively expensive and cannot be used easily with all microcomputers. They are most beneficial when the tasks the computer will perform require access to a large amount of data or the need to store a large number of programs, records, etc., in one location.

Hardware, Software, and Courseware

A very common distinction when dealing with computers is that between hardware and software. *Hardware* refers to all of the physical components of a computer. The CPU, disk drives, monitor, memory chips, and the like are all hardware. The computer itself and all of its peripherals fall into the hardware category. By contrast, *software* is the term for all of the instructions that are used to tell the computer what to do. Some of these instructions can be stored in ROM so that the computer will, for example, automatically know what to do when the power is turned on. Other examples of software are the commercial programs, which are sets of instructions that tell the computer what to do and the order in which to do them. A computer cannot do anything without software; that is, computers must be instructed to perform tasks, and those tasks must be described in explicit detail in the software.

For educational materials, there is a third category, called *courseware*. Courseware represents all of the supplemental materials that can be used to help integrate the computer-based instruction into the curriculum. Courseware might include teachers' manuals, additional readings for students, follow-up activities, or cross references to other materials that might teach related skills or content. In short, courseware explains how the software can or should be used educationally.

What Is Needed to Use a Computer for Educational Purposes?

There is no simple answer to this question because the type of computer that one needs for a specific educational purpose will depend entirely on what the purpose is. Many educational programs can be run on small-capacity, inexpensive computers. Some applications that are extremely sophisticated or that involve a great deal of record keeping or other management activity can only be accomplished on computers with greater capacity and are consequently more expensive. This is but one of the reasons it is imperative that the prospective user of computers in education must carefully determine the purposes and goals of the computer-based instruction before committing to purchase computer hardware.

COMPUTER-ASSISTED INSTRUCTION

Since the middle of the 1960s, some educators have assumed that it would be possible one day to teach by computer. The idea was that computers would make it feasible to provide every student with an individualized program of instruction. In addition, the thought was that computers could take over much of the management of instruction by providing the appropriate educational plans for students, based on their performance. It was hoped that eventually the computer could assume the role of a teacher and provide instruction with minimal teacher intervention.

Computer-assisted instruction (CAI) remains a major goal of computer uses in education. Current results indicate that, under certain circumstances, computers may be extremely effective for CAI, but not for other purposes. It seems that on the average CAI can increase student performance by about 10 percent over conventional teaching methods. On the other hand, when we examine the effects of computer-managed instruction, we find that there is no difference between conventional management and computer management. Thus, the conclusion is that there is no advantage in terms of student achievement to using the computer to manage instruction.

Increased Memory Capacity

One bottleneck for microcomputers has been their limited memory and capacity to store information. Recent technological developments have changed this somewhat, and memory capacity in computers has almost ceased to be an issue. Machines routinely come equipped with megabytes of memory rather than the 64K that was standard only a few years ago. A single floppy diskette can hold 720K or more of data compared with less than 100K only a few years ago. Hard disk drives have the ability to hold upwards of 20MB of data. New optical CD ROM disks will hold as much as 500MB of data.

What this means is simply that there is less need for economizing on the resources available to the computer program. In the past, programs had to be carefully limited in the amount of memory they occupied both in the computer and on a diskette. As those limits have eased, software has become more sophisticated and complex, to the benefit of teachers and students.

Software Innovations

The newest software innovations have produced changes in instructional capabilities that may hold great benefits for CAI. The first of these developments is the increased sophistication of artificial intelligence.

In the past, computer programs have been flawed mainly because they were rigid and could not anticipate unusual responses from students. With the use of artificial intelligence techniques, software can be produced that overcomes this limitation. The program can learn from student responses and can react to them in ways that will let the program learn to help "teach" the student. As these techniques continue to develop, it will eventually be possible for software to approximate closely the behavior of teachers.

A second innovation is hypertext. This is the contemporary instance of an older concept, Dynabook. *Hypertext* is a program that allows information to be connected to other information in any way in which the author wishes. For example, a hypertext passage about the Civil War might contain a mention of Appomattox. Students who did not know what Appomattox was could select an option that presented them with basic information about Appomattox. Of course, they would not have to select that information; they might select more advanced or detailed information. Unfamiliar words or concepts in the hypertext explanation could also be elaborated in the same way. This system provides a way to account for the variety of student ability and interest levels with great efficiency.

The program could contain a wide variety of types of information—dictionary definitions to encyclopedic information or graphics of any sort.

The hypertext program is recent and there are presently few commercial applications on the market, but there will be many in the future. Coupled with a CD ROM disk, a hypertext program could give a computer user access to an entire library connected to the text being read at the computer.

COMPUTERS AS EDUCATIONAL TOOLS

Several things have become apparent in the past few years: The attempts at using computers as devices to present CAI have not been as successful as had originally been hoped. At the same time, the development of software that allowed microcomputers to perform a wide range of tasks has focused attention on the role of computers as educational tools.

In this regard, there are three types of computer software that perform tasks unequaled in any other manner. These are word processing, data base, and spreadsheet programs. All three of these are often regarded as business-oriented software. However, they are coming to have dramatic influences in the classroom.

Word Processing

Word processors are programs that manipulate text. All word processors are comprised of two separate components, an editing program for inputting text and a formatting program for printing copies of the text. Often a particular program does not seem to have these two discrete components because they are connected by a *menu* that allows the user to choose between them.

An editor allows the user to input text, revise it, and rearrange and manipulate it in almost any conceivable manner. Editors range from extremely complex to very simple. The more complex an editor is, the longer it usually takes to learn how to use it—and often the complexity is unrelated to the most common tasks of editing and revising. Similarly, formatters vary in what they will allow the word processing program to do—everything from simple printing to producing graphics embedded in the middle of text.

The educational appeal of word processors is that they are a perfect tool for using in a process writing environment (see Chapter 4). That is, word processors almost perfectly reflect the notion that a draft is just that. It is malleable and never has to be printed until the author is comfortable with its form. There is no limit to the number of revisions that can be made to a document before it is printed. Even after a printed copy is produced, corrections can be entered easily by using the editor to make any revisions that are necessary.

With a word processing program a teacher can make comments on the electronic version of a text (stored on a diskette) and have the student read those comments and make corrections, all without producing a printed copy.

Moreover, there are other components that often accompany word processing programs that can be educationally useful. Foremost among these

A word processor allows unlimited revisions of a document before a student prints it. (Robert Bawden)

are *spelling checkers*, which can be used to check electronic versions of documents for spelling errors. They do this by checking the words in a document on a diskette against a dictionary stored in the computer or on diskette. Some are very sophisticated, prompting the user to replace words from a list of options that are common errors or similar in appearance to the questionable word. Simple spelling checkers only tell the user that a word is not in the computer dictionary. Most spelling checkers operate after a document has been created. Still others will signal the user as a word is being entered that it is not in the dictionary used for the spelling check.

Although spelling checkers seem very useful, they are not a substitute for knowing how to spell. Computer dictionaries are relatively limited and will only be able to tell the user that the word is not in the dictionary. It would not give any differential help if the word is uncommon and properly spelled or common and spelled incorrectly. Spelling checkers are not able to distinguish between typographic errors that produce real words and correctly spelled words—e.g., *tow* for *two*. So long as the word in the text is a real word, the spelling checker does not signal it as incorrect.

Another type of word processing aid is a *mechanics checker*, which checks for many of the mechanical features of writing—grammatical usage, complexity or readability of the text, and elements such as repeated words or noncapitalized beginning words of sentences. Because the rules for these sorts of features are not absolutely defined in English, these programs have only moderate success, but can call attention to problem areas for students.

Prewriting software formalizes prewriting activities in programs that force the writer to go through steps that will lead to appropriate ideas for writing. These include, for example, describing the audience, brainstorming about the topic, reducing the brainstorming ideas into manageable units, and the like. Some of these programs allow the user to create an outline that can be used in the main word processing program. The writer can then expand on the outline as needed. Obviously, these activities can also be used to check a composition against the original intent to make certain that the purposes have been fulfilled.

A final writing aid is an *outliner*. This is a part of the word processing program that allows the user to create an outline of what is to be written. The headings can be rearranged, deleted, revised, and automatically re-numbered as needed. Sophisticated outliners will allow the user to display more or less complexity in the outline, as desired. For example, a writer might want to display only the main headings. When completed, the outline can be used in the word processor and fleshed out until the writer is satisfied. Outliners can serve as useful guides so that writers are reminded of important topics that should not be left out of final composition.

Some Important Considerations in Using Word Processing

There are three important cautions that must be observed when using word processing in an educational setting. First, students must be able to keyboard to make the most effective use of word processors. Second, there must be sufficient numbers of computers and software packages to allow students sufficient access to the machines. Third, the curriculum must support the use of word processing.

Keyboarding Keyboarding skills are critical to good, efficient word process-ing. Even if students cannot keyboard, they could do some rudimentary word processing, but it will probably be frustrating and almost as difficult as hand-writing. Students can be taught to do keyboarding beginning at least in second grade. There are a number of software packages on the market that teach these skills, mostly in an independent manner. However, they require a great deal more teacher supervision and guidance than might be imagined.

What is required for keyboarding instruction? First, each student must have access to a single computer for reasonable amounts of time during the instruction. This can vary anywhere from several weeks to longer. Second, the teacher must be available for supplementary instruction when the stu-dents cannot make use of the instruction delivered by the program. There are just some times when the concepts that are being taught are too abstract to be conveyed by the program. Besides, the feedback is often fairly low level. For example, several of these programs illustrate a hand and indicate which finger is to be used to press the appropriate key. If a student is having difficulty, this might not be sufficient to help. Most of the other feedback is about time (speed) and errors (accuracy). The emphasis is definitely on speed and accuracy.

Because of the intensive nature of computer use during the learning of keyboarding, several alternative methods of teaching these skills have been proposed. Among these are paper keyboards to allow students to familiarize themselves with the finger positions on the keys and typing keyboards that function almost like a typewriter. It is unlikely that these alternatives are very effective, since the look and feel of them are sufficiently different to make transfer to a real computer keyboard unlikely. What we are certain of is that it takes consistent practice and real computer feedback to produce successful learning in these situations.

Numbers of Computers How many computers will be required for what is to be taught using computers? This is both a simple and a complex question. And the answer can be either simple or complex. The calculation of how many computers are required is based on what is to be taught and how much time it will take to teach it. (Also included should be the amount of time the computers will be used for nonteaching, management purposes.) Once you know how much computer time is required, the calculation can be made by the formula:

$$\text{Number of computers} = \frac{(\text{Minutes per day per student}) \times (\text{Number of students})}{\text{Number of minutes per day}}$$

That is, the total amount of computer time required for all uses is divided by the time available. Thus, if teachers want to give students 30 minutes of computer time each day, they can calculate the number of computers that will be required for, say, 50 students if the computers are available for 6 hours a day:

$$\text{Number of computers} = \frac{30 \times 50}{360} = \frac{1500}{360} = 4.2$$

Five computers (4.2 rounded up to the next highest whole number) would be needed if they were to be used for every minute of all 6 hours each day. In reality, you would need at least one spare computer (approximately 10 percent of the total number) so that you would not lose instructional time if one of the machines malfunctions or goes down.

Be careful, for this is not the only hardware need. For every two or three computers, a printer is necessary, since the effectiveness of word processing ultimately depends on obtaining final paper copies. There are some other needs, furniture, electrical supply, and the like, which are equally important to add to these calculations.

One difficult part of this calculation is determining just what it is that needs to be taught by computer and how much time to allot to it. The time must include all of the CAI, word processing, and other uses of the computer.

A second difficult part of this calculation involves the arrangement of computers in a school setting. Computers are either placed in a laboratory or they are located in a classroom. Obviously, more computers can be placed in a laboratory than in a classroom. Laboratory arrangements are useful when entire classes are to be given instruction in the same material. Such grouping, however, can make scheduling more complicated if several classes have to be scheduled into the laboratory at the same time. Classroom placements are more useful when students can be allowed to work on projects at odd times throughout the day. Perhaps the optimal arrangement is to have some computers in a laboratory and others decentralized in classrooms. It is probably important to have excess computer capacity to loosen the scheduling requirements.

Once a sufficient number of computers is available, it is important to guarantee availability of software packages to allow students to use them whenever they need to. There are several alternatives to making this a reality. The first is simply to buy enough individual software packages for each potential student user. A second is to purchase a site license, which either gives the purchaser a large number of copies (at a discount) or the right to make an agreed-upon number of copies. Most software is protected by copyright and the copying of it is illegal, except for backup copies made for emergency use. The simple test is that a single software package should run on no more than one machine at a time.

The final alternative is to develop a network system in which all of the computers can be linked to a central data bank in which programs are stored. When one is needed, it can be loaded directly from the network and used on the computer. At the same time, other students at other computers in the network can be using the same program on different machines. The use of programs in this way often requires a special license from the publisher.

Curricular Concerns The curriculum has been mentioned as an important element in the use of word processing. Research has shown that students who use word processing do not automatically get better at writing or editing. Under certain circumstances, they do less writing than with paper and pencil when they use computers. If word processing is to have its maximum effects, students must learn about revision and editing strategies, they must be able to keyboard effectively, and they must be allowed to use word processing for many of their assignments.

Writing must be taught in conjunction with reading and it must be used beyond the original teaching situations. In short, for transfer of the learning to take place, students must be encouraged to use the skills in a variety of situations. This requirement dictates something about the arrangement of computers. It suggests that at least some of the computers be decentralized so that students have access to them when they have time to write during the day. It also suggests that students should have access to the computers at times when they might be required to complete assignments outside class— like before or after school or during study periods.

If full advantage of the power of the word processor is to be taken, students must also learn about process writing. They must be encouraged to make use of revision and editing capabilities of word processors. Students must also understand that drafts are just that, and that printed copies do not have to be made at intermediate stages. Note, though, that drafts are useful for proofreading, revising, and so forth when corrections can be entered into the computer at a later time. The use of intermediate hard copies can help alleviate the problem of reading speed at the computer noted earlier. It will also decrease the number of computers required for student uses.

Data Bases

A *data base* is simply a collection of related information organized in records. Every *record* in a data base is composed of *fields*, which are pieces of information related to the record. For example, a telephone book is a data base. Each entry in a telephone book is a record, with the fields name, address, and phone number. In a data base, each record must have the same fields, although all of them do not have to be complete.

A computerized data base has advantages over conventional ones like collections of file cards: It is easier to use and manipulate. Information can be scanned rapidly and organized in almost any way conceivable. Search criteria can be established to search for records that meet specific criteria. For example, if the phone book were computerized, it could be searched to print out a list of all people with the last name of, say, Smith. Or, it could find all of the people who had telephone numbers beginning with the prefix 555, for example.

How Can Data Bases Be Used in Educational Settings? Data base programs can be used in any educational context where it is important to organize and later retrieve information. In reading and writing, this comes most clearly under the prewriting or revision stages of writing. A student who was going to write a paper about dinosaurs could easily begin the process by using a data base program to store information about dinosaurs. Once the outline of the paper were determined, the student could use the data base program to selectively retrieve the information collected earlier, organized according to the needs of the paper.

This same example can be replicated in any content area. The skills that a student must exercise include reading the material to extract the information to place it into the data base. In addition, the student must organize the data base records and fields—a task not unlike that of generating semantic maps. That is, the student must decide what categories of information about the topic should be included in the data base. Finally, higher level thinking skills must be involved as the student organizes the manner in which the material will be retrieved.

Rudimentary data base programs can easily be learned by students in second or third grade, although a great deal of teacher assistance may be required to organize the data base. Once that is accomplished, students can easily learn how to do simple *reports* (a formatted subset of information retrieved from the data base) on the content of the data base. As students become more sophisticated in the use of computers, their use of the information in data bases will also become more sophisticated.

So far, the discussion has emphasized having students create their own data bases. It is equally useful at times to have students use a data base that someone else has created (a teacher, other students, etc.). With a modem and a telephone link, students can access commercial data bases (for a fee) and retrieve information of wider scope and greater diversity. As CD ROM technology becomes more common, there will be immense amounts of data organized in data bases available to almost every computer user. To date, there have been few of these applications, beyond an electronic version of an encyclopedia and a set of reference books, for use in instruction. However, the future potential may be nearly unlimited.

Spreadsheets

A *spreadsheet* is a program that manipulates numerical and other data in a matrix of cells. Data can be entered directly in the cells or can be calculated from the results of data entered in other cells. The major advantage of a spreadsheet is that it handles numerical data in a highly efficient manner. In particular, spreadsheets have the ability to adjust all the data in a calculation when any individual number is changed. That is, if the spreadsheet is used to add a group of numbers, it automatically corrects the sum when any of the individual entries is changed or corrected. The most sophisticated of these programs include data base functions as well as mathematical operations. These programs have few applications for reading and writing instruction, although they have been adapted successfully for use with word problems in mathematics. They are mentioned here simply because they should be a part of any general curriculum that includes computers. Their introduction should be delayed until after students have become comfortable with computers in general.

Integrated Programs

Integrated programs are mentioned here because they are a special case of the programs we have been discussing. An *integrated program* consists of several different types of programs linked together. For example, a word processor, spreadsheet, and data base might all be combined in a single program. The advantage of this arrangement is that data can be easily moved from one to the other function, whereas this might not be the case with three separate programs. Another advantage of integrated programs is that learning the commands for each of the different functions may be easier, since they are usually the same (or similar) for similar operations in each of the different components. For example, the command for deleting a word in the word processor might be the same as deleting a cell in the spreadsheet or a record in the data base. Educational applications have been written for use with some of the more common integrated programs found in school settings.

Computer Literacy Revisited

Where does this notion of using the computer as a tool leave us? We have to consider whether or not we really want to use the computers we have to teach the traditional sorts of computer literacy topics. It is probably best to teach students only what they need to know about computers to be able to use them. That is, students should be taught about what a diskette is and what goes on it in the context of actually using the computer. Thus, we should have a curriculum that includes CAI and using the computer as a tool to do word processing, data base tasks, and even spreadsheet manipulations.

In this context, students will learn what they need to learn about the computer because it relates to completing the assigned work, not because it was something else to learn.

EVALUATING READING AND WRITING SOFTWARE

Software for use in language arts is only one instance of computer software in education. There are some considerations when evaluating software that are common to all fields. There are also some unique considerations in evaluation of reading and language arts software.

General Considerations in Evaluating Software

The primary concern in evaluating software for any area of instruction should be its consistency with the remainder of the curriculum. That is, whatever else enters into an evaluation, the software must deliver instruction that is consistent with the other forms of instruction a student will receive. For example, software that presents individual skill-based drill and practice exercises would be useless in an environment where the remainder of reading instruction was done from a whole language perspective. In other words, the teaching goals of the computer-based instruction should be the same as, or similar to, those for the other types of instruction in the school setting.

A second concern is that the software should do its task better than could be done in another teaching or instructional mode. If the computer-based instruction has no advantage over other instruction, it should be rejected out-

Curricular goals are an important consideration in choosing software suitable for classroom needs. (J. R. Holland/Stock, Boston)

of-hand. "Better" is not a precise criterion. Its meaning will depend on the details of the type of software and the particular schools in which the evaluation is conducted. "Better" as a criterion should serve primarily to remind an evaluator that a piece of software *must* have some advantage over other instruction before it should be implemented.

Because curricular goals are critical in assessing the value of computer software, the very first step in conducting an evaluation is to specify those goals as completely as possible. This entails specifying the beginning state of knowledge of the students, the desired outcomes of instruction, and the resources (e.g., amount of time, number of teachers) available for accomplishing the task. Only when all of these are specified can an evaluation match the software to individual school or classroom needs.

The diversity of curricular goals and types of computer software means that each type of software may have to be evaluated along a different set of criteria. This means simply that there is no single evaluation form that will be appropriate for all software. Each evaluation should be tailored to local and individual needs. However, all software of a given type, for a given purpose, should be evaluated along the same set of criteria.

Specific Criteria for Reading and Writing Software

There is an important characteristic that is often overlooked when evaluating language arts software: It is extremely important to assess the readability level of the text that is presented on the screen. Although this is usually a primary criterion in evaluations of conventional materials, it is almost always neglected in software evaluations.

Similarly, one should be careful to assess the level of prior knowledge and cognitive abilities that are assumed by the program. These will be critical to the success of a student using the program, and the time to find out about them is during the evaluation, not during instruction.

Drill and Practice Software For drill and practice software, important criteria include the appropriateness of feedback. Does the program let the student know what was right and wrong at the appropriate time? Do the exercises get easier if the student misses a few and harder if the student succeeds? In general, software, to be most effective, should go beyond simple drill and practice and include elements of instruction when the student is not performing at acceptable levels. However, much of the drill and practice software is an improvement over conventional forms. If your teaching style incorporates drill and practice, computers may help you do it more effectively.

CAI Software Evaluating CAI software requires examination of the instructional strategies and the presentation modes, as well as all the other criteria discussed above. The clarity of the instruction is important. Does the program teach, rather than just talk about or mention content? Does the instruction adjust to the level of the students by branching to segments that are either easier or harder? As in other materials, feedback should be appropriate to performance; it should not demean the student or be unrealistically optimistic (particularly when the student has not done well).

In addition the program should help maintain the student's attention by using sound, graphics, or animation wherever appropriate. These elements should not distract from the basic goal of the program, however. Good software will allow the user to select options like turning sound on or off.

Students should be able to leave the program in the middle of it and return at a later time (e.g., after recess). They should also be able to get help by asking for it (usually by pressing a special key). And, they should not have to spend an inordinate amount of time reviewing instructions if they already know them.

Good CAI software will incorporate a management system so that both students and teachers will know what progress has been made and what remains to be done. This can also serve as a motivational device for students to work at an optimum pace. The management system should be easy to use and understand. It should also be consistent with what is done in noncomputer contexts.

Finally, the CAI software should be factually accurate. While this seems obvious, even conventional textbooks have been published with errors in them. The programs should also be examined for appropriate grammar, syntax, spelling, and the like. It is desirable that the programs be modifiable, but at the very least, a good evaluation will make the user aware of limitations that have to be considered. Teachers may have to go so far as to produce auxiliary materials to correct deficiencies in software.

Simulation Software Simulations are the most difficult sort of software to evaluate. The important criterion to remember in evaluating simulations is that they must actually accomplish the purpose for which they are being used. If the simulation is only partly relevant to the curriculum goal, it may be more work to incorporate the simulation into your instruction than to teach without it.

A second consideration is the amount of time it takes to participate in a simulation compared to the amount of learning. While it may be enjoyable for students to simulate certain aspects of their learning, if the achievement is not commensurate with the time, an alternative approach might be more sensible.

Other Evaluations Evaluating software as tools for other tasks can take almost as many forms as there are tools or pieces of software. As an example, evaluation of a word processor should be done in light of the students' abilities and time they will have available for using it. Ideally, word processors should be easy to use, require little or no specialized computer knowledge, be able to produce all of the effects the user wants, and make editing simpler than by conventional means.

Optional but desirable features include spelling checkers and even some sorts of stylistic analyses. Again, the importance of these features will depend to a large degree on the particular aims of an individual teacher in a given classroom environment.

These examples of criteria important for evaluating software for reading and language arts are meant to be merely examples. As indicated above, there is no one evaluation. Each situation is different, and the evaluation must ultimately be based on the students, the teaching environment, the resources, and the curricular goals.

When you find good software, then try to find a machine that can run it. If you don't find software that meets your needs, it is reasonable to use it *if you can adapt it (or change your other instruction) to make up for the deficiencies.* Most importantly, though, don't use poor software simply because there is nothing better.

CAUTIONS AND LIMITATIONS REGARDING COMPUTERS

When using computers in reading and language arts instruction, there are several important limitations and cautions. One of the most basic of these limitations is that, at the present time, the capacity of computers to "speak" and "listen" is relatively primitive. This means that students who have not achieved at least an acceptable level of literacy skills will not be able to make full use of much of the available software.

Problems of Speech Input and Output

There is a set of problems that attend the speech production element of CAI for reading. Several approaches have been used. The simplest technique has been to tape record whatever speech or language the computer program is going to present. The computer then controls the tape and plays the appropriate segments during the lesson. However, there are difficulties in returning to or skipping ahead of segments on the tape.

A second alternative has been to attempt to *synthesize speech* so that the computer could produce any segment at any point in the program. Votrax technology has been used for a long time in the PLATO system, even though the voice quality is not as good as what would often be desired.

A third alternative has been to *digitize speech*. That is, speech is converted to computer codes (0s and 1s) and is reconstructed when needed. The voice quality of the best digitized speech is as good as a tape recording. The limitation is that the codes for digitizing speech take up a great deal of storage space, and space is usually at a premium in the microcomputers commonly used in educational environments.

Speech input (or speech recognition) is much more limited than speech output. Technology has provided us with computers that are capable of recognizing small, limited sets of words. However, it is not possible, at present, for computers to recognize any random word by any student with 100 percent accuracy. If there is a "training" phase, during which the computer can "listen" to a student speak the words to be used, accuracy for a small set of words can be almost perfect.

Thus, for most practical purposes, it is not possible, at present, for a computer to listen to a student read and make consistently accurate judgments about fluency and accuracy. It is only possible to have a computer "speak" to a student by using relatively sophisticated microcomputers. Advances in technology may make dramatic improvements in this area.

Problems with Visual Display

Other problems for reading instruction with computers center on the quality of the displays. That is, many computer users report that they have visual problems, fatigue, headaches, and other ailments after working with and reading from a computer video display. Some research has shown that the speed of reading from computer displays may be as much as 25% slower than from a similar, but conventionally printed, hard copy. These problems may be accentuated by the tendency for less expensive microcomputers to use television sets or inexpensive color monitors rather than higher-resolution monitors. Note that this is often the case in school settings where funds are tight. It may be a "false" economy to save on this aspect of hardware.

Transfer Problems

The final set of problems concerns the applicability of computer instruction to other, noncomputer situations. That is, students who learn material in CAI settings may not make the connection between performance during the lesson and application of that learning elsewhere. Although transfer of learning is critical for sound teaching, students rarely transfer learning spontaneously.

Because many studies show only moderate achievement gains in CAI programs, it is essential that teachers using CAI constantly evaluate and monitor student progress for both original achievement and transfer of learning.

HARDWARE EVALUATION

In an ideal situation, users would first make decisions about the software in which they were interested and then make a decision to purchase hardware to accomplish the task of running the software that had been judged best. However, the realities of most situations are that the user often finds the hardware in place. What we will describe in this section is what to do in either case.

If you have examined software and have decided that there are pieces of it that are really critical to your implementation, the hardware decision is very simple: Find a computer or computers that will run the software you have selected. Remember, the primary goal is to teach students. The hardware will only deliver the instruction. If you do not concentrate on the instructional aspects, your efforts will be doomed from the beginning.

However, many computer users find themselves already confronted with hardware. If that is the case, the situation should be reversed from that described in the paragraph above. You should examine all of the pieces of software that are available for the hardware that is in place and determine whether any of it is worth using. Do not be afraid to reach a negative decision. There may be times when your curricular needs are not met by the available software.

In the event you are lucky enough to be able to make the choices for hardware, you must evaluate it along many dimensions, much the same as you did for software. The importance of the dimensions will differ for each educational environment, just as the importance of the criteria for software varied for different types of software.

Price is always an important consideration, particularly in times of tight fiscal policy. However, what is available for the money is equally important. In an evaluation, you must consider what the hardware will be able to do: How much memory does the machine have? Is it expandable? Can periph-

FIGURE 19.1   Periodicals

The following are general computer publications that contain information on a wide variety of computers. The articles range in difficulty from novice level to advanced-user level.

A+ Magazine	InCider
Byte	InfoWorld
Commodore: The Microcomputer Magazine	PC Magazine
Creative Computing	PC World
80 Micro	Popular Computing

The following publications are specifically designed to cover educational topics as they relate to computers.

Classroom Computer News	Educational Computer
Computer Curriculum Resources	Electronic Education
Computers, Reading and Language Arts	Electronic Learning
The Computing Teacher	Teaching and Computing

The following periodicals deal with theory and research in computers and education.

AEDS Journal	Journal of Computer-Based Instruction
AEDS Monitor	Journal of Educational Computing Research
Educational Technology	T.H.E. Journal

erals be added a few at a time? Does the machine have color and/or graphics capabilities? Can it produce sound, voice, or music? How legible is the screen display? (Note how important this last is for the teaching of reading and writing.) How compatible is the hardware with other hardware in the same schools or in schools nearby? What kind of repair or service facilities will be available for the machines? Finally, the question of how much software support is available is important. That is, you must ask how much new software is likely to be produced for the machines. This last can only be estimated, but it is important.

To gather data, you should examine the hardware yourself—in the configuration you want to use, not a simpler or a more sophisticated version. You should also try to find users of the hardware and determine what their experiences have been. There are also reviews of hardware published in many of the computer magazines listed in Figure 19.1.

WHAT ABOUT THE FUTURE?

For the novice computer user, the array of equipment, software, possible uses, and choices that must be made are overwhelming. Beginning computer users are also overwhelmed by the rate of introduction of new hardware and software. It will take a great deal of effort to keep up with new developments while learning about those that already exist.

What is in store for the future? In terms of hardware, we should expect to see better sound quality integrated into computer software. Speech recognition capabilities are likely to be added to microcomputers as well. In short, we may soon see computers that can "listen" as well as "speak" to students during reading instruction. The development of the videodisk will allow more realistic graphic displays to be presented. The amount of information that can be stored on videodisks will allow far more realistic simulations and more extensive lesson activities for CAI. Of course, computers will become cheaper with more memory capacity and flexibility. Most of the limitations mentioned above should be overcome shortly. Once the hardware limitations are gone, it will be up to software developers to provide sound instructional programs that can make use of the capabilities of the computer.

In software, we should see the development of better instructional programs that are closely related to curricular concerns. The likelihood is that computers will be used for certain instructional tasks they enhance, like word processing, and restricted in others. As greater hardware capacity becomes available, the software will take advantage of it. Programs will be able to provide a greater range of instruction, remediation, and management than before. As computer networks develop, students will have easy access to data bases, other computer users, and instruction that would not otherwise be available at a local site.

Input for software content will be sought from teachers and students, and the emphasis should be on curricular unity rather than on isolated bits of software. Learning in the ultimate computer environment will be free from many of the constraints of the conventional classroom. Teachers will be free to deal with many of the more difficult instructional problems like teaching cultural appreciation, values, and the like. Although this attractive goal is possible, it is still some distance away, and we will need even better hardware and software than we have today to reach it. It is important that teachers prepare for the proliferation of computers by learning what they are and using them when and where they are appropriate.

SUGGESTED ADDITIONAL READING

COBURN, P., KELMAN, P., ROBERTS, N., SNYDER, T., WATT, D., & WEINER, C. (1985). *Practical guide to computers in education*, 2d ed. Reading, MA: Addison-Wesley.

DAIUTE, C. (1985). *Writing and computers*. Reading, MA: Addison-Wesley.

GEOFFRION, L., & GEOFFRION, O. (1982). *Computers and reading instruction*. Reading, MA: Addison-Wesley.

KNAPP, L. (1986). *The word processor and the writing teacher*. Englewood Cliffs, NJ: Prentice Hall.

PETERSON, D. (1984). *Intelligent schoolhouse*. Reston, VA: Reston Publishing Co.

RESEARCH BASE

KULIK, J., KULIK, C., & BANGERT-DROWNS, R. (1985). Effectiveness of computer-based education in elementary schools. *Computers in Human Behavior, 1*, 59–74.

MASON, G., BLANCHARD, J., & DANIEL, D. (1987). *Computer applications in reading*, 3d ed. Newark, DE: International Reading Association.

NIEMEC, R., & WALBERG, H. (1987). Comparative effects of CAI: A synthesis of reviews. *Journal of Educational Computing Research, 3*, 19–37.

Special Language Issues | 20

Maria Torres

GETTING READY

As a teacher, you must become aware of Black English and bilingualism because more than one fourth (27 percent) of the total enrollment in United States public elementary and secondary schools represents a racial or ethnic minority. Nineteen of the 50 states in the United States have a minority population of 25 percent or more, and 12 states increased in minority populations by 6 percent or more between 1970 and 1980. Specifically, the black population accounted for 16 percent of the total public school enrollment in 1980. Between 1976 and 1982, the number of children between 5 and 14 years of age who spoke a language other than English at home increased by 27 percent. Thus, at some point in your career, you will be faced with students who are bilingual or speak Black English. Whether you make a difference in these students' chances to blossom into fully literate individuals may well depend on what you know about special language issues.

FOCUS QUESTIONS

- What is a social dialect? How is the concept of social dialect different from regional dialect?

- How is bilingualism defined? Will bilingualism confuse a student?

- Is more standard English the solution to success in reading for Black English-speaking students?

- What are the four major goals of bilingual education programs?

- What instructional strategies can you use to adapt instruction to meet the needs of Black English-speaking students? of language minority students?

MAJOR TYPES OF LANGUAGE DIFFERENCES

When people speak it is like choosing the right outfit from their wardrobe for a special occasion. They choose what to wear depending, for instance, on

413

whether they want to impress someone or want to feel comfortable. Each situation calls for a series of choices. Furthermore, what a person wears for one occasion is not necessarily the best choice for another. It is all right to be different, of course, but if someone wore evening clothes to go skiing, he or she would stick out like a sore thumb. Thus, people change clothes to fit new situations. Moreover, there are limits to or a range of appropriateness of dress.

This is also so when people are speaking. There are choices about the manner of speaking, the words to use, the emphasis, and the intonation. Choice of language can be influenced by the formality of a situation. Imagine how students would speak in response to a classmate's question of a formal presentation as opposed to the way they would speak to that same classmate if they met casually in the hall. Everybody can recall a case in which formality prompted a change in how they spoke. The person one is speaking to can also influence the way one talks. For example, talking to a minister is different from talking to one's sister. Talk can also be affected by what is talked about or where the conversation takes place. The choices people make are not always made consciously, but it is possible to trace the patterns of how they speak and why they intuitively know when it is appropriate or not. People learn all this by acquiring natural language as they are growing up.

Variations in language can also be connected to social group membership. For example, at a national conference in the Midwest, you may easily notice how the pronunciation or choice of words differs among the persons present. Midwesterners speak differently from New Yorkers or Texans. These different ways of speaking are called regional varieties, or dialects. Differences in racial or ethnic background, in social class background, in whether a person is male or female, or in what kind of job the person holds may also result in different ways of speaking.

This chapter concentrates on two language situations that have been the focus of discussion and inquiry particularly as they relate to educational attainment and achievement of racial and ethnic minorities in the United States. Specifically, this chapter focuses on Black English and bilingualism, some of the myths and realities associated with these language situations, and the implications these have for organizing and planning for instruction.

Black English

In 1979, Judge Joiner concluded in the landmark decision of *King vs. Ann Arbor* that schools did not recognize the differences in dialects between standard English and Black English; that Black English was a consistent, systematic, rule-governed, and different form of speech; that the problem was not that black children possessed a different speech but that the schools did not take speech into account in teaching black students the literacy skills needed to achieve in school; and that it was the schools' obligation to make teachers knowledgeable about Black English and to train them to use this knowledge in the instruction of black children. How these conclusions were reached is discussed here.

Black English is a name given to a variety of dialects. In general, Black English speakers across the United States are said to use the same features when speaking; the pronunciation, the sentence structure, and the vocabulary are generally the same. However, there are differences across regions, social class, and educational experience. In this sense it is not very different from the standard English varieties mentioned earlier. New Yorkers speak a Black English different from people from New Orleans or Atlanta.

Not all black Americans speak Black English, although the majority may be familiar with it. Some individuals use only one or two features of Black English. Some blacks use Black English features as they speak, but feel very comfortable with reading and writing in standard English. Yet again, some blacks speak Black English in some circumstances and standard English in others. Furthermore, Black English is spoken by Puerto Ricans and other children in many urban settings. Thus, it is important for teachers to be aware of such possibilities when assessing the language needs of black children, in particular, and Black English speakers in general.

Various interpretations have been offered about the origin of Black English. What does this have to do with teaching? The way teachers look at the origin of Black English may have an impact on what they do in their classrooms. One such interpretation is that Black English is a corruption of standard English, and from this perspective, the Black English features found in standard English are stressed. Another more recent view is based on the strong links between Black English in the United States and on the African continent. A third perspective takes aspects of both views and looks at the interactional nature of Black English development.

There are incidents supporting each of these views. The first perspective, also known as the *deficit model,* presents the following evidence: there are similarities between Black English features and "errors" made by foreigners in their attempt to learn standard English; the noise level in homes of black Americans prevent children from hearing certain sounds; black mothers have been found to speak to their children with less frequency than do white middle-class mothers; and blacks consistently score low in verbal sections of standardized tests.

The counterargument is guided by what is known as the *difference theory,* which assumes equality of languages. It holds that the African slaves brought to the United States did not have a common African language that facilitated communication across tribes. Faced with the need to communicate among themselves as well as with whites, a common language was established. Development of this common language went through the following stages. The first phase was a simplified language that contained elements of the several languages of its speakers, also known as pidgin. The second phase, development of Creole, resulted when a new generation accepted the simplified language as a native language. In other words, the language of communication between the slaves and their children was the simplified common language of slaves; then the children who spoke this common language as their native language expanded its use and transformed it into a bona fide communication system. Thus Black English differs systematically from the languages from which it originates, but it continues to share many of its original features.

The third perspective emphasizes that the simplified language system and its development interacted with a foreigner's type of English to produce what today is known as Black English. Because there is a common core in syntax, vocabulary, and sound system, it may appear solely as a corruption of the first, but it is actually a different language system from English. Furthermore, it has been found that many researchers did not take into account the fact that when parents and children are taken out of their homes and put in a laboratory situation they are inhibited and speak less. In fact, tremendously elaborate use of language can be found in oral rituals of Black English speakers. For instance, *the dozens* is an exchange of verbal insults that usually takes place among young black males who know each other well and frequently involves the mother as a target of insults although it can, and does, focus on other topics as well. Whether one agrees with the appropriateness of this language or not, it counters the deficit theory and testifies to the high verbal performance of blacks.

One of the major points Judge Joiner made was that Black English was not inferior, but was a consistent, systematic, rule-governed form of communication. Such findings are important for instruction because the way teachers act toward the use of Black English in the classroom, consciously or unconsciously, can be the result of thinking about Black English as an imperfect acquisition of English resulting from a nonsupportive home environment. Some teachers immediately correct a student who uses a final possessive *s*, such as "I sees," without stopping to think that this is a feature of Black English. Rather than correct the student, the teacher should use a context in which the final possessive *s* is deleted to determine whether the meaning of the sentence conveys the same message in spite of the deletion of possessive *s* and whether pointing out the difference between standard English and Black English is essential to the lesson.

It is possible to agree that Black English is a bona fide communication form but to be convinced that a distinction needs to be made about when Black English is appropriate and when it is not. This is indeed a different matter and will be treated as a distinct concern at a later point in the chapter.

Bilingualism

Bilingual language situations in the United States result when an individual speaks a language other than English—such as Chinese, Japanese, French, Spanish, or Croatian—some or all of the time at home or in the community and, either through formal or informal schooling, is proficient at some level in English. Generally, the home or community language is the native language and English is the second language. Individuals are usually categorized in groups according to the language spoken; these groups are called *language minorities.* Any one of the many language minority populations in the United States must be considered within the context of their sociohistorical conditions and, more specifically, in relation to the language attitudes of the community. Both the historical conditions and the attitudes have implications for determining how to deal with language diversity in your classroom. For example, some of the language minority groups are also historically disenfranchised racial or ethnic minorities, such as the Puerto Ricans. Not only may the native language be instructionally appropriate for the individual child, but it may also be culturally and politically symbolic of ethnic identification for the group. However, not all language minorities share the same historical conditions nor are language issues equally important across ethnic groups. However, the fact is that a student with another language brings greater complexity to the classroom. Under these circumstances, how well the student knows the native language or the second language are specific educational questions that teachers must learn to deal with.

One can also find differences in the degree of bilingualism. At the individual level, for example, a teacher may find that one child responds when told in English to get in line, but that same child has a blank expression during most of the reading lesson. Another child of the same language minority may be in the high reading group and be as engaged as any other student in the group. What causes this? Although there may be more than one explanation, consider the following. The first child is probably non- or limited-English proficient, and the other, although possibly bilingual, is not limited in his or her knowledge and use of English. In other words, not all members of a language minority group have equal difficulty in understanding, speaking, reading, and writing English. As a matter of fact, English may be the dominant language for individuals of a language minority group.

How well individuals know the language can be explained by thinking of bilingualism as a continuum. Chinese offers a good illustration. At one extreme, there is the monolingual Chinese speaker who has just arrived in the United States and does not have a working knowledge of English. At the other extreme, there is the monolingual English-speaking person of Chinese descent. In between these two extremes there are many possibilities, including a person of Chinese descent who uses a mixture of English and Chinese to communicate with others on a daily basis. Furthermore, it is possible that the degree of bilingualism is related to an individual's ability to understand or speak the language or to their ability to read and write it. Many United States-born Hispanics, for example, understand and speak Spanish well, but are less proficient in reading and writing Spanish. On the other hand, there are individuals who can read and write Spanish comfortably in church or at home, but are unable to do so when faced with the task of translating in a courtroom or teaching a lesson in science. Not only are they at a loss for words, but they cannot understand or write the specialized language of these fields.

The number of language minority speakers who are limited in their proficiency of English is estimated to be as high as 8,034,000 in the United States. Approximately 60 percent of the language minority school-age children are from a Spanish-language background. Thus, most of the knowledge about bilingualism in the United States is drawn from Hispanic children. This discussion, then, uses Hispanics as the primary examples, although examples of other language minorities are noted, where appropriate.

Hispanic is an umbrella term that refers to Spanish-speaking populations that come from 21 different countries, including the Mexican-Spanish-origin population that originally resided within the boundaries of what once was Mexican territory and today is the southwestern United States. Hispanic is not a well-received term by some groups because it is a political term associated with government funding and does not originate from the people themselves. The term, and the degree of its acceptance, is subject to regional and ethnic variation. Some people prefer the term *Latino* or *La Raza*. Suffice it to say that teachers should ask a student or the parents to self-identify. For our purpose, the term Hispanic will be used interchangeably with Spanish-speaking, although not all Hispanics are Spanish-speaking, or vice versa.

There is a richness of cultural diversity among Hispanics. At a national level, the largest Hispanic groups are Mexican-Mexican Americans, Puerto Ricans, and Cubans. The largest concentration of Mexican-Mexican Americans is in the southwest, of Puerto Ricans is on the East Coast, and of Cubans is in Florida. Each group has a history, political perspective, literary tradition, and language and cultural style that is different and unique. Hispanics draw from these rich traditions as they interact with the institutional mandates of everyday life in the United States. However, the interaction tends to reinforce the use of oral language more than the written form.

Many Hispanics are not first generation, but they speak Spanish in their home or community. Is this any different from Italian, Polish, or other ethnic groups in the United States? The answer is yes and no. The affirmative aspect is that, as with the Italians and Polish, there is a loss of the native language with each passing generation. What then accounts for the continued maintenance of Spanish, unlike other language groups? There are two factors. First, the rate of language loss over generations is not only slower than that found in other groups but is coupled with a higher birthrate among Hispanics, meaning that the number of individuals who speak Spanish is growing. Second, the combined efforts of the constant flow of immigration from all parts of Latin America, the proximity of the Mexican border, the settlement patterns of Hispanics, and the segregation policies and practices against Hispanics that continue in many American cities also serve to give the impression of enormous growth among the Spanish-speaking population in the last couple of years.

In 1980, a little less than one-third of the Spanish-speaking school-age population was estimated to speak only English at home. This suggests the widespread use of the native language among Spanish-speaking children, but does not give any indication of their ability to work in a totally English setting. Furthermore, it is recognized that the widespread use of Spanish does not mean that all Spanish-speaking Hispanics do not know English.

In a classroom, then, a teacher cannot assume that a language minority child does not know English well; nor is it safe to assume that they can understand all that is going on when English is the language of instruction. It is important to find out how well they know English, what skills they have, and ultimately, how instruction can be adapted to meet their needs. Furthermore, it is important to understand what they use their native language and second language for, whether they mix the languages, and how they change from one language to the other.

EIGHT MYTHS ASSOCIATED WITH SPECIAL LANGUAGE ISSUES

There are many myths associated with language and the education of blacks and language minorities. The following section compares and contrasts the myths or variants thereof.

1. *Teaching students in their native language will confuse them intellectually.* This is a myth that comes from the language minority children's failure to achieve at the same rate as Anglo children and from a long tradition of studies beginning in the 1920s that hypothesized that bilingual children were at a disadvantage when tested because intelligence tests were so heavily based on language performance. When bilingual children were found to have more grammatical errors, reduced vocabulary, and deficiencies in articulation, it was concluded that bilingualism was a negative condition, and thus it needed to be eliminated. The tests were not questioned, nor was the possibility explored that bilingual people were not only cultured but perhaps more intelligent.

As scholars searched for evidence to demystify this tradition, they began by accounting for the flaws that resulted from how the research was done. The research studies had not taken into account the effects of social class or the complexity of definition posed by bilingualism. Sorting out these factors and looking closely at the phenomena has resulted in the conclusion that bilingual children were more mentally flexible than monolinguals. How could this be, when previous evidence showed deficiencies? Researchers have found that greater mental flexibility was more frequently found when learning a second language did not result in sacrificing the first language. In other words, if an individual learned a second language and became fully proficient in both languages, the ability to use both languages would result in greater mental flexibility. Furthermore, it was found that the existence of bilingualism in an individual is more likely to cause mental flexibility than the reverse.

In addition, literacy skills in a first language appear to help academic achievement in a second language. For example, experience with reading in English gives a student an advantage when faced with a French text. The student knows that a cluster of letters make up a word and that the word means something, the space between a cluster of letters means that it is a word separate and distinct from other words, the capital letter at the beginning of a cluster of letters followed by a space and other clusters of letters that end up with a period at the end indicate a sentence, and thus a thought. A student knows these words convey a message and once the key to the pronunciation is known words can be decoded, and so forth. In other words, there are concepts that need not be taught to a child who already knows one language and is learning another. There are, however, some differences depending on the language group being taught. For example, the general notion that one reads from left to right is different from Arabs and Asians, who read from right to left. However, the point is that teaching someone who has some concepts for the printed word can save a teacher some steps. This is why children who have been in school in their native countries for 4 or 5 years come to the United States and learn to read and write at a much more rapid pace than children who did not have school experience in their language.

There is no clear equivalent to this myth in the case of Black English. However, as is true in the bilingual situation, blacks who have poor auditory discrimination or articulation as measured by standardized tests have been labeled as intellectually deficient, immature thinkers, and learning disabled. Very few scholars bothered to look at the biases of the test until relatively recently. Even present-day tests that include natural writing samples have failed to take into consideration that the tone, organization, and style of written work can be influenced by cultural aspects. What is also similar in both cases is the interference issue. A Black English speaker, when reading orally, may not pronounce a sentence as written in a standard English text. Most of the time, teachers immediately conclude that the speaker does not know how to decode and that the lack of decoding skills affects comprehension. There is no evidence of interference when a child transforms standard English text into Black English. On the contrary, it is evidence of a very sophisticated mental process. Not only do the children demonstrate an understanding of the text by producing sentences that mean the same thing in their dialect, but they also demonstrate an act of immediate translation from one dialect to another in order to produce a new sentence.

2. *Students need more English in bilingual education classrooms.* This myth at first glance seems logical. If practice makes perfect, then the more students practice hearing and speaking English, the more likely they will learn it faster. Just think about listening to a different language radio show while traveling abroad, or when in the presence of two individuals who are speaking a language a person does not know. Do you understand? Do you pay very much attention? Probably after noting that what you are hearing is in an unfamiliar language and not comprehensible you would tune out and not listen anymore. This form of language is called *incomprehensible input,* because what was said cannot be understood. Thus, more is not better under all circumstances. In the case of teaching a non- or limited-English-speaking student, it is important to think about *how* to teach English.

A second reason why more English is not better is illustrated in the

It is important to think about *how* to teach English to non- or limited-English-speaking students. (Elizabeth Crews)

following example. Teachers very often tell parents that they should stop talking to their children in the native language and should expose their children to more English because they need more practice. The probability is very high that the parent is limited-English proficient. Imagine the parent and the student at home sitting at the kitchen table and the parent putting the teacher's advice into practice. What kind of experience can this parent have with the child? Imagine that the parent has a blue coffee mug in his or her hands. The parent can probably say *cup, blue, coffee,* or *cup blue coffee.* If the parent decides to extend the "lesson," the parent might say *inside coffee* or *inside cup coffee,* and so forth. Very soon, the parent will run out of anything to say. On the other hand, if the parent were to speak in the native language, he or she could make more sophisticated comments about the color and function of the cup, the weight with or without coffee or other liquid, the shape of the cup, the size of the cup relative to other cups, and so forth. The difference in experience is clear. The amount of language exposure in the first situation is limited to approximately 10 words, as opposed to 250 words in the second, and the difference in intellectual and conceptual exposure is like day and night.

There is another practical matter to consider. Previous "sink-or-swim" methods, where only English was spoken, were not successful in schooling language minorities.

The variant myth for Black English is to teach standard English, or as a teacher from Detroit put it in reference to standard English in a 1982 article, "They need to be taught, corrected, and properly directed in mastering their native tongue." Again, this stems from failure to recognize Black English as a different language system.

It is true that unlike the bilingual situation, standard and Black English share a common core of syntax and sounds. This makes black speakers proficient in understanding standard English speakers. However, similar to the second-language learner, there is a need to lower what is called *the affective filter*. In other words, there are invisible barriers that create favorable or unfavorable conditions for learning a language. Some teachers have proposed to teach standard English by making blacks feel ashamed of the way they talk. The results for the majority of children have been disastrous. When children are threatened by the feeling that their language and culture are not as good, their defenses arise, creating a barrier for learning. Encouraging greater pride and awareness about the black language and culture has proven to be more successful. As a result of the Civil Rights and Black Power Movements, more and more black youth developed positive views about Black English, and this reinforced its use. This reinforcement seems to have had positive effects. Although not nearly as satisfactory as they should be, there are reports of improvements by blacks in language arts and reading scores at the national level.

3. *Previous generations of immigrants learned English and were successful without special school programs.* Early immigrants had bilingual schools in many states. One example is the German population, which between 1838 and World War I had what they called German schools. Many laws were passed during this period that provided options for teaching in a language other than English. One such law, passed in Ohio in 1839, stated that in any district where there was an English school that did not have branches taught in German, it would be lawful for students in those districts who desired to learn in the German language to attend a district German school. It was more the result of the anti-German and antiforeign sentiments than a concern for educational achievement of Germans that later resulted in the prohibition of teaching in a language other than English in public schools.

The second related point is that the immigrants who came to this country in the early part of this century did not "make it" on the basis of education. The most common road to success was through the pooling of family resources to buy a small plot of land or to establish a business. The success rate of immigrants of first- and second-generation children through schooling may not have been as high as is popularly believed.

A third argument related to this myth is that the labor economy has changed. In the past, the nature and amount of entry jobs were significantly different. Today, most jobs require some degree of training. Unemployed nonskilled workers, such as from the auto and steel industries, are presently faced with the need for retraining to qualify for jobs. Furthermore, the job-training and retraining opportunities usually require some knowledge of English, again posing a barrier that adds to the complexity of making it. Thus, it is more difficult for today's immigrants to find jobs.

Many critics of bilingual education point to the phenomena of Vietnamese students who graduate *magna cum laude* from American schools. They are faced with the same conditions as other non- or limited-English speakers, so why are they so successful in school? Although very few scholars have focused on this, there are some immediate issues that come to mind. Most of the first wave of Vietnamese to come to the United States were connected with the United States military in Vietnam, were of middle or upper-middle class, and had a favorable disposition toward English and the United States. They were political refugees, and did not come to the United States for economic survival. This occurrence is similar to the early wave of Cuban immigrants, a middle-class professional or upper-class group, who were very successful in educational attainment, in contrast to the Puerto Rican or Mexican immigrant populations who are having more difficulty. These differences suggest that factors other than language are at work that account for the failure or success of language minorities in the educational system. Thus, in evaluating the success of Vietnamese students it is important to find out if they were first- or second-wave immigrants and whether they previously had the benefit of a middle-class environment.

It has been found that a strong base in the first language as well as previous schooling are helpful in learning a second language and promote successful achievement in that language. Closely related to the advantage of previous schooling is the age of the child. It has been found that older students are more efficient language learners than younger children. In the past, experts thought that the best time to introduce a second language to children was when they were young because a more nativelike pronunciation and use of the language resulted. Although this is true, it is also true that older children have more experience as well as conceptual and intellectual knowledge that permits them to learn a new language in relatively less time, even though a noticeable accent may remain.

A fourth point is that when a language learner is highly motivated and unthreatened, language learning is facilitated, resulting in a lower affective filter. Furthermore, when individuals are learning a language because it will help integrate them socially, it is more likely that they will be more favorably disposed to the new language than when they feel they have to do it for economic survival.

4. *Fostering native language learning will lead to separatism.* This is the same kind of thinking that led to the elimination of language schools in the United States during World War I. To impose one language over another because the two languages cannot coexist is not a universal solution; there are many other alternatives. In India there are 12 official languages; in Tanzania there are two official languages, Swahili and English, and many hundreds of tribal languages; in China there are 54 different nationality groups,

most of whom are educated at an elementary level in their native language in the autonomous regions. In a great majority of the countries of the world, similar language differences exist. Some countries opt for coexistence of languages at a state level, others opt for a language that serves to bridge all other languages, known as a *lingua franca*. In the case of the Philippines, English and Filipino serve as lingua franca. There are cases in which minority languages coexist within the boundaries of a region, as in the Yunan province of China, where 22 language groups live side by side. In other cases there are distinct language areas, as in Switzerland where the country is divided into cantons, and each canton has an official language—German, French, or Italian.

To illustrate the point about separatism, take the case of Quebec, in which the situation stems from complex political, social, and economic factors of which language is only a part. Recognizing language as a symbolic issue in the resolution of the Quebec situation is correct. However, to boil down the issue of separatism in Quebec to one of language is to diminish the sociohistorical conditions that have led to the explosive conditions present today.

5. *Bilingual education is nothing more than a jobs program.* This myth does not focus on students or on the instruction a school provides but on the displacement of white teachers by language minority teachers, a possible side effect of special programs. One of the original claims of ethnic and racial minorities was that there was a lack of teachers who were sensitive to the children's needs. Training and hiring more knowledgeable and sensitive teachers was attempted. In some cases this meant teachers from the language minority group; it also meant teachers trained in teaching language minority populations. It was preferable that a trained language minority teacher who met both conditions be hired. A great number of language minority individuals participated in these training programs, but not all the teachers trained were language minority.

Between 1980 and 1981, four out of five teachers who had limited-English-proficient students did not have the basic preparation to meet their needs. In 1984 it was estimated that the nation needed 52,000 to 56,000 bilingual teachers. The number of trained teachers still does not meet the growing needs of language minority children. In California, the largest recipient of federal funds for language minority schooling, the proportion of white teachers has remained constant throughout the years, although the actual number of Hispanic teachers has increased tremendously. The need is growing at a much faster rate than the number of graduating teachers.

6. *Children are being taught an "incorrect" Spanish.* It is very likely that a professional from a Spanish-speaking country could walk into a bilingual classroom and come out with the impression that the Spanish spoken in the classroom is incorrect. If they were to pick up the materials sent out by bilingual programs, they would be even more adamant. The concern reflected in this argument is similar to that of the standard English and Black English situation. It is not true for all programs, and it is more true for bilingual

programs with a Mexican-American population. Why? First, every language has a variety of dialects. In Spanish, there are more than 20 varieties reflecting the number of countries whose official language is Spanish. Each one of these countries has its own standard. Within each country, however, there are varieties associated with the social group membership and from regional, gender, racial, ethnicity, and occupational differences. In the United States, the Mexican-American population claims its own Spanish dialect, which has many varieties including a mixture (code switching) of English and Spanish that has its own system. In other words, this variation puts together English and Spanish words at random that make up a complete thought but violate the rules used by people who are knowledgeable in one or another variety.

The second factor is that many teachers were not Spanish-dominant speakers on entering the bilingual education program and have only had on-the-job training. The teachers who were trained in English-speaking schools know how to talk about their subjects in the language they were taught—English. The language minority children's needs, however, necessitate that teachers learn the language and style appropriate for teaching these subjects in the native tongue as well.

7. *Children of language minority groups are proficient in their native language, therefore content should be taught in the native language.* This is a generalization to which, when applied to individual children, the general truth does not apply. Some language minority children are not proficient in their native language and some do not perform like native speakers in either the native language or the second language but speak a mixture of the two. The most common proficient native-language speaker is a newly acquired immigrant student.

Assessment is required to find out a student's proficiency level. There are oral-language proficiency tests, such as the Bilingual Syntax Measure, that take into account the fact that a child may code switch. Some oral-language tests combine both a natural-language sample with the more traditional ways of measuring language, such as the Language Assessment Scale (LAS). These two tests, when appropriately administered, can give a fair understanding of a child's ability to understand and speak English, and in the case of Spanish speakers, the oral-language performance. However, there is some caution to be exercised with any test. For example, it has been found that the scores in Spanish on the LAS may be somewhat depressed. The kind of language measured by the LAS may not reflect that spoken at home or in the community. No matter how much testers try, they face variations of language from area to area.

A similar kind of myth can be found in Black English. It is based on the assumption that black children who speak Black English will be able to read texts written in Black English. What is not considered is that white students, when they go to school, must be taught to read in standard English. Why should Black English speakers not require reading instruction in their own dialect? The other related implication is that the sound-symbol correspondence simplification will itself make reading possible. In this regard, the example of the Initial Teaching Alphabet (ITA) is appropriate. Sir James Pitman, who designed the ITA, produced an alphabet of 44 written symbols that correspond on a one-to-one basis to the sounds in English. His premise was that this simplification would help beginning readers during the early stages of reading and would not interfere in the transfer to traditional orthography. Today this method is no longer used, testifying to the fact that reading is not merely the decoding of written symbols, even when there is instruction in this method.

8. *Parents want their children to learn English, so why put their children in bilingual education programs?* There are differences in opinions about how to go about educating children among language minority populations. However, there is no disagreement about parents wanting their children to learn English. This strong desire is anchored in the parents' belief that a better education and better job will result from learning English. However, this does not necessarily mean the parents want the native language eradicated. All surveys of parents done in the last decade have indicated that they would like their children to maintain the native languages not only because it helps maintain family and social ties but also because it is thought to increase their children's potential economic opportunity. In other words, there is an advantage to knowing two or more languages when you apply for a job.

Black parents, like language minority parents, want their children to obtain a better education and occupation. Knowing the school language, standard English, is viewed as a prerequisite or at least as potentially leading to educational and economic improvement. Black parents do not favor teaching Black English as much as language minority parents do, although this often depends on the subgroup one refers to.

A more parallel situation is found among Mexican-American parents. They too want their children to learn to speak correctly, not *pocho*. A recent survey of parents in San Jose, California, indicated that nearly 65 percent preferred that standard Spanish be taught in the schools. However, in this same group of parents there were people who expressed some strong opposition because they felt at a loss with standard Spanish. Generally, these parents are second or third generation and do not identify with the Mexican standard Spanish.

MEETING SPECIAL LANGUAGE NEEDS THROUGH BILINGUAL EDUCATION

As teachers, administrators, government officials, parents, and communities began to recognize that many Hispanic school children were not working at grade level and dropped out of school at a younger age and more often than their Anglo counterparts, they began to search for alternatives. One such alternative was to teach academic content in the native language. This alternative was labeled *bilingual education*. Bilingual education molded itself to fit the American educational system with the particular aim of educating language minority school children. In other words, it aimed at improving the academic achievements of language minorities and at decreasing the drop-out rate. The way bilingual education proposed to meet these goals was by teaching students English as a second language, teaching academic subjects in the students' native language, developing positive self-concept in the students, and, in some instances, maintaining the native language through enrichment activities.

English as a Second Language

English had been previously taught by the sink-or-swim method, which consisted of putting children in an all-English classroom environment in which they had to learn not only the English language but also the subject matter being taught. English as a second language is viewed as a method for teaching children who have a native language other than English. It is different from the regular English course in that it introduces language in a more systematic and planned way. Additionally, it is different from foreign language learning in that there is a viable context for the use of English in natural settings.

Academic Subjects

The continuation of academic subjects in a student's native language was based on two premises: when a child is burdened with learning what is being taught while at the same time learning the language, there will be considerable loss of content; and the native language is assumed to be the stronger language.

Thus, concepts of math, social studies, science, and other content areas are introduced in the stronger language. The amounts of time in the native language or the form the lesson takes can vary.

Self-Concept

Why children do well in school subjects or why they continue their education is influenced by the way they feel about themselves, that is, their self-concepts. If Annie likes herself, and if she believes that she can do the work well or go to college, there is greater self-motivation and greater enthusiasm in doing so. Liking themselves or feeling good about themselves is related to how people feel about their families and their cultures. All people belong to a cultural group and their belongingness partially determines how they act in social situations. In every school, classroom culture is at work. Culture affects how teachers organize their classrooms and how classroom rules, as well as what will be taught in the classroom, are developed. Culture also creeps into the way the teachers teach and how they perceive their students' progress.

A positive self-concept is important when a student is learning a second language. (Elizabeth Crews)

When cultures come in contact with each other and rejection or intolerance results, the members of the less powerful group suffer. Thus, in many classrooms, the power lies with teachers, and when they are not aware of cultural differences, intentionally or not the clash of cultures may interfere with student learning.

One clear example of culture at work is the preference of Mexican-American children for working in groups. To some teachers, cooperation without permission is cheating, but teachers who are in tune with the Mexican-American culture do not have trouble here. Not only do they perceive nonsanctioned cooperation as an appropriate method of learning but organize their classrooms to permit such cooperation. Thus, bilingual education not only brings into the classroom knowledge about the child's history, music, dance, foods, and holidays, which is the usual way culture is perceived in the schools, but also provides for children to incorporate their ways of learning into the classroom.

Maintenance

Finally, the maintenance of the native language is seen to be a way to ensure higher levels of literacy in both languages, and to extend the positive self-concept argument by appreciating the language associated with a cultural group. This entails learning subject matter in the native language as well as learning the native language as a subject matter.

There have been many problems of implementation for bilingual education programs. It is easier to state goals than to put them into effect. It is also easier to identify the complexities that contribute to the problems of implementation than to find solutions to the problems. It takes time, trial and error, and knowledge resulting from experience, as well as new thinking to get these problems resolved.

MEETING SPECIAL LANGUAGE NEEDS OF BLACK ENGLISH

In the early 1970s, some attempts were made to develop programs for Black English speakers that specifically centered on language issues. One was the development and implementation of a black dialect reading program. This program assumed that if the mismatch between the spoken language and the written language were reduced, greater comprehension and fewer errors in oral reading would result. The goal of this program was to improve the reading of Black English speakers. Another strategy was the development of English as a second dialect program of instruction. It was assumed that the distance between standard English and Black English was sufficient to merit the development of a program that would build on the similarities between the two dialects while systematically presenting the differences. The aim of the program was to teach standard English.

One of the strategies was based on the affirmation of Black English as a legitimate instructional language medium, and the other recognized Black English as a base for learning standard English but did not confirm or deny its legitimacy as a language to be used as a means of instruction. Whereas neither one has had wide acceptance, some useful principles can be derived from the experience and incorporated into lesson planning. One of the principles is part of the multicultural education movement that purports to teach students about diversity of cultures and equity. What this has actually meant for teachers is the use of culturally diverse materials in their teaching. This is especially true when the student population itself is from different cultural backgrounds. The limitations of most multicultural programs in this respect is that many have not gone beyond the level of surface culture. The need to incorporate cultural forms more appropriate to black culture still needs to be addressed.

The second principle regards language. Teachers are being taught, as part of their language arts and reading courses, that language dialects exist and that rather than ignore language varieties in the classroom they should think about adaptations in teaching that would encourage expression of concepts, thoughts, ideas, and emotions in whatever languages students bring with them. The degree to which teachers can implement these principles is regulated by their knowledge of the language and culture, the classroom composition, and the curriculum goals. However, at minimum, a teacher should include some materials written in Black English and expose all children to the power of a June Jordan or a James Baldwin as part of the language arts program. Teachers should refrain from correction of Black English features; they should introduce Black English features as a different way of communicating, when appropriate; and they should use individual conference periods to point out the differences between the two dialects in a sensitive fashion.

PROVIDING INSTRUCTION FOR SPECIAL LANGUAGE SITUATIONS

Language instruction in schools has been enriched by educators' reflection on the implications of language acquisition research. Here is an illustration of how teachers can begin to think about applying language knowledge to the instruction of Black English-speaking and language minority children. The discussion is organized around three notions: language is a means of communication; language is developmental; and meaning is constructed by verbal and nonverbal cues.

Language Is a Means of Communication

Language when spoken in a natural context, as when you talk to your mother, a next-door neighbor, or the store clerk, is governed by the need to communicate. As children grow they acquire the language of their surroundings as a means of conveying their desires and figuring out the meaning of utterances spoken by others. This is true whether the child is learning English, Croatian, or Arabic. Children, as they interact with adults and other children, make many grammatical errors that are ignored. The emphasis is on the meaning. Corrections by adults occur when there is an error in content. As a matter of fact, parents usually attribute meaning to nonsensical utterances a child makes. It is natural, then, that black children speak in the dialect spoken at home and that a transformation from the standard English text to Black English occurs when reading aloud. They are trying to make sense, to construct meaning from the text, and they are using their own language variety to do so. There are implications for teaching. First, literacy, reading, and writing should be primarily organized for making sense of the world. It must be interesting, purposeful, and meaningful and, thus, an act of giving or receiving through a written text. Second, the pronunciation or use of a dialect in oral reading should not be corrected as decoding errors. Emphasis should be placed on meaning.

Language Is Developmental

Before children as infants acquire their native language, there is usually a period of silence. In other words, they are not born today and speaking tomorrow. Usually it takes 12 to 18 months before children start one-word utterances. During the 12 to 18 months before producing an utterance, they acquire what is called *receptive knowledge* of the language. That is to say, they can understand what is spoken to them, but they cannot yet produce language. Receptive knowledge of the language is also found in a second-language situation. When learning English as a second language, students should not be expected to speak it immediately. You will soon see how their need to communicate with peers and adults will motivate them to speak English or to incorporate standard English features when they speak a non-standard variety.

Furthermore, the production of language starts out with what is called a *one-word stage*. At this point, children produce words that are meaningful in the environment, such as *mama, ball, eat, milk*. At a later point children produce two-word phrases such as *Daddy go* and *pretty boy*. As they continue to engage in the mastery of their language, children go through a process of self-correction and engage in the production of more and more complex utterances.

In a similar way, second-language learners go through various phases of acquisition, producing more complex, longer, and nativelike utterances after systematic exposure to the language. Black English speakers have also been found to incorporate features of standard English into their speech gradually. Thus, teachers' anxiety about the errors produced should be eased by looking at non-nativelike structures as developmental.

Meaning Is Constructed by Verbal and Nonverbal Cues

An adult interprets what a child says by looking around for contextual cues. A smile and a pointing finger from a toddler may be sufficient indicators for an adult to understand that the child wants to draw attention to an object or occurrence of interest. A child learns how to interpret utterances spoken to them by using contextual cues also. For example, to find out whether the command "Come here" really means "I would like you to come here whether you want to come or not" or "You may choose to come here if you want," the child uses facial gestures, tone of voice, and other contextual cues to interpret the meaning of what was said. A very similar situation occurs when learning a second language. The learner tries to make sense of utterances spoken in the second language by using context, gestures, movement, and so forth.

There are a few implications for organizing instruction of students from different dialect or language backgrounds. For example, one such implication is related to auditory discrimination. The contrasts made by standard English speakers may be different for black or language minority students. In Black English, words such as *pen, pin* and *toll, told* are not as distinguishable from each other as in standard English. Thus, caution is required when planning instruction to determine whether what is to be taught really provides cues for correct interpretation. In second-language learning, there is an increasing use of a function (or social purpose) of language as a way of organizing the curriculum. A social situation is developed so that the context provides the basis for interpreting the meaning of the utterances. It also helps organize lessons or units that emphasize communication over grammatical forms.

This in no way exhausts the implications for instruction or the principles of language acquisition that need to be considered in teaching the linguistically different student. Nonetheless, it provides a way of thinking about language teaching-learning processes and the linguistically different child.

RESOURCES

Where do teachers get more information, materials, and experts to help with special language in the classroom? There are a few places that can offer assistance including university English departments and colleges of education. Local experts are also found through state educational agencies in cultural and bilingual divisions and among elementary or secondary language arts and reading personnel. Nationally, there are a few networks, such as the Title IV National Origin and Race Desegregation Assistance Centers and the Title VII Multifunctional Bilingual Education Centers. A school district can request technical assistance and training and provide searches for materials at minimal cost. A key source for information about these networks and other resources is the National Clearinghouse for Bilingual Education (NCBE), 1555 Wilson Boulevard, Suite 605, Rosslyn, Virginia 22209, (800) 336-4560. The NCBE can provide information about the nearest Title IV and Title VII service center.

Two other sets of people are potentially helpful: students and parents. Children from the same language and cultural backgrounds as a student a teacher is concerned about can be great resources as tutors. They can transform an instructional task, making it culturally and linguistically more appropriate for the student needing help. Furthermore, tutoring also allows tutors to review the content of the lesson and improve their own skills. A good peer or cross-age tutoring system in a classroom can help use this resource better.

Parents can also be of great help. They can be used in a way similar to the buffer described in Chapter 8. Although teachers may have to spend some time recruiting parents who will be dependable, the efforts result in great benefits for students. Remember to encourage parents to visit the classroom and to show them that their help is appreciated. Initially, if a teacher does not know their language, search for a bilingual person who can help communication. Elicit from the parents ways they think they can help and encourage them to do so. Remember, parents want a better life for their children. Capitalize on this desire.

SUMMARY

Special language problems involve a wide variety of difficulties, including social and regional dialects, bilingualism, and non-standard English. Bilingual education is enhanced when English is viewed as a second language, when effort is made to teach academic subjects in a student's native language, when efforts are made to accommodate cultural characteristics of bilingual students, and when efforts are made to extend bilingual students' self-concepts. Instruction for Black English-speaking students is enhanced when Black English is recognized as a legitimate language medium and when teachers help students distinguish differences between the standard dialect and the dialect of Black English. All instruction for special language instruction should emphasize communication, the developmental nature of language, and the way in which both verbal and nonverbal cues are used to communicate.

SUGGESTED ADDITIONAL READINGS

BARNITZ, J. G. (1982). Orthographies, bilingualism, and learning to read English as a second language. *Reading Teacher, 35*(5), 560–567.

BRESNAHAN, M. (1976). Selecting sensitive and sensible books about blacks. *Reading Teacher, 30*(1), 16–20.

DOWNING, J. (1984). A source of cognitive confusion for beginning readers: Learning in a second language. *Reading Teacher, 37*(4), 366–372.

EBEL, C. W. (1980). An update: Teaching reading to students of English as a second language. *Reading Teacher, 33*(4), 403–407.

FEELEY, J. T. (1983). Help for the reading teacher: Dealing with the Limited English Proficient (LET) child in the elementary classroom. *Reading Teacher, 36*(7), 650–655.

GAMEZ, G. I. (1979). Reading in a second language: "Native language approach" vs. "direct method." *Reading Teacher, 32*(6), 665–670.

GILLET, J. W., & GENTRY, J. R. (1983). Bridges between nonstandard and standard English with extension of dictated stories. *Reading Teacher, 36*(4), 360–364.

HEATHCOTE, O. D. (1982). Sex stereotyping in Mexican reading primers. *Reading Teacher, 36*(2), 158–165.

HU-PEI AU, K. (1979). Using the experience-text-relationship method with minority children. *Reading Teacher, 32*(6), 677–679.

KUPINSKY, B. Z. (1983). Bilingual reading instruction in kindergarten. *Reading Teacher, 37*(2), 132–137.

MINKOFF, D. (1984). Game activities for practicing English as a second language. *Journal of Reading, 28*(1), 40–42.

MOUSTAFA, M., & PENROSE, J. (1985). Comprehensible input PLUS the language experience approach: Reading instruction for limited English speaking students. *Reading Teacher, 38*(7), 640–647.

PEREZ, S. A. (1979). How to effectively teach Spanish-speaking children even if you're not bilingual. *Language Arts, 56*(2), 159–162.

PREWITT DIAZ, J. O. (1982). The effects of a dual language reading program on the reading ability of Puerto Rican students. *Reading Psychology, 3*(3), 233–238.

SCHON, I. (1985). Remarkable books in Spanish for young readers. *Reading Teacher, 38*(7), 668–670.

STAUFFER, R. G. (1979). The language experience approach to reading instruction for deaf and hearing impaired children. *Reading Teacher, 33*(1), 21–24.

TOMKINS, G. E., & MCGEE, L. M. (1983). Launching nonstandard speakers into standard English. *Language Arts, 60*(4), 463–469.

WHEAT, T. E., GALEN, N. D., & NORWOOD, M. (1979). Initial reading experiences for linguistically diverse learners. *Reading Teacher, 33*(1), 28–31.

WIESENDANGER, K. D., & BIRLEM, E. D. (1979). Adapting language experience to reading for bilingual pupils. *Reading Teacher, 32*(6), 671–673.

RESEARCH BASE

ASCHER, C. (1983). Writing instruction for dialectally different youths. *Urban Review, 5,* 69–73.

BARNITZ, J. G. (1980). Black English and other dialects: Sociolinguistic implications for reading instruction. *Reading Teacher, 33,* 779–786.

BONGERE, M. B. (1981). Dialect and reading disabilities. *Journal of Research and Development, 14,* 67–73.

BRUNTRESS, N. G. (1982). Educational implications of the Ann Arbor decision. *Educational Horizons,* 79–82.

CRONNELL, B. (1984). Black English influence in writing of 3rd and 6th grade black students. *Educational Research, 77,* 233–236.

CRONNELL, B. (1983). Dialect & writing: A review. *Journal of Research and Development in Education, 17,* 58–64.

DAVIS, B. G., & ARMSTRONG, H. (1981). The impact of teaching Black English on self-image and achievement. *Western Journal of Black Studies, 5,* 208–218.

DENNARD, K. (1981). Black educator speaks about Black English. *Reading Teacher, 35,* 133.

DONALD, B. (1983). Black English—heritage, help or hindrance? *Principal, 61,* 45.

DURKIN, D. (1984). Poor black children who are successful readers: An investigation. *Urban Education, 19,* 53–76.

EDWARDS, V. (1983). Dialect speakers: Fact and fantasy. *Early Childhood Development and Care, 11,* 79–87.

EHERWEIN, L. (1982). Do dialect speakers' miscues influence comprehension? *Reading World, 21,* 255–263.

FERGUSON, A. M. (1982). A case for teaching standard English to black students. *English Journal, 71,* 38–40.

FREEMAN, E. (1982). The Ann Arbor decision: The importance of teachers' attitudes toward language. *Elementary School Journal, 83,* 41–47.

GEMAKE, J. S. (1981). Interference of certain dialect elements with reading comprehension for third grade. *Reading Improvement, 18,* 183–189.

GENTRY, R. (1983). What reading teachers should know about dialect. *Reading World, 23,* 108–115.

GILLET, J. W., & GENTRY, J. R. (1983). Bridges between non-standard and standard English with extensions of dictated stories. *Reading Teacher, 36,* 360–364.

GUILLARY, S. F., & CLIFFORD, C. S. (1980). What is being done for black children in reading? *Reading Horizons, 21,* 22–27.

JOHNSON, F. L., & BUTTAY, R. (1983). White listeners' responses to sounding black and sounding white: The effects of message content on judgment about language. *Communications Monographs, 49,* 33–49.

JONES, C. D. (1979). Ebonics and reading. *Journal of Black Studies, 9,* 423–448.

MARKHAM, L. R. (1984). "De dog and de cat": Assisting speakers of Black English as they begin to write. *Young Child, 39,* 15–24.

MCPHAIL, I. P. (1982). Toward an agenda for urban literacy: The study of schools where low income black children read at grade level. *Reading World, 22,* 132–149.

MONTEITH, M. K. (1980). Implications of the Ann Arbor decision: Black English and the reading teacher. *Journal of Reading, 23,* 556–559.

PADAK, N. D. (1981). Language and educational needs of children who speak Black English. *Reading Teacher, 35,* 144–151.

PALMER, B. C., & HAFNER, L. E. (1979). Black students get an edge in reading. *Reading Horizons, 19,* 324–328.

POLITZER, R. L., ET AL. (1981). Teaching standard English in third grade: Classroom functions of language. *Language Learning, 31,* 171–193.

RAMSEY, P. A. (1979). Teaching the teacher to teach black dialect writers. *College English, 41,* 197–201. (1981). *Discussion, 43,* 633–638.

SCHWARTZ, J. I. (1982). Dialect interference in attainment of literacy. *Journal of Reading, 25,* 440–446.

SMITH, R. P., & DENTON, J. J. (1980). Effects of dialect, ethnicity, and orientation of sociolinguistics on perception of teaching candidates. *Educational Research Quarterly, 5,* 70–79.

SMITHERMAN, G. (Ed.). (1981). *Black English and education of black children and youth.* Detroit: Harlo.

STEFFERSEN, M. S., ET AL. (1982). Black English vernacular and reading comprehension: A close study of 3rd, 6th, and 9th graders. *Journal of Reading Behavior, 14,* 285–298.

STOCKMAN, I. J., & VAUGHN COOKE, F. B. (1982). Re-examination of research on language of black children: The need for a new framework. *Journal of Education, 164,* 157–172.

TAYLOR, J. B. (1983). Influence of speech variety on teacher evaluation of reading comprehension. *Journal of Educational Psychology, 75,* 662–667.

THOMAS, G. E. (1983). Deficit, difference, and bicultural theories of black dialect & non-standard English. *Urban Review, 15,* 107–118.

TORREY, J. W. (1983). Black children's knowledge of standard English. *American Education Research Journal, 20,* 627–643.

TROUTMAN, D. E., & FALK, J. I. (1982). Speaking Black English and reading: Is there a problem of interference? *Journal of Negro Education, 51,* 123–133.

WANGBERG, E. G. (1982). Non-standard speaking students: What should we do? *Clearinghouse, 55,* 305–307.

YELLIN, D. J. (1980). Black English controversy: Implications for the Ann Arbor case. *Journal of Reading, 24,* 150–154.

21 Exceptional Children and Mainstreaming

Sandra Michelsen

GETTING READY

It is a classroom reality that not all students have "normal" developmental reading growth. A related reality is mainstreaming, in which students with diverse needs are integrated into a regular classroom environment. This chapter provides background information concerning students with special learning problems and offers suggestions about reading instruction for these students when they are mainstreamed with normal students.

FOCUS QUESTIONS

- What is PL 94–142?

- What are the implications of this law for classroom teachers?

- What are the categories of diversity that you may encounter in your classroom?

- What are the major instructional considerations to keep in mind when teaching exceptional children?

Exceptional, diverse needs, normal, and *gifted* are very difficult terms to define. From a broad perspective, all children are exceptional and have diverse needs. For the purposes of this chapter, an exceptional child is one who has learning problems, has been legally so identified, and thus requires special education services in addition to those offered in the regular classroom environment. More than one out of ten children require such extra educational service during some or all of their years in school and are considered exceptional. Children whose needs are above that offered in the regular school curriculum are known as gifted. They, too, require special instructional consideration, even though many states do not require that they be legally identified.

In this chapter, a normal student receives regular educational instruction and has not been legally identified for special education services; an exceptional, or special education, student has diverse needs to the degree that special educational services have legally been identified as required; and a gifted child is, despite the absence of legal identification, a child with diverse needs requiring educational services beyond the regular curriculum.

STUDENTS WITH DIVERSE NEEDS

To appreciate how a student with a diverse learning need views a regular classroom environment, imagine the following situations:

- Rub cold cream on a pair of eyeglasses and try to read with them. Imagine sitting in a small reading group taking turns reading aloud. Your turn comes, you hesitate between words, and you even skip some. The teacher tells you to hurry up while other students begin calling out the words before you can identify them. Then some giggles erupt within the group, and you hear whispers of "stupid," and "dummy." How would you feel at this time? Would you like to read?

- Imagine you are a second grader. You are asked to read a list of vocabulary words that includes *chersonese, exuvial*, and *syzygy*. You can actually read words like *cat, bed*, and *deep*. When you hesitate or make a mistake, the teacher chastises you and accuses you of not really trying. Imagine how you would feel. Would you want to continue to try? Would you be eager for reading group tomorrow?

- Turn down the volume on the TV so that you cannot quite hear every word. Pretend this is your reading lesson and the teacher is introducing a strategy to identify words using context clues. Listen for five to ten minutes. Would you be able to explain the strategy when the teacher called on you? Due to your inability to do this task successfully, you are told that you did not listen hard enough and you cannot go out for recess. How do you feel about reading? Was reading group a successful experience for you?

- Imagine that your reading group meets from 10:00 to 10:30 a.m. At that time you always have a difficult time concentrating. Your blood sugar is very low because you are a diabetic. You really need a snack. You cannot answer some of the teacher's comprehension questions about the story. You are told that you need to think harder. You must answer the next three questions before you can go down to the office to get your orange juice. How would you feel about reading?

- Imagine you are asked to read a story with sentences like, *The cat sat on a fat rat*. At home you are currently engrossed in a book about how to write a trigonometry program on your microcomputer. How would you feel about attending reading group? Would you be eager to find out what happened when the cat sat on the fat rat?

These five instances highlight some diversities found in many regular class-rooms. As a teacher, you must recognize these needs and deal with the reading instruction for each particular need. This chapter assists you in this.

HISTORICAL BACKGROUND OF SPECIAL EDUCATION

Early in our nation's history, residential schools were established for the physically handicapped and mentally impaired to provide for housing, care, and education. Before this time, these citizens largely had been ignored by society. The residential placement kept the handicapped out of the main-stream of everyday life. Some individuals with milder handicaps were taught skills to cope with their handicap, the aim being to return this group of individuals to society. For the most part, institutionalization meant a lifetime placement without reprieve.

Around the turn of the century, a trend to establish special public school classrooms for handicapped children emerged. This eliminated the need for full-time institutional placement for such children. These special classes

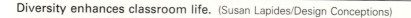

Diversity enhances classroom life. (Susan Lapides/Design Conceptions)

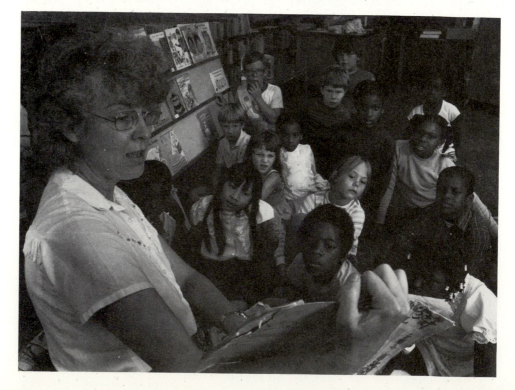

within the public education framework were not immediately accepted or successful. It was at this time that the classes for the mentally handicapped became known as *special education*. Although this stigma remains today, special education now has a much broader role than just involving the mentally handicapped.

After World War I and World War II, a new feeling about handicapped citizens began to emerge. Normal young adults returned from the wars handicapped. The general public became more accepting and willing to provide for these people. Also, parents of handicapped children brought the issue of educating handicapped persons to the forefront. The number of special education classes increased.

Until the 1960s, these classes were generally self-contained. A handicapped child placed in a special education classroom remained there for the entire school day. There was no association with the regular classrooms within the same building even for lunch or recess. With the civil and human rights movements in the 1960s and 1970s, a new concept of the educational plight of the handicapped emerged. Equality of education became a major theme of educational planning. The strengths of learners were emphasized instead of their handicaps, with educational experiences and materials adapted to the learner. Every attempt was to be made to have the "special" learner take part in as much regular education as possible. Important state and federal court decisions encouraged the inclusion of the mentally, physically, and emotionally handicapped children in regular classroom public education. This program is called *mainstreaming*. This led to the congressional passage of the Education for All Handicapped Children Act in 1975, known as Public Law 94–142. This law became effective in 1977 and dramatically changed the educational experiences of diverse learners or special education students.

PL 94–142

The Education for All Handicapped Children Act, PL 94–142, requires an appropriate public and free education for all children in the United States between the ages of 3 and 21 years of age. The key word is *appropriate*. The most suitable education for children with diverse needs is sought. A classroom teacher should be familiar with four of the major aspects of PL 94–142.

1. An important aspect of PL 94–142 is "the least restrictive environment." This phrase means that students must be placed in the regular classroom unless the total evaluation of the student indicates otherwise. At times, a combination of special classes and regular classroom instruction more appropriately fits a student's needs.

2. The law mandates certain requirements for testing measures and evaluation. Placement testing must be free from racial and cultural bias and

must be appropriate for the handicapped student. No one testing instrument or evaluation can be used as the sole determiner of placement.

3. A statement must be written about the student's educational needs and a plan to meet these needs. This statement is developed through the combined efforts of specialized personnel, the classroom teacher, and the parents and is known as an Individualized Education Program (IEP). The IEP must be reviewed and updated annually. Although the exact format of the IEP form is not specifically mandated, it must include the child's current educational levels, short-term objectives and annual goals, the special services and personnel required, programs/methods to be used, the initiation date of special services and expected termination dates, and tests, measurements, and other information to be used to assess progress.

4. To protect the students' rights, parents have access to the student's records. If the parents desire, they can request other evaluations. Parents also have the right to appeal decisions regarding placement of the student.

About 12 percent of the school-age population fall within the guidelines of PL 94–142. The emotional, physical, and mentally handicapped guidelines include the mentally impaired, hard of hearing or deaf, speech impaired, visually impaired, orthopedically and health impaired, and learning disabled.

Mental Impairment Mental impairment refers to a general intelligence level that is not within the average IQ range of 90 to 110. The terms *educable mentally impaired* (or EMI) and *trainable mentally impaired* (TMI) are educational levels. EMI children are thought to have IQs within the 75 to 50 range, and TMI children are considered to have IQ ranges of 25 to 50. Generally, a TMI child is not placed in a regular classroom. Despite the tendency to use IQ scores, it must be emphasized that there is not a specific IQ number to determine classroom placement. According to the guidelines of PL 94–142, the whole child must be evaluated.

Hearing Impaired The hearing impaired child is deaf or hard of hearing. A hard of hearing student has defective hearing but is functional for ordinary purposes with or without the use of a hearing aid. A deaf student's disability precludes successful linguistic formation. Testing for intensity or loudness of sounds measured by decibels is required to determine placement for the hearing impaired child.

Speech Impaired This category is also called *communication disorders*. A child with a disorder in this category has difficulty with oral communication, which may be linked to other handicaps such as mental retardation. Speech impairments can result from a physical problem such as cleft palate, a disease such as cerebral palsy, or from other functional factors. Impairments fall within three categories: articulation disorders, which consist of errors in production; voice disorders, which include difficulties in pitch, intensity, quality, and flexibility; and functional disorders, which involve the interruption of the flow of speech such as stuttering.

Visually Impaired The visually impaired child is partially sighted or blind. A partially sighted student has a visual acuity of 20/70 after correction and the blind student has a visual acuity of 20/200 or less after correction. The partially sighted student usually is able to read regular or large print. The blind child usually will read only braille.

Physically or Health Impaired This category includes many orthopedic, neurological, and health impairments. An orthopedic disability also includes congenital malformations. Physical impairments encompass chronic ailments, such as diabetes, and terminal diseases, such as cancer.

Learning Disabled The category of learning disabled includes a whole range of disorders that affect a student's ability to learn. These problems include difficulty in listening, thinking, talking, reading, writing or doing mathematics. Learning disability conditions include brain dysfunctions. A student may have a learning disability despite a normal or above average IQ range. In essence, learning disability refers to students who are not achieving their academic potential.

In summary, PL 94–142 means that a classroom teacher may be required to teach students with these diverse educational needs because they will be mainstreamed into the classroom. Consequently, the classroom teacher must be knowledgeable about general principles and specific instructional strategies to assist these students. Since gifted students are not specifically included within PL 94–142, they are discussed later in this chapter.

GENERAL SUGGESTIONS FOR HELPING MAINSTREAMED STUDENTS

The following suggestions are useful when instructing mainstreamed students:

1. Do not worry about how many children will be mainstreamed into your classroom. The hearing impaired, visually impaired, learning disabled, and physically handicapped are not all placed in the same classroom. Generally, only one or two mainstreamed children are placed in a particular classroom.

2. Most mainstreamed students are more *like* the normal students than

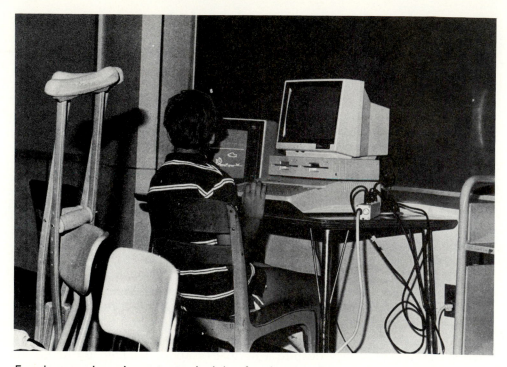

Equal access is an important principle of mainstreaming. (Robert Bawden)

they are *different* from them. The student has more similarities with other students in the regular classroom and needs to be treated as such.

3. Maintain high student expectations. High expectations and positive attitudes are particularly important for diverse learners.

4. PL 94–142 mandates that teachers must participate in the planning of the annual IEP. However, you should exceed this requirement and work on a day-to-day basis with the specialized personnel and parents to understand student's diverse needs and to suggest methods for the classroom. You should coordinate instructional materials or procedures with the specialized personnel who helped develop the IEP so the child does not get confused. A simple term such as the "silent e" rule can confuse the student if it is referred to in different ways by different personnel.

5. You need not change your view of reading instruction and reading outcomes when instructing a child with diverse needs. You should still instruct students to work out their own problems when blockages in comprehension occur and to have them enjoy reading. You must, how-

ever, set high expectations for their developmental reading growth no matter what their disability.

SPECIFIC SUGGESTIONS FOR READING INSTRUCTION

The following suggestions for reading instruction are useful in pursuing the goals specified earlier in this book.

Mentally Impaired

When planning reading instruction for a mentally impaired student, you need to realize that the student probably will have a low tolerance and get frustrated easily. Also, it is likely that the student will have a short attention span, a below-average language ability, a below-average ability to generalize and to conceptualize, and a poor self-concept. You must plan for the student to reach his or her highest potential, but also be aware of the student's role in the classroom in relationship to his or her self-concept. Thus, plan individually for the child so that instruction is at the appropriate level. Since these students do not learn at the same pace as others, they need systematic instruction. The teacher also must include them in other reading activities so they can share some reading experiences with other members of the class.

When instructing mentally impaired students in reading, "real" reading such as telephone books and magazines should be used as much as possible to remind them of the wholistic and meaning getting features of reading. Also, have them listen to tape recordings of other groups' stories so they can participate later in discussions. Language experience activities are also useful because they emphasize that reading is connected with background experience, and is wholistic and meaningful.

Hearing Impaired

A hearing impaired student placed in a regular classroom will communicate by speech (lip) reading or through the use of a hearing aid, or a combination of a hearing aid and speech reading. You need to know what the student is using. If the student is watching the teacher's lips, then be sure this student always is placed within sight of you and remember to speak slowly and distinctly. If the student is using a hearing aid, place the student near you and away from distracting sounds.

Since a hearing impaired child has difficulty with sounds, a phonics approach to reading instruction is not very helpful. Emphasize a strong sight word vocabulary and contextual meaning. Use many visual materials and teaching aids. Make sure that the steps of a reading strategy are listed on the board for the student to read. When giving directions, write them as well as say them. Since a hearing impaired child generally has a language disability also, practice with various kinds of speaking activities are helpful.

Speech Impaired

For speech-impaired students, you must know from the student's speech pathologist what type of assistance the child is receiving. It is very important that the student be encouraged and reminded, but not badgered, to use appropriate speech in reading class. You should consistently require that the child read and answer questions like any other child in the reading group. You should encourage the student to read and talk without interruption. Strive to develop an attitude of acceptance among the child's peers. For instance, if the student's disability is stuttering, do not eliminate the child's turn during oral reading. The rest of the group should be encouraged to listen to the child and to refrain from calling out the words before the stuttering student has time to speak. For other speech disabilities, the teacher can be an important model in emphasizing correct speech. Frequent use of a tape recorder is an excellent instructional tool to reinforce correct speech patterns.

Vision Impaired

For students with low vision, use a multisensory approach to reading instruction. A child with impaired vision needs to feel objects and how words and letters are formed. Place the student in the reading group and in the classroom so that you or other students can read to him or her. Tape recordings also may be used. As with any other student with a diverse need, you must be aware of the extent of the student's disability and make sure that the child properly uses any special devices or materials suggested in the IEP. Similarly, you need to know if regular reading materials are appropriate, or if the child should use large print books. In the case of a blind child, braille is needed. A pair of glasses in a desk will not assist a low-vision student to read.

Physically or Health Impaired

Since this category covers many diverse needs, it is very difficult to offer specific instructional methods for teaching these children to read. Many of the health impairments will not affect the student's ability to learn. Others, such as cerebral palsy, can affect the child's ability to communicate and to interact with text. In this regard, you need to be acquainted with the rate of deterioration accompanying the physical condition and to modify expectations accordingly.

Remember that a student with an orthopedic disability must not be excluded from a reading group just for convenience sake. Every possible effort should be made to physically include that child in the reading group. These children may not spend as much time in active play as others and may actually have more time to read than "normal" children. Use this as an opportunity to suggest many different and interesting books for the child to read. A child who does not participate in physical education should not be expected to do extra work sheets.

A student with a health impairment involving highs and lows of efficiency levels such as diabetes should receive reading group instruction during one of the high efficiency periods. Thus, if a child with diabetes needs nourishment at 10:30 a.m., 10:00 a.m. would not be a good time for the reading group to meet. If the child's physical impairment decreases his skill in communicating, such as being unable to write, certain technological devices or a tape recorder may be used for oral responses. Remember that because a child has difficulty communicating answers about what he knows and what he is thinking does not necessarily mean that the cognitive processes are impaired or that reading developmental growth is impeded.

Learning Disabled

If you have a student classified as learning disabled (LD), it means that there is a discrepancy between what the child's potential ability is and what the child actually is achieving. There are many conditions that account for this disability, including perceptual handicaps and brain injury. A learning disabled child most likely has one or more problems in perceptual motor skills, thought processes, communication problems, or general learning difficulties. There is no single reading method or technique that can be uniformly applied to a learning disabled child. There are, however, some general guidelines that can assist you in planning a reading instructional program for such a student.

1. Since the child usually has some confusion in learning, tasks need to be simplified and broken down into smaller steps than with "normal" children. Shorter assignments can be given and less work put on a page. Instead of assigning ten fill-in sentences on a page, you could divide this in half and only give five at a time.

2. The teacher should structure the environment for the student. The child needs to know specifically where the materials are located, the procedures to follow, and how the tasks are to be completed.

3. Give more frequent positive feedback to a learning disabled child. Such students often have a failure syndrome and need to feel more positive in their learning efforts. A star or sticker can be given for each correct answer instead of one for an entire page.

4. To reduce learning confusion and to establish a more structured environment, establish a specific, quiet, private place for the child to do his or her reading. This will help eliminate minor distractions. This does

not mean segregation from the reading group. As with other main-streamed students, the learning disabled should be included in group reading activities whenever possible.

A learning disabled student's main problem is one of learning confusion. The more the classroom teacher can do to eliminate that confusion, the more the LD student is assisted. The classroom teacher also needs to communicate frequently with the specialized personnel involved in this child's IEP and use suggestions from them for reading instruction.

THE GIFTED CHILD

This section of the chapter discusses historical influences upon gifted education, discusses characteristics of giftedness, and makes instructional suggestions to assist in planning reading experiences for gifted students.

Historical Foundation of Gifted Education

Attention to gifted education has been sporadic during the past 60 years, depending upon the social and political climate of the times. For example, during World War I and World War II, interest in gifted education declined. With attention focused on Sputnik in the 1950s, there was renewed interest in developing intellectually superior students. Concern about the space race led to many special programs for intellectually endowed children in the areas of math and science. Even though it is generally thought that the top 2 to 5 percent of the nation's school population is gifted, these children were not identified as such at that time.

With the move toward equity during the 1960s, gifted education again declined. The problem of elitism was a major difficulty in gifted instruction. It was thought that a gifted child should be educated like "normal" children and should not be given anything extra in education. It was also felt that gifted children could make it on their own and that they should not need any additional attention in school. In the early 1970s, interest was rekindled with the establishment of a Directorship of Gifted Education in the U.S. Office of Education.

PL 94–142 does not especially mandate programs for gifted children. However, by the early 1980s, many states had authorized gifted education as a requirement for high ability students. Some states even authorize IEPs for their gifted children. Most states now have guidelines for gifted programs.

Opponents of gifted education believe that it is elitism education; teachers cannot be prepared adequately to deal with gifted students; there is not enough funding; students are too difficult to identify; and gifted students can make it on their own. Proponents of gifted education, in contrast, believe that gifted learners are the most retarded of our school population in respect to the difference between the groups' potential achievement and actual achievement level. Believers in gifted education feel that a resource in this nation is being lost by failing to provide appropriate education for gifted children.

Identifying the Gifted Student

Identification of giftedness varies. There is no single set of characteristics to identify a child as gifted. There are, however, accepted areas that are usually used. These include general intellectual ability, specific academic aptitude, aptitude in the visual and performing arts, creative or productive thinking, and leadership ability. Many data need to be considered to identify gifted students. They include the student's past performance, standardized test scores, teacher evaluation and progress reports, parent reports, and language ability. All this information may be assembled into three areas: intellectual ability, task commitment, and creativity.

The classroom teacher does not have the responsibility for singularly deciding if a student is gifted or not. Usually other educators and specialized personnel assist in this recommendation.

Reading Instruction for the Gifted

The foremost principle in planning reading instruction for gifted students is to differentiate instruction and not just give more work. A student who has already mastered a reading skill does not need to be given a second work sheet on that same skill. A gifted child needs something different. Teachers should plan a combination of enriched and accelerated experiences.

Enrichment experiences involve going deeper and more thoroughly into what is presently being studied. If a reading group is studying Mexico in the reading basal text, the gifted student can go to the library and do a research report on certain aspects of Mexico. Acceleration involves going ahead of the grade level. If a third grader is reading at a fifth grader level, then that child may go on and read higher grade level materials. It is important for the classroom teacher to realize that pure acceleration for the high ability child is not totally appropriate. A third grade high ability student reading an eighth grade level novel may not find the subject matter relevant or suitable. Thus, the classroom teacher needs to seek a balance between providing experiences that enrich at the gifted child's present grade level but also offer acceleration into a high ability level.

When providing differentiated learning experiences, you must consider the student's higher levels of cognitive ability. There are six levels of thinking: knowledge, comprehension, application, analysis, synthesis, and evaluation. Most "normal children" are taught and learn predominantly at the levels of knowledge, comprehension, and application. These levels involve convergent thinking and center around finding an answer. Gifted youngsters need to be provided with instruction at the levels of analysis, synthesis, and evaluation. These levels emphasize divergent thinking rather than simply finding an answer. At the analysis level, the student discusses information implicit in the reading. To synthesize, the student compares and contrasts subject areas using a number of materials and media. At the evaluation level, the student makes judgments about the information. Remember the gifted instruction needs to emphasize the depth and quality of thinking and learning, rather than the quality of work completed. Too many times gifted children become unmotivated because they are expected to do more of the same.

Differentiated instruction for the gifted also must include direct instruction. Gifted students do not get everything on their own. They need instruction in how to analyze, synthesize, and evaluate. The classroom teacher cannot confuse practice and drill, which the gifted student usually does not need, with direct instruction.

The available literature presents a wide range of opportunities for the classroom teacher to plan differentiated learning experiences for the gifted student. One book can provide access into many different subject areas and several modes of language. Do not have the gifted student read just for the sake of reading or to occupy time.

Reading experiences for the gifted should also include critical and creative reading. The student is reading critically when the higher level thinking skills are being used. The student is reading creatively when a reorganization of reading material takes place. The student may rewrite or elaborate upon a story, or transform a story into a puppet show or a musical.

As with other special education students in the classroom, there should be a balance between including the gifted child in "normal" reading group activities and in individual independent activities to meet the diverse instructional needs of the gifted.

An Instructional Model for Educating the Gifted

To plan for gifted students, a systematic model is needed. The one recommended here consists of three stages of learning.[1] Type 1 is called exploratory. At this stage, the student learns at the lower levels of knowledge acquisition. Type 2 includes higher level thinking skills and more open-endedness of involvement for the student. Type 3 is the stage when the individual applies this knowledge to a real life purpose with the ultimate goal of a real product and a real audience.

For instance, a student at the Type 1 stage may read a book of poetry. At the Type 2 stage, the student might analyze the meaning of selected poems, compare and contrast types of poems, and make personal judgments about them. At the Type 3 stage the student could write original poetry and send it to a child's newspaper or magazine for possible publication. The student could also make an entire collection of poetry, put the poems into book form, and place it in the school's library. Using these three stages of experiences, the student explores and reads poetry at the Type 1 stage, examines it at

[1] Renzulli, J. (1977). *Enrichment triad model.* Mansfield Center, CT: Creative Learning Center Press.

stages of higher levels of thinking at the Type 2 stage, and produces a real product with a real audience at the Type 3 stage.

SUMMARY

The Education for All Handicapped Children Act, PL 94–142, requires teachers to teach students with diverse educational needs because they are to be mainstreamed into regular classrooms rather than being taught separately. This means that you need to be able to teach students with diverse needs including the hearing impaired, speech impaired, visually impaired, physically impaired, learning disabled, and gifted.

SUGGESTED ADDITIONAL READINGS

BURG, L., & KAUFMAN, M. (1980). Laws about special education: Their impact on the use of reading specialists. *Reading Teacher,* 34(2), 187–191.

CARLSEN, J. M. (1985). Between the deaf child and reading: The language connection. *Reading Teacher,* 38(4), 424–426.

CARR, K. S. (1984). What gifted readers need from reading instruction. *Reading Teacher,* 38(2), 144–146.

GAUG, M. A. (1984). Reading acceleration and enrichment in the elementary grades. *Reading Teacher,* 37(4), 372–376.

GREENBAUM, J., VARAS, M., & MARKEL, G. (1980). Using books about handicapped children. *Reading Teacher,* 33(4), 416–419.

GUTHRIE, F. M., & CUNNINGHAM, P. M. (1982). Teaching decoding skills to educable mentally handicapped children. *Reading Teacher,* 35(5), 554–559.

HANSEN, J., & HUBBARD, R. (1984). Poor readers can draw inferences. *Reading Teacher,* 37(7), 386–589.

LANQUETOT, R. (1984). Autistic children and reading. *Reading Teacher,* 38(2), 182–186.

LUKASEVICH, A. (1983). Three dozen useful information sources on reading for the gifted. *Reading Teacher,* 36(6), 542–548.

MOLLER, B. W. (1984). An instructional model for gifted advanced readers. *Journal of Reading,* 27(4), 324–327.

MONSON, D., & SHURTLEFF, C. (1979). Altering attitudes toward the physically handicapped through print and non-print media. *Language Arts,* 56(2), 163–170.

PRICE, E. H. (1976). How thirty-seven gifted children learned to read. *Reading Teacher,* 30(1), 44–49.

SINATRA, R. C., GEMAKE-STAHL, J., & BERG, D. N. (1984). Improving reading comprehension of disabled readers through semantic mapping. *Reading Teacher,* 38(1), 22–34.

SMITH, J. P. (1982). Writing in a remedial reading program: A case study. *Language Arts,* 59(3), 245–253.

SPECKELS, J. (1980). "Poor" readers can learn phonics. *Reading Teacher,* 34(1), 22–26.

RESEARCH BASE

CARTWRIGHT, G., CARTWRIGHT, C., & WARD, M. (1984). *Educating special learners* (2nd ed.). Belmont: Wadsworth.

GEARHEART, B. R. (1983). *Education of the exceptional child: History, present practices, and trends.* Lanhorn, MD: University Press of America.

GEARHEART, W. (1984). *The exceptional student in the regular classroom* (2nd ed.). St. Louis, MO: Times Mirror/Mosby.

GEASS, R. M., CHRISTIANSEN, J., & CHRISTIANSEN, J. L. (1982). *Teaching exceptional students in the regular classroom.* Boston: Little, Brown.

HENNINGER, M. L., & NELLSEROOD, E. M. (Eds.) (1984). *Working with parents of handicapped children: A book of readings for school personnel.* Lanhorn, MD: University Press of America.

MORSINK, C. V. (1984). *Teaching special needs students in the regular classrooms.* Boston: Little, Brown.

How to Avoid Burnout | 22

GETTING READY

As lifelong learners, professional teachers make a conscious effort to remain professionally fresh and vibrant. Learning how to continue your professional growth throughout your career is an important part of being a teacher. This chapter describes why continued professional growth is important and makes suggestions about how to ensure that your teaching remains fresh and vital throughout your career.

FOCUS QUESTIONS

- What happens when teachers do not make conscious efforts to continue their professional growth?

- How can you assess your professional growth?

- What are some professional activities that ensure your continued professional growth?

- What personal things can you do to maintain your freshness and vibrancy as a teacher?

- What are the rewards of continuing your professional growth?

This book began by pointing out two truths about reading instruction in today's schools: First, some teachers are more effective than others, and, second, many teachers teach more like technicians than professionals. Consequently, this book has emphasized what makes teachers effective and how they can become professional decision makers who maintain cognitive control of their instruction rather than technicians who merely follow the directions in a teachers' guide.

However, no single book, course, or degree program can do all that is needed in this regard. Rather, professional decision making in teaching requires a lifetime commitment to new learning and a career-long effort to grow as a teacher. In short, when you receive your initial certification to teach, you have not finished your preparation—you have just begun it. The following sections describe some of the ways to continue your professional growth throughout your career.

ASSESSMENT PLAN

Continued professional growth depends upon how well you assess your capabilities so you can use your strengths and overcome your weaknesses. While preparing for a teaching position, you need to ask yourself: "What are my strengths and weaknesses? What needs to be worked on now? What needs to be worked on later?" This self-assessment can be structured around the following four areas: students and their needs; the reading curriculum; the role of the teacher; and the classroom environment.

Students and Their Needs   This category involves assessing what you know about reading growth and your ability to apply this knowledge to students' reading needs. Do you feel knowledgeable about reading stages, instructional reading levels, the influence of verbal aptitude on reading growth, student interests, etc.? Can you effectively use these concepts in classroom teaching? Organize these into two lists, one labeled Strengths and one labeled Needs.

Reading Curriculum   This category involves assessing what you know about and what you can do to improve the typical reading curriculum. Are you knowledgeable about the three instructional goals of reading? Do you have objectives and activities for each instructional goal? Are you familiar with the strengths and weaknesses of basal reading materials? Do you understand state assessment tests and standardized tests and their role in the reading curriculum? Can you effectively use these in your instruction? Add these items to your list of strengths and needs.

Role of the Teacher   This category involves assessing your knowledge of the teacher's role and your ability to perform it. Can you assess students in terms of the three curricular goals? Can you provide instruction for the three goals? Can you find, develop, and organize materials for instruction? Which of the above can you do effectively? Which are you concerned about? Add these to your list of strengths and needs.

Classroom Environment   Finally, assess your ability to create a literate classroom environment? Do you know what constitutes a literate environment? Can you create one? Do you know how to account for and create good social-emotional, physical, and intellectual environments? Add these to your list of strengths and needs. Figure 22.1 is a check list you can use to assess yourself.

PROFESSIONAL DEVELOPMENT PLAN

Once your self-assessment is completed, use the data to create a professional development plan. Your plan for continued professional growth can be divided into two areas. Begin by setting goals for yourself. How can you improve your classroom work based on your assessment of yourself? Your

Teachers must be able to assess their knowledge of their role and their ability to perform it. (Susan Lapides/Design Conceptions)

planning should include both long- and short-term goals, since both are crucial to lifelong professional growth. Successful completion of short-term goals provides incentive and rewards for continuing the effort, and successful completion of long-term goals provides a pattern of thinking and action that supports lifelong professional growth.

You set goals as you search for ways to improve. In fact, the heart of professional growth is the ongoing search for improvement. The best teachers are the ones whose motivation to excel has them constantly looking for ways to improve. In short, they are always experimenting with better ways to do things.

RESOURCES FOR IMPROVEMENT

The teaching profession offers both formal and informal resources for improvement and updating.

FIGURE 22.1 Teacher Self-Assessment

	Strength	*Need*
A. Student variables		
1. Do I have knowledge of		
a. Reading stages		
b. Instructional reading levels		
c. Independent reading levels		
d. Influences on verbal learning and aptitudes		
e. Student interests		
B. Curriculum variables		
1. Do I have knowledge of		
a. Instructional goals		
b. Objectives and activities for goals		
c. Strengths and weaknesses of basals		
d. State assessment test		
e. Standardized tests		
2. Can I use		
a. Reading stages		
b. Instructional reading levels		
c. Independent reading levels		
d. Influences of verbal learning and attitudes		
e. Student interests		

Formal Resources

The primary resources in this category include professional organizations, professional journals, and graduate work in universities. Professional organizations tend to divide into ones with an interest in particular kinds of problems (for example, reading problems or early childhood problems) and those with an interest in particular curricular areas (social studies, language, mathematics, etc.). All these organizations have annual conferences where teachers gather to exchange ideas and to hear speakers present information on the most recent innovations in the field. These conferences are often highly exciting, intense, and satisfying experiences where teachers obtain many ideas and return to the classroom stimulated and renewed. A list of organizations that have a particular interest in the teaching of reading are included in Figure 22.2.

Second, teachers can get new ideas and innovations from various professional journals, of which many are associated with professional organizations such as those noted in Figure 22.2, but others are published independently.

FIGURE 22.1 continued

	Strength	Need
C. Teacher variables		
1. Do I have knowledge of		
a. Student assessment		
b. Student instruction		
c. Environment conducive to learning		
d. Developing and organizing materials		
2. Can I use		
a. Student assessment data		
b. Instructional strategies		
c. Classroom environments conducive to learning		
d. Developed and organized materials		
D. Classroom environment variables		
1. Do I have knowledge of		
a. A literate environment		
b. Social-emotional environment		
c. Physical environment		
d. Intellectual environment		
2. Can I use		
a. Literate environment		
b. Social-emotional environment		
c. Physical environment		
d. Intellectual environment		

In either case, these journals contain teaching and curriculum ideas that have been submitted from all over the country and, sometimes, from all over the world. By subscribing to one or more of them, you are assured of intellectual stimulation and continued growth as a teacher. Figure 22.3 contains a list of journals of particular assistance to teachers interested in improving reading and writing instruction.

Finally, many colleges and universities offer programs of graduate study for teachers. These institutions offer a wide range of courses and workshops relating recent trends and findings to the problems of teaching. Participation in such graduate education is an effective way of pursuing both short-term and long-term goals. It not only broadens your perspective on your classroom work, but serves as the basis for salary increases in many states.

Informal Resources

Helpful ideas can come from a variety of informal sources: students, colleagues, your school district, and your own travel. The most accessible and

FIGURE 22.2   Professional Organizations

Association for Supervision and Curriculum Development
125 N. West St.
Alexandria, VA 22314–2798

International Reading Association
800 Berksdale Road
PO Box 8139
Newark, NJ 19711

State affiliates of International Reading Association

National Council of Teachers of English
1111 Kenyon Road
Urbana, IL 61801

State affiliates of National Council of Teachers of English

possibly the most overlooked resource is your students themselves. By listening to students and questioning them about their interests and concerns, you can get many useful ideas for modifying your instruction and for incorporating student interests into your materials and activities.

A second informal resource is other teachers. Teaching is an isolated profession in which you spend most of your professional time with children, and very little with professional colleagues. Yet, colleagial interaction is one of the most helpful ways to maintain professional growth. One way to ensure colleagial interaction is to have a "buddy system" in which you team with another teacher from your own school or from another school in the area. You can periodically exchange ideas, materials, and innovations that have worked. This plan can also include exchange visits to one another's classrooms. Adapting good ideas of other teachers is encouraged in teaching. If somebody else has a good idea, borrow it and see if you can make it fit your own situation; if you have a good idea, encourage your colleagues to use it with their classes. This kind of exchange promotes the growth essential for teaching.

School districts also provide informal sources for professional growth. Most school districts, for instance, provide resource centers where the most recent ideas about instructional improvements are cataloged and displayed so that teachers can use them. Many districts have "professional days" in which teachers can take time off for professional growth. A visit to another teacher's classroom is an excellent way to spend this time because it gives you another perspective on your own work. Finally, school districts offer various in-service programs. Whether attendance is voluntary or mandatory, these programs are an excellent way to develop yourself professionally. Also, many of these in-service programs are backed up by a formal, district-wide

FIGURE 22.3   Professional Journals

Elementary School Journal
University of Chicago Press
PO Box 37005
Chicago, IL 60637

Instruction
PO Box 6099
Duluth, MN 55806-9799

Journal of Reading
IRA 800 Berksdale Road
PO Box 8139
Newark, NJ 19711

Learning Magazine
530 University Avenue
Palo Alto, CA 94301

Reading Psychology
1010 Vermont Avenue, NW Suite 612
Washington, DC 20005

Reading Teacher
IRA
800 Berksdale Road
PO Box 8139
Newark, NJ 19711

School Library Journal
PR Bowher Co.
PO Box 67
Whitinsville, MA 01588

staff development program where participation can earn you salary increases or other incentives. All such district-level activities are excellent sources of ideas and innovations.

Finally, your own travel can be a resource for growth. For instance, you could plan your travel around a professional theme, such as traveling in foreign countries to visit and compare school systems or traveling through our country with the goal of collecting local folk lore for use in your classes. In short, there are many formal and informal resources available to teachers who want to grow and get better at their profession.

MONITORING AND EVALUATING PROGRESS

In addition to taking advantage of available resources for professional growth, you need to monitor and evaluate your progress toward the goals you have set as part of your professional plan. At designated points, you should sit down and examine the data you have collected regarding how well or how poorly you are achieving your goals. Data gathering and evaluation need not be formal. However, it does need to be regular and honest.

Increasing Your Impact on Students

There are many ways to collect data about your impact on students. One way is to keep careful records of your students' progress toward the goals you have set and to evaluate yourself in terms of how well your students achieve these goals. For instance, if you want students to develop certain concepts

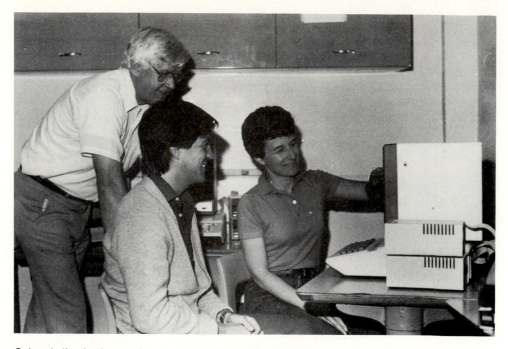

School district in-service programs help keep teachers current. (Robert Bawden)

about reading, you must keep records of their progress and review these periodically. Likewise, if you want students to develop certain attitudes or to become more aware of how reading works, you must keep track of this. If you want students to become better writers, you must keep samples of their writing throughout the year and periodically review their progress. By setting goals and then reviewing the data regarding how well your students are achieving these goals, you will find yourself modifying your teaching in order to meet these goals. Such change is evidence of professional vitality and growth.

In addition to keeping track of student progress on academic work, you should also keep track of their awareness of lesson content. It is a good practice to periodically interview students after lessons, asking them what they think you were teaching, why you were teaching it, and how to do it. If several students give responses which indicate misconceptions about the lesson, you should re-evaluate your teaching and make changes that will improve your students' awareness of what is going on during instruction.

Reflective Journals

A second way to keep track of your professional growth is to keep a reflective journal. Either daily or several times a week, write your thoughts about your progress. Note what is going well and what is not going so well. Include your ideas, thoughts, and feelings and periodically evaluate your journal and yourself. Ask yourself if you are progressing the way you want to or if there is a problem that needs to be resolved. If possible, share this information with another professional and have that person help you evaluate it. Decide with that person whether to continue as you have been or to make changes.

Self-Monitoring

A third way to monitor and evaluate your professional growth is to taperecord (or videotape) your own instruction. It is very difficult to be aware of what you are doing while engaged in the act of teaching. However, you can be much more objective and perceptive when you listen to yourself or watch yourself. It is particularly helpful if you look for only one thing at a time. For instance, listen to the tape once to determine how many times you were distracted from the main focus of the lesson; listen another time to determine whether each student was given an equal opportunity to respond, listen another time to see how explicit you were in showing students how to do the task, and so on. Each time you will note things to improve your teaching. Once you are aware of these shortcomings, you can take steps to improve them. If you are not aware, however, you can never improve. Again, sharing and discussing the results of these analyses with a colleague is better than solitary evaluation.

IMPORTANCE OF PERSONAL GROWTH

Teachers should be well-balanced people. They must not only be competent professionals, but also be interesting persons. This means that professional development is not enough—it must be accompanied by personal development.

Because teaching is such a demanding task, it can become all-absorbing. You can become so devoted to helping students achieve and grow that all of your time is allocated to professional tasks. In short, you can become a highly professional drudge.

This must be avoided. Teaching is person-to-person interaction and, in the final analysis, your impact on students will depend both on your professional competencies and on how interesting you are as a person. Your students' desire to interact with you will depend on how they see you as a person. Attention and respect is not awarded to drudges, it is given to teachers who are alive and vital in their private lives as well as their professional lives.

To achieve vitality as a person, you have to cultivate interests beyond the classroom. You have to know what is going on in the world around you, and you should become involved in community, state, and national affairs. This does not necessarily mean that you must be a political activist, merely

Having a variety of personal interests helps balance the demands of classroom teaching. (Robert Bawden)

that you should take an active interest in contemporary affairs. You do this by reading more than just professional journals.

Your personal development means developing your own interests and aptitudes. Because teaching is stressful and absorbing work, it is particularly important that you have a rich family and social life and that you have hobbies and activities that absorb your energies and attention once school is done. In short, you should be a multidimensional person who has a variety of interests—someone who paints, or gardens, or flies airplanes, or refinishes furniture, or runs marathons, or explores caves. These other interests will help balance the professional devotion required to be a classroom teacher.

FACING THE REALITIES

All the previously mentioned plans for continuing your professional growth are helpful. However, one major problem remains. It involves the realities of classroom life, which often force otherwise dedicated teachers to become technicians who follow prescriptions rather than professionals who exercise professional control.

It is alarming that so many teachers act like technicians. At a time when the teaching of reading must be thoughtful, we find too many teachers who are mechanical, routinized, and procedural. The result is students who respond to reading in mechanical ways, who see reading as tasks to be completed rather than genuine communication, and who rarely choose to read once school is over.

It is not accurate to say that such technical teachers are simply unwilling to put forth the necessary effort. Most teachers try hard and want to do well by their students. However, the complexities of the job simply overwhelm many teachers. There just seems to be too much to attend to and not enough help, too many demands and not enough time, too many pressures and not enough reward, and too many students who have difficulty learning and not enough techniques that work. Eventually, some teachers stop trying to be innovative and fall back on prescriptions of others, which they can follow in routinized ways.

The typical scenario proceeds something like this. A new teacher accepts a position in a school district that uses a mandated basal text program and expects high achievement on the state assessment test. The principal frequently visits the new teacher's classroom to ensure that the basal is being followed and the students are being prepared for the test. Following the lead of the veteran teachers in the building, the new teacher uses the basal text prescriptions and prepares students for the test. Instruction lacks interest or relevancy, students get bored, the success rate is low, and students become unmotivated. Soon the teacher becomes discouraged and casts about for "the answer." The school district and the state either encourage the use of another prescription or closer adherence to the one already in use. The teacher follows these directions but the results are the same. Yet another prescription is suggested; the teacher tries to implement it but has little success. The teacher's frustration and boredom continue, and eventually all signs of freshness, innovation, and vibrancy disappear. The teacher either gives in to mindless technical behavior, or gives up the profession entirely.

This is a dim picture. Does it have to be this way? We think not. The source of technical behavior in teachers is rooted in the reality of the workplace, but there are ways to deal with these realities and to fight off the pressures to become a technician. Three suggestions follow.

Be Realistic Classroom teaching in our society *is* difficult. The pressures are great and the rewards in terms of money and prestige are small. Teachers are expected to be public servants who can work miracles with large numbers of students with a minimum of resources. They must have the strength to maintain cognitive control over their own teaching while fighting off the pressures for conformity and regimentation that come from school and society. They are expected to resolve inherently unresolvable problems while working in isolation from their colleagues.

The task is difficult, and you must be realistic. You need to understand that students will not always respond with enthusiasm, that not all students make dramatic progress, that there is a bureaucracy in teaching, and that classroom teachers often seem powerless. You must also understand that there are no panaceas in teaching. There will never be one right way to teach reading to all students; we will always be seeking better ways. The nature of teaching is to constantly strive to improve.

Accept Dilemmas You must also learn that teaching is full of dilemmas. You must understand that survival in the classroom demands keeping students busy, but that this is not necessarily teaching. You must understand that your task is to demonstrate how to cognitively process language, even though no one knows for sure how this cognition occurs for different people. You must think in terms of "real world" applications of reading, even though the school district, the state, and our society seem to place more value on test scores that measure the performance of isolated skills. And you must stress cognition, strategic awareness, and mental processing when the instructional materials you are required to use often stress memory, rote, and accuracy.

Maintain a Vision Finally, you should have a vision that transcends the constraints of the workplace. Reading is more than skills and more than a subject; you must see it as part of a language communication system. You must view the goals of reading not only as getting the message but also as positive responses and accurate concepts of what reading is. Teaching is a person-to-person interaction that no script or machine or prescription will ever replace. It will be helpful to keep the following in mind:

1. The rewards of teaching lie in presiding over nondramatic growth, which you witness daily in various kinds of students.

2. No outside authority governs what happens when you close your classroom door and begin teaching.

3. No day will be like any other.

4. No matter how long you teach, there will always be new challenges.

5. The cliché "the youth of America is in the hands of its teachers" is not a cliché at all but the truth.

To summarize, you must love and value teaching but not romanticize it. It is a demanding and difficult task, and progress results more from diligent planning, the reflective application of pedagogical knowledge, and tenacity in making and sticking with decisions than from flashy demonstrations, intuitive interactions, or dramatic confrontations. It can demand all your time and effort and produce few tangible results. When these realities are consciously acknowledged and dealt with, teachers can fight off burnout and the temptation to be technicians. To know what the realities are is to arm against them. If your expectations are realistic and you are prepared to deal with them you cannot be surprised.

SUMMARY

Effective teaching is associated with vital teachers who make their own decisions and, in so doing, maintain control of their instruction. Teachers who do not make conscious efforts to remain vital by continuing their professional growth become professionally stale. Consequently, the best teachers continually search for better ways to do things, develop realistic ways to assess their own work, and develop programs of professional development for themselves. In addition, the most effective teachers make conscious efforts to be well-rounded, interesting human beings since personal development often carries over into professional work. And, finally, effective teachers are realistic about the demands of teaching. When you make the effort to continue your professional growth while also being realistic, teaching can offer you a fulfilling professional life.

SUGGESTED ADDITIONAL READINGS

BAILEY, M. H., & GUERRA, C. L. (1984). Inservice education in reading: Three points of view. *Reading Teacher, 38*(2), 174–176.

BEAN, R. M., & EICHELBERGER, R. T. (1985). Changing the role of reading specialists: From pull-out to in-class programs. *Reading Teacher, 38*(7), 648–653.

CASSIDY, J. (1977). Reporting pupil progress in reading—parents vs. teachers. *Reading Teacher, 31*(3), 294–296.

CHARNOCK, J. (1982). Notes from the reading-language skills teacher. *Reading Teacher, 36*(2), 132–135.

CRISCUOLO, N. P. (1980). Effective ways to communicate with parents about reading. *Reading Teacher, 34*(2), 164–166.

CUNNINGHAM, P. M. (1977). Match informal evaluation to your teaching practices. *Reading Teacher, 31*(1), 51–56.

DREHER, M. J., & SINGER, H. (1985). Parents' attitudes toward reports of standardized reading test results. *Reading Teacher, 38*(7), 624–632.

GUTHRIE, J. T. (1983). TV effects on achievement. *Reading Teacher, 36*(7), 732–734.

JONGSMA, E. (1985). Homework: Is it worthwhile? *Reading Teacher, 36*(7), 702–704.

LAPP, D., FLOOD, J., & GLECKMAN, G. (1982). Classroom practices can make use of what researchers learn. *Reading Teacher, 35*(5), 578–585.

RHODES, L. K., & HILL, M. W. (1985). Supporting reading in the home—naturally: Selected materials for parents. *Reading Teacher, 38*(7), 619–623.

SITTIG, L. H. (1982). Involving parents and children in reading for fun. *Reading Teacher, 36*(2), 166–169.

VUKELICH, C. (1984). Parents' role in the reading process: A review of practical suggestions and ways to communicate with parents. *Reading Teacher, 37*(6), 472–477.

RESEARCH BASE

BARNES, H., PUTNAM, J., & WANOUS, D. (1979). Learning from research adaptation. *Adapting educational research: Staff development approaches.* Norman, OK: University of Oklahoma Teacher Corps Research Adaptation Cluster.

DUFFY, G., & ROEHLER, L. (1986). Constraints on teacher change. *Journal of Teacher Education, 37*(1), 55–59.

DUFFY, G., ROEHLER, L., & PUTNAM, J. (1987). Putting the teacher in control: Instructional decision making and basal textbooks. *Elementary School Journal, 87*(3), 357–366.

JOYCE, B., & SHOWERS, B. (1983). *Power in staff development through research on teaching.* Alexandria, VA: Association for Supervision and Curriculum Development.

ROEHLER, L. (1983). Moving toward integration through inservice. In B. Busching & J. Schwartz (Eds.), *Integrating the language arts in the elementary school.* Urbana, IL: National Council of Teachers of English.

ROEHLER, L., WESSELMAN, R., & PUTNAM, J. (1984). *Training teachers for instructional change in reading: A descriptive study* (Research Series No. 143). East Lansing: Michigan State University, Institute for Research on Teaching.

SCHWAAB, J. (1969). The practical: A language for curriculum. *School Review, 79,* 1–23.

Glossary

Ability group Teacher-assigned instructional group in which all student members have about the same ability; used primarily for developing *content and process goals;* contrasted with collaborative groups.

Academic task The work students engage in.

Acountability Holding teachers and students responsible for student achievement; frequently associated with assessment testing mandated by state law.

Activate background knowledge Accessing prior knowledge about *topic,* author's *purpose,* and text structure for the purpose of making initial predictions about what will happen; *initiating strategy.*

Activity flow Maintaining a smooth, uninterrupted flow of classroom activities as a way of keeping students on task.

Affix A prefix, suffix, or inflectional ending added to a root word; used in *structural analysis* for *decoding.*

Allocated time Designated amount of time assigned to academic content; the time when reading is normally taught, for instance.

Application Ability to *transfer* what has been learned from the classroom to the real world; using reading strategies for reading *recreational* or *functional text.*

Application stage *Stage of developing reading growth* typically associated with grades 5 through 8; curricular emphasis is on *content,* such as social studies or science; contrasted with *readiness, initial mastery, expanded fundamentals,* and *power stages.*

Assessment Collection of data to be used in making decisions; crucial to instruction, especially *direct instruction,* because good decisions cannot be made about instructional objectives until student performance is assessed; may involve *formal* or *informal tests.*

Attitude Concepts and feelings one possesses about a particular activity or idea; in this book, the concepts and feelings students possess about reading and writing.

Attitude goals One of the three major curricular goals in reading; consist of developing a positive response to reading and an accurate *concept* of what reading is; viewed as the foundation of an effective instructional program because little can be learned unless students have accurate concepts and positive feelings about reading.

Auditory discrimination Ability to distinguish one sound from another; in reading, for example, the ability to distinguish the sound of the letter *d* from the sound of the letter *b;* contrasted with *visual discrimination.*

Author's chair A technique in which a student writer is interviewed by student peers about something he or she has written.

Author's purpose Author's reason for composing *text;* readers analyze author's purpose to aid in understanding text meaning; contrasted with *topic* and *text* structure.

Basal reading textbook The reading textbook used in most U.S. classrooms; each text program consists of a students' edition of stories written to match the average ability level of the grade at which it is to be used, a teachers' edition containing instructional suggestions, and a variety of supplementary materials.

Basal text approach Organizing reading instruction around the stories and books in a basal text series; students read each story in each *basal* reading *textbook* and complete associated workbook and text materials under the supervision of their teachers; contrasted with *language experience* and *personalized reading approaches.*

Book part strategy *Locational study strategy* used to find information in books; includes table of contents, index, glossary, etc.; contrasted with *library, reference source,* and *graphics strategies.*

Buffer Person recruited by a teacher to assist with routine classroom tasks; can be an adult, an older student, or a student in the class.

Cognition Act of knowing; associated with the *mental processing* readers do to make sense out of *text.*

Collaborative group/sharing Teacher-assigned or self-started temporary grouping structure used primarily for developing *attitude goals;* students with varying abilities work together to solve a problem or to complete a project; important aspect of the *social-emotional environment;* contrasted with *ability groups.*

Combined approach Organizing reading instruction by combining a variety of approaches; occurs both directly (with *basal text* activities) and less directly (with *language experience* and *personalized reading* activities); teachers use each approach to develop specific reading goals.

Comprehension Process of making sense of an author's or speaker's message; reconstructing an author's message for *recreational* or *functional* purposes.

Comprehension strategy Used by readers to determine text meaning; includes *initiating*, *during-reading*, and *post-reading strategies*; all are metacognitive.

Concept Understanding students have of a particular phenomenon; the sum of one's *direct* and *vicarious experiences* with that phenomenon; organized into a network of related understandings (the *schema/schemata* for the phenomenon).

Concept book Children's book written to help preschool and primary grade students develop a particular idea; examples: a book on colors or a book on clouds.

Connected text Printed matter that represents a complete message being communicated within a meaningful environment.

Connotative language Using words that trigger emotional responses; example: "arrogant" has a negative connotation, but "confident" has a positive connotation.

Constraint Limits on a teacher's freedom to perform various tasks of teaching; example: society has certain expectations that teachers must take into consideration when making instructional decisions.

Content Message conveyed by a *text* or speech.

Content area reading Textbook reading done in various content areas such as science, social studies, etc.

Content goals One of the three major curricular goals in reading; consist of guiding students to an understanding of the messages conveyed by particular *functional* or *recreational* texts.

Context *Semantic* elements of *text* or speech that immediately precede or follow a sentence or word and can be analyzed to predict meaning.

Context clue Clue embedded in *text* that helps readers decode unknown words; contrasted with *structural analysis* and *phonics*.

Contract Written agreement between a teacher and a student stating what a student will be accountable for on a particular project.

Controlled text Text created by teachers for purposes of providing students practice with a particular skill or strategy; contrasted with *natural text*.

Cooperative group See *collaborative group*.

Critical question Question that requires students to make a judgment about the meaning an author is conveying in *text;* requires readers to go beyond reconstructing the author's message to make a value judgment about the message; contrasted with *inferential* and *literal questions*.

Critical reading Making a judgment about the meaning an author is conveying in *text;* requires readers to go beyond reconstructing the author's message to make a value judgment about the message; usually associated with *post-reading strategies;* emphasized in upper grades.

Curriculum That which is to be taught and how it is organized for instruction; in reading, it includes *attitude*, *process*, and *content goals*.

Decode To figure out what an unknown word is; to use *context clues*, *structural analysis*, or *phonics* or a combination of these to identify an unknown word.

Denotative language Using neutral terms that tend to be objective in nature; example: referring to a person as "slim" rather than "skinny."

Developmental progression The steady, progressive pattern that most students follow in learning to read; the instruction provided in a particular grade is part of a development progression; the different points along this line of development are called *stages of development reading growth*.

Direct experience An experience one actually has; contrasted with a second-hand, or *vicarious*, experience; example: seeing the Empire State Building.

Direct instruction Developing curricular goals by overtly interacting with students; often characterized by an abundance of teacher talk; used primarily for *process* and *content goals;* contrasted with *indirect instruction*.

Direct teacher mediation Teachers' attempts to guide students' understanding; usually through instructional dialogue; contrasted with *indirect instruction*.

Directed listening activity (DLA) A technique for structuring listening activities to ensure that students understand the content; includes introduction, purpose setting, listening, discussion, and closure.

Directed reading lesson (DRL)   Structuring reading activities to ensure that students understand the content; includes introduction (*topic*, words, *purpose*), reading, and discussion (clarifying, summarizing, extending understanding).

Directed reading-thinking activity (DRTA)   Structuring reading activities; similar to the Directed reading activity, except that students are involved in making predictions about the purposes for reading.

Drafting stage   Stage of the writing in which the writer composes a first draft of the message.

Drill-and-practice model   Technique for teaching *routine skills* through *direct instruction;* emphasis is on repetition and memory; format includes introducing, *modeling, practice,* and *application.*

During-reading strategy   *Metacognitive strategy* readers use while reading text to monitor their understanding and to repair any blockages to meaning; contrasted with *initiating, post-reading,* and *study strategies.*

Editing stage   Stage of the writing process in which writers revise drafts of the message for purposes of clarity and precision of meaning; contrasted with *planning* and *drafting stages.*

Evaluating strategy   *Post-reading strategy* used to make judgments about the text's message; example: discriminating fantasy and reality; see *critical reading.*

Expanded fundamentals stage   Stage of *developmental reading growth* typically associated with grades 3 and 4; curricular emphasis is on learning and applying the fundamental skills of reading, particularly comprehension; contrasted with *readiness, initial mastery, application,* and *power stages.*

Expectation   Tendency of humans to do what is expected of them; example: children from homes where reading and learning are valued tend to have positive expectations about learning to read.

Explanation   Process of providing students with information and assistance needed to construct a *schema* about a particular phenomenon; associated with *direct instruction;* uses explicit statements, *modeling,* and *guided practice.*

Expository text   *Text* written primarily to inform; contrasted with *narrative text.*

Expressive language mode   The language modes of speaking and writing, both of which are used to express meaning; contrasted with *receptive language mode.*

Fix-it strategy   *During-reading strategy* used to repair a meaning blockage; contrasted with *fluency* and *monitoring.*

Fluency   Relative smoothness of constructing meaning from *text;* fluent reading reflects the reader's clear understanding of the vocabulary used, the *topic,* the author's *purpose,* and the *text structure* and is evidenced by correct intonation and an absence of interruptions.

Formal test   *Assessment* device published by testing companies and used by teachers in accordance with specified procedures; contrasted with *informal test.*

Frustration reading level   Traditionally, reading materials too difficult for a particular student to read; student fails to recognize at least 95 percent of the words instantly or fails to answer 75 percent of the questions posed about the content of the text; contrasted with *instructional* and *independent reading levels.*

Functional text   Created to inform; examples: textbooks, encyclopedias, and catalogues; see *expository text;* contrasted with *recreational text.*

Function word   In the English language a word that signals a *syntactic* meaning as opposed to a *semantic* meaning; example: prepositions are function words because they signal the beginning of a prepositional phrase rather than provide a lexical meaning.

Graphic strategies   *Locational study strategies* used to find information in graphics such as maps, tables, charts, and graphs; contrasted with *book part, library,* and *reference source strategies.*

Guided practice   Attempting to move students gradually to a point where they can use strategies independently.

How-to-change pattern   Routine teachers establish regarding what students are to do when changing from one activity to another.

How-to-start pattern   Routine teachers establish regarding what students are to do when starting new activities.

How-to-stop patterns   Routine teachers establish regarding what students are to do when they finish their work.

Independent activity/practice Activities students do by themselves while the teacher is teaching other students in a reading group; often referred to as *seatwork*.

Independent reading level Traditionally, reading materials comfortable for a particular student to read; student recognizes at least 99 percent of the words instantly and answers 90 percent of the questions posed about the content of the *text;* contrasted with *frustration* and *instructional reading levels.*

Indirect instruction Developing curricular goals by providing a *literate environment* designed to help students "discover" certain things; characterized by an absence of direct guidance by the teacher; used primarily for *attitude goals;* contrasted with *direct instruction.*

Individualized reading Synonym for *personalized reading.*

Inference/Inferential Process of constructing the meaning an author implies but does not state explicitly; requires readers to make predictions using a combination of *prior knowledge* and text-based clues.

Inferential question Question that requires students to make an inference; students must determine the meaning an author implies but does not state explicitly; contrasted with *critical* and *literal questions.*

Informal test *Assessment* device that depends heavily on teacher judgment; these are often teacher-made tests; contrasted with *formal tests.*

Initial mastery stage *Stage of developmental reading growth* typically associated with grades 1 and 2; curricular emphasis is on learning and applying the fundamental skills of reading, particularly *word recognition;* contrasted with *readiness, expanded fundamentals, application,* and *power stages.*

Initiating strategy Metacognitive strategy readers use as they begin to read a text; involves making initial predictions about *topic,* author's *purpose,* and *text structure;* contrasted with *during-reading, post-reading,* and *study strategies.*

Instruction Intentional use of academic work, *presentations,* and interactive dialogue to provide information students need to build *schemata* regarding desired curricular goals; contrasted with *learning* and *teaching.*

Instructional reading level Traditionally, reading materials that a student can read with teacher assistance; student recognizes 95 to 99 percent of the words instantly and answers 75 to 90 percent of the questions posed about the content of the *text;* contrasted with *frustration* and *instructional reading levels.*

Integration Forming into a whole all four language modes in the classroom; listening, speaking, reading, and writing are interrelated; an important characteristic of the *literate environment.*

Intellectual environment Part of the classroom *literate environment;* characterized by expectations that language will be used meaningfully and by challenges to get involved with meaningful language communication; integrated with *physical* and social-emotional environments.

Interaction pattern Routine teachers establish regarding conversation and other socialization in the classroom.

Internal motivator Motivator teachers can use to stimulate particularly good responses from students; examples: giving students choices, opportunities to act like adults, and opportunities to alter or create language.

Invented spelling Unorthodox spelling of words that young children invent during *preliterate stages.*

Language arts Curriculum subject that integrates listening, speaking, reading, and writing.

Language convention Procedure for dealing with language that has been agreed on in the interest of expediting communication; example: left-to-right progress across a line of print; *routine skill;* contrasted with *linguistic unit.*

Language experience approach (LEA) Organizing reading instruction around materials written by students; students engage in experiences, talk about the experiences, write about the experiences, and then read what they have written; contrasted with *basal text* and *personalized reading approaches.*

Library strategy Locational study strategy used to find information in the library; includes looking at the card catalog and knowing the Dewey Decimal system; contrasted with *book part, reference source,* and *graphics strategies.*

Linguistic unit Units of printed symbols associated with written language; examples: letters, words; *routine skill;* contrasted with *language conventions.*

Literacy Ability to successfully communicate

using the four *language modes* (reading, writing, speaking, and listening).

Literal question   Question that requires students to answer in terms of what is written on the printed page; contrasted with *critical* and *inferential questions.*

Literate environment   Classroom environment permeated with examples of literacy and language in action; various kinds of student communications, both oral and written, are encouraged; *integration* of the four *language modes* is emphasized in classroom activities; includes the *physical, intellectual,* and *social-emotional environments;* contrasted with *direct teacher mediation.*

Locational strategy   *Study strategy* used to locate information; examples: *book part, library,* and *graphic strategies;* contrasted with *rate, remembering, organizing,* and *study habit strategies.*

Long-term memory   Information accessible to recall for long periods of time after experiences; contrasted with *short-term memory.*

Look back   Used during reading; a *fix-it strategy;* when a problem is encountered in reading *text,* readers look back in the text for *semantic* and *syntactic* cues.

Mainstreaming   Placing students with special learning problems (and who would normally be taught by special education teachers) in regular elementary classrooms.

Mediation   Thinking about something and, in the process, constructing an altered meaning; see *direct teacher mediation.*

Mental modeling   Teachers explain their own thinking process identified in a *task analysis* by showing students how they themselves use it.

Mental processing   Reasoning done to construct meaning from text; associated with *metacognitive strategies.*

Metacognition   Conscious awareness of how thinking is done; in this book, conscious awareness of the reasoning involved in making sense out of written text.

Metacognitive control   Being consciously aware of how reasoning is done so that it can be monitored and controlled; see also *self-regulation.*

Metacognitive strategy   Strategy students use in a conscious way to meet *process goals;* awareness of what to do and how to do it; includes *initiating, during-reading, post-reading,* and *study strategies.*

Model   Showing students how to do a task with the expectation that they will then emulate the model; in reading, modeling often involves teachers' talking about how they think through a task, since much of reading is *cognitive.*

Modified directed reading lesson (MDRL)   Structuring a reading lesson so that skills and strategies are taught before reading the story in which they will be applied; format includes an introduction of the story, instruction of the skill or strategy, purpose setting for both story content and skill or strategy application, reading, discussion of the story and the skill or strategy application, and closure.

Monitoring   *During reading strategy;* process of keeping track of one's own meaning getting while reading; includes monitoring for unknown words, unrecognized words, author's meaning, and beyond author's meaning; contrasted with *fluency* and *fix-it strategies.*

Motivation   Condition affecting student perseverance; affected primarily by the degree to which students value the activity being pursued and by the amount of success experienced while pursuing it.

Narrative text   *Text* written primarily to entertain, contrasted with *expository text.*

Natural text   *Text* that has not been altered from the form in which the author(s) published it; contrasted with *controlled text.*

Nook-and-cranny time   Short periods of time during the school day when no academic tasks are being pursued; useful for additional reading instruction.

On-your-own strategy   Strategy readers use to relate questions about *content* to answers in the *text;* readers rely on their background knowledge; contrasted with *right-there* and *think-and-search strategies;* see QARs.

Oral round-robin reading   Traditional technique for listening to students read orally—each student reads aloud in turn while the teacher listens.

Organizing strategy   Includes *study* and *post-reading strategies.*

Personalized reading approach   Organizing instruction around materials students select from the school or room library; students select a book of their choice, read at their own pace, and receive individual help from teachers in conferences.

Phonics/Phonic analysis   Process of using letters and letter sounds to sound out and *decode* an unknown word; contrasted with *context clues* and *structural analysis.*

Phonogram   Common phonic spelling pattern; examples: *at* in *cat, bat,* and *sat* and *et* in *bet, met,* and *set.*

Physical environment   Part of the classroom *literate environment;* characterized by physical evidences of literacy and by physically attractive areas that encourage students to engage in meaningful reading; integrated with *intellectual* and *social-emotional environments.*

Planning stage   Stage of the writing process in which writers gather and organize information in preparation for composing; contrasted with *drafting* and *editing stages.*

Post-reading strategy   *Metacognitive strategies* readers use after reading a selection; involves reflecting about a selection's content for purposes of reorganizing and evaluating what was read.

Power stage   *Stage of developmental reading growth* typically associated with grades 9 through 12; curricular emphasis is on the highly technical aspects of reading and studying; contrasted with *readiness, initial mastery, expanded fundamentals,* and *application stages.*

Practice   Repetition and drill of an act to make it habitual.

Preliterate writing   Doodling preschoolers and kindergarteners do to "write" stories before they learn how printed language works.

Preprimer   First book in the *basal text approach;* consists of pictures and a limited number of words and short sentences.

Presentation   Part of the lesson in which teachers present information to students; usually includes lesson introduction, *modeling,* and demonstrations.

Primer   Book after the *preprimer* in the *basal text approach;* an easy reading book.

Print awareness   Awareness of what printed symbols are and how they work; first stage in *word recognition;* associated with *language conventions* and *linguistic units.*

Prior knowledge   Background experience (*direct* and *vicarious*) accessible for use in making sense out of text.

Procedural pattern   Predetermined organizational procedures that become classroom routines.

Process   Means by which students attain a goal; in this book, the means by which students comprehend *text.*

Process goals   One of the three major curricular goals in reading; consist of understanding how the reading system works and how to apply strategies when reading.

Purpose   In this textbook, why students read a particular text; the particular information being sought from a printed text reflects the purpose; see also *author's purpose.*

Question-answer relationship (QAR)   Technique for comprehending *functional text* in which students analyze the relationship between what the question asks for and what the text offers; includes *right there, think-and-search,* and *on-your-own strategies.*

Rate strategy   Study strategy in which students decide the most efficient rate of reading for the situation; examples include *scanning, skimming,* and careful pacing; contrasted with *locational, remembering, organizing,* and *study habit strategies.*

Readiness   Curricular content in reading designed to get young students ready to read; see *readiness stage.*

Readiness stage   *Stage of developmental reading growth* typically associated with preschool and kindergarten; curricular emphasis is on building positive responses to reading and accurate concepts of what reading is; contrasted with *initial mastery, expanded fundamentals, application,* and *power stage.*

Reading program   Organizing structure used to teach reading; most teachers use either the *basal text approach,* the *language experience approach,* the *personalized approach,* or a *combined approach.*

Receptive language mode   The language modes of listening and reading, both of which are used to receive meaning; contrasted with *expressive language modes.*

Recreational text   *Text* created to entertain or enrich; examples: stories, poems, and plays; see also *narrative text,* contrasted with *functional text.*

Reference source strategies   *Locational study strategy* used to find information in reference sources; includes dictionaries, encyclopedias, atlases, etc.; contrasted with *book part, library,* and *graphics strategies.*

Remembering   Recalling at a later time information comprehended in reading or listening situations.

Remembering strategy   *Study strategy* in which students consciously attempt to retain information; includes *SQ3R,* summarizing, and stating main ideas; contrasted with *locational, rate, organizing,* and *study habit strategies.*

Repeated reading   Technique for developing fluency; students are directed to read a passage over and over again until they can read it smoothly.

Restructuring   Combining prior knowledge with new knowledge; the result is usually a somewhat different meaning from what the author or speaker intended, or a "restructured understanding."

Right-there strategy   *Strategy* readers use to relate questions about *content* to answers in the text; readers examine what is right there on the page for clues to disrupted meaning; contrasted with *think-and-search* and *on-your-own strategies;* see also *QAR.*

Routine skill   Procedure readers can employ from memory without conscious awareness of what they are doing; a *process goal;* includes *language conventions* and *linguistic units.*

Safety valve   Learning center or activity available to students; not changed daily; need not be associated with academic work in the classroom; tends to be viewed by students as fun; examples: vocabulary games, board games, journal writing, and recreational reading.

Scanning   Very fast rate of reading; used as a *study strategy* to quickly locate sections of *text* that are likely to contain desired information.

Schema, pl. schemata   Mental structure of one's concepts about a phenomenon; based on *direct* and *vicarious experiences;* see also *concept.*

Scope-and-sequence chart   Chart published by *basal text* companies that visually displays all the skills and strategies taught throughout students' K–8 reading programs.

Seatwork   Work teachers give students when they are not working under the teacher's direct supervision.

Self-concept   Image that people hold of themselves; developed from perceptions of what they and other people think of them.

Self-fulfilling prophecy   Phenomenon of human behavior characterizing the tendency of hu-

mans to fulfill the expectations they set for themselves.

Self-regulation   Imposing personal control over comprehension of text; see also *metacognitive control.*

Semantic   Meaning associated with words or clusters of words.

Semantic map   *Organizing study strategy;* requires grouping *concepts* and labeling the grouped concepts.

Short-term memory   Information accessible to recall for only short periods of time after experiences; contrasted with *long-term memory.*

Sight word   Word readers recognize instantly when encountered in *text;* a routine skill.

Skimming   Method of moving eyes rapidly over text; used as a *rate study strategy* to search likely sections of *text* for key words that signal the desired information; contrasted with *scanning* and careful pacing.

Social-emotional environment   Part of the classroom literate environment; characterized by warmth, acceptance, and agreed-on procedures for the interchange of ideas; factors include social interactions and *collaborative sharing;* interchanged with *physical* and *intellectual environments.*

SQ3R   *Remembering study strategy;* SQ3R stands for survey, question, read, recite, and review.

Stages of developmental reading growth   Different points along the line of *developmental reading;* includes *readiness, initial mastery, expanded fundamentals, application,* and *power stages.*

Standardized tests   Developed by testing companies; field-tested on large samples of students; used to measure ability; norms are established and used to compare students' performance with students in other places.

Story structure   Elements that organize a story; usually include setting, character(s), problem, story events, and resolution of the problem.

Story map   Analysis of a story according to its structure; usually based on elements such as setting, character(s), problem, story events, and resolution of the problem.

Strategic   Flexible, adaptable, and conscious use of knowledge about reading and how it works.

Strategic behavior   Actions and thoughts in which students use strategies.

Structural analysis   Using prefixes, suffixes, inflectional endings, and root words to identify words and decode their meanings; contrasted with *context clues* and *phonics.*

Structured overviews   Technique for graphically displaying key words associated with a topic and how they are related; used primarily with *functional text;* contrasted with *QARs* and *study guides.*

Student engagement   Getting students to focus attention on the academic task and to keep on that task.

Study habit   *Study strategies* that aid in organizing time and promote efficient study; examples: prioritizing study assignments, allocating time, following directions, and test taking; contrasted with *locational, rate, remembering,* and *organizing strategies.*

Study strategy   *Metacognitive strategies* expert readers use to efficiently gather and use information from a variety of text sources in response to the demands of study; includes *locational, rate, remembering, organizing,* and *study habit strategies.*

Survey, question, read, recite, and review (SQ3R)   Five-step process used in teaching *content goals;* designed to help readers recall information.

Syntactic   Meaning associated with the grammatical structure of a language; includes word order, function words, and so on.

Task analysis   Process in which teachers decide what steps are involved in performing a particular task.

Teacher-pupil planning   Process by which teachers and students, through discussion, decide what will be studied and how it will be studied.

Teaching   All the tasks associated with being a classroom teacher; does not necessarily refer to developing intended curricular goals; contrasted with *learning* and *instruction.*

Text   Sum of the message being read or spoken; authors compose text to communicate messages or ideas; the meaning is the author's; the text carries the meaning, but readers must reconstruct the author's meaning from the cues embedded in the text.

Text structure   Way a written text is organized; example: newspaper articles have a structure different from epic poems, plays, and so on; readers use *prior knowledge* about text structure to aid in constructing meaning from text; contrasted with *topic* and *purpose.*

Think and search strategy   Strategy readers use to relate questions about *content* to answers in the *text;* readers examine and think about information implied by the author as a means of repairing disrupted meaning; contrasted with *right-there* and *on-your-own strategies;* see also *QAR.*

Topic   What a written selection is about; readers use *prior knowledge* about topic to aid in constructing meaning from *text.*

Transfer   Ability to use in one situation what was learned in another situation; in reading, the goal is that strategies learned in school will be used in reading done outside school; see also *application.*

Typographic cues   Punctuation (such as question marks and exclamation points) and other devices (such as underlining and italics) that help readers determine an author's meaning.

Uninterrupted sustained silent reading (USSR)   Activity during which all students and the teacher read books of their choice; often called sustained silent reading or DEAR (drop everything and read).

Unit   Unified learning experience that may encompass several days or weeks; develops a variety of related objectives; includes several lessons; characterized by a logical progression of activities moving toward predetermined goals; often offers opportunities for integration of language.

Verbal learning   Aptitude for learning language; characterized by the ability to understand and respond to language instruction; influenced by background experience, culture, and language.

Vicarious experience   Not a *direct experience;* experience that replaces a *direct experience;* example: seeing the Empire State Building is a real experience but seeing a picture of the Empire State Building is a vicarious experience.

Visual discrimination   Ability to distinguish one visual form from another; in reading, for example, the ability to distinguish the printed form of *d* from the printed form of *b;* contrasted with *auditory discrimination.*

Vocabulary   Knowing the meaning of words; contrasted with *word recognition.*

Vocabulary strategy   Used to figure out the meaning of unknown words.

Whole language approach   Reading instruction that projects an *integrated* conception of language; emphasis is placed on using all language modes for genuine communication purposes; instructional activities focus on meaningful uses of language in pursuing genuine literacy events.

Word analysis/attack Category of *fix-it strategies* that focus on what to do when a word is not recognizable at sight; also called *decoding;* three major methods of word attack are *context clues, structural analysis,* and *phonics.*

Word caller Students who accurately pronounce words encountered in text but do not know what the words and the text mean.

Word recognition Recognizing the printed form of a word; successfully pronouncing a word.

Word recognition strategy Used to identify unknown printed words.

Index

About the Authors

GERALD G. DUFFY and LAURA R. ROEHLER are both former elementary and middle school teachers and are now professors of education at Michigan State University, where he teaches graduate and undergraduate reading and language arts courses and she is Assistant Chair of the Department of Teacher Education. Drs. Duffy and Roehler have collaborated on several instructional research projects in the last 15 years under the auspices of the Institute for Research on Teaching at Michigan State University, with the results of these studies having been published in a variety of scholarly and practical journals. In addition, they coauthored (with George Sherman) a book entitled *How To Teach Reading Systematically* and coedited (with Jana Mason) a volume entitled *Comprehension Instruction: Perspectives and Suggestions.*